shiho. sugiura's
Silver diamond
3: switch all on

By Shiho Sugiura

🐌 TOKYOPOP®

HAMBURG // LONDON // LOS ANGELES // TOKYO

SILVER DIAMOND Vol. 3
Created by Shiho Sugiura

Translation - Shirley Kubo
English Adaptation - Karen S. Ahlstrom
Fan Consultant - The SD Fan Advisory Group
Retouch and Lettering - Star Print Brokers
Production Artist - Vicente Rivera, Jr.
Graphic Designer - Chelsea Windlinger

Editor - Alexis Kirsch
Pre-Production Supervisor - Vicente Rivera, Jr.
Pre-Production Specialist - Lucas Rivera
Managing Editor - Vy Nguyen
Senior Designer - Louis Csontos
Senior Designer - James Lee
Senior Editor - Bryce P. Coleman
Senior Editor - Jenna Winterberg
Associate Publisher - Marco F. Pavia
President and C.O.O. - John Parker
C.E.O. and Chief Creative Officer - Stu Levy

A  Manga

TOKYOPOP Inc.
5900 Wilshire Blvd. Suite 2000
Los Angeles, CA 90036

E-mail: info@TOKYOPOP.com
Come visit us online at www.TOKYOPOP.com

ISBN: 978-1-4278-0967-4

First TOKYOPOP printing: January 2009
10 9 8 7 6 5 4 3 2 1
Printed in the USA

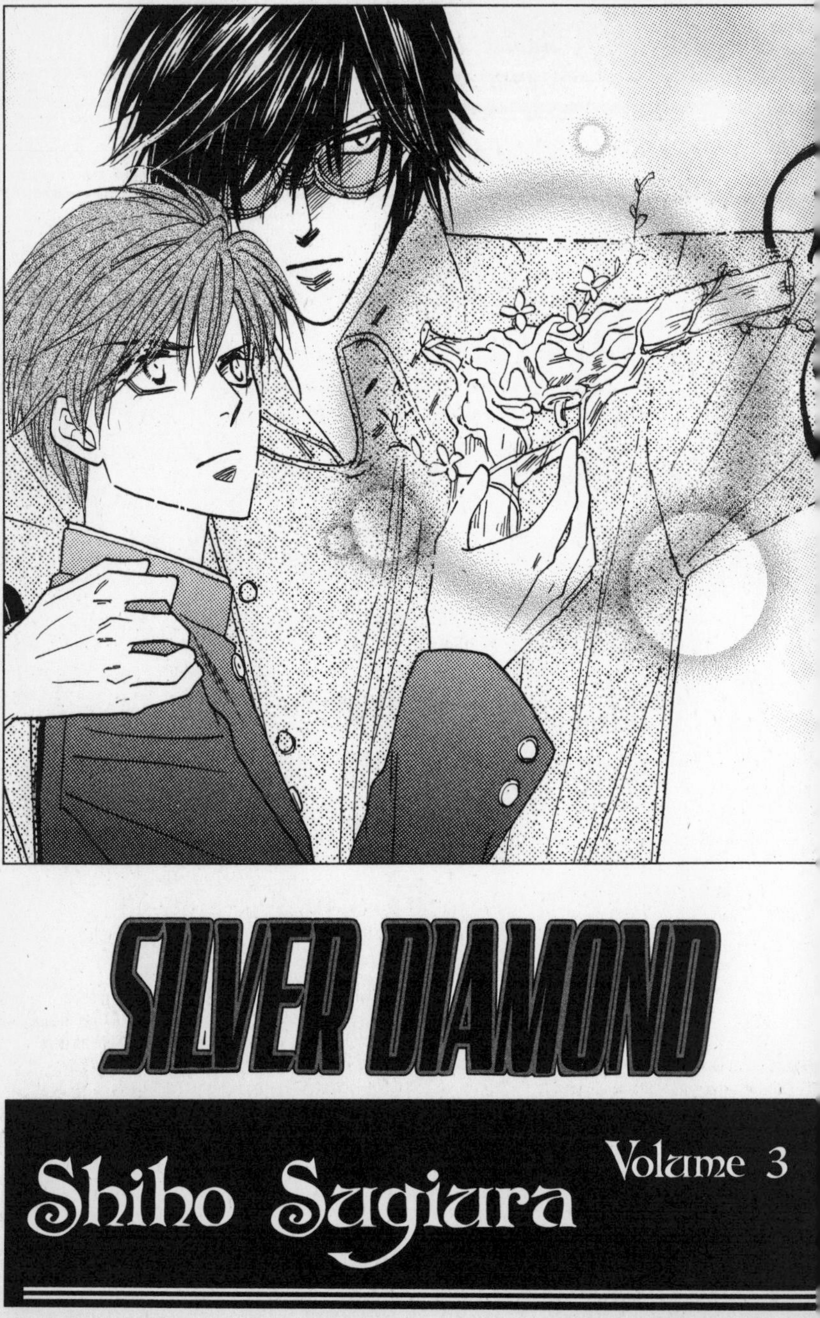

SILVER DIAMOND

Shiho Sugiura

Volume 3

Contents

Silver Diamond

*TO KEEP *SILVER DIAMOND* AS AUTHENTIC AS POSSIBLE, JAPANESE NAME ORDER (FAMILY
AME FIRST) AND HONORIFICS WILL BE MAINTAINED THROUGHOUT THE TEXT. FOR FURTHER
XPLANATIONS OF SPECIALLY-MARKED DIALOGUE(*), PLEASE CHECK THE GLOSSARY AT THE END
F THE VOLUME.

SILVER DIAMOND

ダイヤモンド

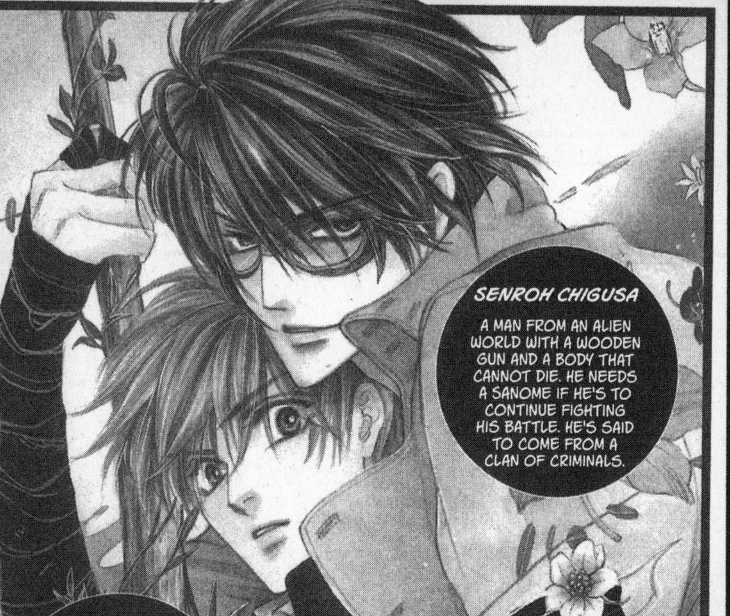

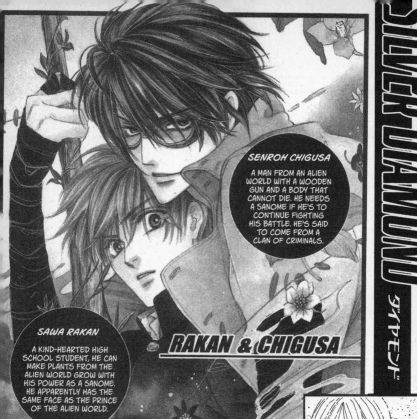

SENROH CHIGUSA
A MAN FROM AN ALIEN WORLD WITH A WOODEN GUN AND A BODY THAT CANNOT DIE. HE NEEDS A SANOME IF HE'S TO CONTINUE FIGHTING HIS BATTLE. HE'S SAID TO COME FROM A CLAN OF CRIMINALS.
RAKAN & CHIGUSA
SAWA RAKAN
A KIND-HEARTED HIGH SCHOOL STUDENT, HE CAN MAKE PLANTS FROM THE ALIEN WORLD GROW WITH HIS POWER AS A SANOME. HE APPARENTLY HAS THE SAME FACE AS THE PRINCE OF THE ALIEN WORLD.

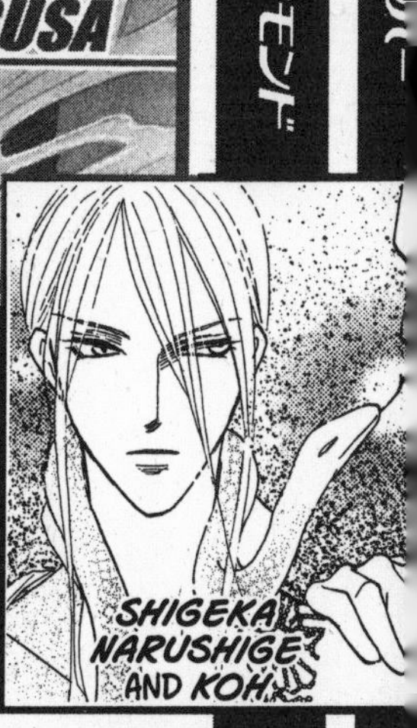

SHIGEKA NARUSHIGE AND KOH

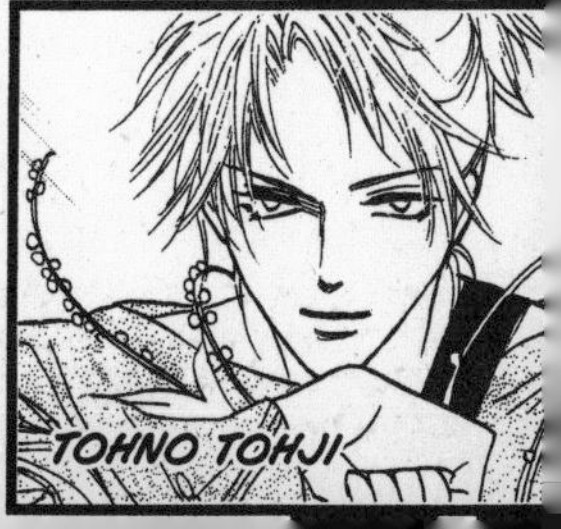

TOHNO TOHJI

STORY and CAST

◆ RAKAN LIVES ALONE IN A HOUSE WITH A JUNGLE-LIKE YARD. ONE DAY, SOMEONE WITH A WOODEN GUN FALLS INTO HIS YARD FROM ANOTHER WORLD. THIS MAN, NAMED SENROH CHIGUSA IMMEDIATELY TRIES TO ATTACK RAKAN, WHO LOOKS EXACTLY LIKE THE PRINCE FROM HIS OWN WORLD. BUT WHEN CHIGUSA SEES THAT RAKAN MADE HIS WOODEN GUN GROW INTO A GIANT TREE, HE RECOGNIZES HIM AS A SANOME AND REALIZES HE'S NECESSARY FOR THE BATTLE HE MUST FIGHT. TO MAKE THINGS WORSE, NARUSHIGE AND KOH FALL IN AS WELL, AND RAKAN'S DAILY ROUTINE TURNS INTO A STRANGE ONE.

◆ AS EVERYONE FINALLY BEGINS TO TRUST ONE ANOTHER, TOHNO TOHJI, AN ASSASSIN FROM THE OTHER WORLD, ARRIVES. TOHJI ATTACKS, USING SPECIAL PLANTS, AND CALLS CHIGUSA AND NARUSHIGE A MONSTER AND A BAD OMEN. RAKAN SIMPLY REPLIES THAT PEOPLE CAN'T HELP HOW THEY'RE BORN. THOUGH TOHJI TAKES RAKAN'S WORDS TO HEART, HE CONTINUES HIS ASSAULT AND RAKAN'S GROUP FINDS THEMSELVES IN A DIRE PREDICAMENT. CHIGUSA TRIES TO FIGHT BACK BY SACRIFICING HIS BODY, BUT RAKAN STOPS HIM, AND ENDS THE BATTLE WITH NO MAJOR INJURIES BY USING HIS SANOME POWERS.

FOR MORE DETAILS, PLEASE READ VOLUMES 1 AND 2!!

SILVER DIAMOND

シルバー　ダイヤモンド

Sugiura Shiho: 2004 JAN

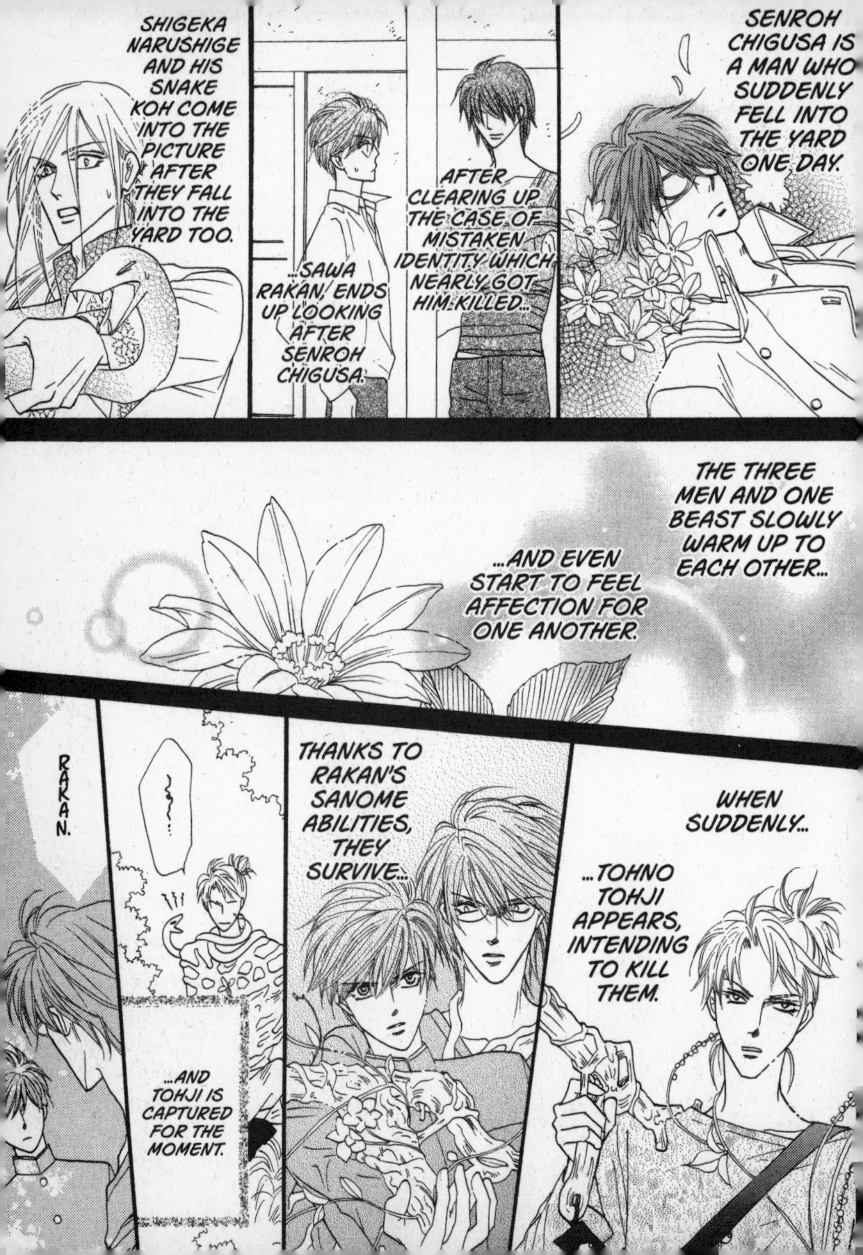
SENROH CHIGUSA IS A MAN WHO SUDDENLY FELL INTO THE YARD ONE DAY.
AFTER CLEARING UP THE CASE OF MISTAKEN IDENTITY WHICH NEARLY GOT HIM KILLED...
...SAWA RAKAN, ENDS UP LOOKING AFTER SENROH CHIGUSA.
SHIGEKA NARUSHIGE AND HIS SNAKE KOH COME INTO THE PICTURE AFTER THEY FALL INTO THE YARD TOO.
THE THREE MEN AND ONE BEAST SLOWLY WARM UP TO EACH OTHER...
...AND EVEN START TO FEEL AFFECTION FOR ONE ANOTHER.
WHEN SUDDENLY...
...TOHNO TOHJI APPEARS, INTENDING TO KILL THEM.
THANKS TO RAKAN'S SANOME ABILITIES, THEY SURVIVE...
...AND TOHJI IS CAPTURED FOR THE MOMENT.
RAKAN.

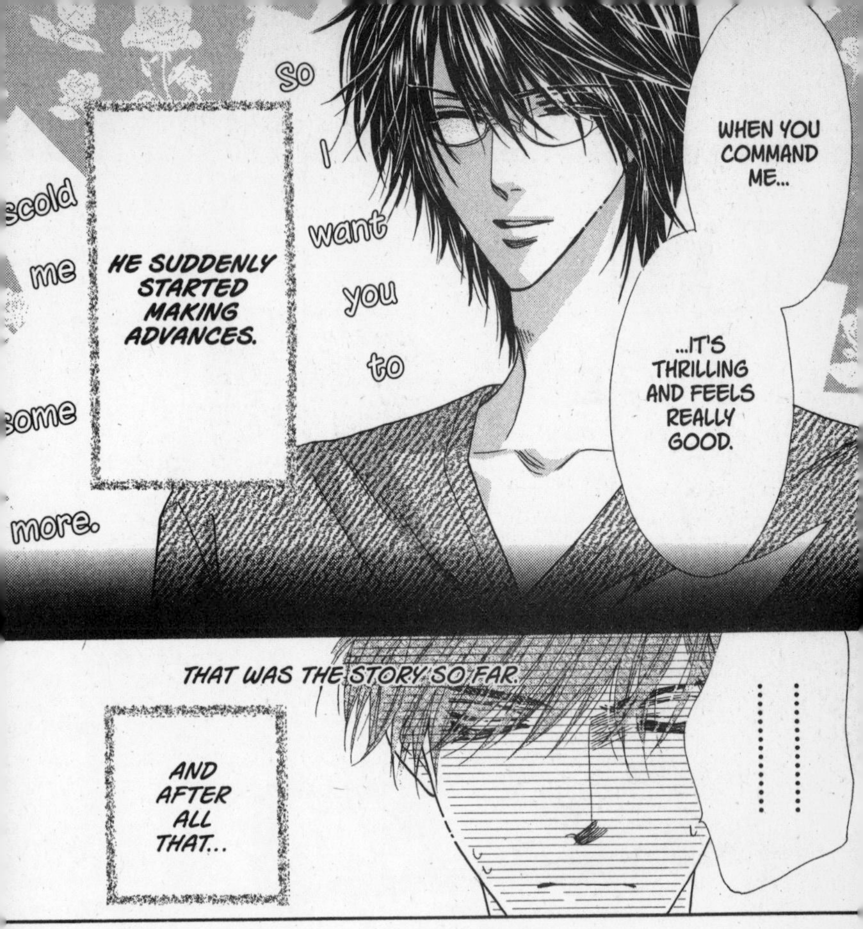
WHEN YOU COMMAND ME...
...IT'S THRILLING AND FEELS REALLY GOOD.
so I want you to scold me some more.
HE SUDDENLY STARTED MAKING ADVANCES.
....
THAT WAS THE STORY SO FAR.
AND AFTER ALL THAT...

Rakan

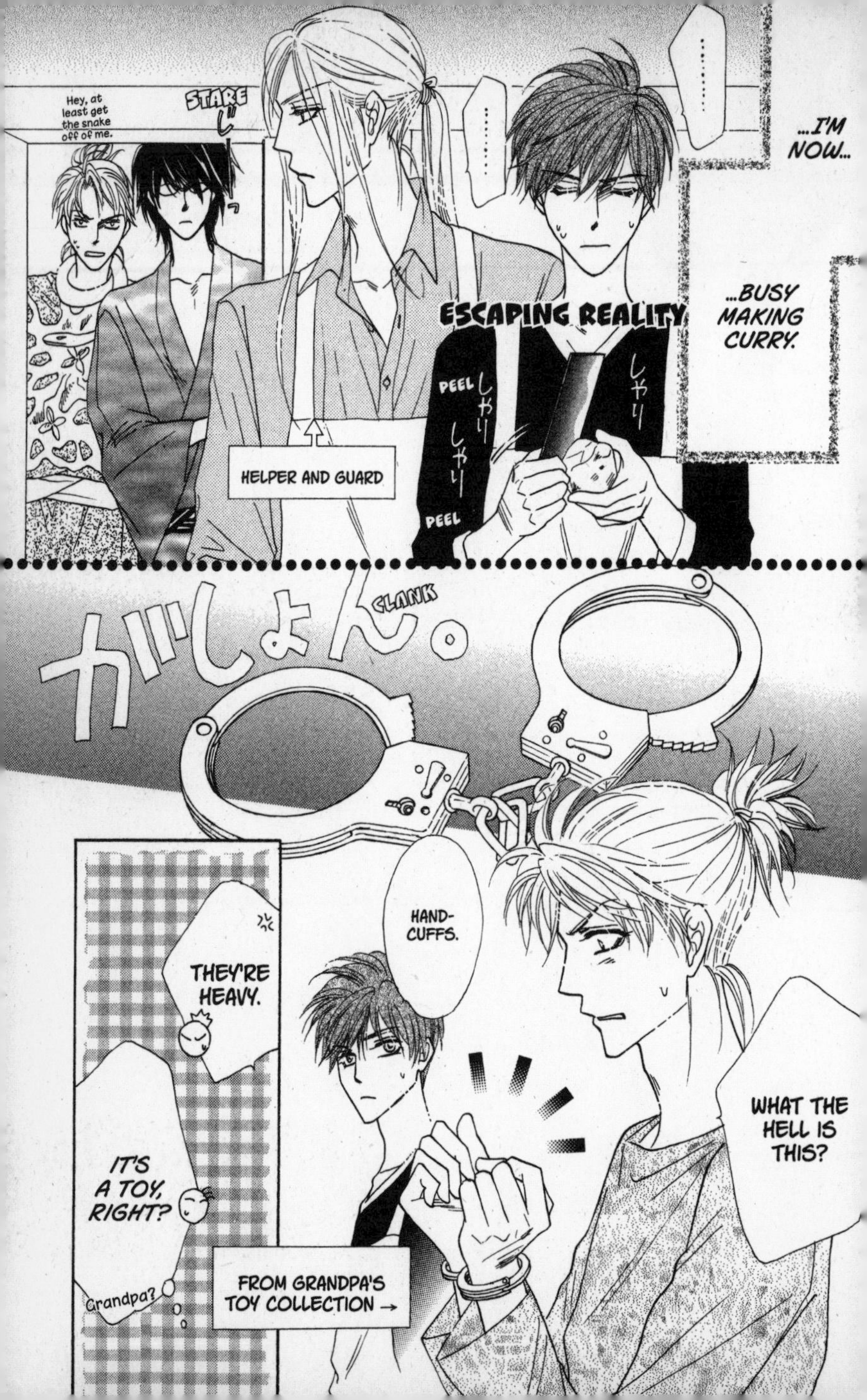
...I'M NOW...
...BUSY MAKING CURRY.
.....
.....
ESCAPING REALITY
PEEL
しゃり
しゃり
しゃり
PEEL
HELPER AND GUARD
STARE
じー
Hey, at least get the snake off of me.
CLANK
がしょん。
WHAT THE HELL IS THIS?
HAND-CUFFS.
THEY'RE HEAVY.
IT'S A TOY, RIGHT?
Grandpa?
FROM GRANDPA'S TOY COLLECTION →

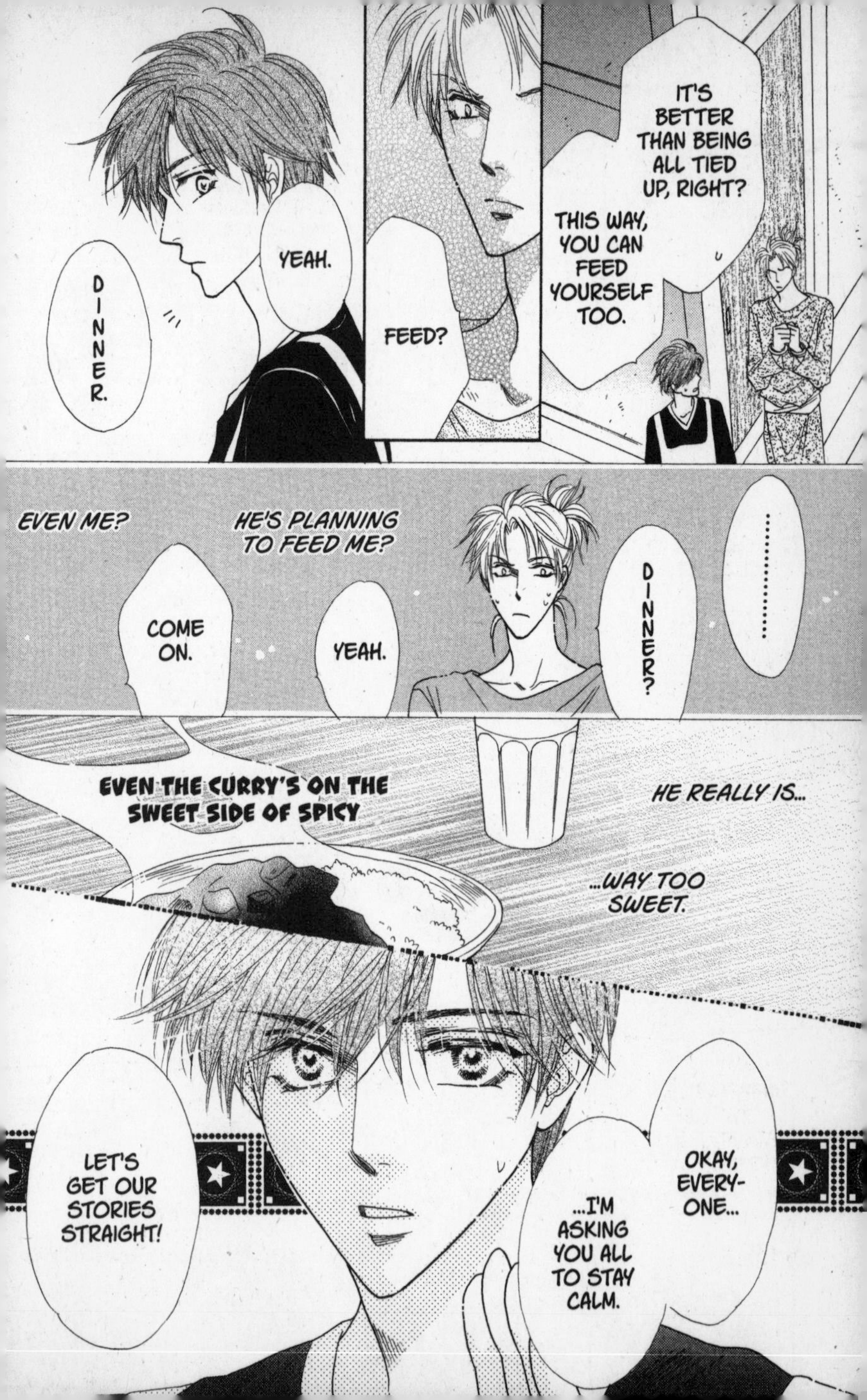
IT'S BETTER THAN BEING ALL TIED UP, RIGHT?
THIS WAY, YOU CAN FEED YOURSELF TOO.
FEED?
YEAH.
DINNER.
......
DINNER?
HE'S PLANNING TO FEED ME?
YEAH.
COME ON.
EVEN ME?
HE REALLY IS...
...WAY TOO SWEET.
EVEN THE CURRY'S ON THE SWEET SIDE OF SPICY
OKAY, EVERYONE...
...I'M ASKING YOU ALL TO STAY CALM.
LET'S GET OUR STORIES STRAIGHT!

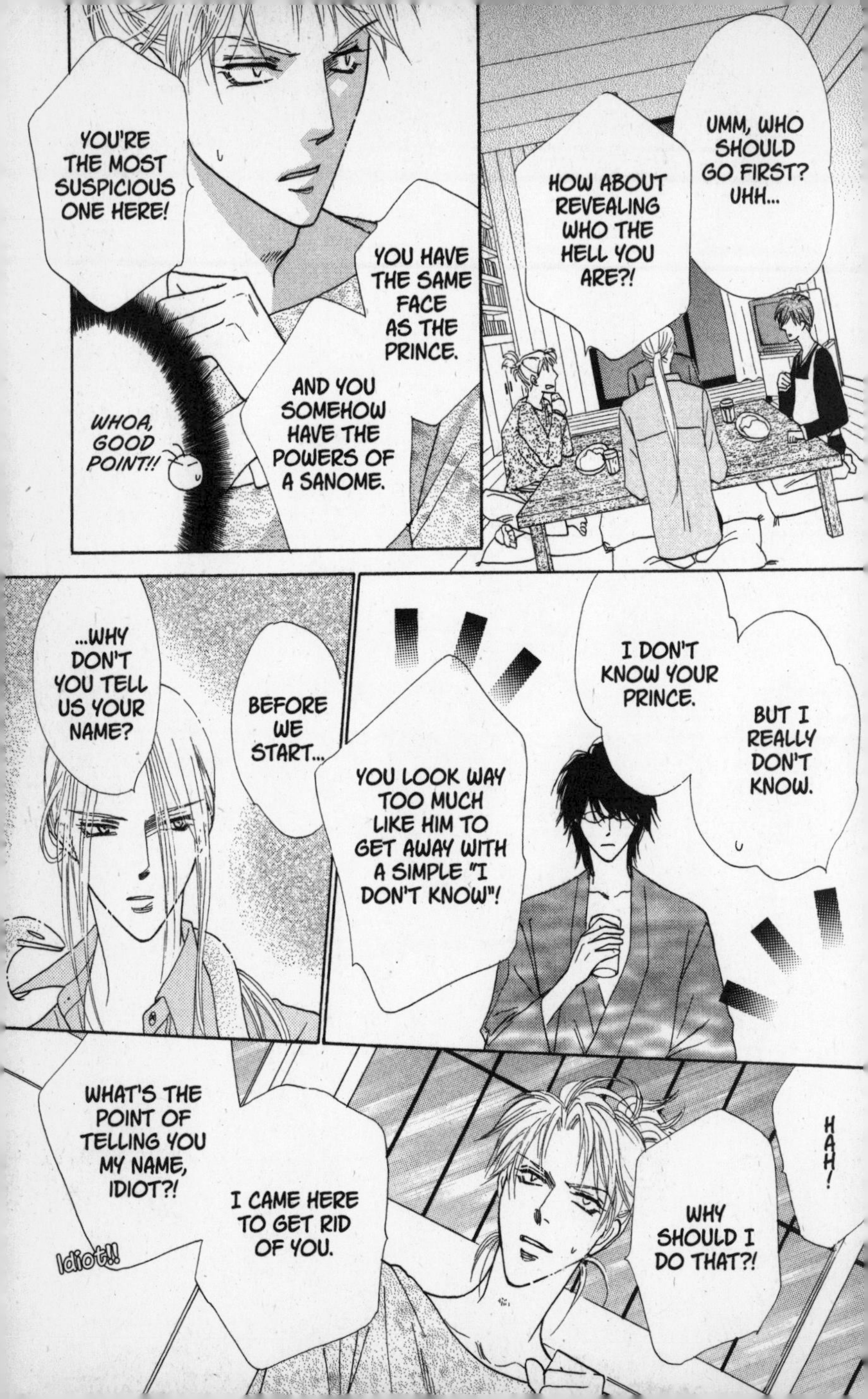
UMM, WHO SHOULD GO FIRST? UHH...
HOW ABOUT REVEALING WHO THE HELL YOU ARE?!
YOU'RE THE MOST SUSPICIOUS ONE HERE!
YOU HAVE THE SAME FACE AS THE PRINCE.
AND YOU SOMEHOW HAVE THE POWERS OF A SANOME.
WHOA, GOOD POINT!!
I DON'T KNOW YOUR PRINCE.
BUT I REALLY DON'T KNOW.
YOU LOOK WAY TOO MUCH LIKE HIM TO GET AWAY WITH A SIMPLE "I DON'T KNOW"!
BEFORE WE START...
...WHY DON'T YOU TELL US YOUR NAME?
HAH!
WHY SHOULD I DO THAT?!
WHAT'S THE POINT OF TELLING YOU MY NAME, IDIOT?!
I CAME HERE TO GET RID OF YOU.
Idiot!!

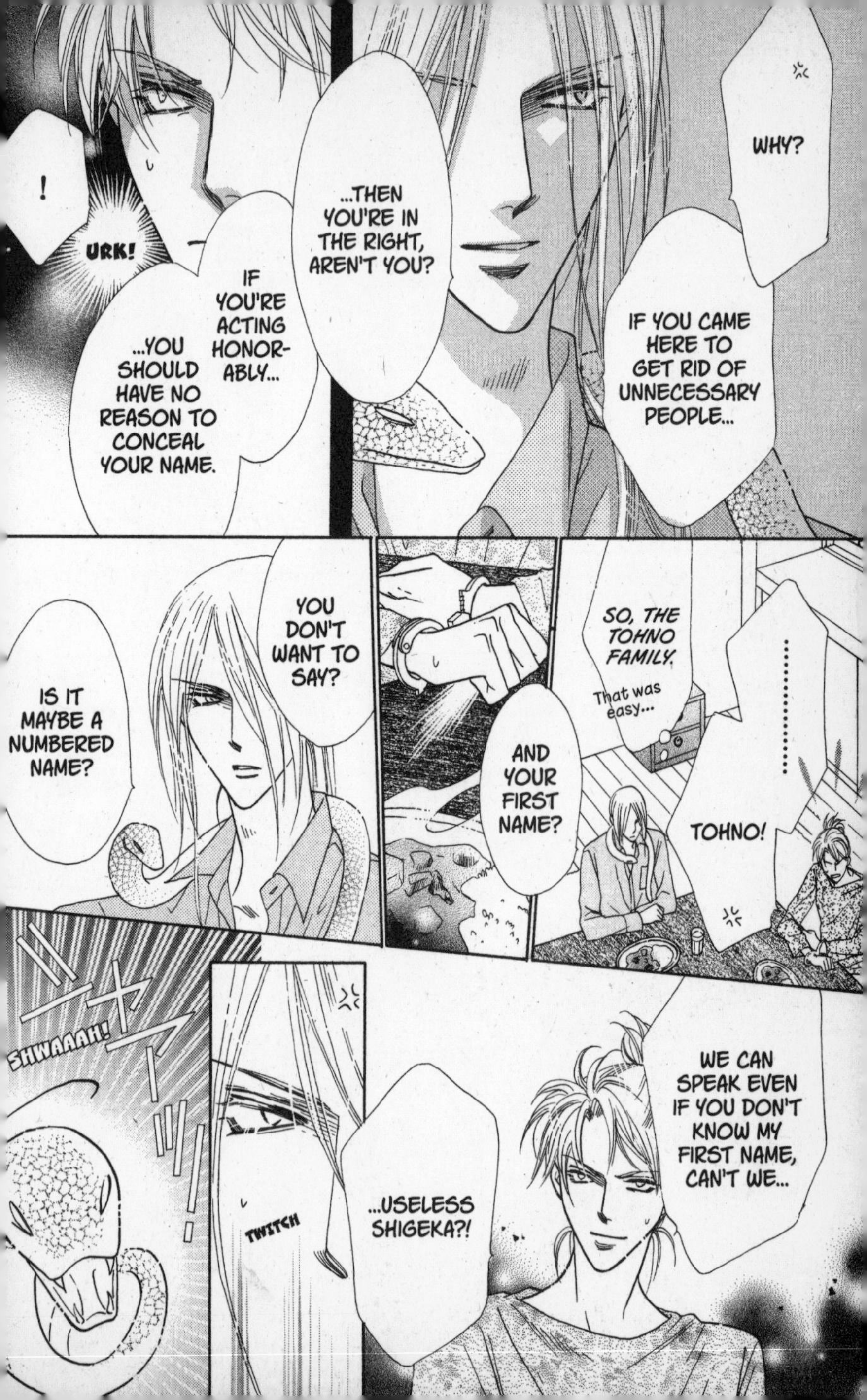
WHY?
IF YOU CAME HERE TO GET RID OF UNNECESSARY PEOPLE...
...THEN YOU'RE IN THE RIGHT, AREN'T YOU?
!
URK!
IF YOU'RE ACTING HONORABLY...
...YOU SHOULD HAVE NO REASON TO CONCEAL YOUR NAME.
SO, THE TOHNO FAMILY.
That was easy...
......
TOHNO!
AND YOUR FIRST NAME?
YOU DON'T WANT TO SAY?
IS IT MAYBE A NUMBERED NAME?
WE CAN SPEAK EVEN IF YOU DON'T KNOW MY FIRST NAME, CAN'T WE...
...USELESS SHIGEKA?!
TWITCH
SHWAAAH!

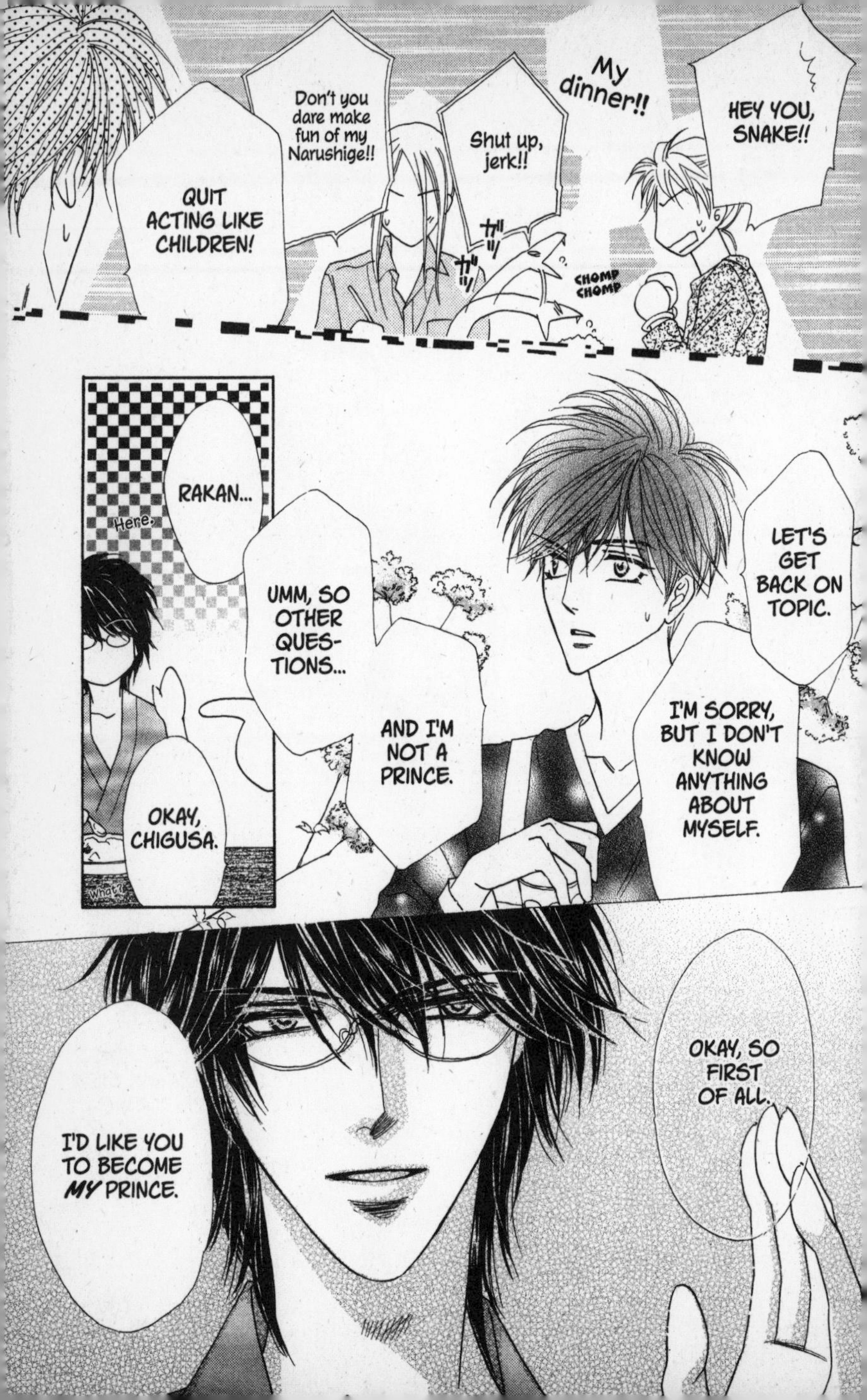
HEY YOU, SNAKE!!
My dinner!!
CHOMP CHOMP
Shut up, jerk!!
Don't you dare make fun of my Narushige!!
QUIT ACTING LIKE CHILDREN!
LET'S GET BACK ON TOPIC.
I'M SORRY, BUT I DON'T KNOW ANYTHING ABOUT MYSELF.
AND I'M NOT A PRINCE.
UMM, SO OTHER QUES-TIONS...
RAKAN...
Here.
OKAY, CHIGUSA.
What?!
OKAY, SO FIRST OF ALL.
I'D LIKE YOU TO BECOME *MY* PRINCE.

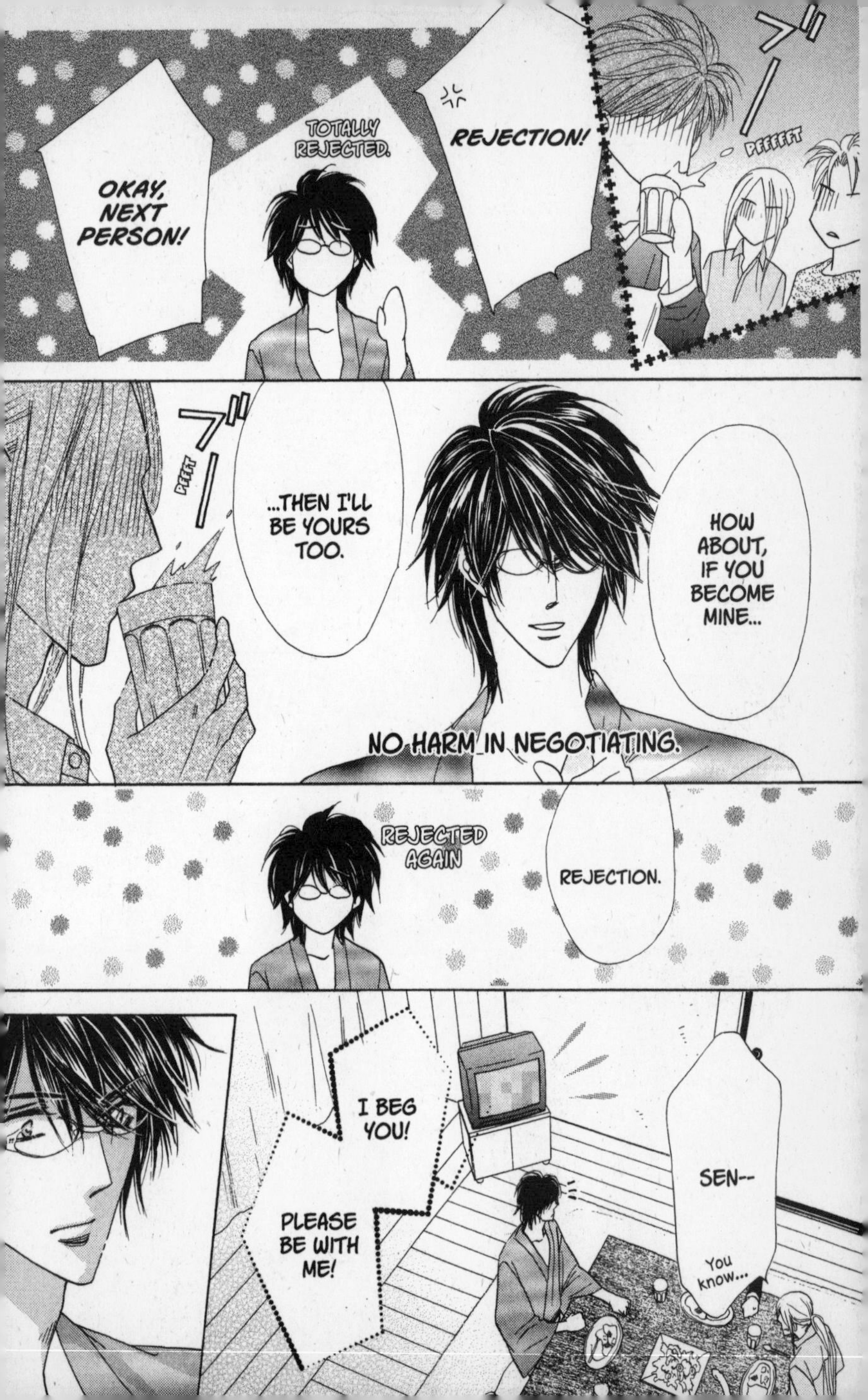
PFFFFFT
REJECTION!
TOTALLY REJECTED.
OKAY, NEXT PERSON!
HOW ABOUT, IF YOU BECOME MINE...
...THEN I'LL BE YOURS TOO.
NO HARM IN NEGOTIATING.
PFFFT
REJECTION.
REJECTED AGAIN
SEN--
You know...
I BEG YOU!
PLEASE BE WITH ME!

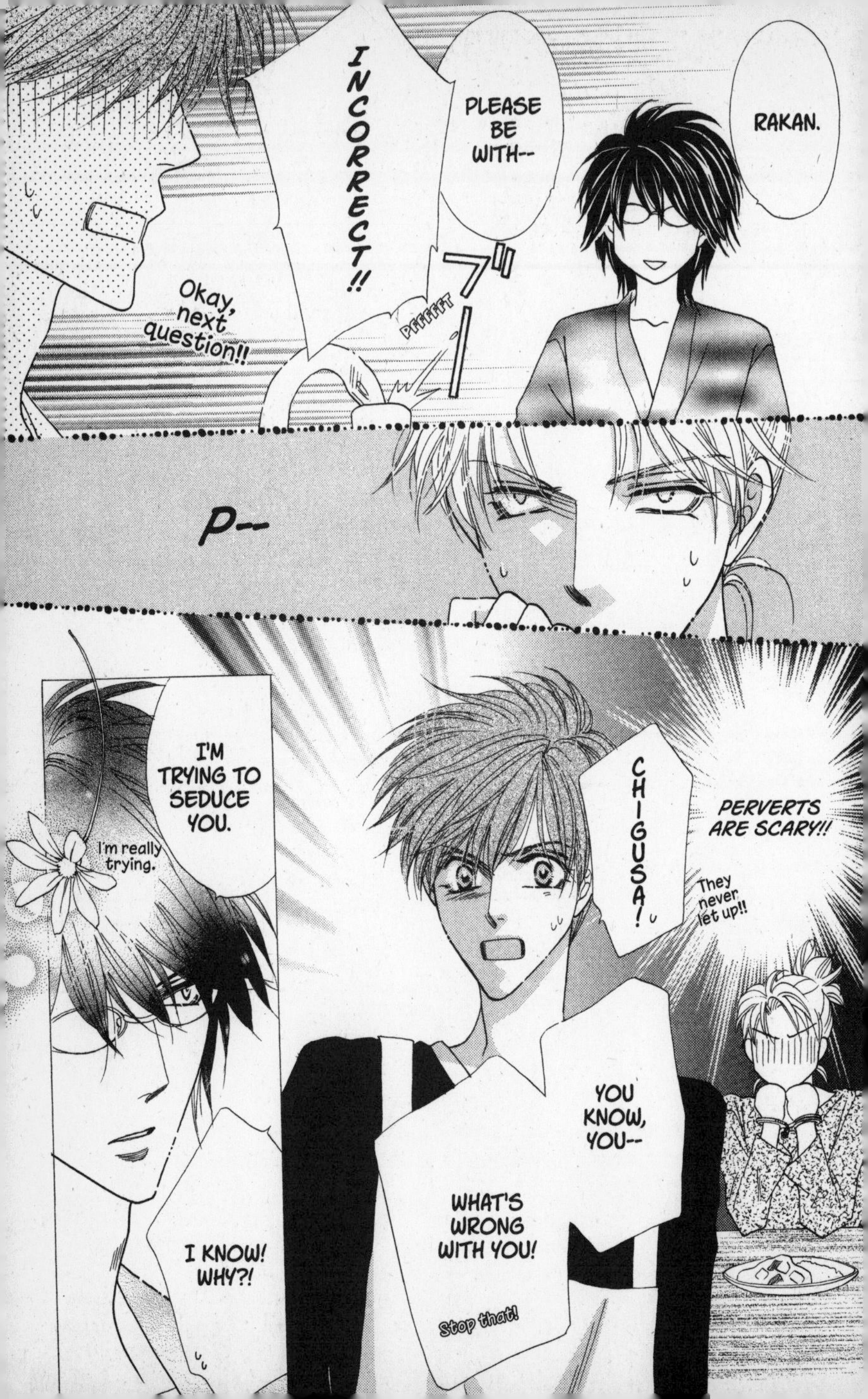
RAKAN.
PLEASE BE WITH--
INCORRECT!!
PFFFFFT
Okay, next question!!
P--
PERVERTS ARE SCARY!!
They never let up!!
CHIGUSA!
YOU KNOW, YOU--
WHAT'S WRONG WITH YOU!
Stop that!
I'M TRYING TO SEDUCE YOU.
I'm really trying.
I KNOW! WHY?!

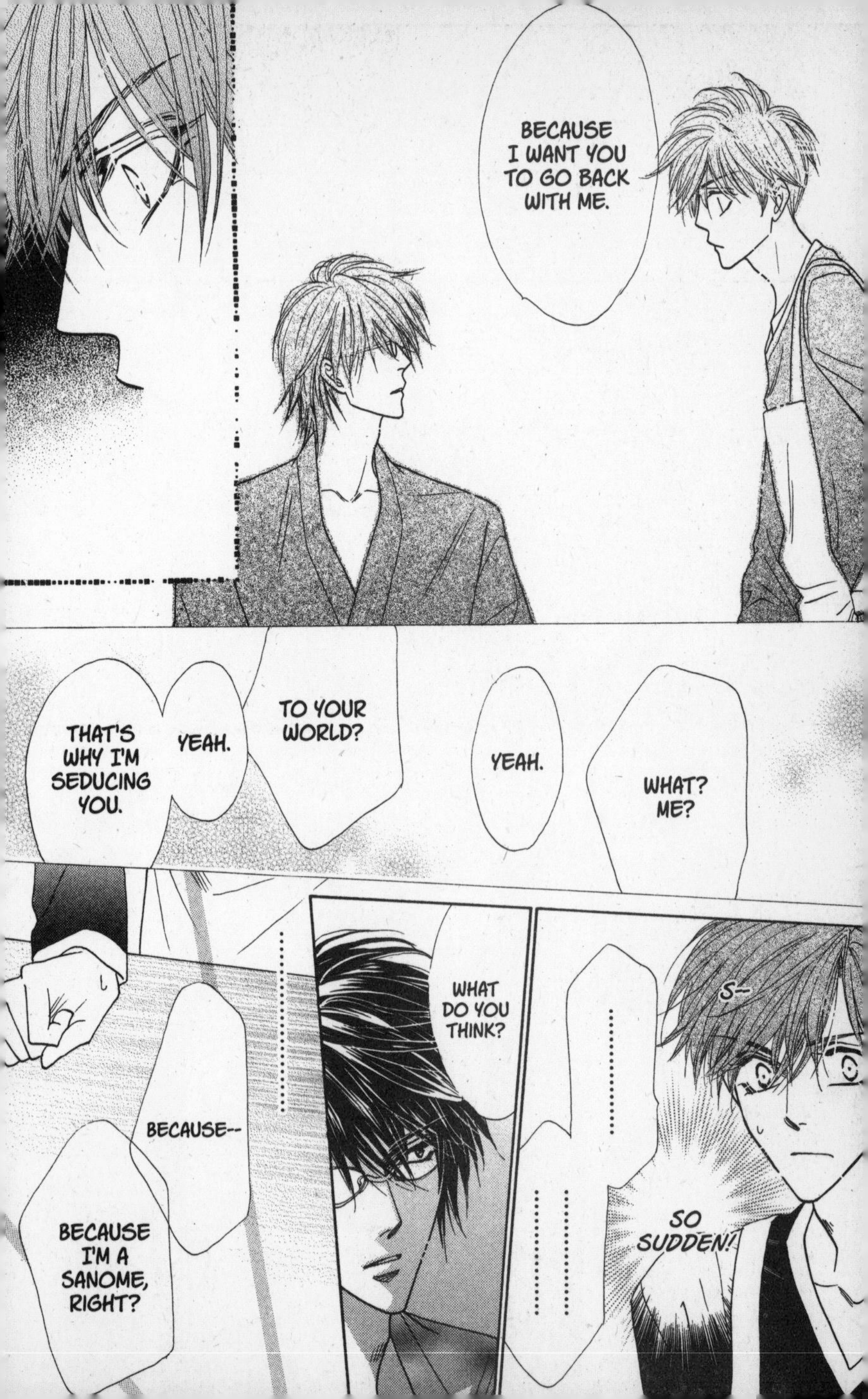
BECAUSE I WANT YOU TO GO BACK WITH ME.
WHAT? ME?
YEAH.
TO YOUR WORLD?
YEAH.
THAT'S WHY I'M SEDUCING YOU.
S--
......
......
SO SUDDEN!
WHAT DO YOU THINK?
......
BECAUSE--
BECAUSE I'M A SANOME, RIGHT?

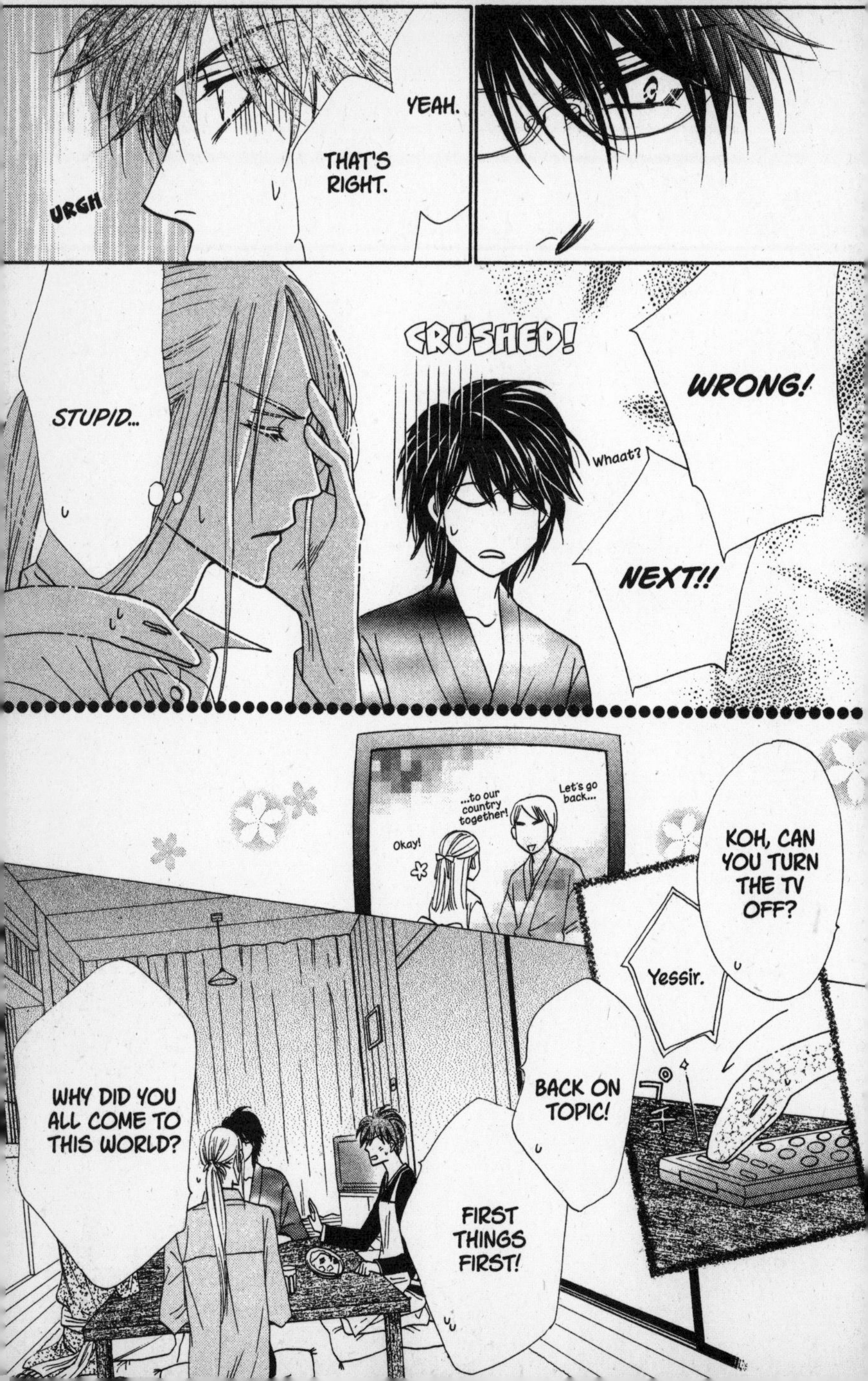
YEAH.
THAT'S RIGHT.
URGH
WRONG!
Whaat?
NEXT!!
CRUSHED!
STUPID...
KOH, CAN YOU TURN THE TV OFF?
Yessir.
Let's go back...
...to our country together!
Okay!
BACK ON TOPIC!
FIRST THINGS FIRST!
WHY DID YOU ALL COME TO THIS WORLD?

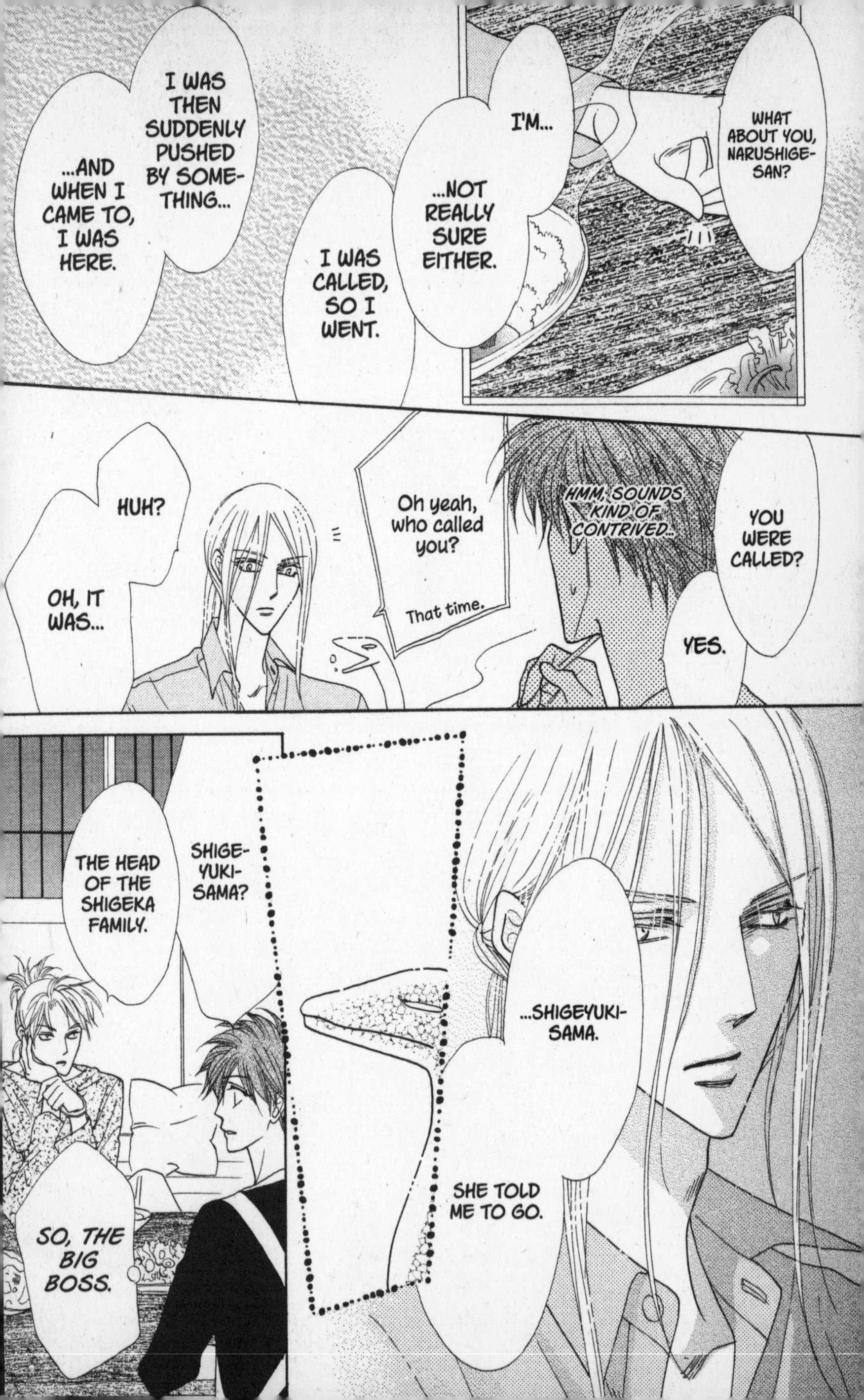
WHAT ABOUT YOU, NARUSHIGE-SAN?
I'M...
...NOT REALLY SURE EITHER.
I WAS CALLED, SO I WENT.
I WAS THEN SUDDENLY PUSHED BY SOMETHING...
...AND WHEN I CAME TO, I WAS HERE.
YOU WERE CALLED?
YES.
HMM. SOUNDS KIND OF CONTRIVED...
Oh yeah, who called you?
That time.
HUH?
OH, IT WAS...
...SHIGEYUKI-SAMA.
SHE TOLD ME TO GO.
SHIGE-YUKI-SAMA?
THE HEAD OF THE SHIGEKA FAMILY.
SO, THE BIG BOSS.

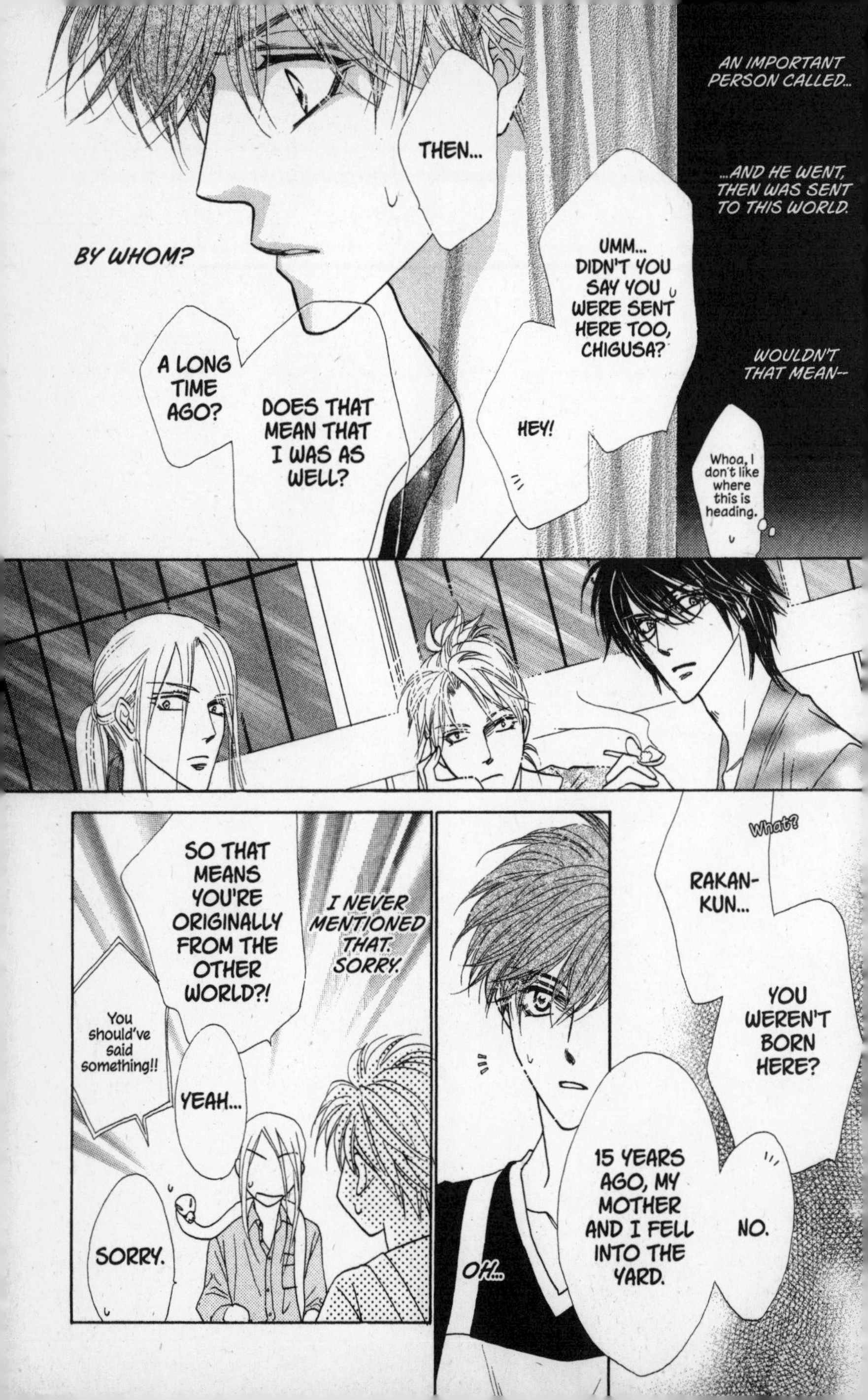
AN IMPORTANT PERSON CALLED...
...AND HE WENT, THEN WAS SENT TO THIS WORLD.
WOULDN'T THAT MEAN--
Whoa, I don't like where this is heading.
UMM... DIDN'T YOU SAY YOU WERE SENT HERE TOO, CHIGUSA?
HEY!
THEN...
BY WHOM?
A LONG TIME AGO?
DOES THAT MEAN THAT I WAS AS WELL?
What?
RAKAN-KUN...
YOU WEREN'T BORN HERE?
NO.
15 YEARS AGO, MY MOTHER AND I FELL INTO THE YARD.
OH...
SO THAT MEANS YOU'RE ORIGINALLY FROM THE OTHER WORLD?!
I NEVER MENTIONED THAT. SORRY.
You should've said something!!
YEAH...
SORRY.

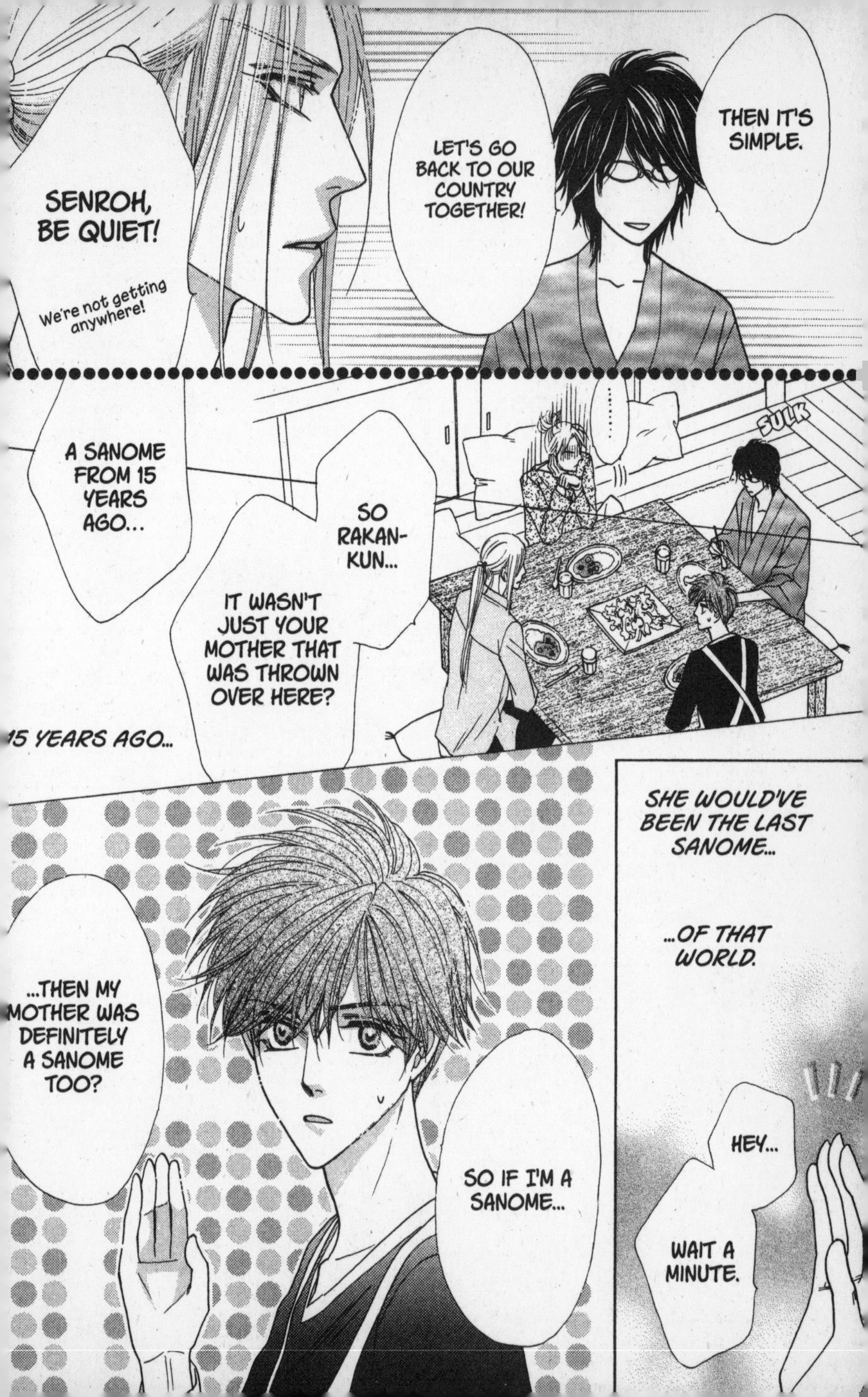
THEN IT'S SIMPLE.
LET'S GO BACK TO OUR COUNTRY TOGETHER!
SENROH, BE QUIET!
We're not getting anywhere!
SULK
...
SO RAKAN-KUN...
IT WASN'T JUST YOUR MOTHER THAT WAS THROWN OVER HERE?
A SANOME FROM 15 YEARS AGO...
15 YEARS AGO...
SHE WOULD'VE BEEN THE LAST SANOME...
...OF THAT WORLD.
HEY...
WAIT A MINUTE.
SO IF I'M A SANOME...
...THEN MY MOTHER WAS DEFINITELY A SANOME TOO?

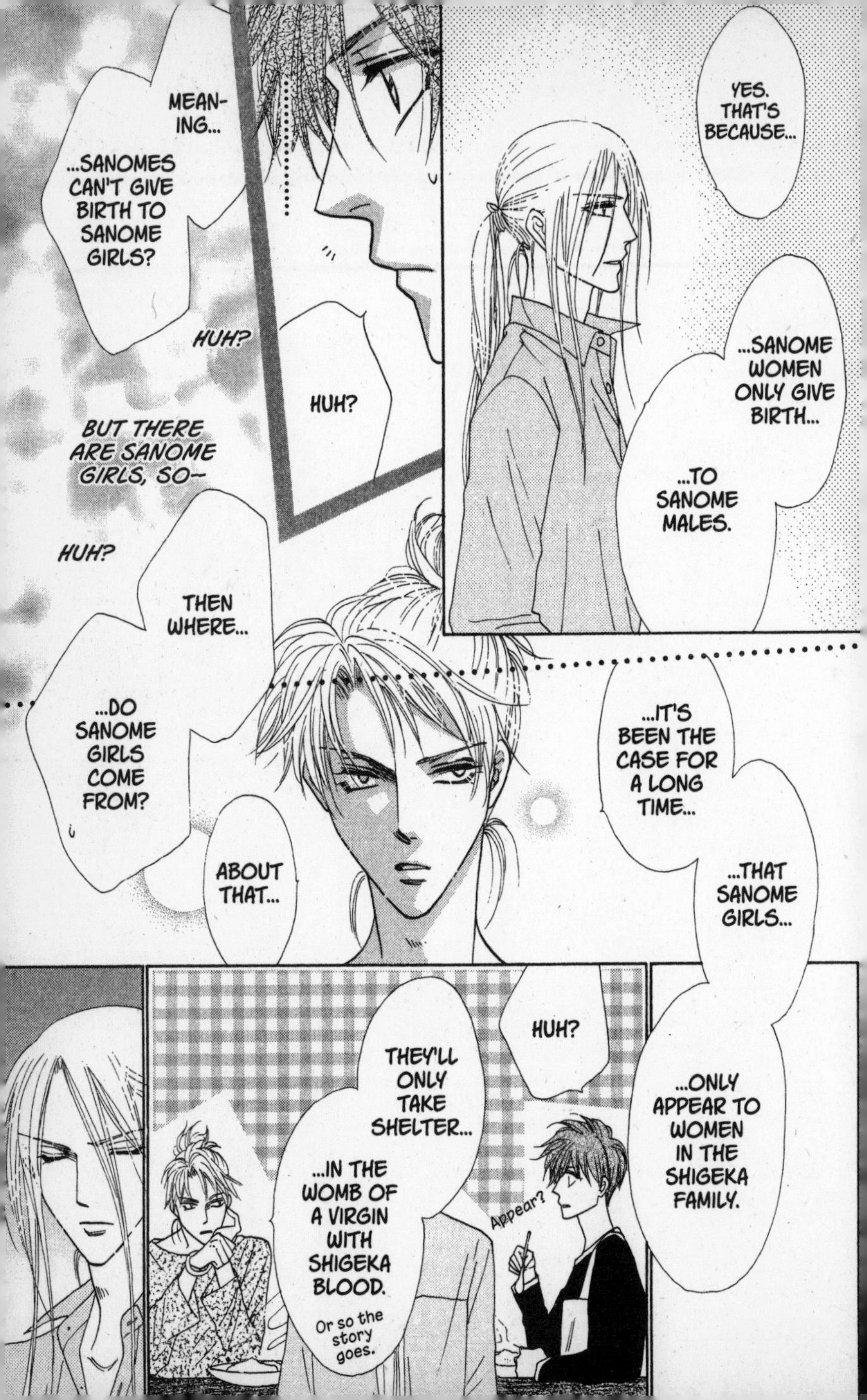
YES. THAT'S BECAUSE...
...SANOME WOMEN ONLY GIVE BIRTH...
...TO SANOME MALES.
MEAN-ING...
...SANOMES CAN'T GIVE BIRTH TO SANOME GIRLS?
HUH?
HUH?
BUT THERE ARE SANOME GIRLS, SO--
HUH?
THEN WHERE...
...DO SANOME GIRLS COME FROM?
ABOUT THAT...
...IT'S BEEN THE CASE FOR A LONG TIME...
...THAT SANOME GIRLS...
...ONLY APPEAR TO WOMEN IN THE SHIGEKA FAMILY.
HUH?
Appear?
THEY'LL ONLY TAKE SHELTER...
...IN THE WOMB OF A VIRGIN WITH SHIGEKA BLOOD.
Or so the story goes.

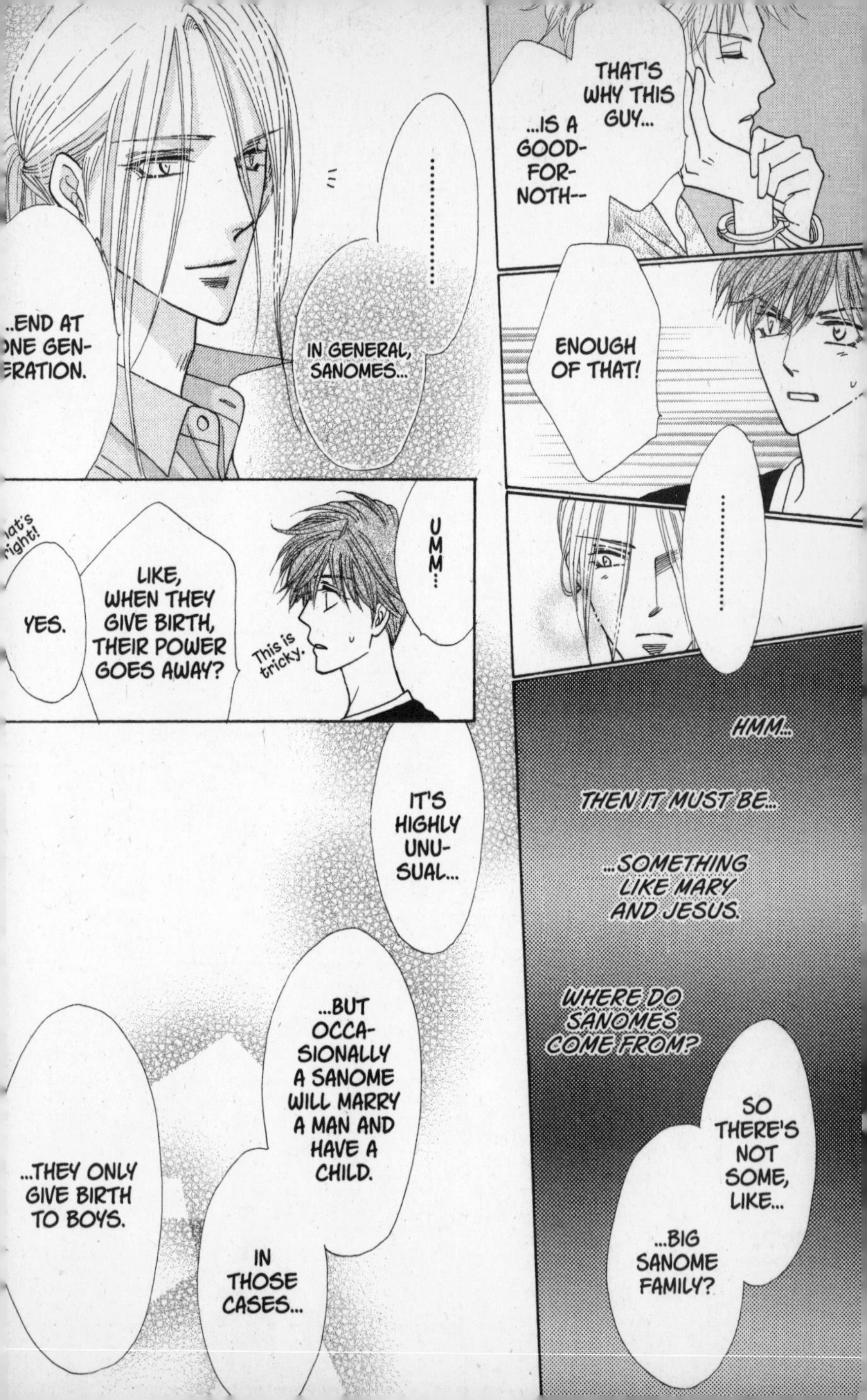

THAT'S WHY THIS GUY...
...IS A GOOD-FOR-NOTH--
ENOUGH OF THAT!
......
HMM...
THEN IT MUST BE...
...SOMETHING LIKE MARY AND JESUS.
WHERE DO SANOMES COME FROM?
SO THERE'S NOT SOME, LIKE...
...BIG SANOME FAMILY?
......
IN GENERAL, SANOMES...
...END AT ONE GENERATION.
UMM...
This is tricky.
LIKE, WHEN THEY GIVE BIRTH, THEIR POWER GOES AWAY?
YES.
IT'S HIGHLY UNUSUAL...
...BUT OCCASIONALLY A SANOME WILL MARRY A MAN AND HAVE A CHILD.
IN THOSE CASES...
...THEY ONLY GIVE BIRTH TO BOYS.

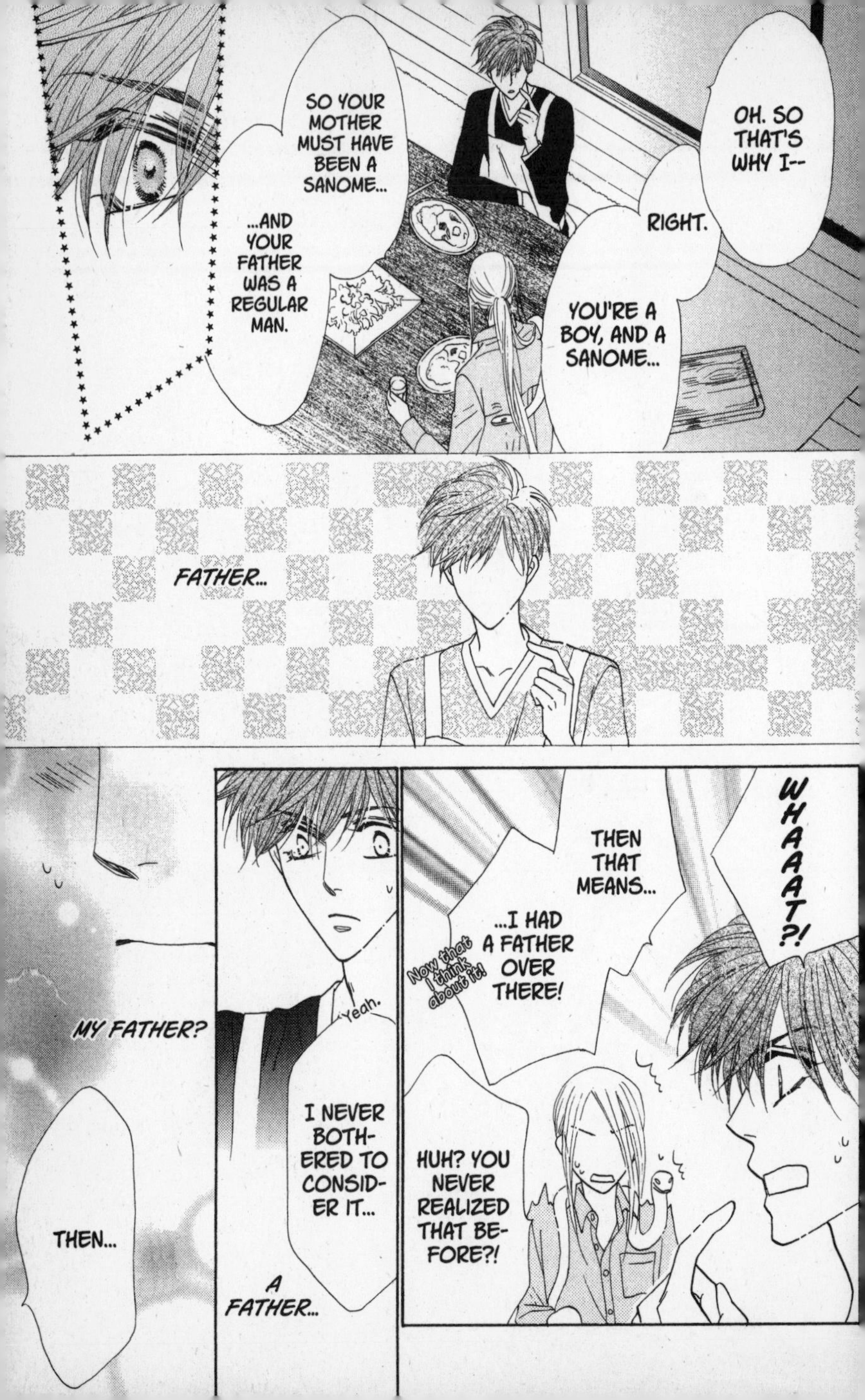
OH. SO THAT'S WHY I--
RIGHT.
YOU'RE A BOY, AND A SANOME...
SO YOUR MOTHER MUST HAVE BEEN A SANOME...
...AND YOUR FATHER WAS A REGULAR MAN.
FATHER...
WHAAAAT?!
THEN THAT MEANS...
...I HAD A FATHER OVER THERE!
Now that I think about it!
HUH? YOU NEVER REALIZED THAT BE-FORE?!
Yeah.
I NEVER BOTH-ERED TO CONSID-ER IT...
A FATHER...
MY FATHER?
THEN...

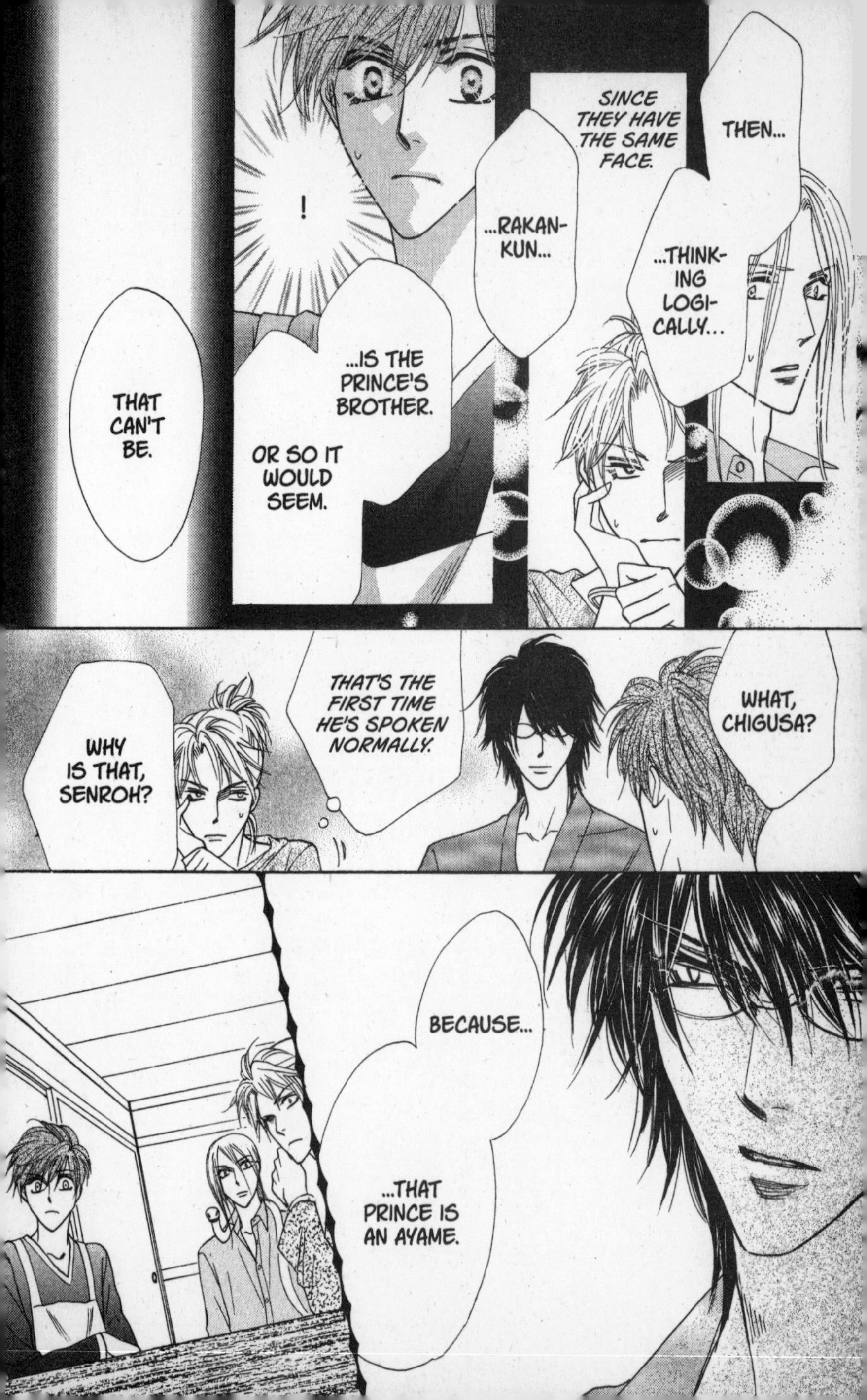
THEN...
...THINKING LOGICALLY...
SINCE THEY HAVE THE SAME FACE.
...RAKAN-KUN...
...IS THE PRINCE'S BROTHER.
OR SO IT WOULD SEEM.
!
THAT CAN'T BE.
WHAT, CHIGUSA?
THAT'S THE FIRST TIME HE'S SPOKEN NORMALLY.
WHY IS THAT, SENROH?
BECAUSE...
...THAT PRINCE IS AN AYAME.

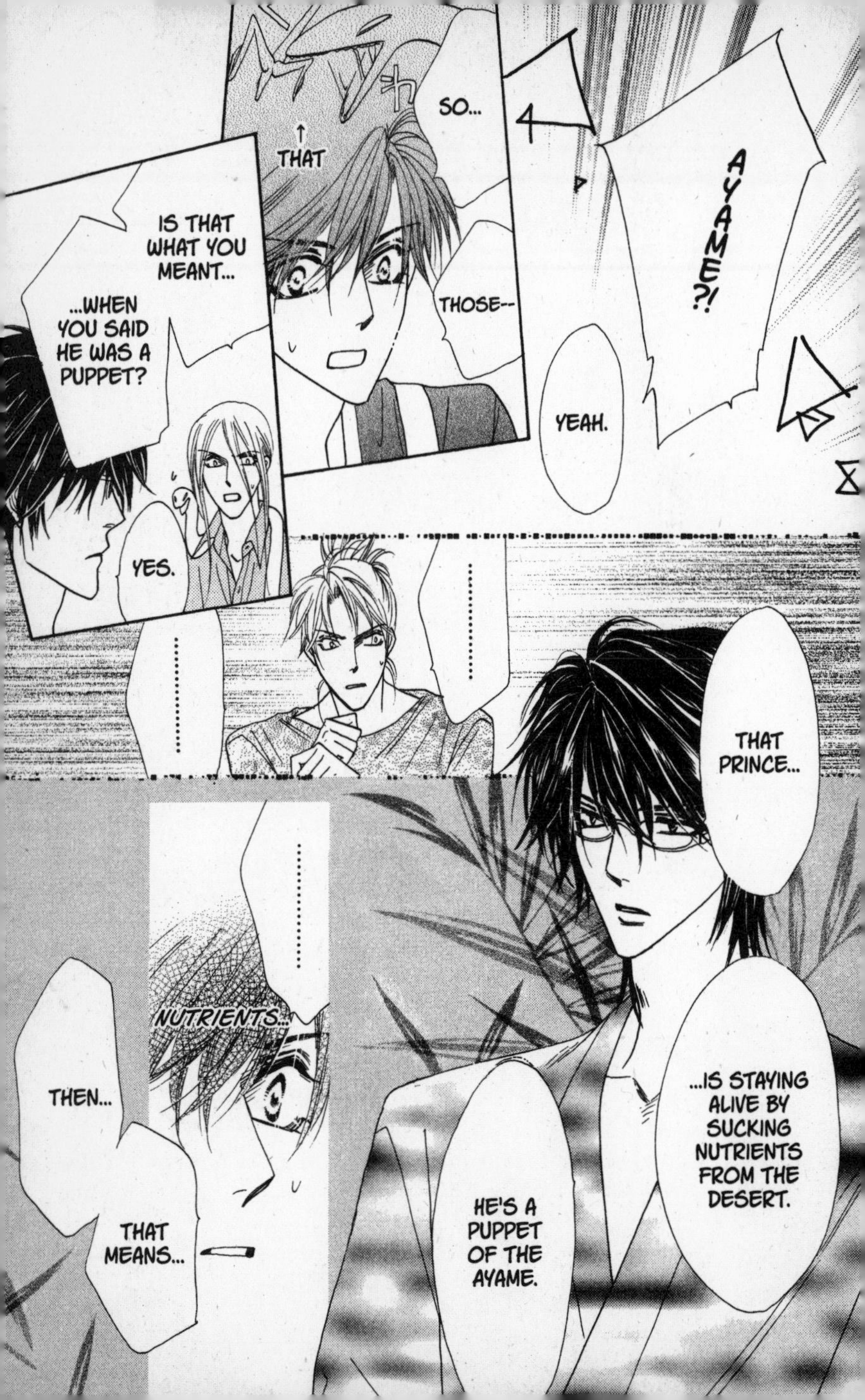
AYAME?!
SO...
THAT
THOSE--
YEAH.
IS THAT WHAT YOU MEANT...
...WHEN YOU SAID HE WAS A PUPPET?
YES.
......
......
THAT PRINCE...
...IS STAYING ALIVE BY SUCKING NUTRIENTS FROM THE DESERT.
HE'S A PUPPET OF THE AYAME.
......
NUTRIENTS...
THEN...
THAT MEANS...

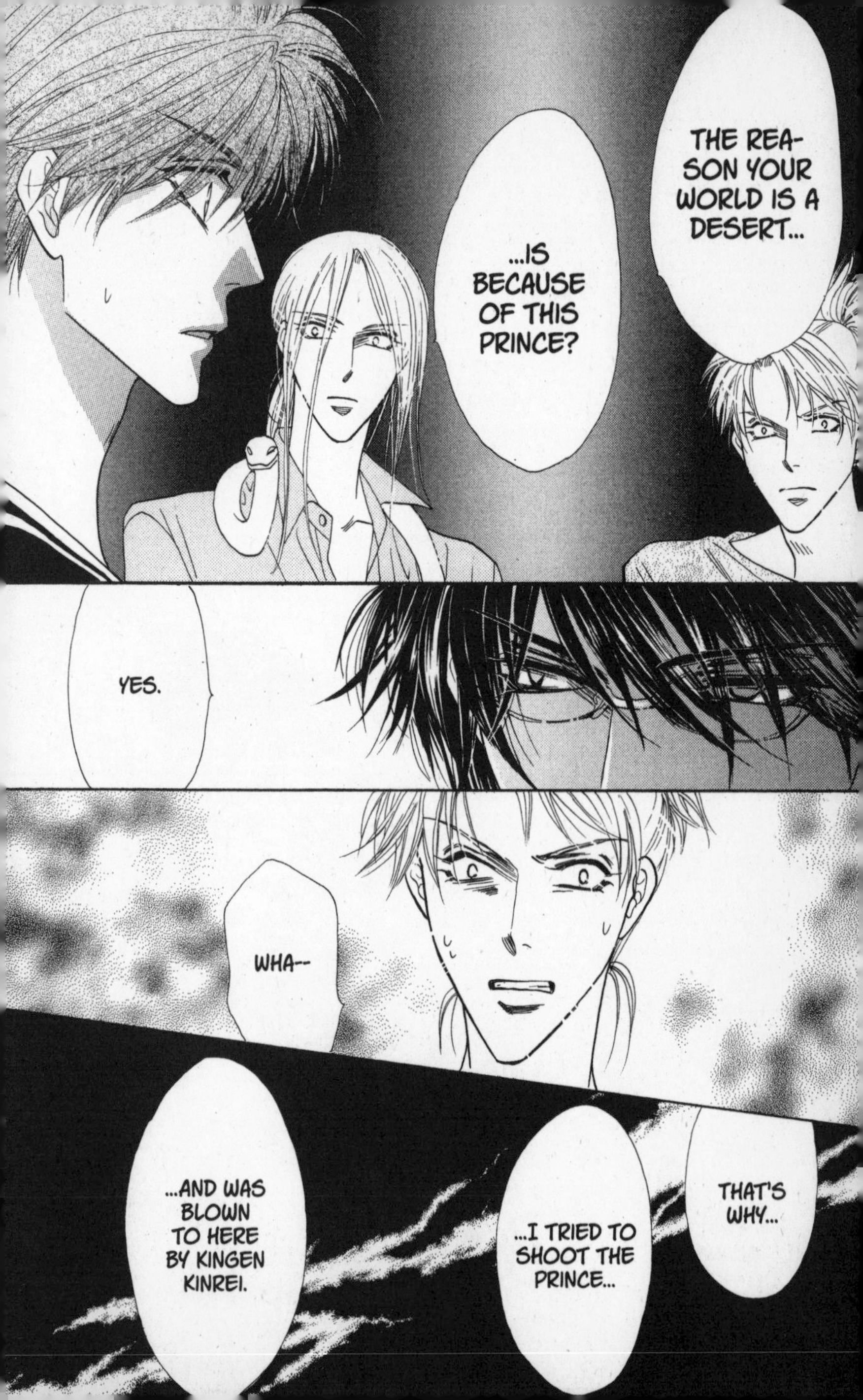
THE REA-SON YOUR WORLD IS A DESERT...
...IS BECAUSE OF THIS PRINCE?
YES.
WHA--
THAT'S WHY...
...I TRIED TO SHOOT THE PRINCE...
...AND WAS BLOWN TO HERE BY KINGEN KINREI.

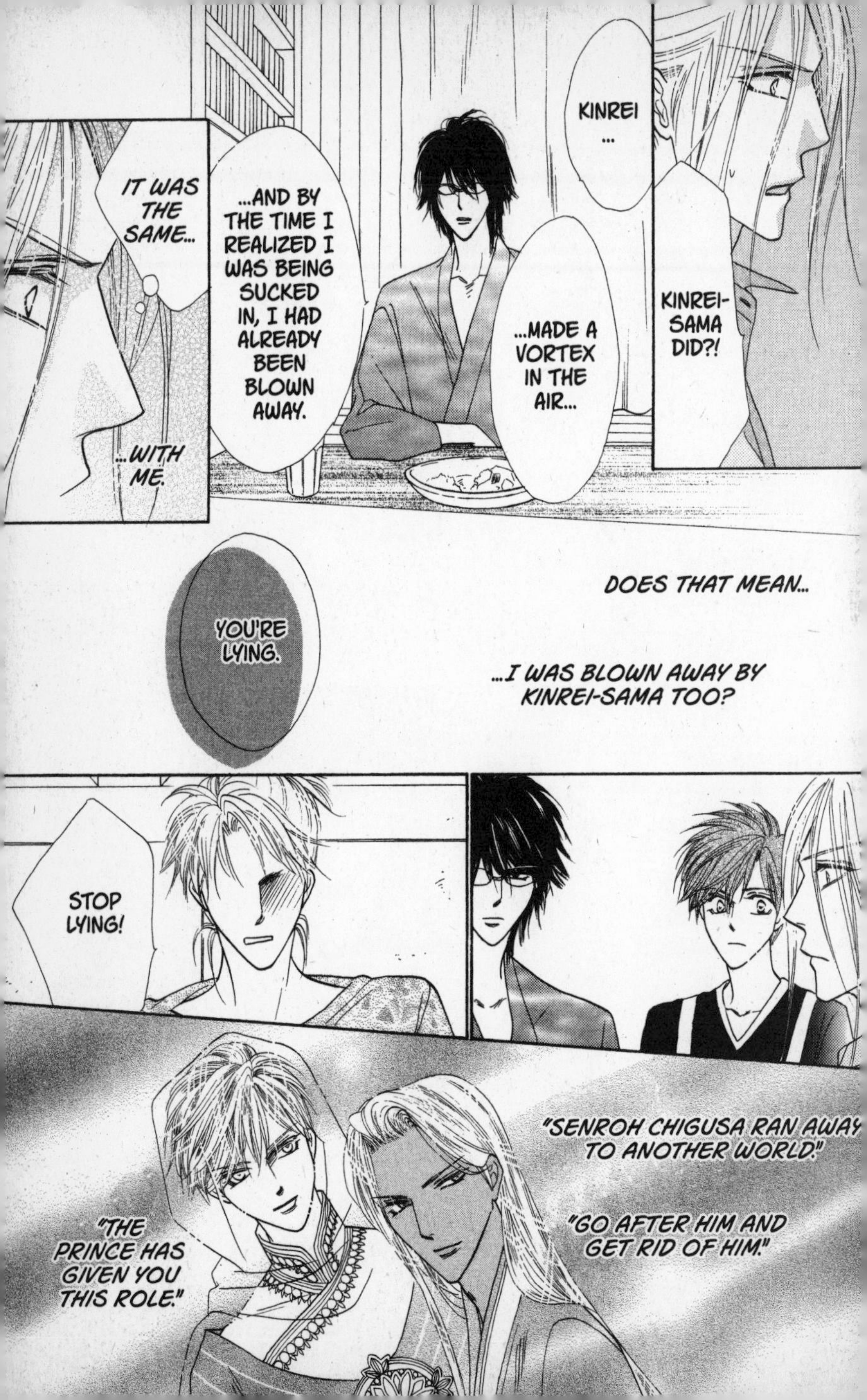
KINREI ...
KINREI-SAMA DID?!
...MADE A VORTEX IN THE AIR...
...AND BY THE TIME I REALIZED I WAS BEING SUCKED IN, I HAD ALREADY BEEN BLOWN AWAY.
IT WAS THE SAME...
...WITH ME.
DOES THAT MEAN...
...I WAS BLOWN AWAY BY KINREI-SAMA TOO?
YOU'RE LYING.
STOP LYING!
"SENROH CHIGUSA RAN AWAY TO ANOTHER WORLD."
"GO AFTER HIM AND GET RID OF HIM."
"THE PRINCE HAS GIVEN YOU THIS ROLE."

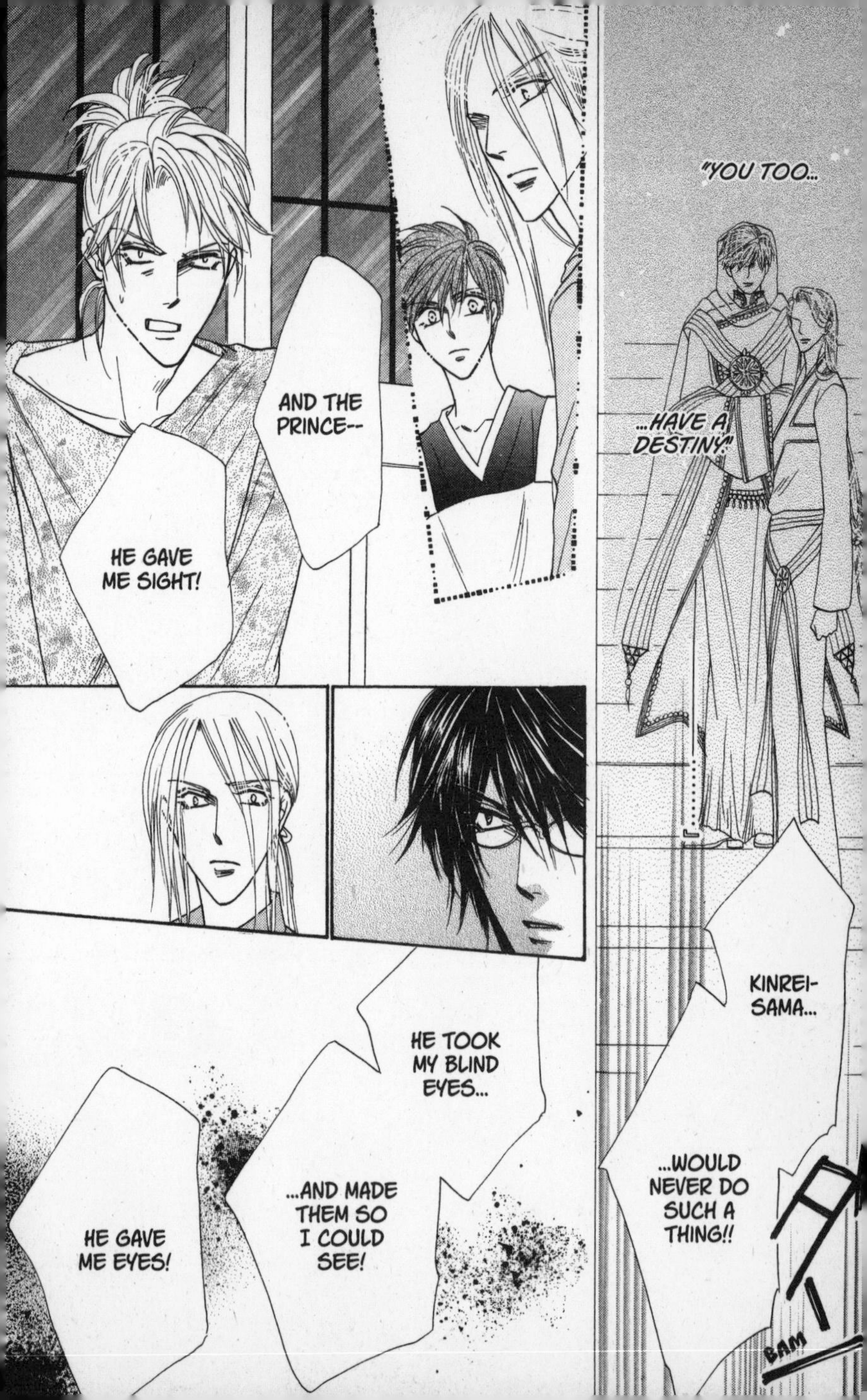
"YOU TOO...
...HAVE A DESTINY."
KINREI-SAMA...
...WOULD NEVER DO SUCH A THING!!
BAM
AND THE PRINCE--
HE GAVE ME SIGHT!
HE TOOK MY BLIND EYES...
...AND MADE THEM SO I COULD SEE!
HE GAVE ME EYES!

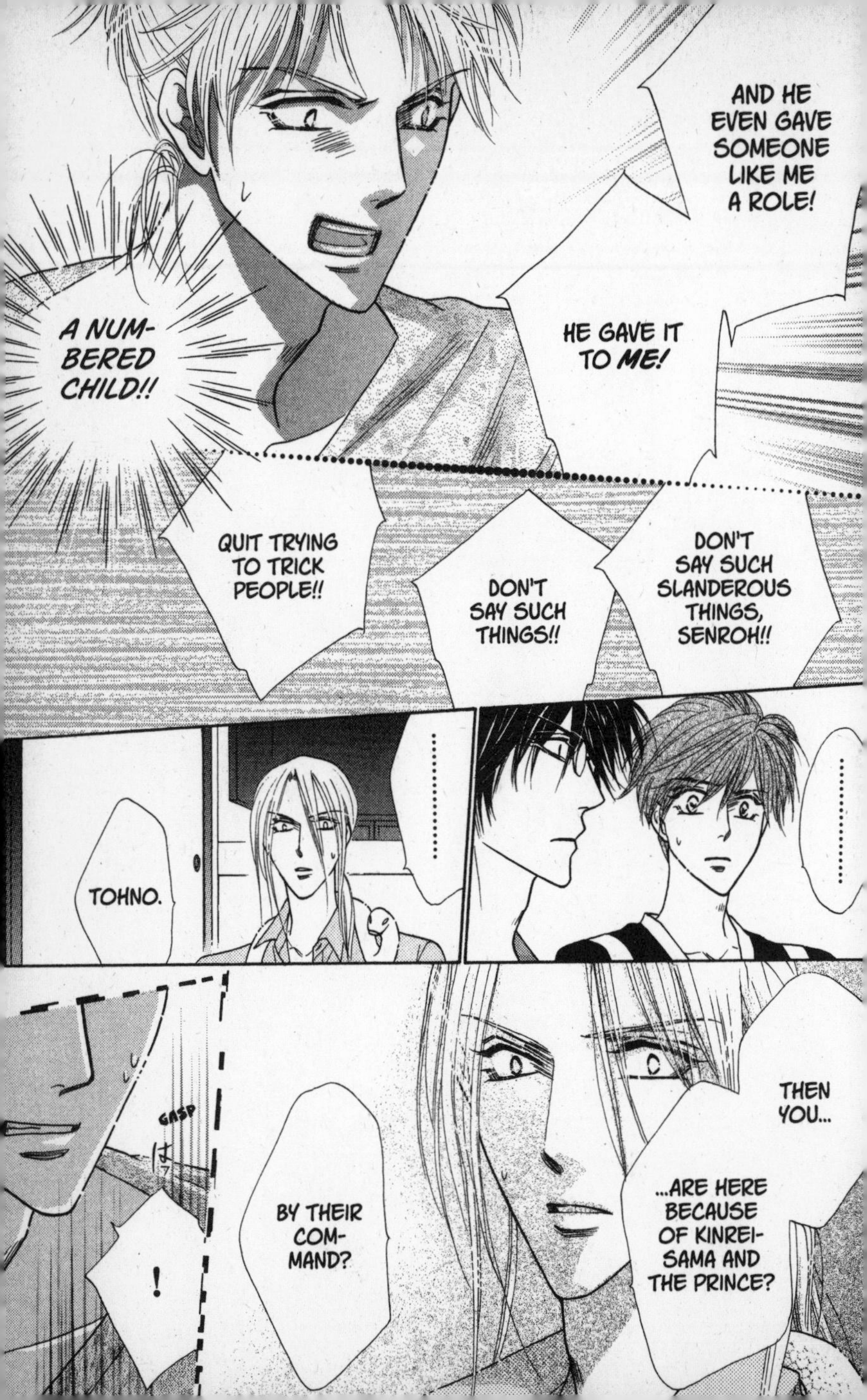
AND HE EVEN GAVE SOMEONE LIKE ME A ROLE!
HE GAVE IT TO *ME!*
A NUM-BERED CHILD!!
DON'T SAY SUCH SLANDEROUS THINGS, SENROH!!
DON'T SAY SUCH THINGS!!
QUIT TRYING TO TRICK PEOPLE!!
......
......
TOHNO.
THEN YOU...
...ARE HERE BECAUSE OF KINREI-SAMA AND THE PRINCE?
BY THEIR COM-MAND?
GASP
は
!

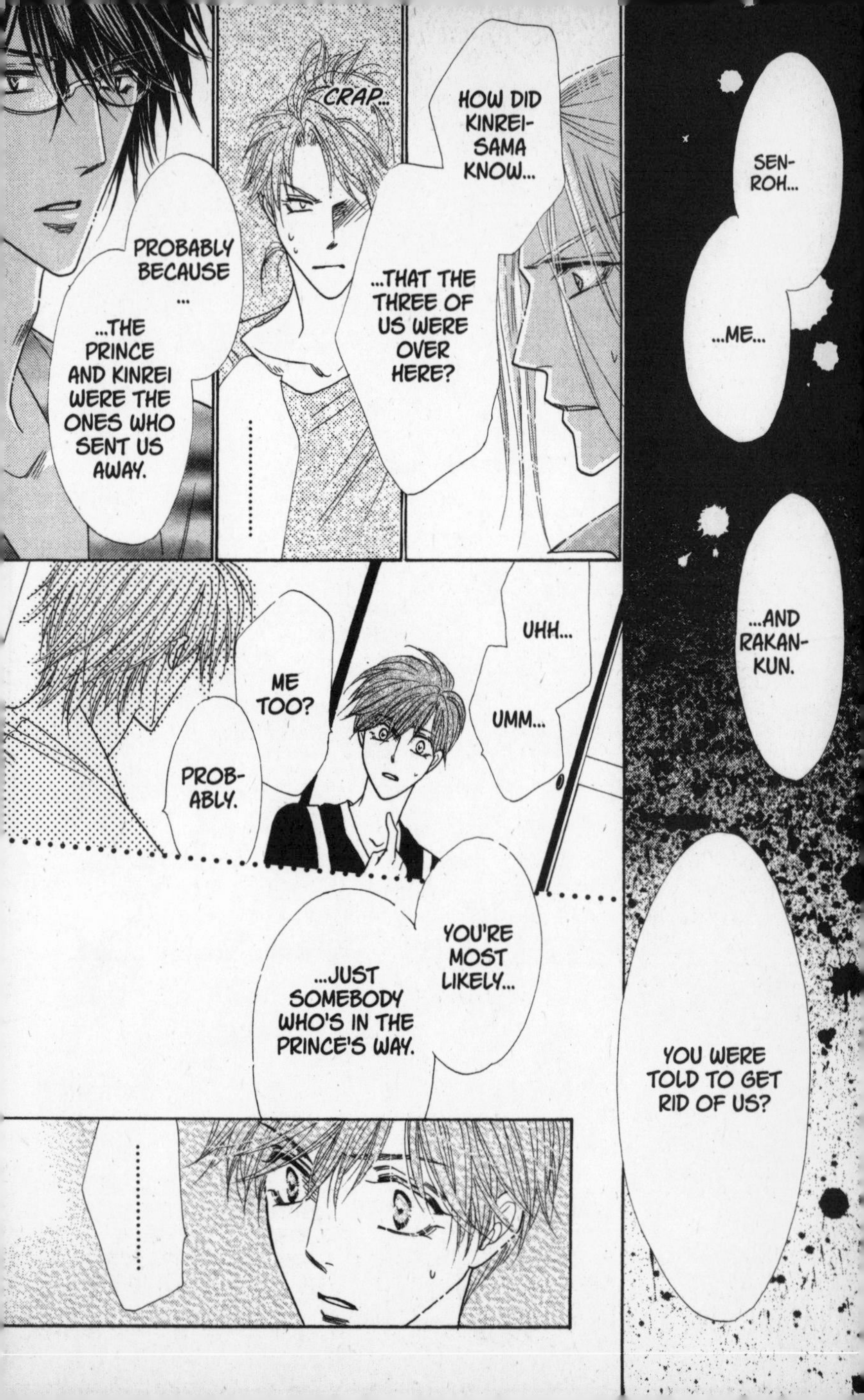
SEN-ROH...
...ME...
...AND RAKAN-KUN.
YOU WERE TOLD TO GET RID OF US?
HOW DID KINREI-SAMA KNOW...
...THAT THE THREE OF US WERE OVER HERE?
CRAP...
......
PROBABLY BECAUSE ...
...THE PRINCE AND KINREI WERE THE ONES WHO SENT US AWAY.
UHH...
UMM...
ME TOO?
PROB-ABLY.
YOU'RE MOST LIKELY...
...JUST SOMEBODY WHO'S IN THE PRINCE'S WAY.
......

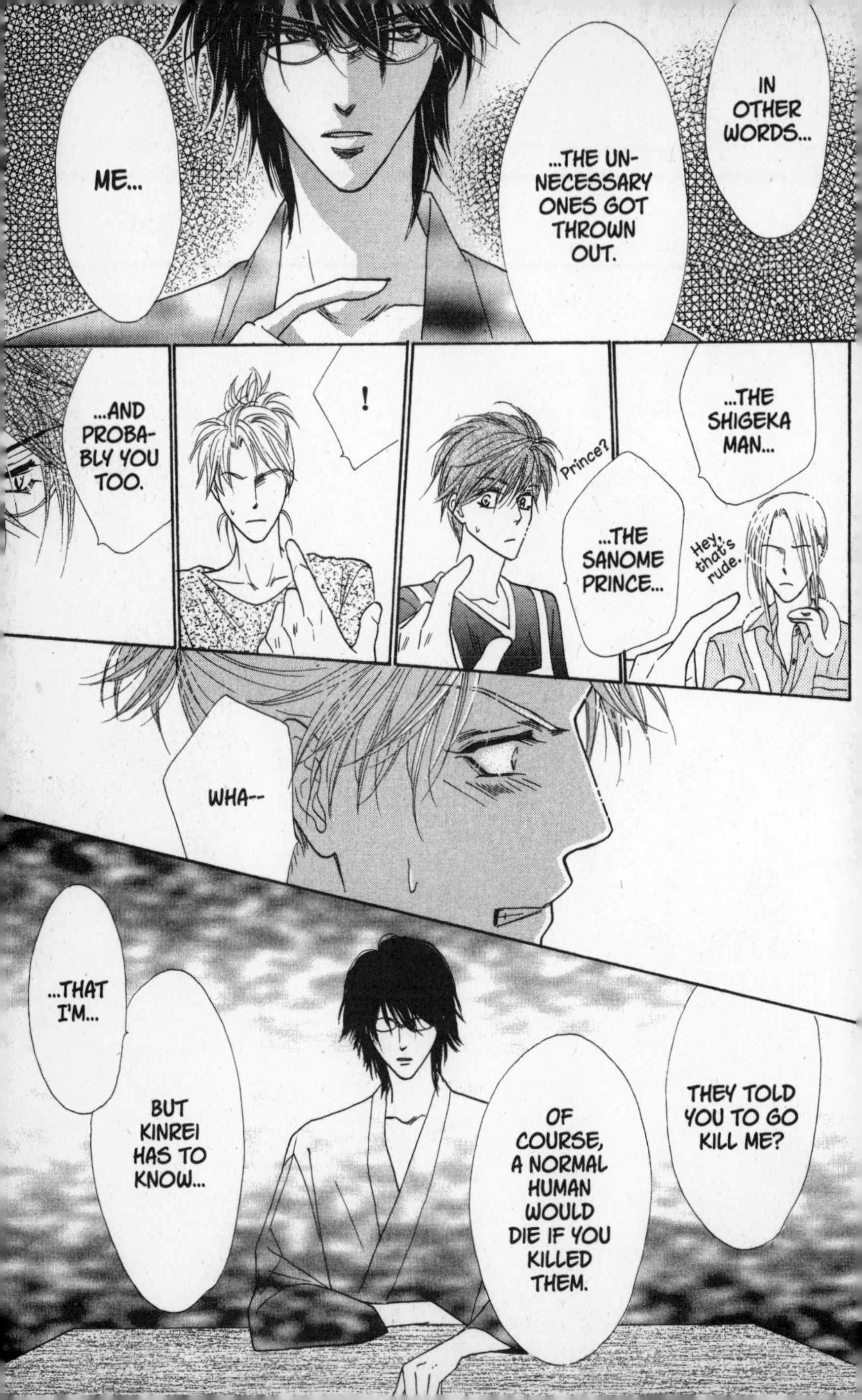
IN OTHER WORDS...
...THE UN-NECESSARY ONES GOT THROWN OUT.
ME...
...THE SHIGEKA MAN...
Hey, that's rude.
...THE SANOME PRINCE...
Prince?
!
...AND PROBA-BLY YOU TOO.
WHA--
THEY TOLD YOU TO GO KILL ME?
OF COURSE, A NORMAL HUMAN WOULD DIE IF YOU KILLED THEM.
BUT KINREI HAS TO KNOW...
...THAT I'M...

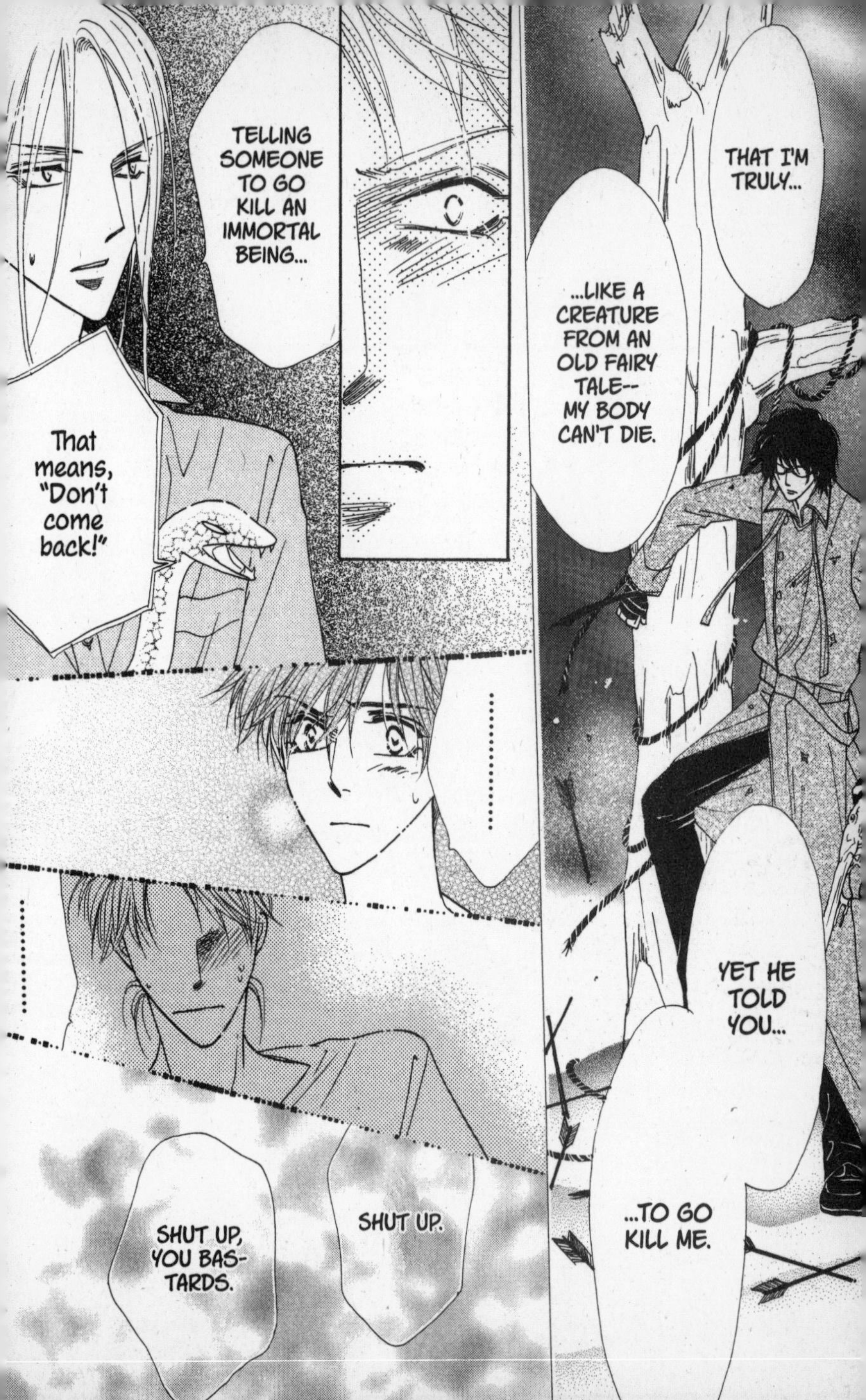
THAT I'M TRULY...
...LIKE A CREATURE FROM AN OLD FAIRY TALE-- MY BODY CAN'T DIE.
YET HE TOLD YOU...
...TO GO KILL ME.
TELLING SOMEONE TO GO KILL AN IMMORTAL BEING...
That means, "Don't come back!"
SHUT UP.
SHUT UP, YOU BASTARDS.

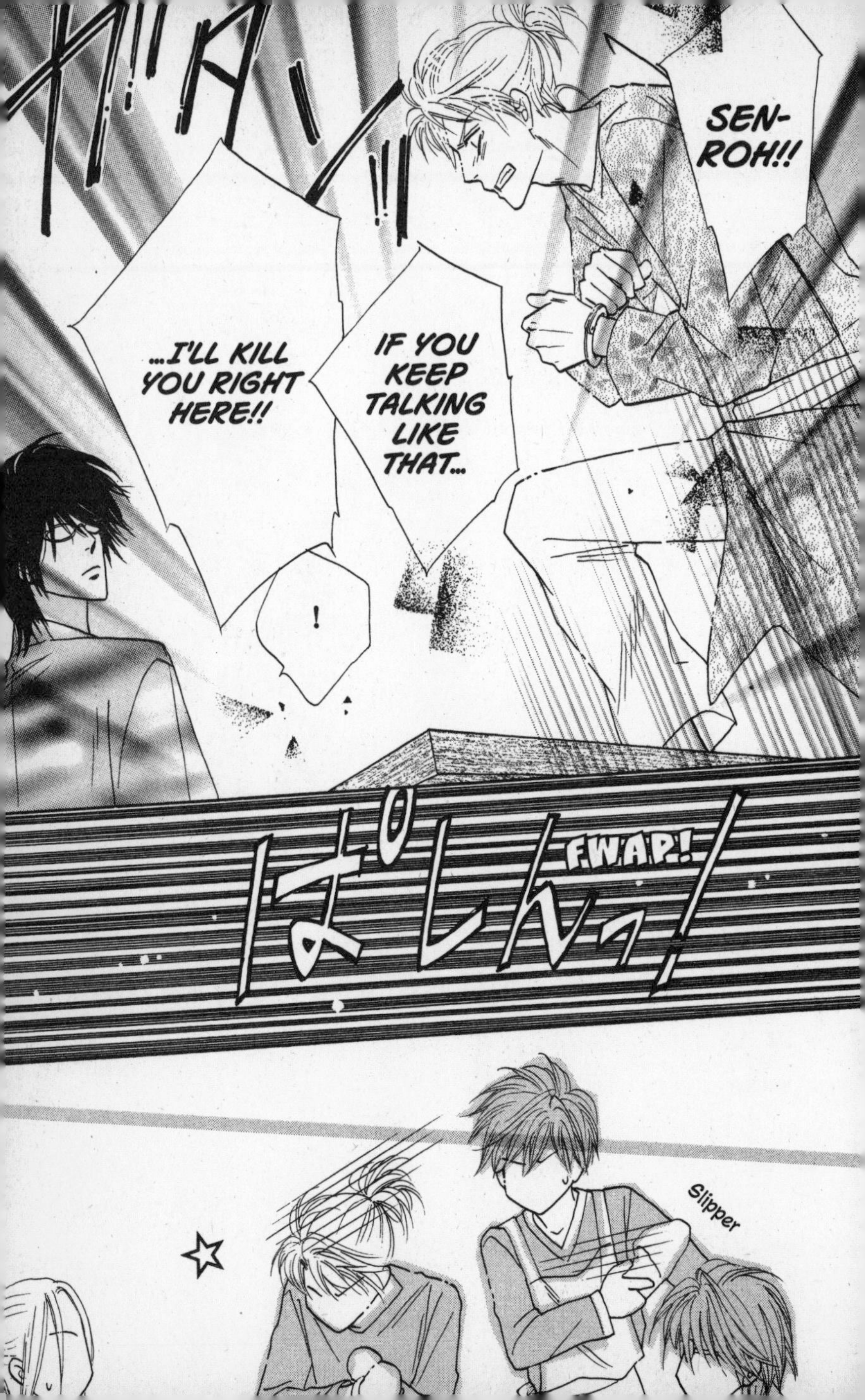
SEN-ROH!!
IF YOU KEEP TALKING LIKE THAT...
...I'LL KILL YOU RIGHT HERE!!
!
ばしんっ!
FWAP!
Slipper

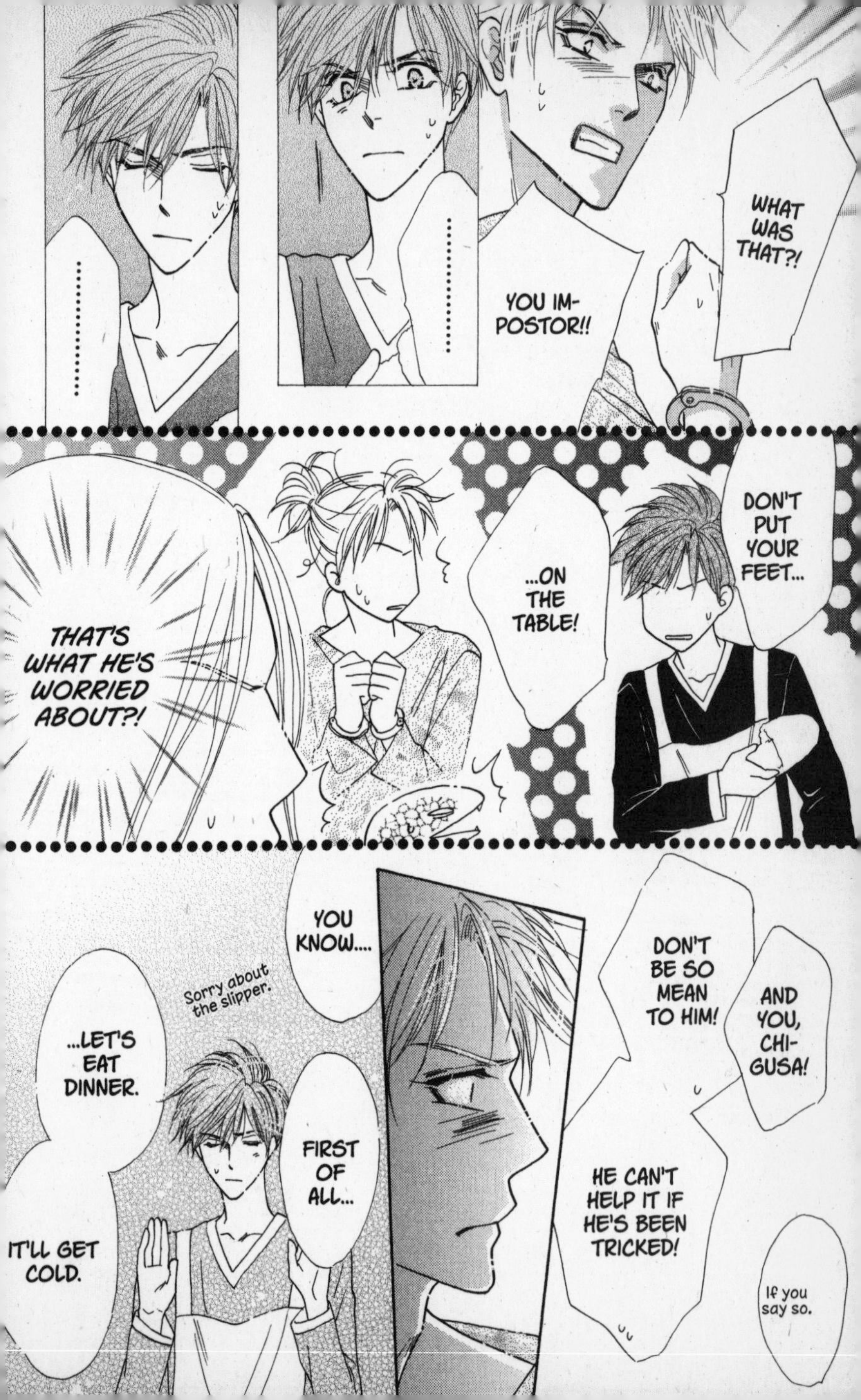
WHAT WAS THAT?!
YOU IM-POSTOR!!
......
......
DON'T PUT YOUR FEET...
...ON THE TABLE!
THAT'S WHAT HE'S WORRIED ABOUT?!
DON'T BE SO MEAN TO HIM!
AND YOU, CHI-GUSA!
HE CAN'T HELP IT IF HE'S BEEN TRICKED!
If you say so.
YOU KNOW....
FIRST OF ALL...
Sorry about the slipper.
...LET'S EAT DINNER.
IT'LL GET COLD.

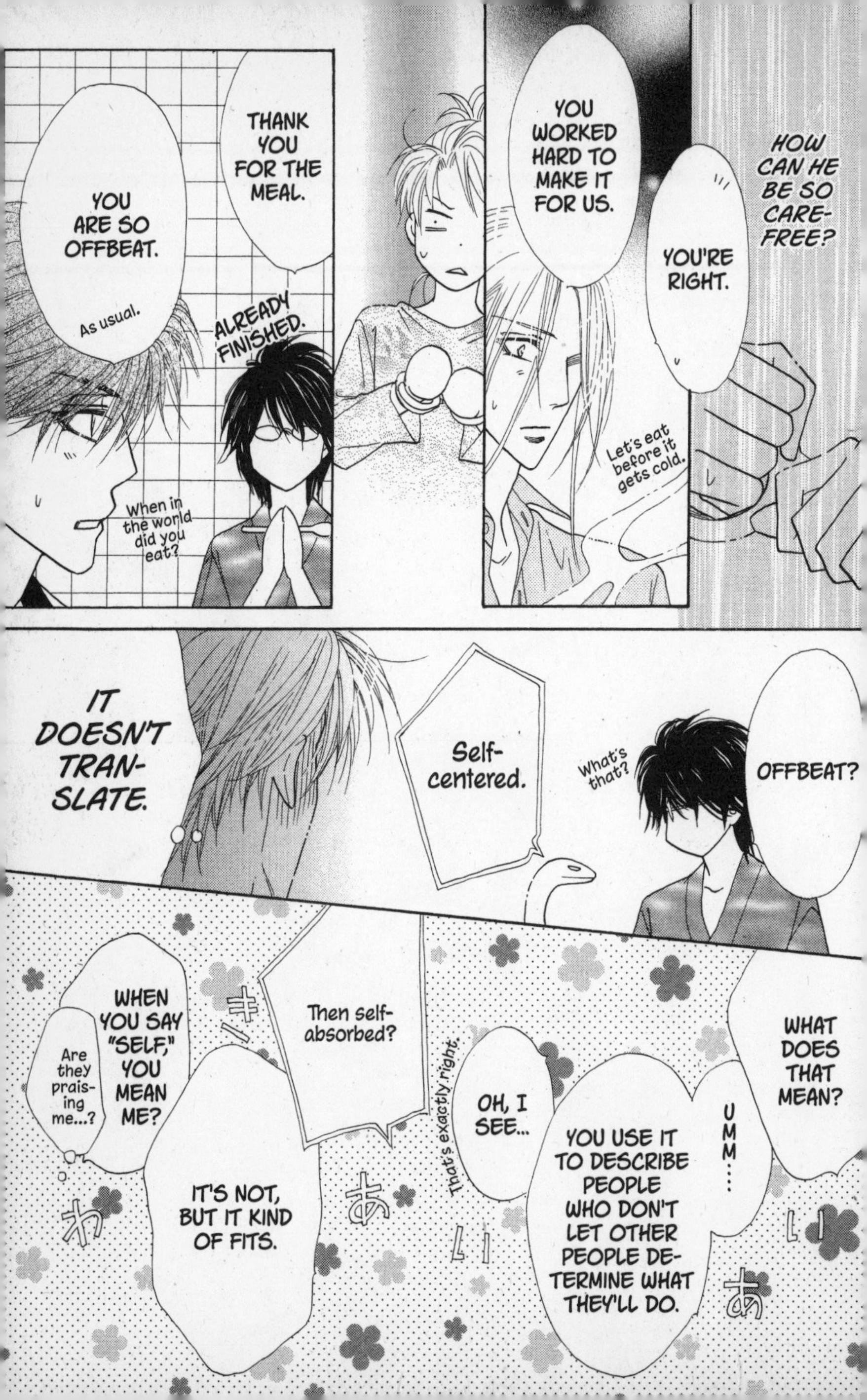
HOW CAN HE BE SO CAREFREE?
YOU WORKED HARD TO MAKE IT FOR US.
YOU'RE RIGHT.
Let's eat before it gets cold.
THANK YOU FOR THE MEAL.
ALREADY FINISHED.
YOU ARE SO OFFBEAT.
As usual.
When in the world did you eat?
OFFBEAT?
What's that?
Self-centered.
IT DOESN'T TRANSLATE.
WHAT DOES THAT MEAN?
UMM....
YOU USE IT TO DESCRIBE PEOPLE WHO DON'T LET OTHER PEOPLE DETERMINE WHAT THEY'LL DO.
OH, I SEE...
That's exactly right.
Then self-absorbed?
WHEN YOU SAY "SELF," YOU MEAN ME?
IT'S NOT, BUT IT KIND OF FITS.
Are they praising me...?

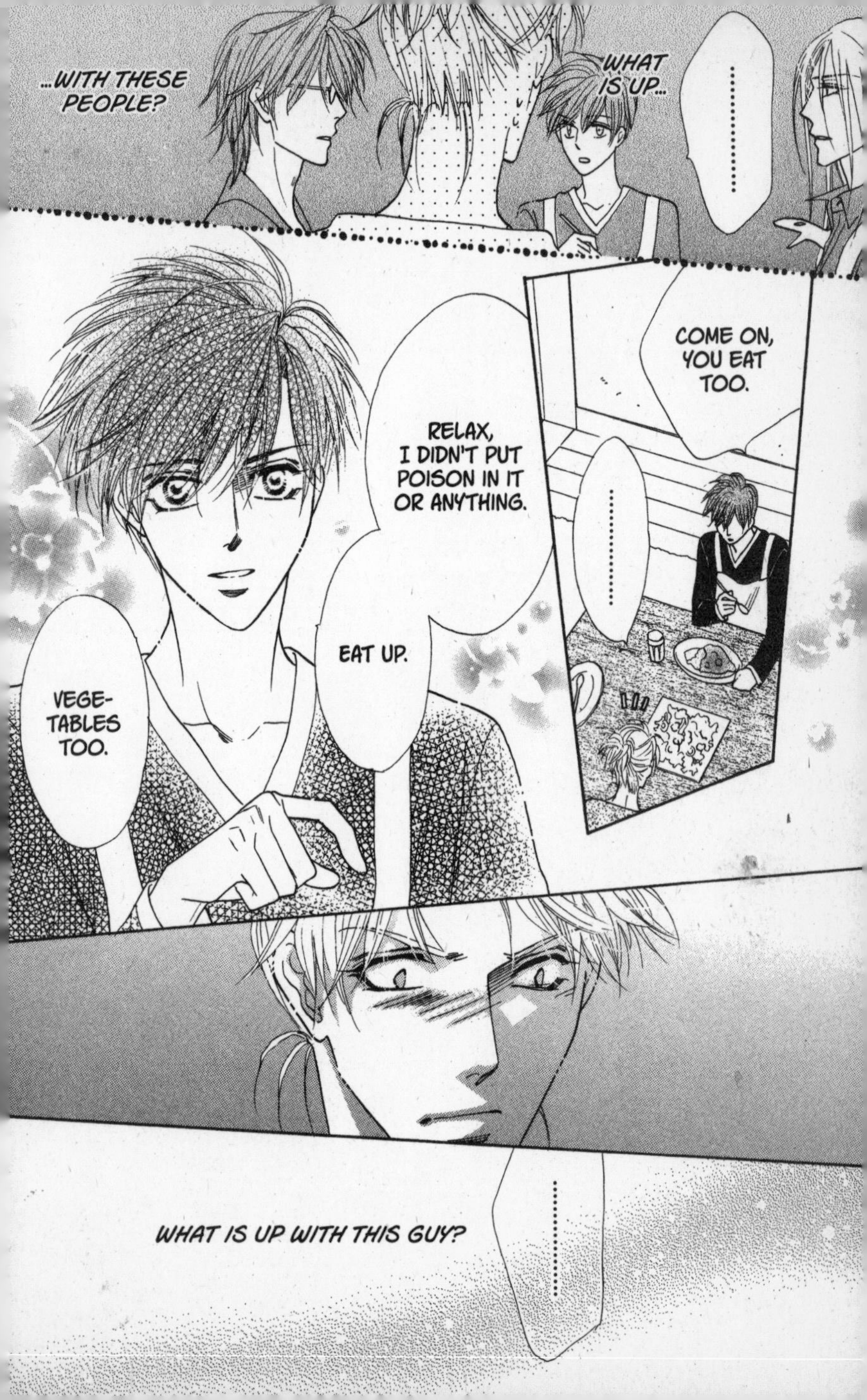
......
WHAT IS UP...
...WITH THESE PEOPLE?
COME ON, YOU EAT TOO.
......
RELAX, I DIDN'T PUT POISON IN IT OR ANYTHING.
EAT UP.
VEGE-TABLES TOO.
......
WHAT IS UP WITH THIS GUY?

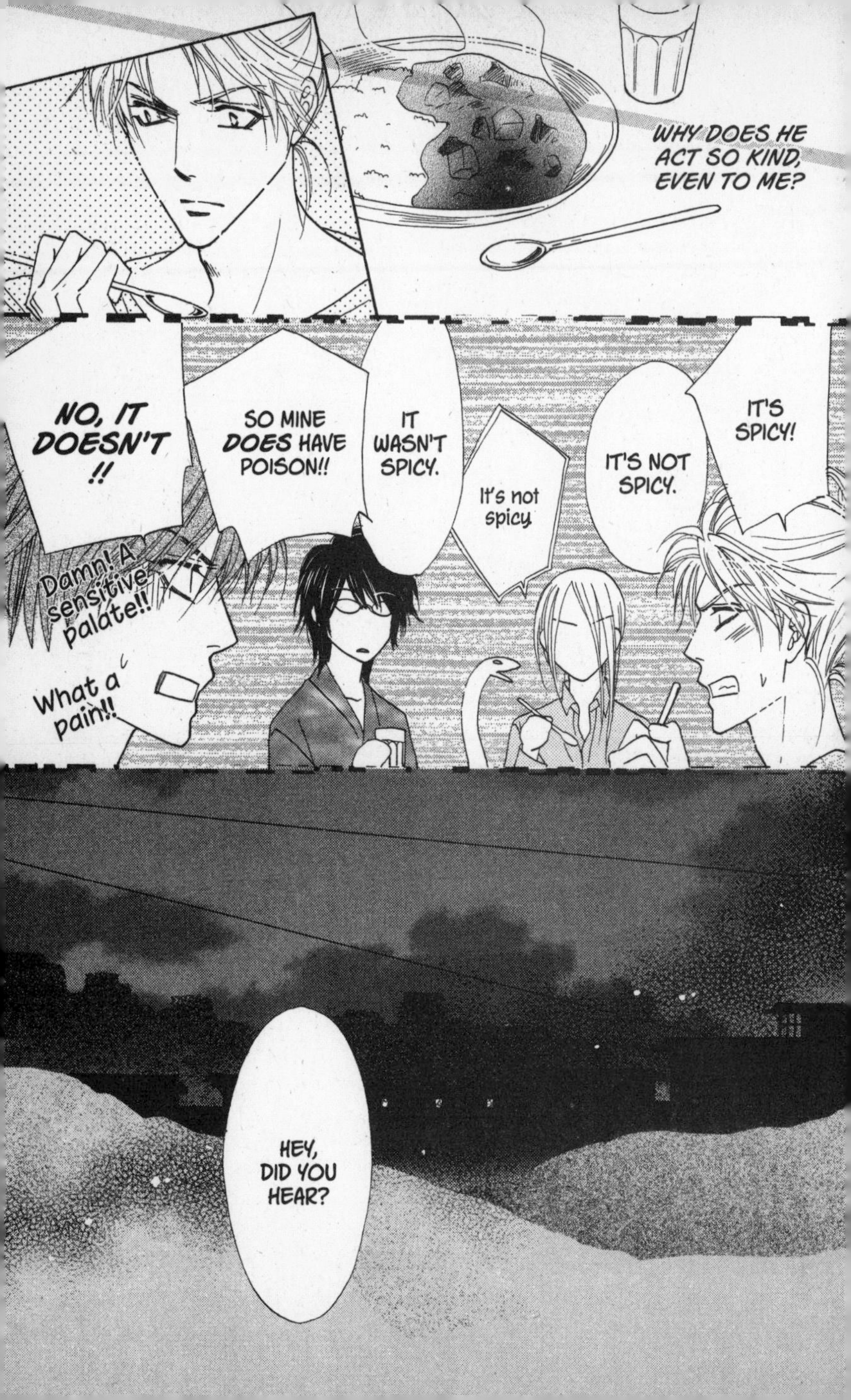
WHY DOES HE ACT SO KIND, EVEN TO ME?
IT'S SPICY!
IT'S NOT SPICY.
It's not spicy.
IT WASN'T SPICY.
SO MINE DOES HAVE POISON!!
NO, IT DOESN'T !!
Damn! A sensitive palate!!
What a pain!!
HEY, DID YOU HEAR?

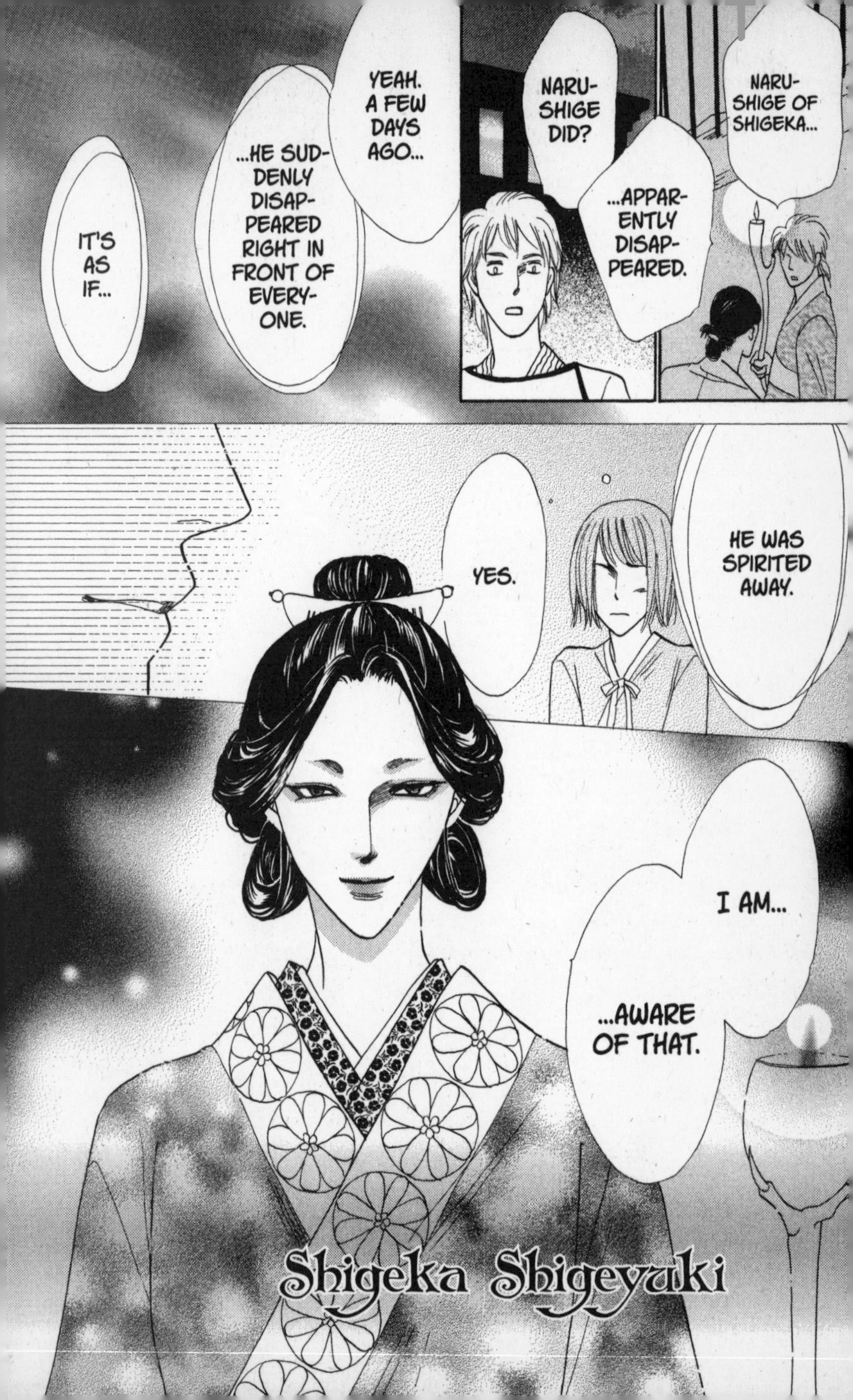
NARUSHIGE OF SHIGEKA...
...APPARENTLY DISAPPEARED.
NARUSHIGE DID?
YEAH. A FEW DAYS AGO...
...HE SUDDENLY DISAPPEARED RIGHT IN FRONT OF EVERYONE.
IT'S AS IF...
HE WAS SPIRITED AWAY.
YES.
I AM...
...AWARE OF THAT.
Shigeka Shigeyuki

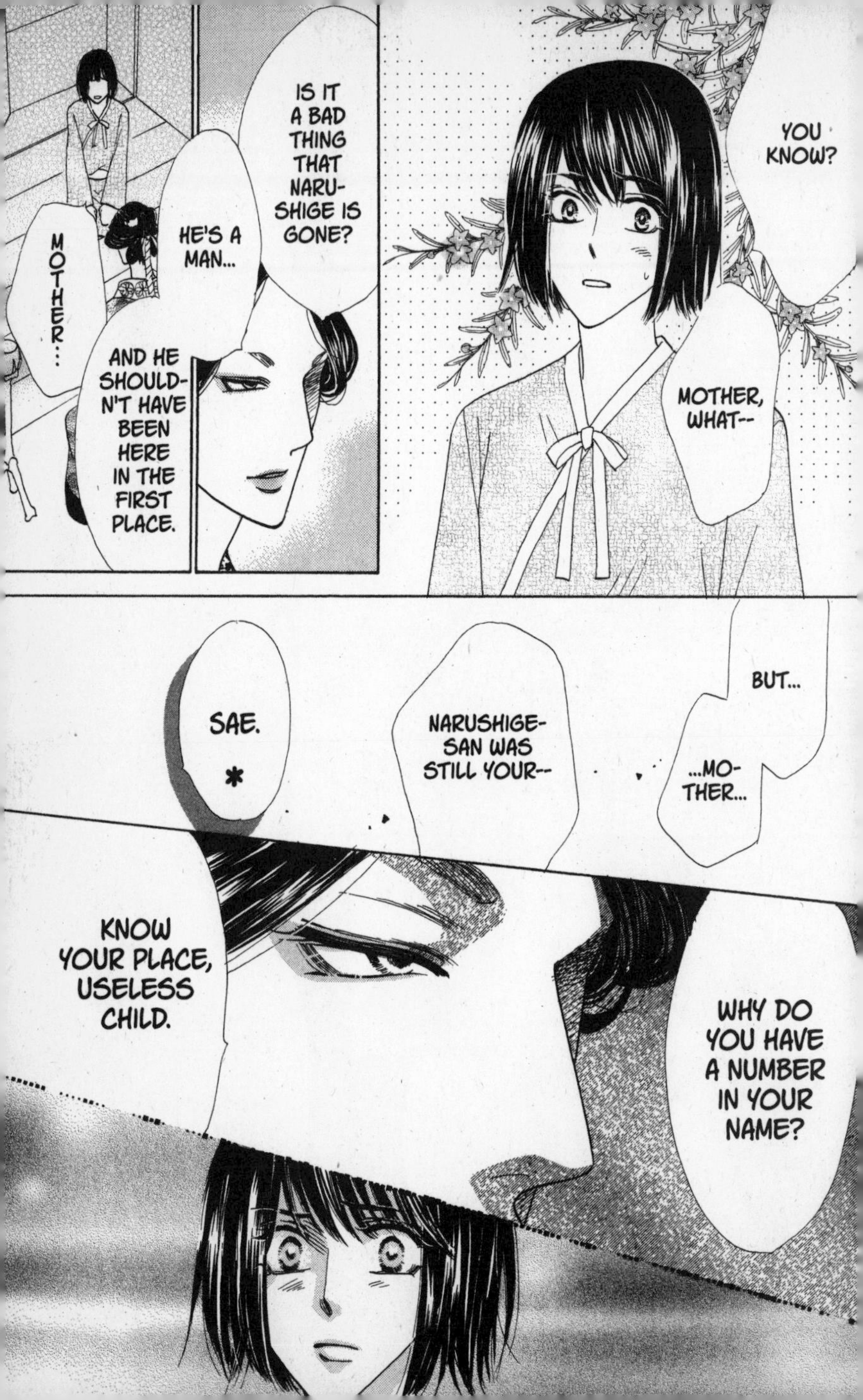
YOU KNOW?
MOTHER, WHAT--
IS IT A BAD THING THAT NARUSHIGE IS GONE?
HE'S A MAN...
AND HE SHOULDN'T HAVE BEEN HERE IN THE FIRST PLACE.
MOTHER...
BUT...
...MOTHER...
NARUSHIGE-SAN WAS STILL YOUR--
SAE. *
WHY DO YOU HAVE A NUMBER IN YOUR NAME?
KNOW YOUR PLACE, USELESS CHILD.

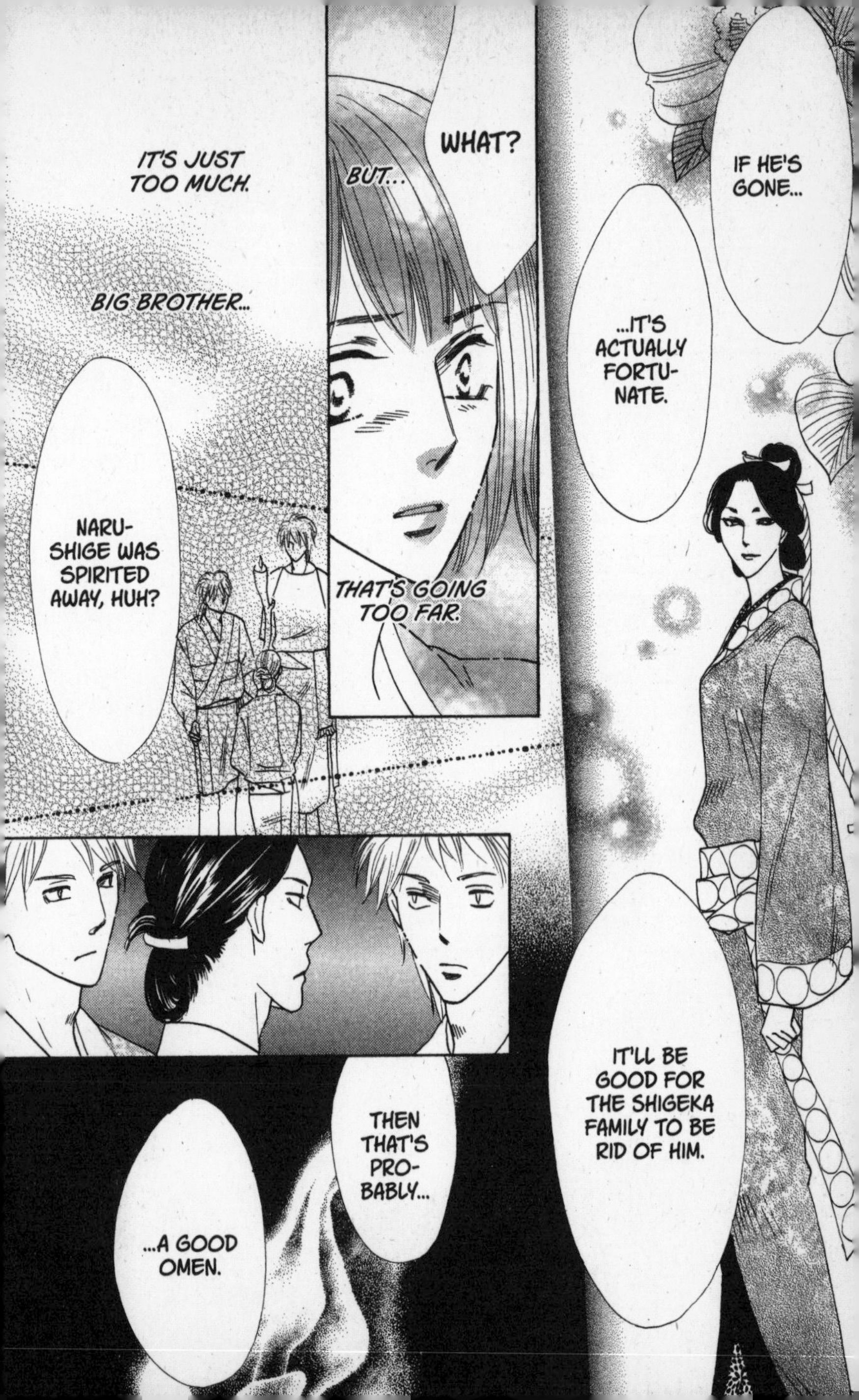
IF HE'S GONE...
...IT'S ACTUALLY FORTUNATE.
IT'LL BE GOOD FOR THE SHIGEKA FAMILY TO BE RID OF HIM.
WHAT?
BUT...
THAT'S GOING TOO FAR.
IT'S JUST TOO MUCH.
BIG BROTHER...
NARUSHIGE WAS SPIRITED AWAY, HUH?
THEN THAT'S PROBABLY...
...A GOOD OMEN.

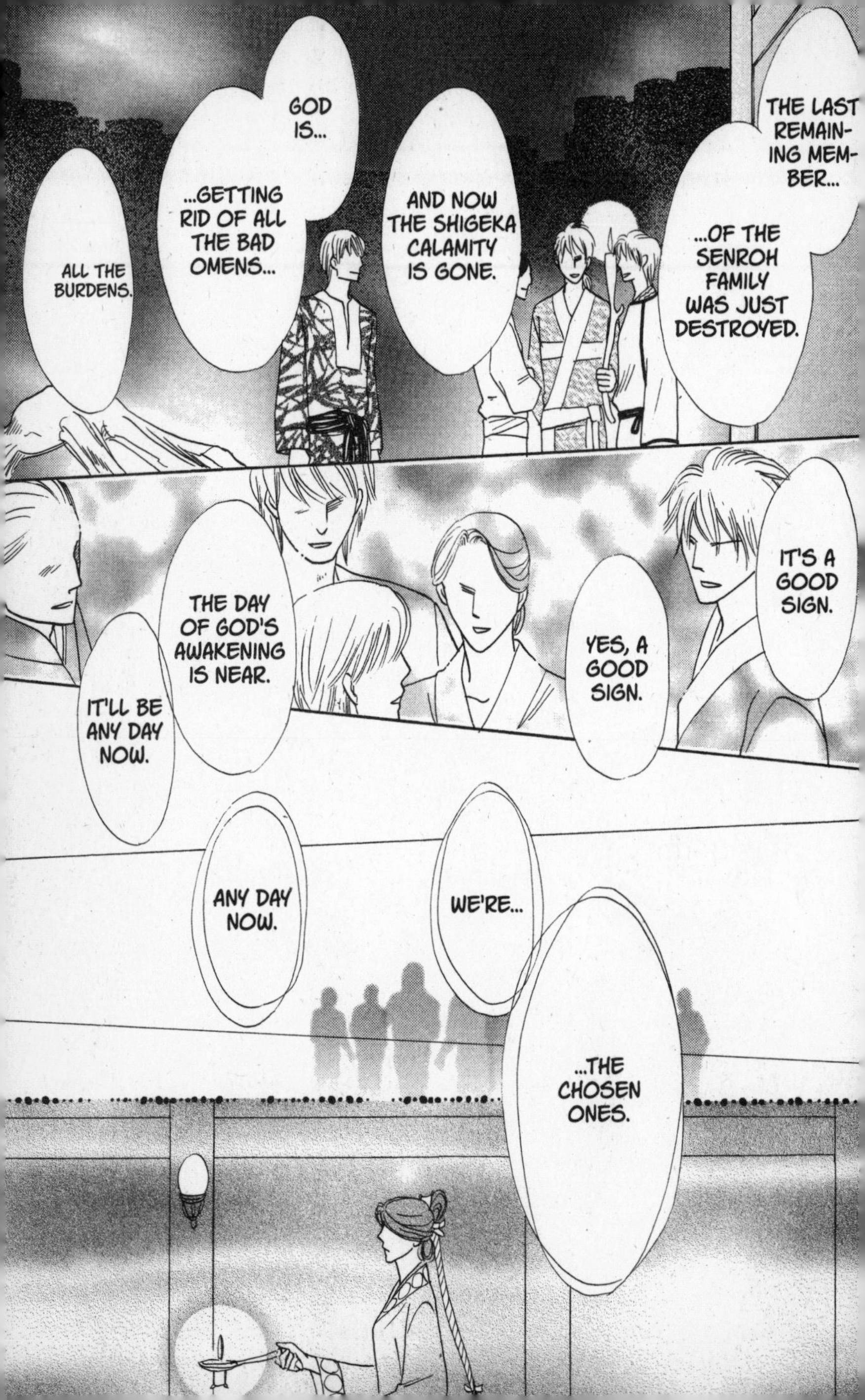
THE LAST REMAINING MEMBER...
...OF THE SENROH FAMILY WAS JUST DESTROYED.
AND NOW THE SHIGEKA CALAMITY IS GONE.
GOD IS...
...GETTING RID OF ALL THE BAD OMENS...
ALL THE BURDENS.
IT'S A GOOD SIGN.
YES, A GOOD SIGN.
THE DAY OF GOD'S AWAKENING IS NEAR.
IT'LL BE ANY DAY NOW.
WE'RE...
ANY DAY NOW.
...THE CHOSEN ONES.

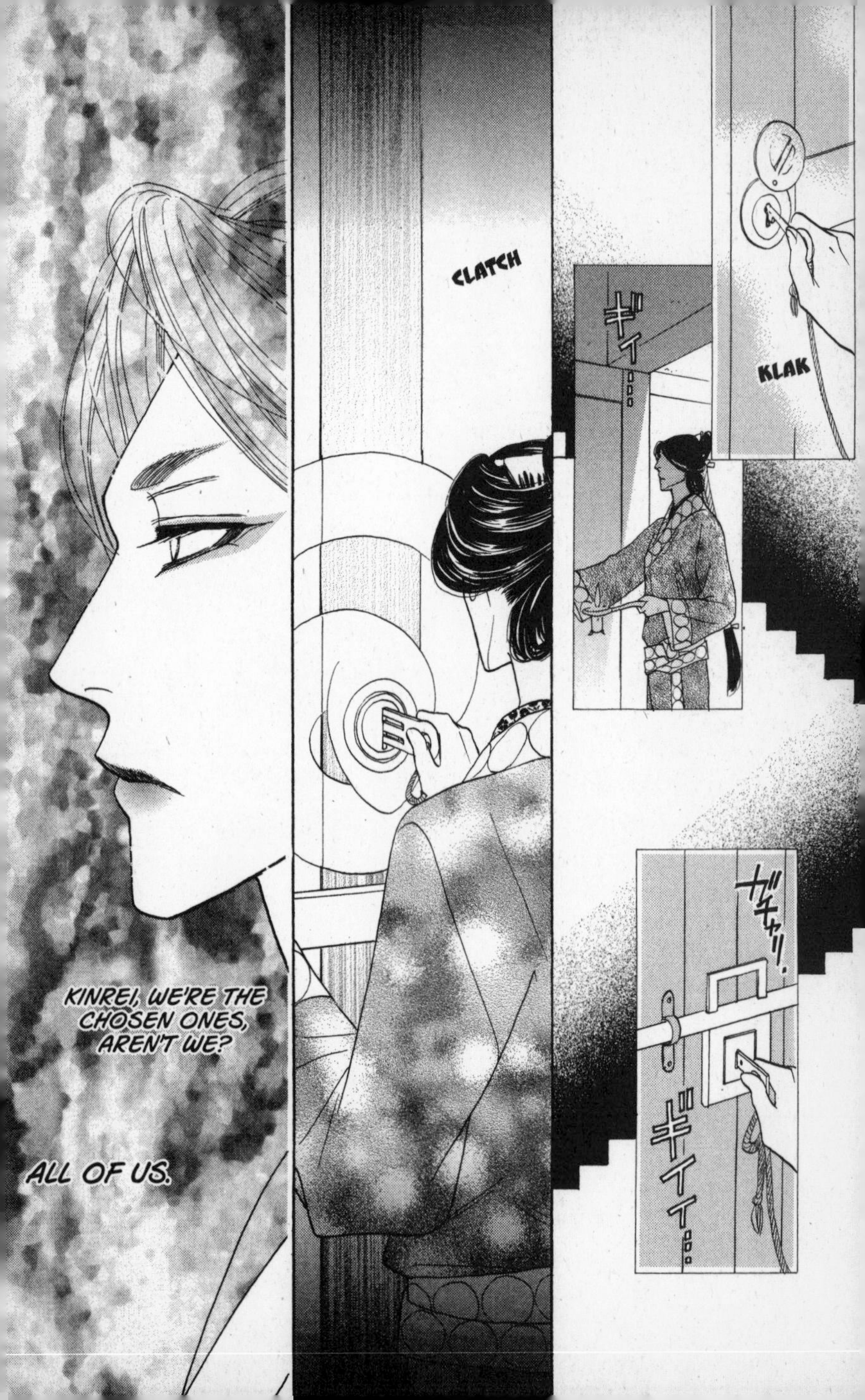
KLAK
ギイ…
ガチャリ.
ギイイ…
CLATCH
KINREI, WE'RE THE CHOSEN ONES, AREN'T WE?
ALL OF US.

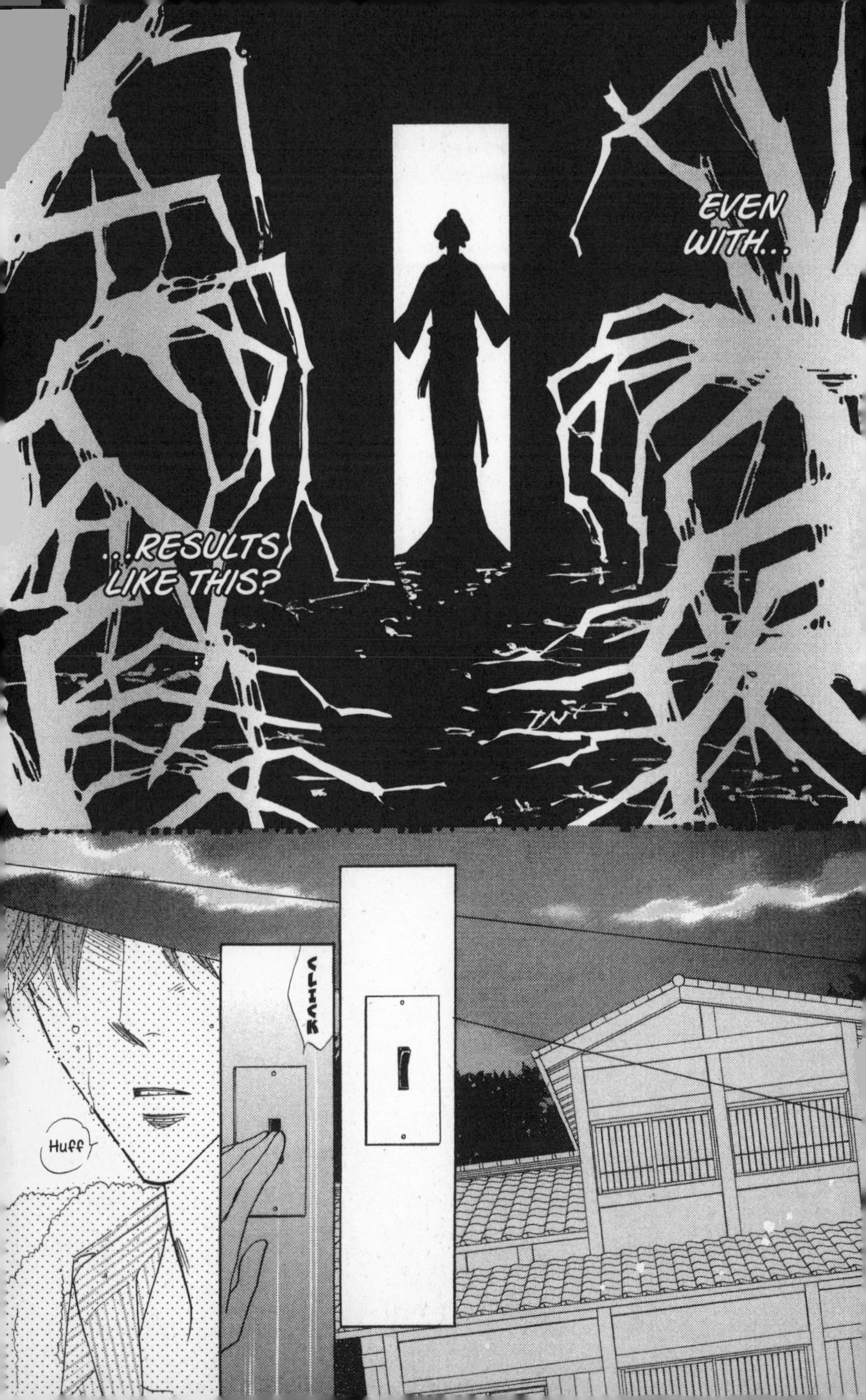
EVEN WITH...
...RESULTS LIKE THIS?
CLICK
Huff

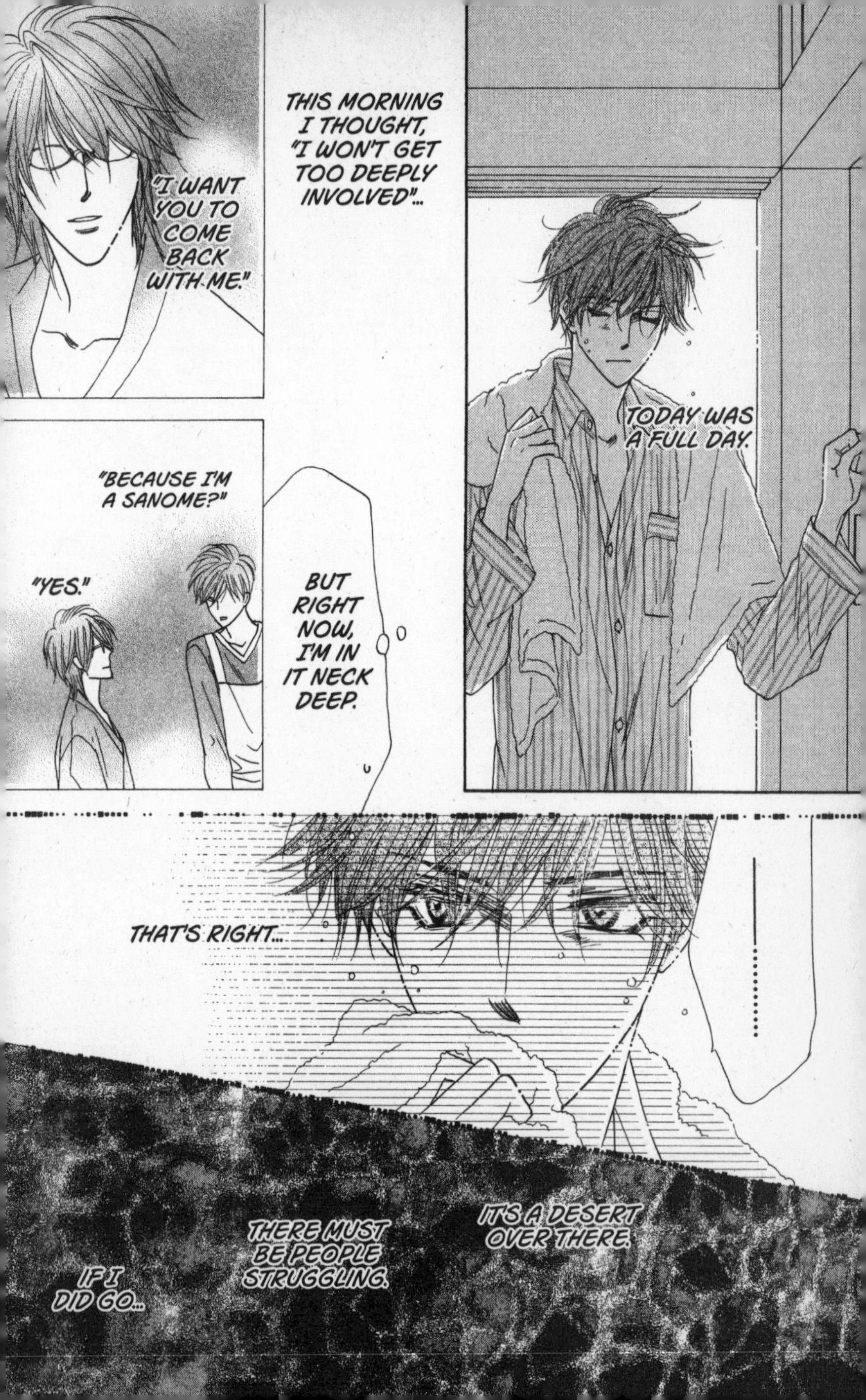
TODAY WAS A FULL DAY.
THIS MORNING I THOUGHT, "I WON'T GET TOO DEEPLY INVOLVED"...
"I WANT YOU TO COME BACK WITH ME."
BUT RIGHT NOW, I'M IN IT NECK DEEP.
"BECAUSE I'M A SANOME?"
"YES."
THAT'S RIGHT...
IT'S A DESERT OVER THERE.
THERE MUST BE PEOPLE STRUGGLING.
IF I DID GO...

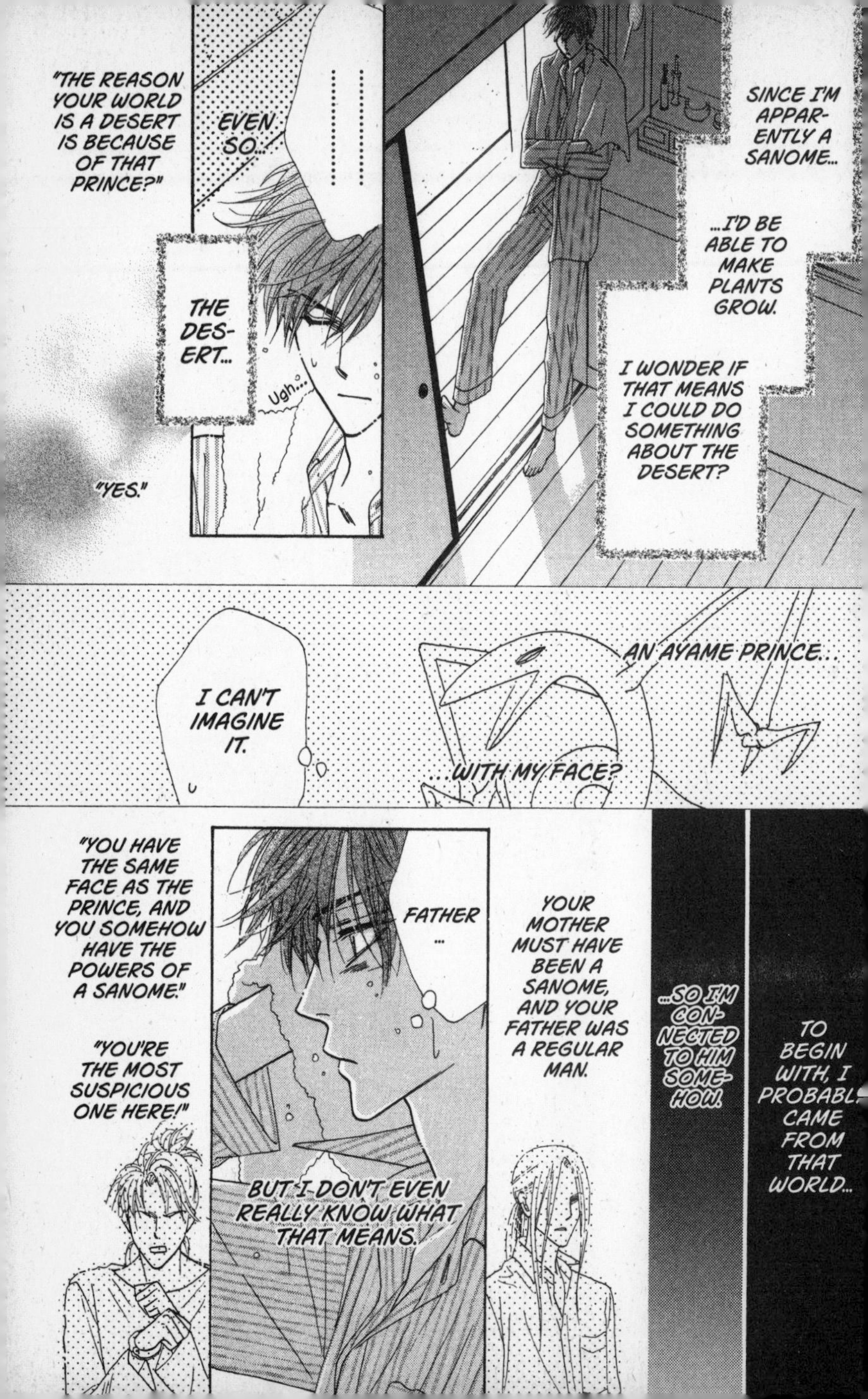
SINCE I'M APPARENTLY A SANOME...
...I'D BE ABLE TO MAKE PLANTS GROW.
I WONDER IF THAT MEANS I COULD DO SOMETHING ABOUT THE DESERT?
......
EVEN SO...
THE DESERT...
Ugh...
"THE REASON YOUR WORLD IS A DESERT IS BECAUSE OF THAT PRINCE?"
"YES."
AN AYAME PRINCE...
...WITH MY FACE?
I CAN'T IMAGINE IT.
TO BEGIN WITH, I PROBABL CAME FROM THAT WORLD...
...SO I'M CONNECTED TO HIM SOMEHOW.
YOUR MOTHER MUST HAVE BEEN A SANOME, AND YOUR FATHER WAS A REGULAR MAN.
FATHER...
BUT I DON'T EVEN REALLY KNOW WHAT THAT MEANS.
"YOU HAVE THE SAME FACE AS THE PRINCE, AND YOU SOMEHOW HAVE THE POWERS OF A SANOME."
"YOU'RE THE MOST SUSPICIOUS ONE HERE!"

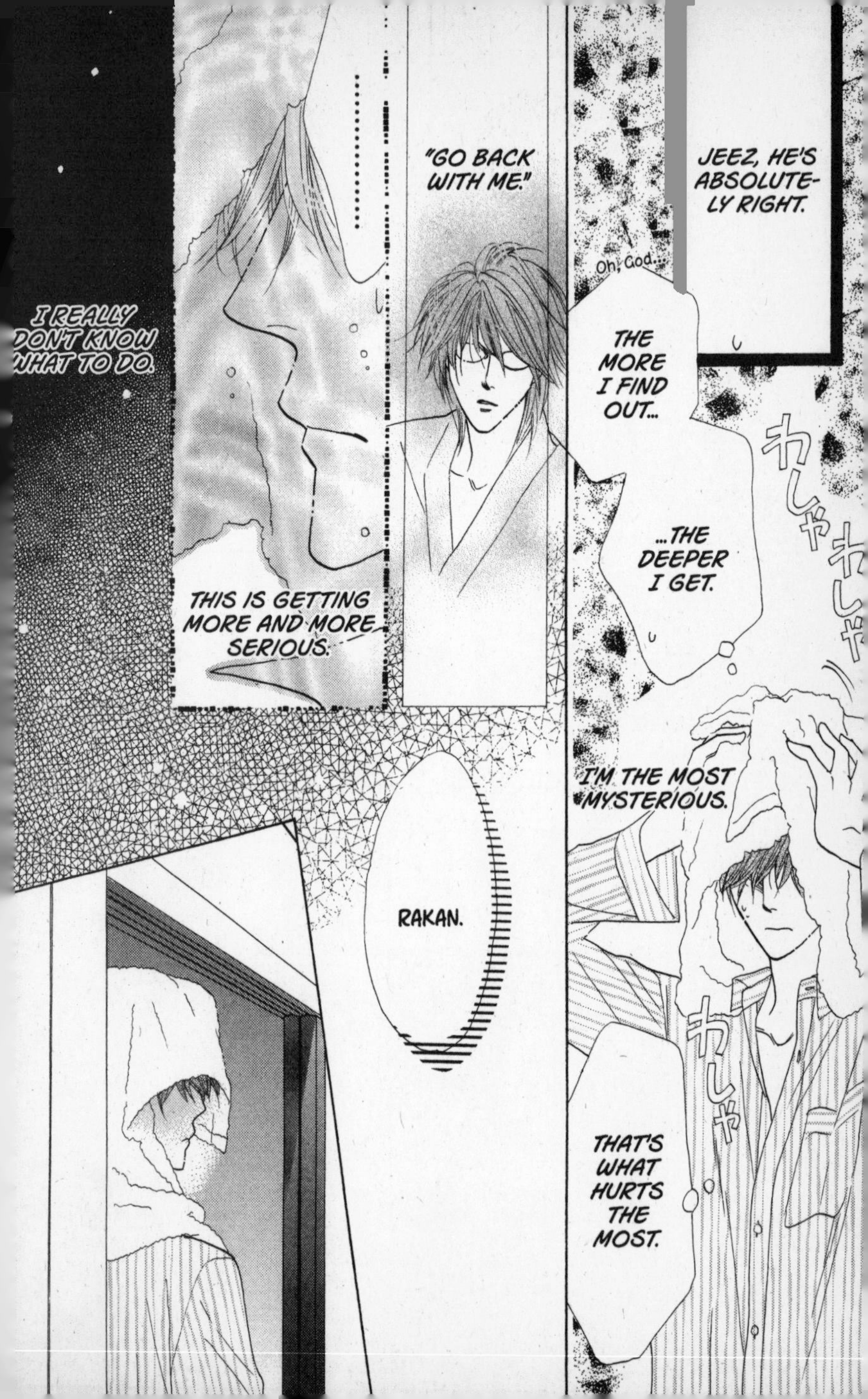
JEEZ, HE'S ABSOLUTE-LY RIGHT.
Oh, God...
THE MORE I FIND OUT...
...THE DEEPER I GET.
わしゃわしゃ
I'M THE MOST MYSTERIOUS.
わしゃ
THAT'S WHAT HURTS THE MOST.
"GO BACK WITH ME."
THIS IS GETTING MORE AND MORE SERIOUS.
I REALLY DON'T KNOW WHAT TO DO.
RAKAN.

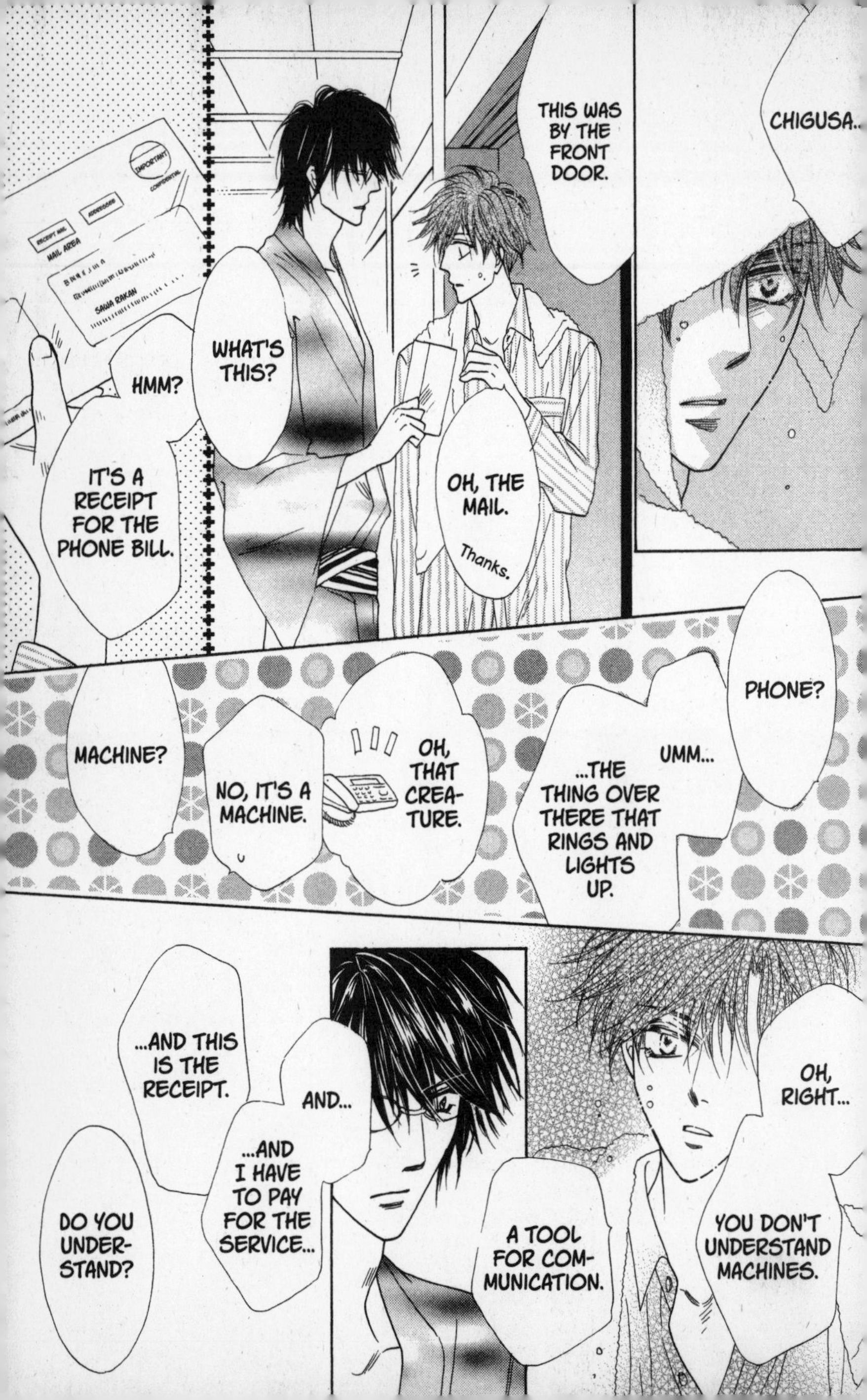
CHIGUSA...
THIS WAS BY THE FRONT DOOR.
WHAT'S THIS?
OH, THE MAIL.
Thanks.
IMPORTANT
CONFIDENTIAL
RECEIPT MAIL
ADDRESSEE
MAIL AREA
SAWA RAKAN
HMM?
IT'S A RECEIPT FOR THE PHONE BILL.
PHONE?
UMM...
...THE THING OVER THERE THAT RINGS AND LIGHTS UP.
OH, THAT CREA-TURE.
NO, IT'S A MACHINE.
MACHINE?
OH, RIGHT...
YOU DON'T UNDERSTAND MACHINES.
A TOOL FOR COM-MUNICATION.
...AND THIS IS THE RECEIPT.
AND...
...AND I HAVE TO PAY FOR THE SERVICE...
DO YOU UNDER-STAND?

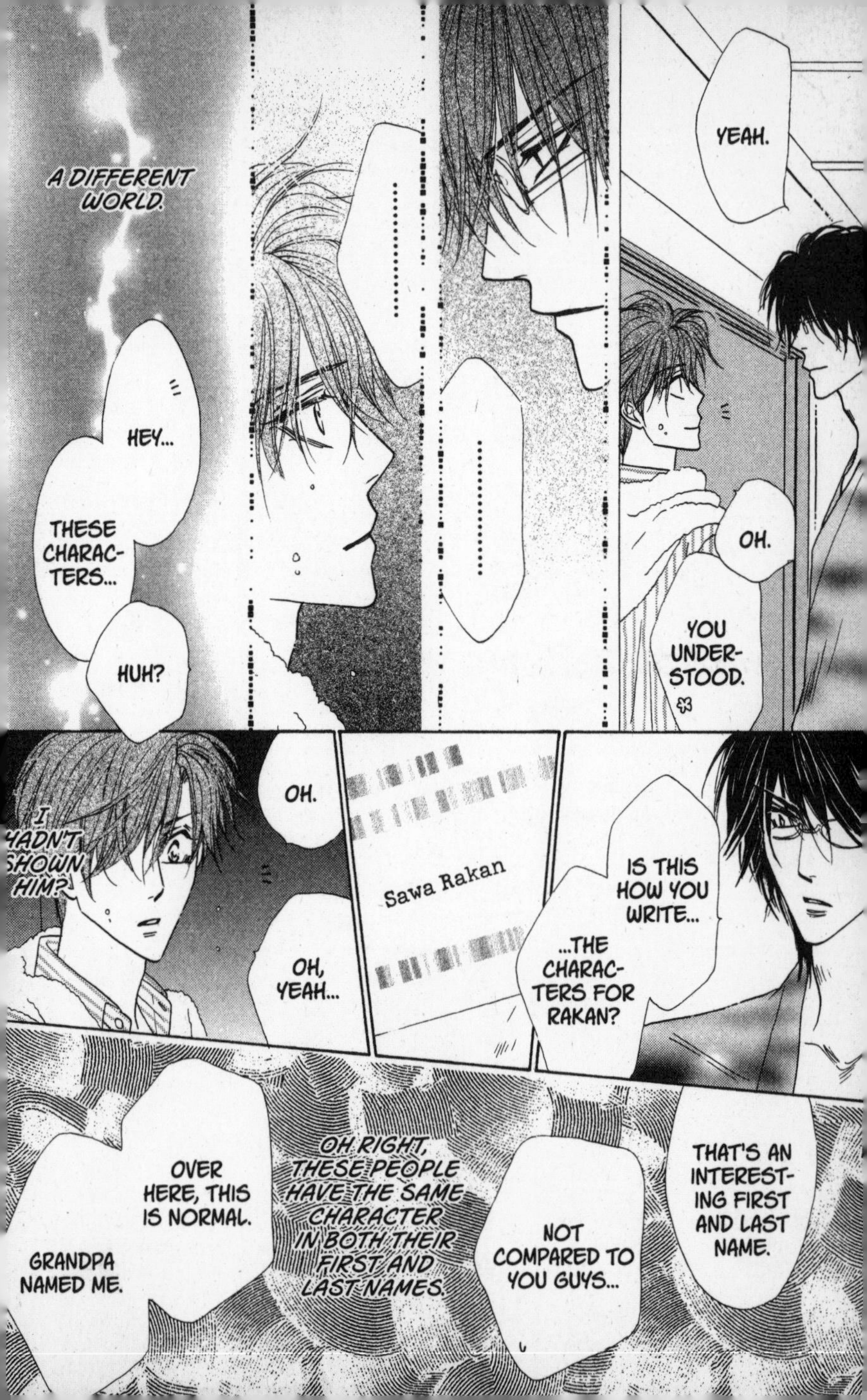
YEAH.
OH.
YOU UNDERSTOOD.
......
......
A DIFFERENT WORLD.
HEY...
THESE CHARACTERS...
HUH?
IS THIS HOW YOU WRITE...
...THE CHARACTERS FOR RAKAN?
Sawa Rakan
OH.
I HADN'T SHOWN HIM?
OH, YEAH...
THAT'S AN INTERESTING FIRST AND LAST NAME.
NOT COMPARED TO YOU GUYS...
OH RIGHT, THESE PEOPLE HAVE THE SAME CHARACTER IN BOTH THEIR FIRST AND LAST NAMES.
OVER HERE, THIS IS NORMAL.
GRANDPA NAMED ME.

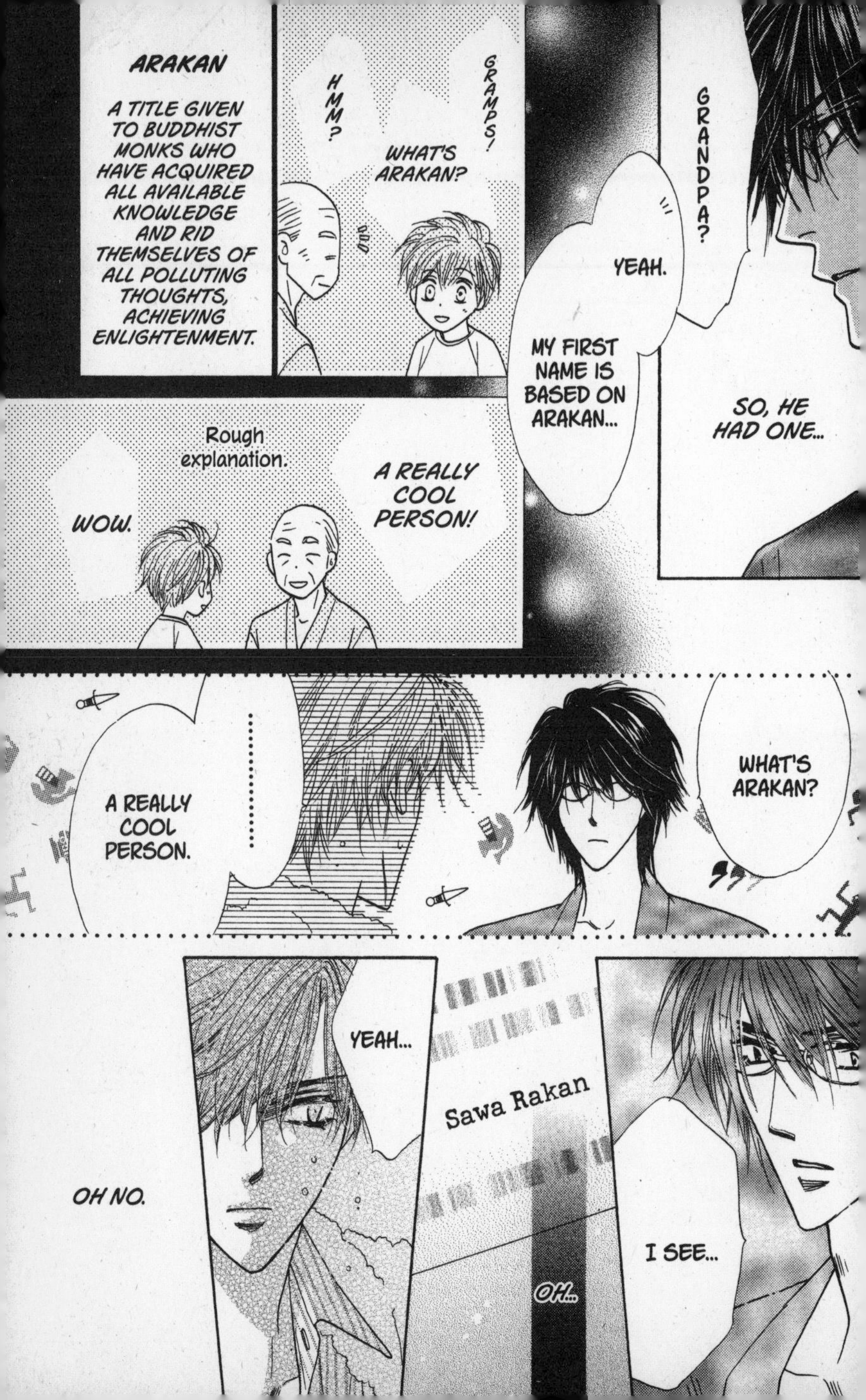
GRANDPA?
SO, HE HAD ONE...
YEAH.
MY FIRST NAME IS BASED ON ARAKAN...
GRAMPS!
HMM?
WHAT'S ARAKAN?
ARAKAN
A TITLE GIVEN TO BUDDHIST MONKS WHO HAVE ACQUIRED ALL AVAILABLE KNOWLEDGE AND RID THEMSELVES OF ALL POLLUTING THOUGHTS, ACHIEVING ENLIGHTENMENT.
A REALLY COOL PERSON!
Rough explanation.
WOW.
WHAT'S ARAKAN?
......
A REALLY COOL PERSON.
I SEE...
Sawa Rakan
OH...
YEAH...
OH NO.

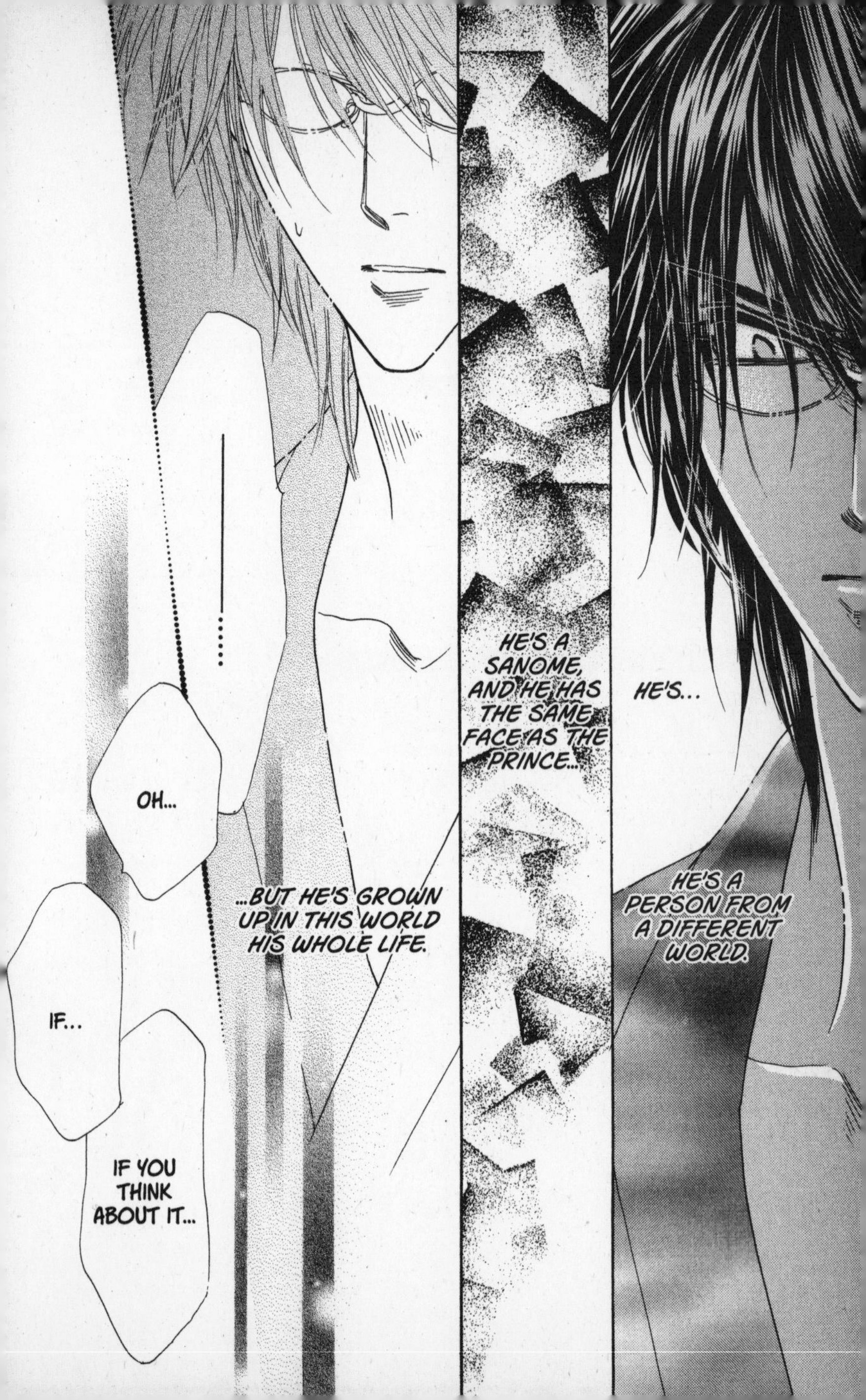
HE'S...
HE'S A PERSON FROM A DIFFERENT WORLD.
HE'S A SANOME, AND HE HAS THE SAME FACE AS THE PRINCE...
...BUT HE'S GROWN UP IN THIS WORLD HIS WHOLE LIFE.
OH...
IF...
IF YOU THINK ABOUT IT...

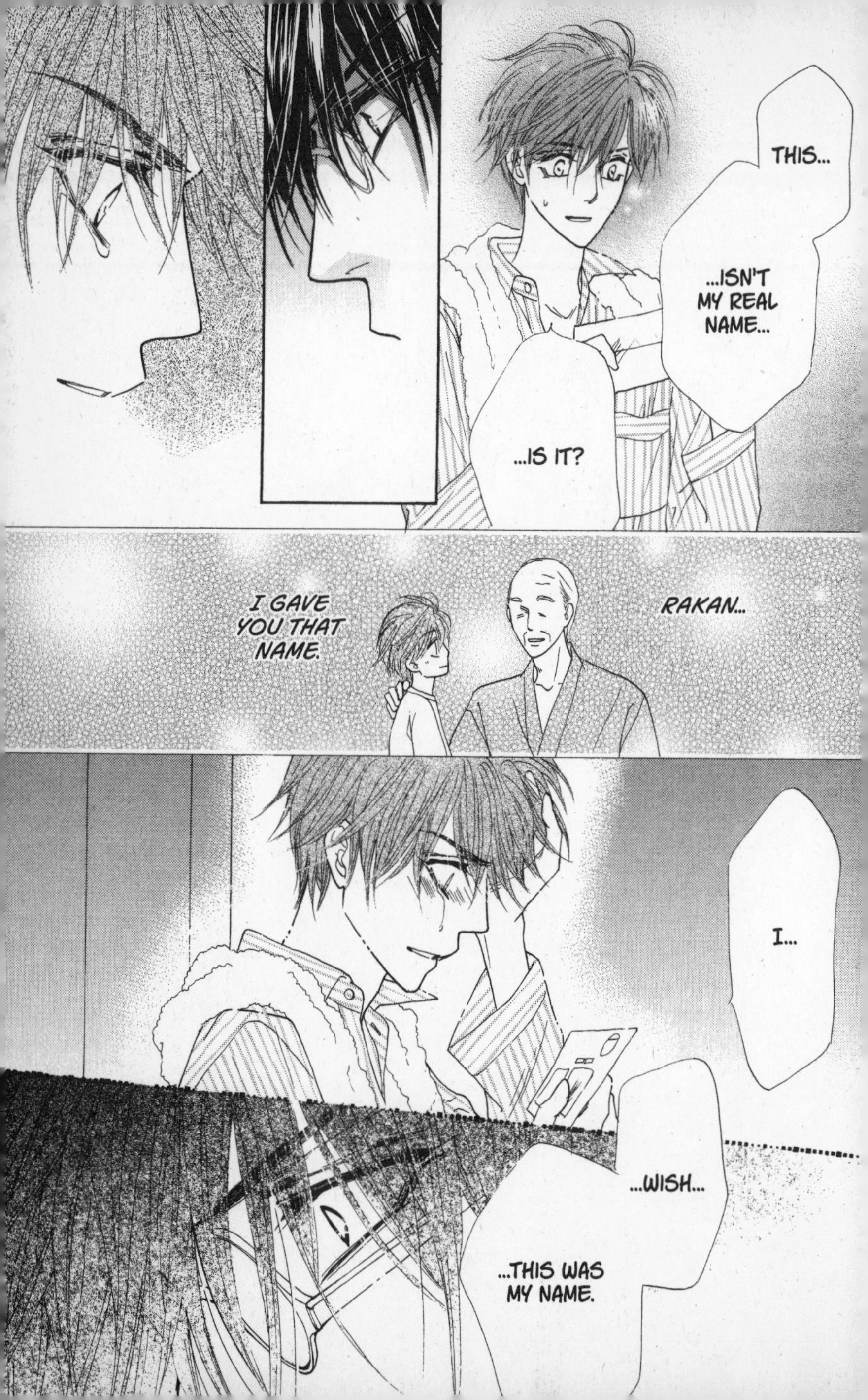
THIS...
...ISN'T MY REAL NAME...
...IS IT?
RAKAN...
I GAVE YOU THAT NAME.
I...
...WISH...
...THIS WAS MY NAME.

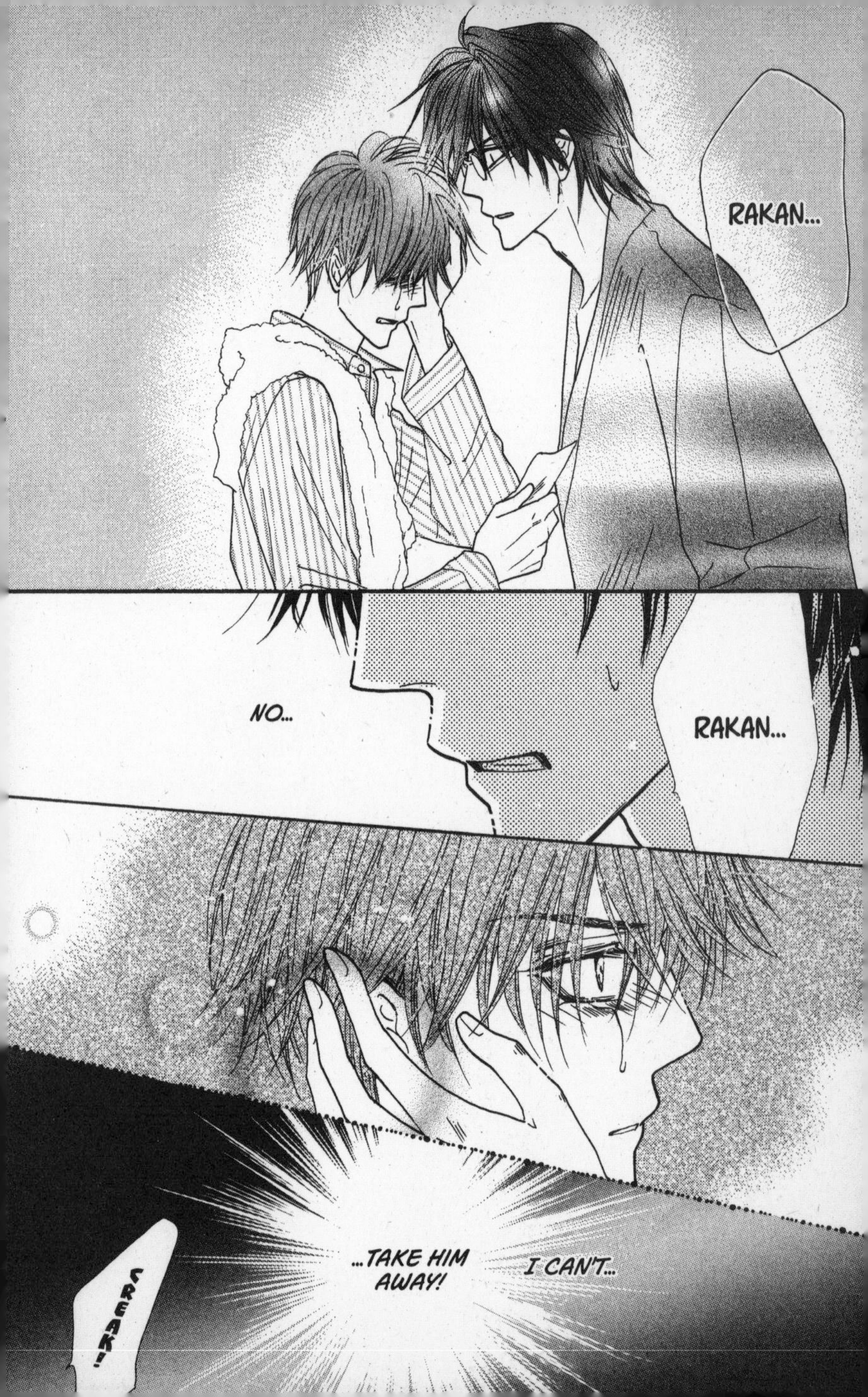
RAKAN...
RAKAN...
NO...
I CAN'T...
...TAKE HIM AWAY!
CREAK!

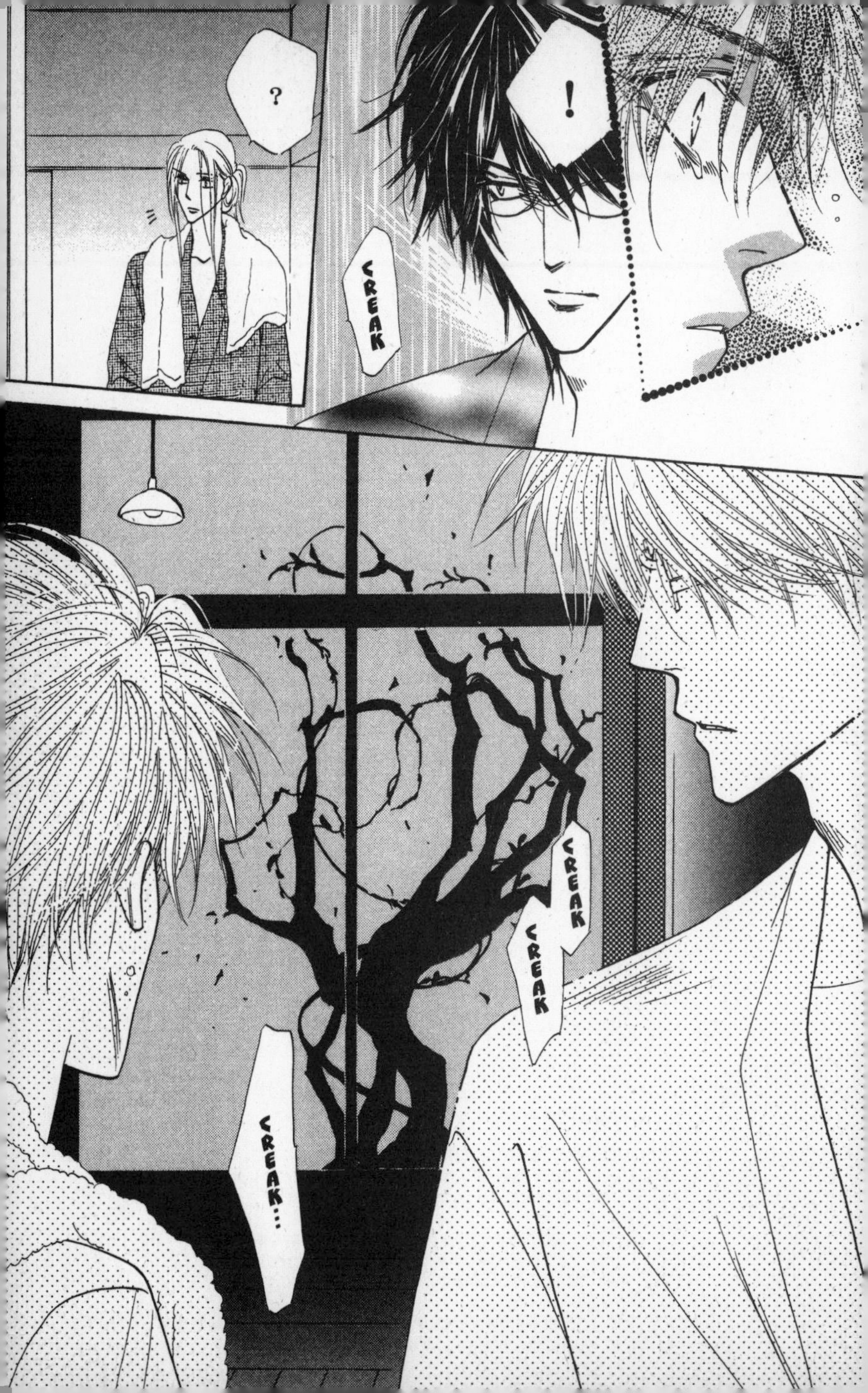
!
CREAK
?
CREAK
CREAK
CREAK...

So here's volume three. Hello! My sister has started calling it "Sil-Peep." It's nice and short. (Is it really nice?) My notes in the last volume were so messy that I freaked out when I saw the book. I thought there was something wrong with my hand. But really, there wasn't anything wrong...

The ink in my pen was just running out and I couldn't write well, that's all.

You should've put some more ink in, you say? No, I didn't even have time to put more ink in. (Then plan your time better when you work!) The pen I'm writing with now is the same pen as the last volume. There's ink in it now. I'm writing neatly enough, for me. I'm so glad.

I have the same lack of time as with the last volume... but I found myself drawing a mosaic tone up there. Umm, why make the mosaic tone, you ask? It's a long story. I'm suddenly into a Disney character lately. ※ Which one it is is a secret. (It's a character that's been around forever, but I'm just suddenly in love with them... Why?)

The other day it was my friend E-san's birthday (Thank you for helping me with the tones in the third chapter!!) and we went to Tokyo Disneyland. After careful contemplation I bought a little stuffed animal of that character. ※

Right now it's sitting right in front of the entryway, and I can see it from my bed and work desk. I'm happy because it's so cute. It's sooo cute! It's so fluffy! ※

I wanted to express my happiness, but of course I can't draw the Disney character, so I made a mosaic instead. Mosaic...

It doesn't really need to become a mosaic, but it would've been nice if it had a shadow...

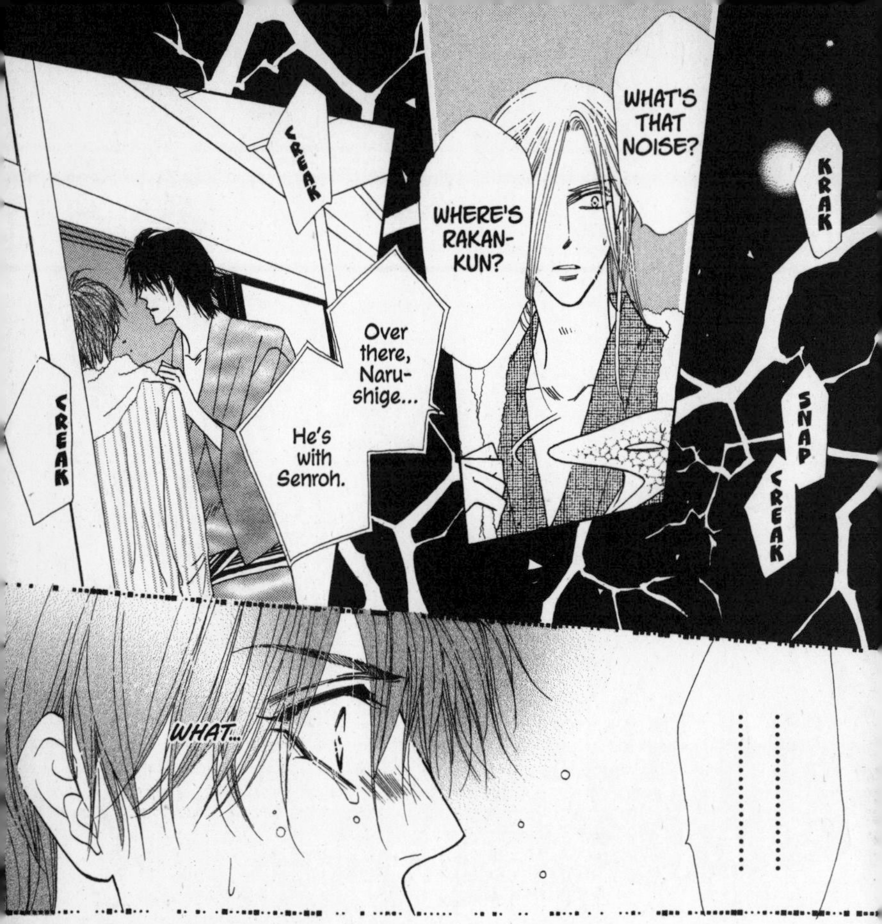
WHAT'S THAT NOISE?
KRAK
WHERE'S RAKAN-KUN?
SNAP
CREAK
CREAK
Over there, Naru-shige...
He's with Senroh.
CREAK
WHAT...

A Quiet Night

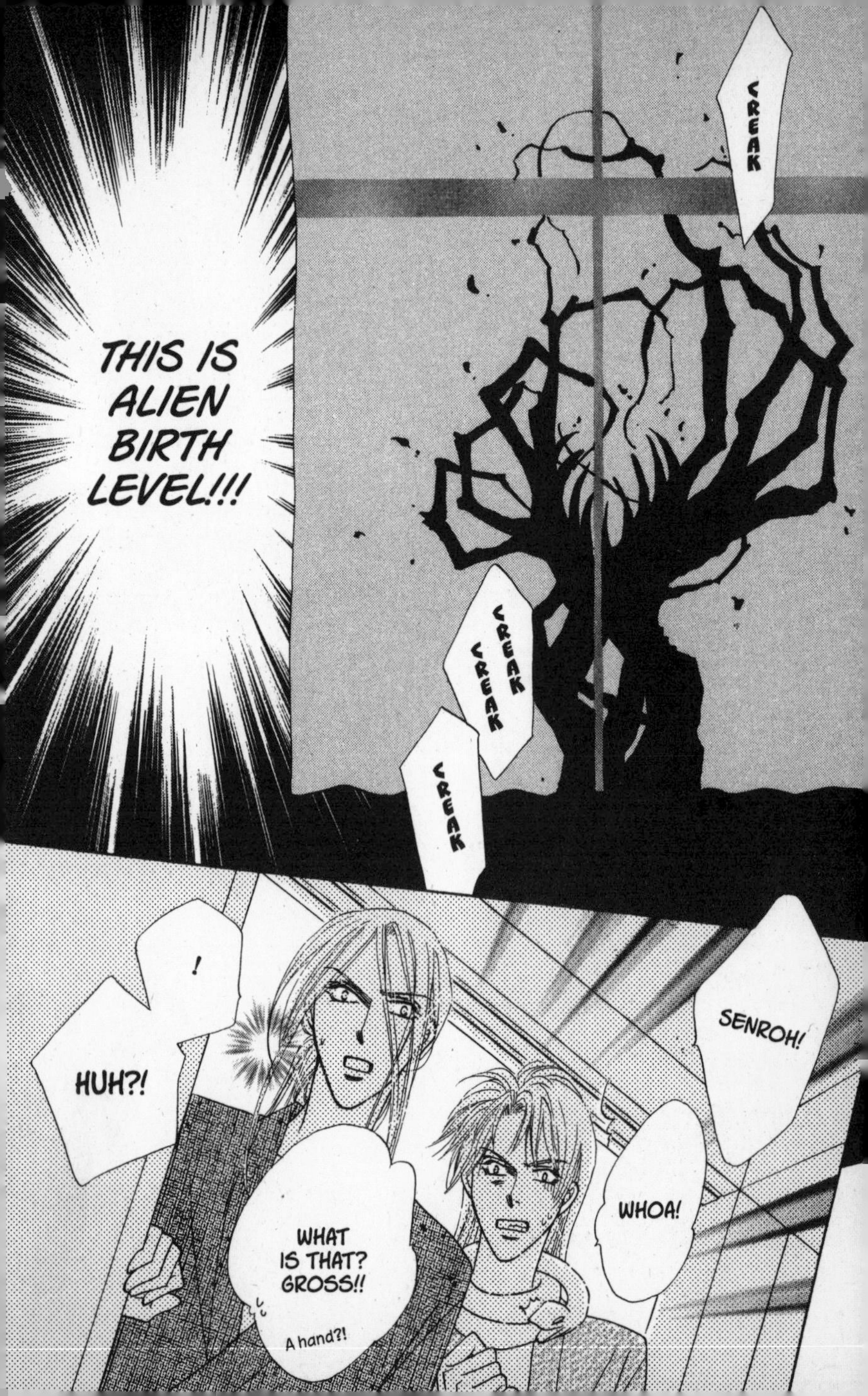
CREAK
CREAK CREAK
CREAK
THIS IS ALIEN BIRTH LEVEL!!!
SENROH!
WHOA!
!
HUH?!
WHAT IS THAT? GROSS!!
A hand?!

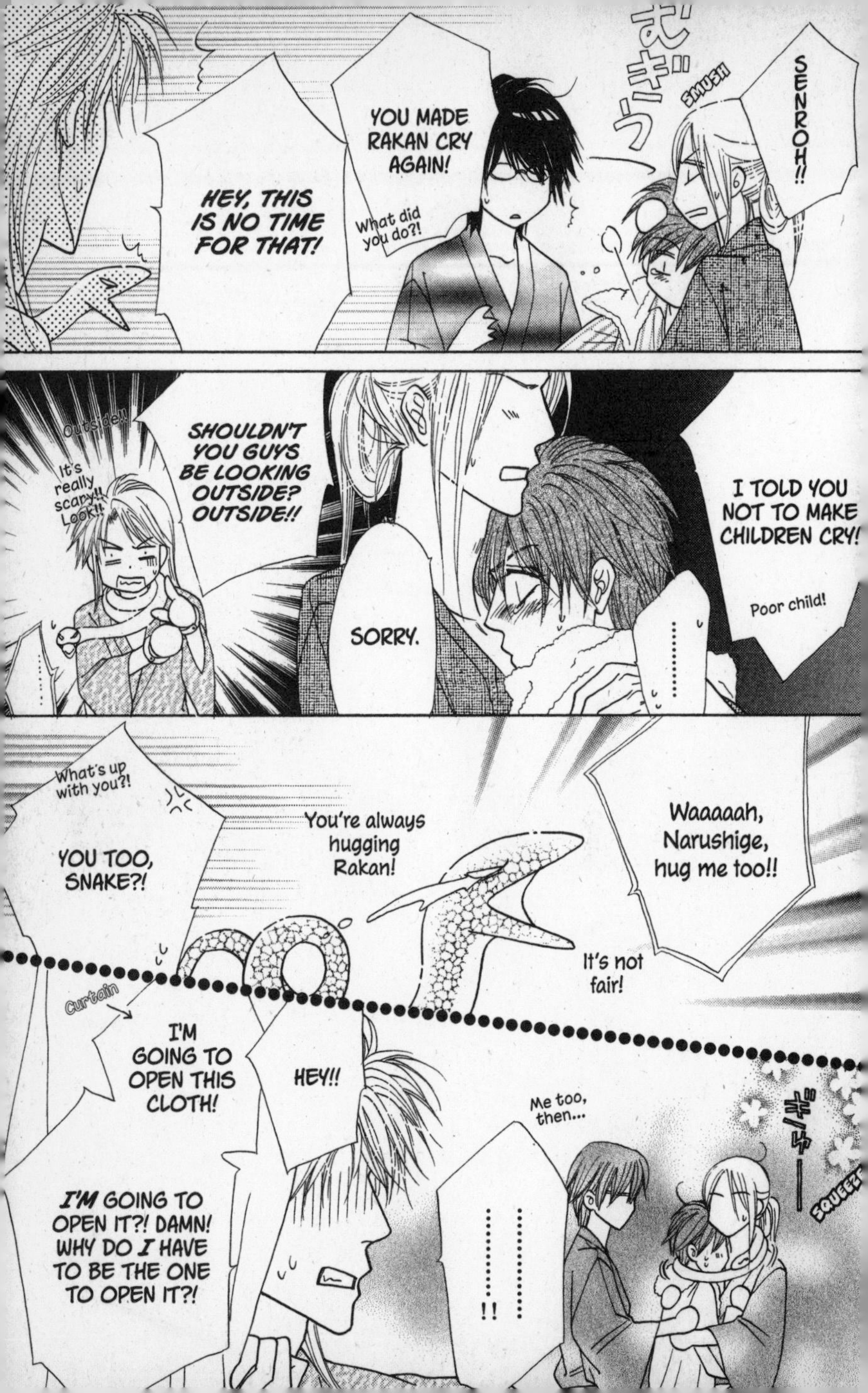
むぎゅう
SMUSH
SENROH!!
YOU MADE RAKAN CRY AGAIN!
What did you do?!
HEY, THIS IS NO TIME FOR THAT!
I TOLD YOU NOT TO MAKE CHILDREN CRY!
Poor child!
......
SORRY.
SHOULDN'T YOU GUYS BE LOOKING OUTSIDE? OUTSIDE!!
Outside!!
It's really scary!! Look!!
......
Waaaaah, Narushige, hug me too!!
It's not fair!
You're always hugging Rakan!
YOU TOO, SNAKE?!
What's up with you?!
ギュー
SQUEEZE
Me too, then...
......!!
HEY!!
I'M GOING TO OPEN THIS CLOTH!
Curtain
I'M GOING TO OPEN IT?! DAMN! WHY DO *I* HAVE TO BE THE ONE TO OPEN IT?!

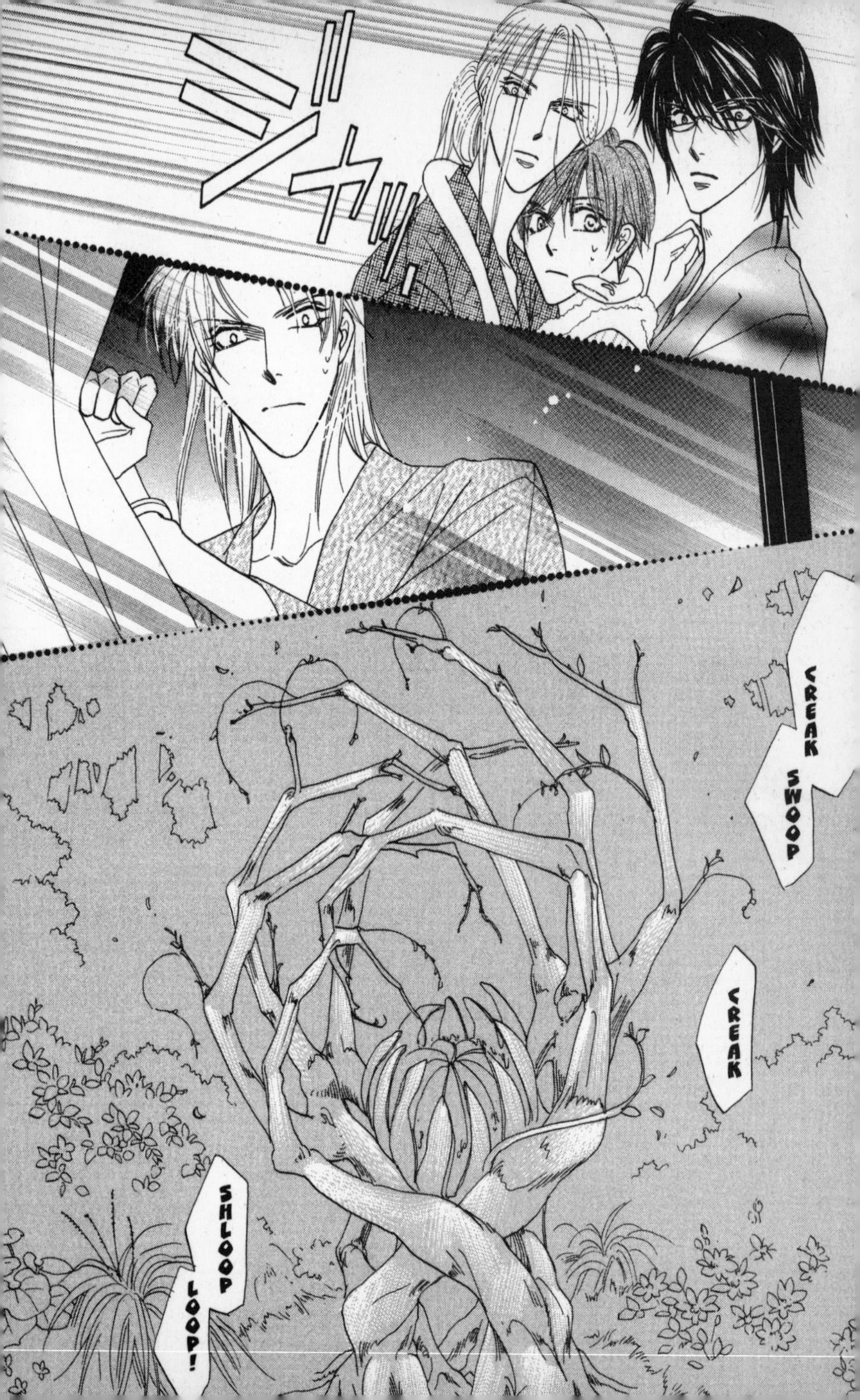
ジャッ
CREAK
SWOOP
CREAK
SHLOOP
LOOOP!

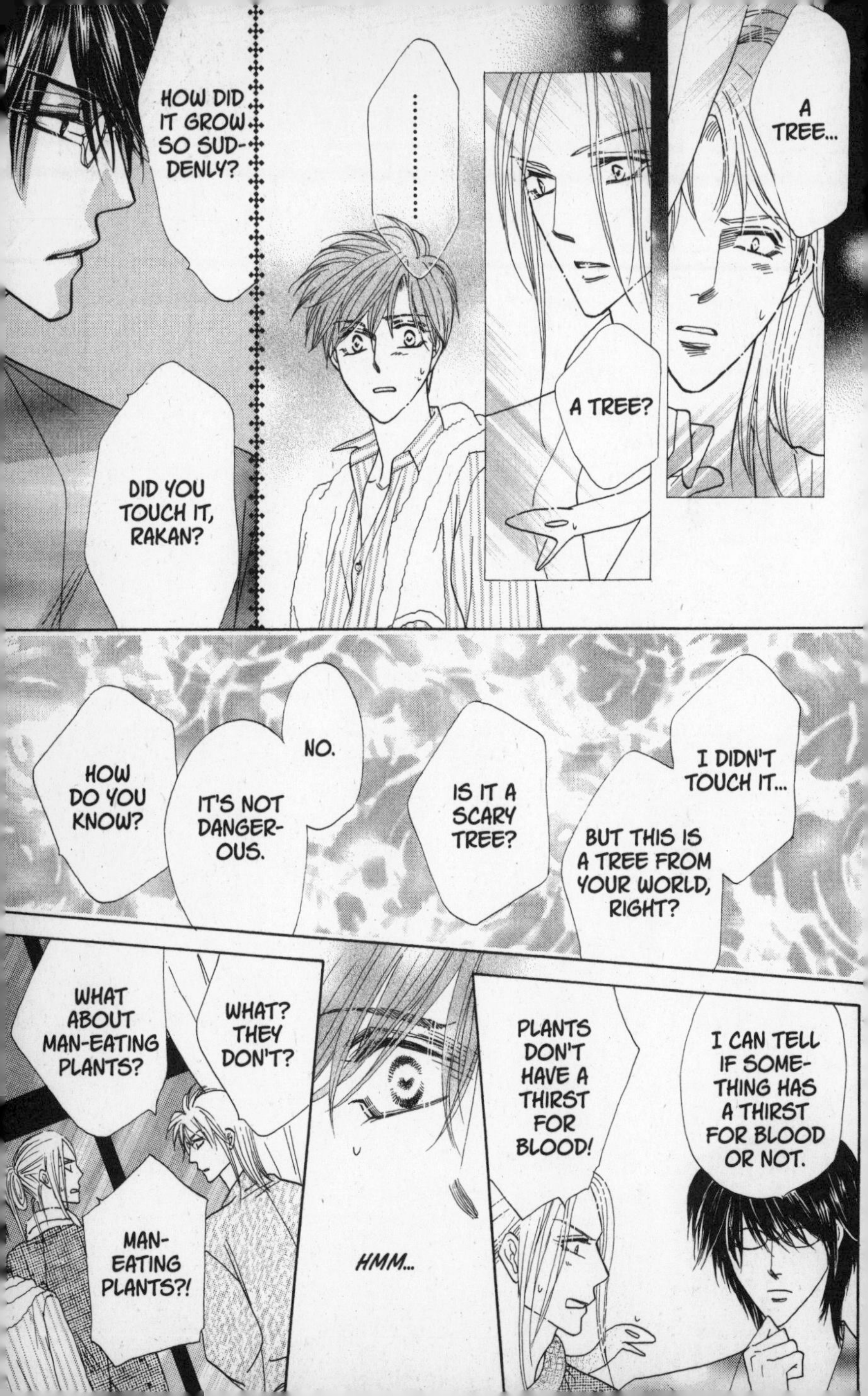
A TREE...
A TREE?
......
HOW DID IT GROW SO SUDDENLY?
DID YOU TOUCH IT, RAKAN?
I DIDN'T TOUCH IT...
BUT THIS IS A TREE FROM YOUR WORLD, RIGHT?
IS IT A SCARY TREE?
NO.
IT'S NOT DANGEROUS.
HOW DO YOU KNOW?
I CAN TELL IF SOMETHING HAS A THIRST FOR BLOOD OR NOT.
PLANTS DON'T HAVE A THIRST FOR BLOOD!
HMM...
WHAT? THEY DON'T?
WHAT ABOUT MAN-EATING PLANTS?
MAN-EATING PLANTS?!

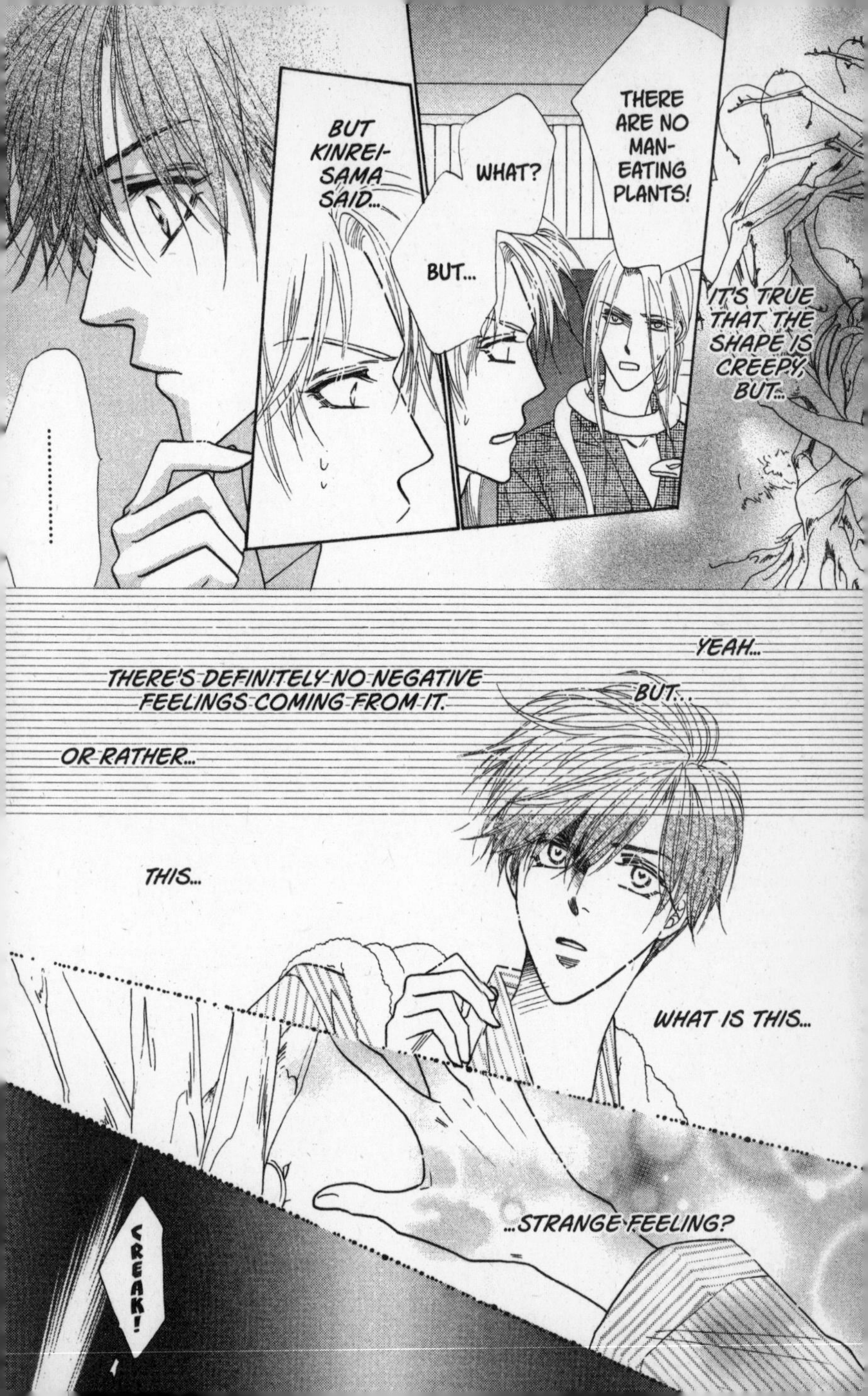

THERE ARE NO MAN-EATING PLANTS!
WHAT?
BUT...
BUT KINREI-SAMA SAID...
IT'S TRUE THAT THE SHAPE IS CREEPY, BUT...
....
YEAH...
BUT...
THERE'S DEFINITELY NO NEGATIVE FEELINGS COMING FROM IT.
OR RATHER...
THIS...
WHAT IS THIS...
...STRANGE FEELING?
CREAK!

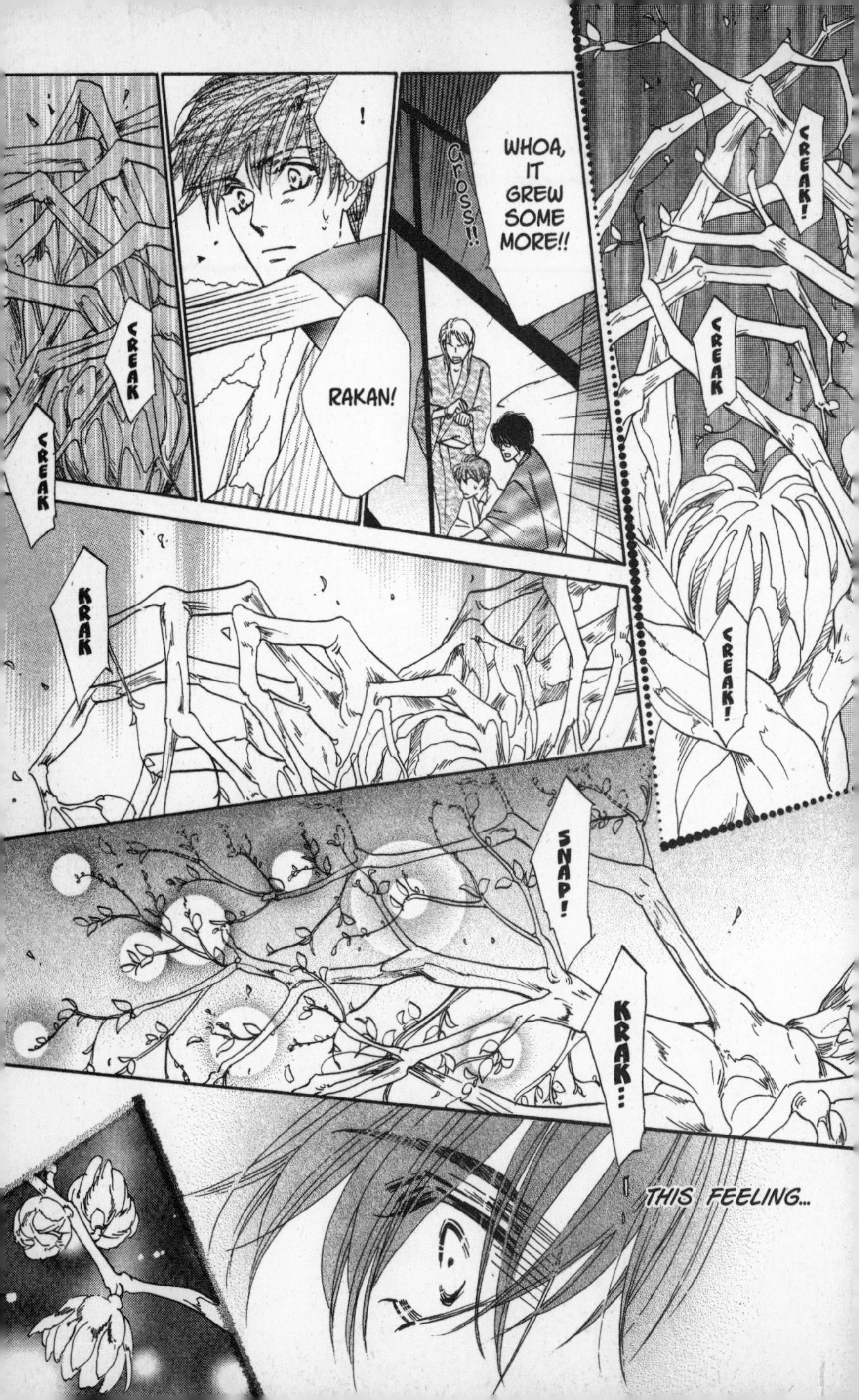
WHOA, IT GREW SOME MORE!!
GROSS!!
!
RAKAN!
CREAK
CREAK
CREAK!
CREAK
CREAK!
KRAK
SNAP!
KRAK!!
THIS FEELING...

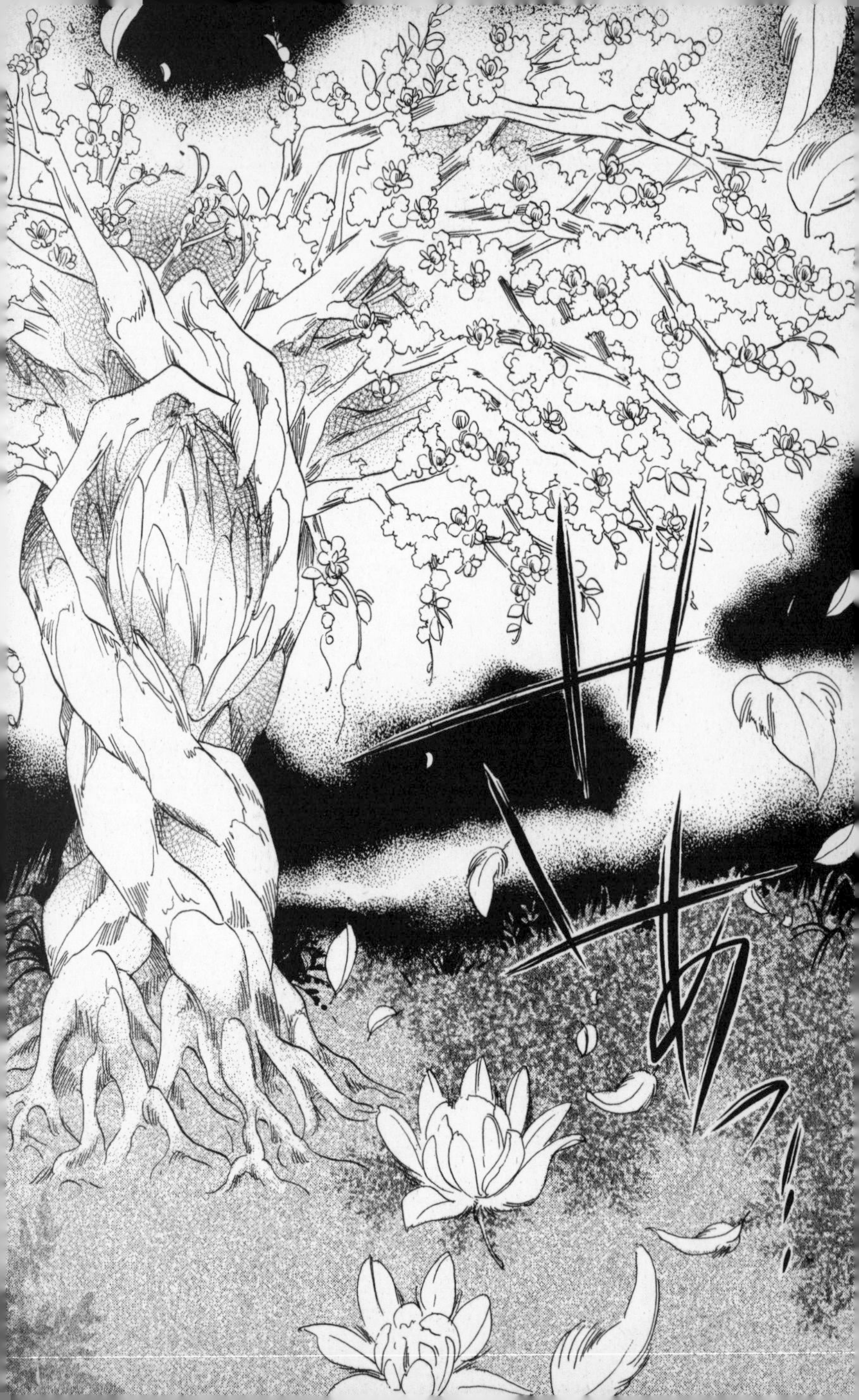

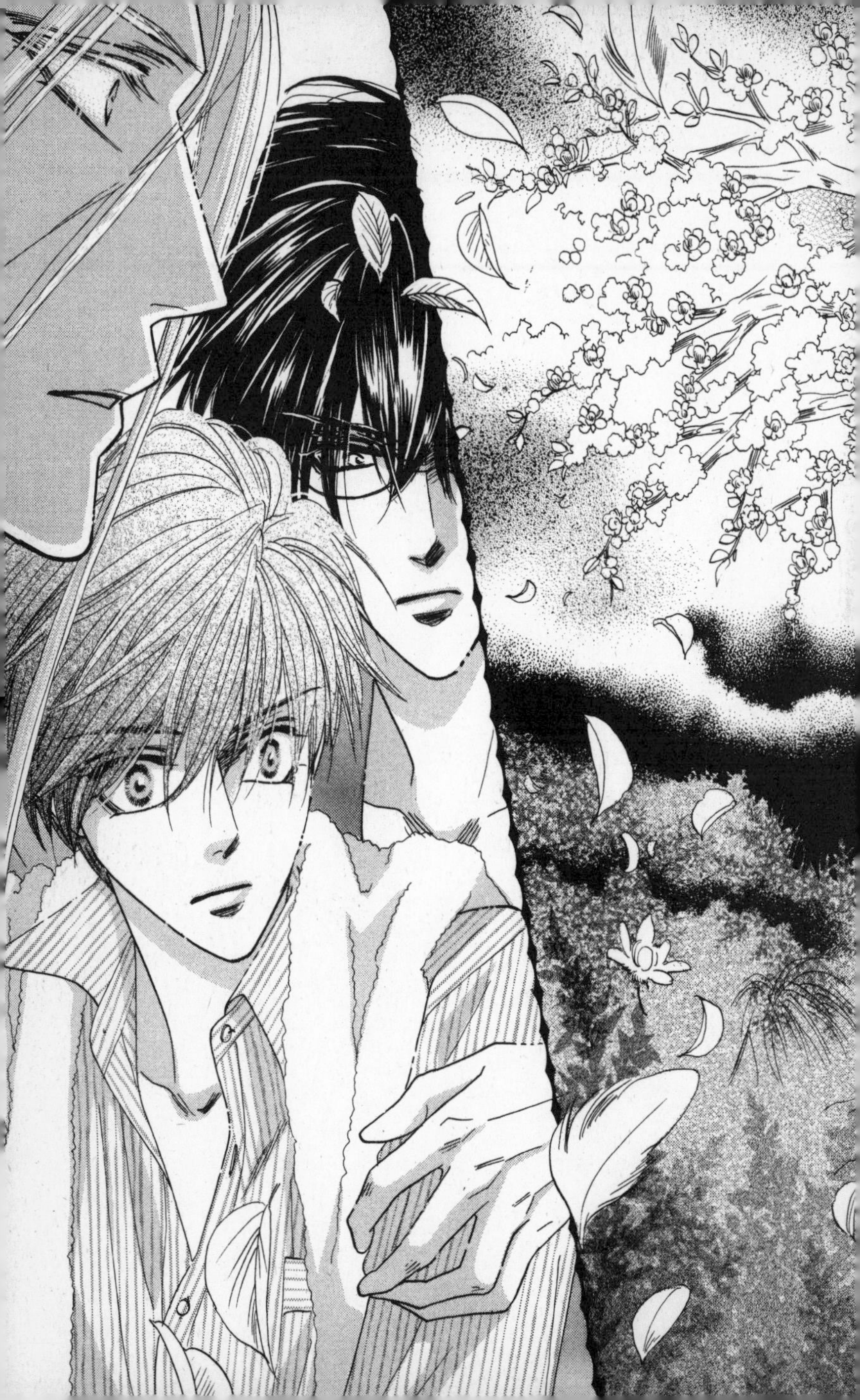

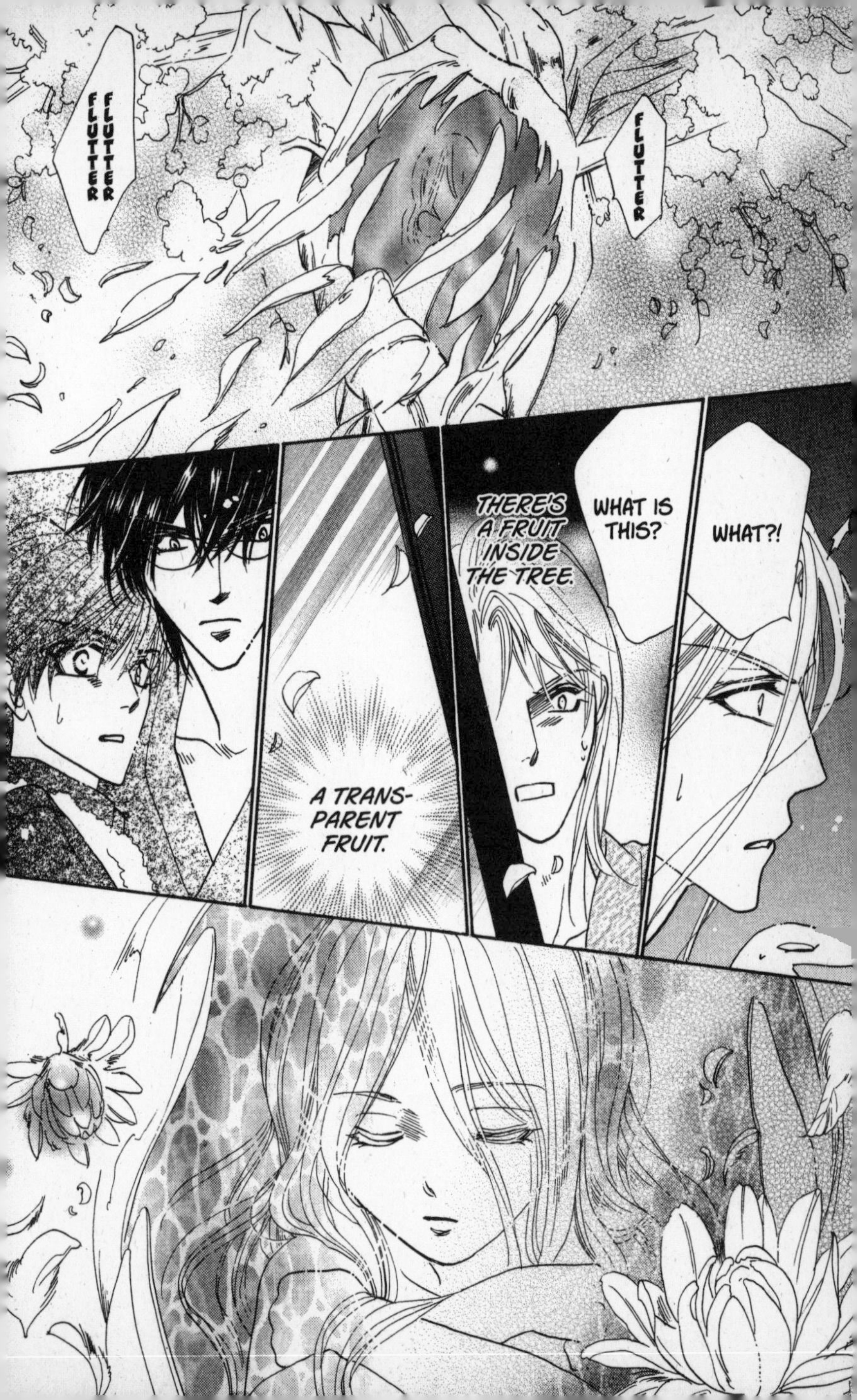
FLUTTER
FLUTTER FLUTTER
WHAT?!
WHAT IS THIS?
THERE'S A FRUIT INSIDE THE TREE.
A TRANS-PARENT FRUIT.

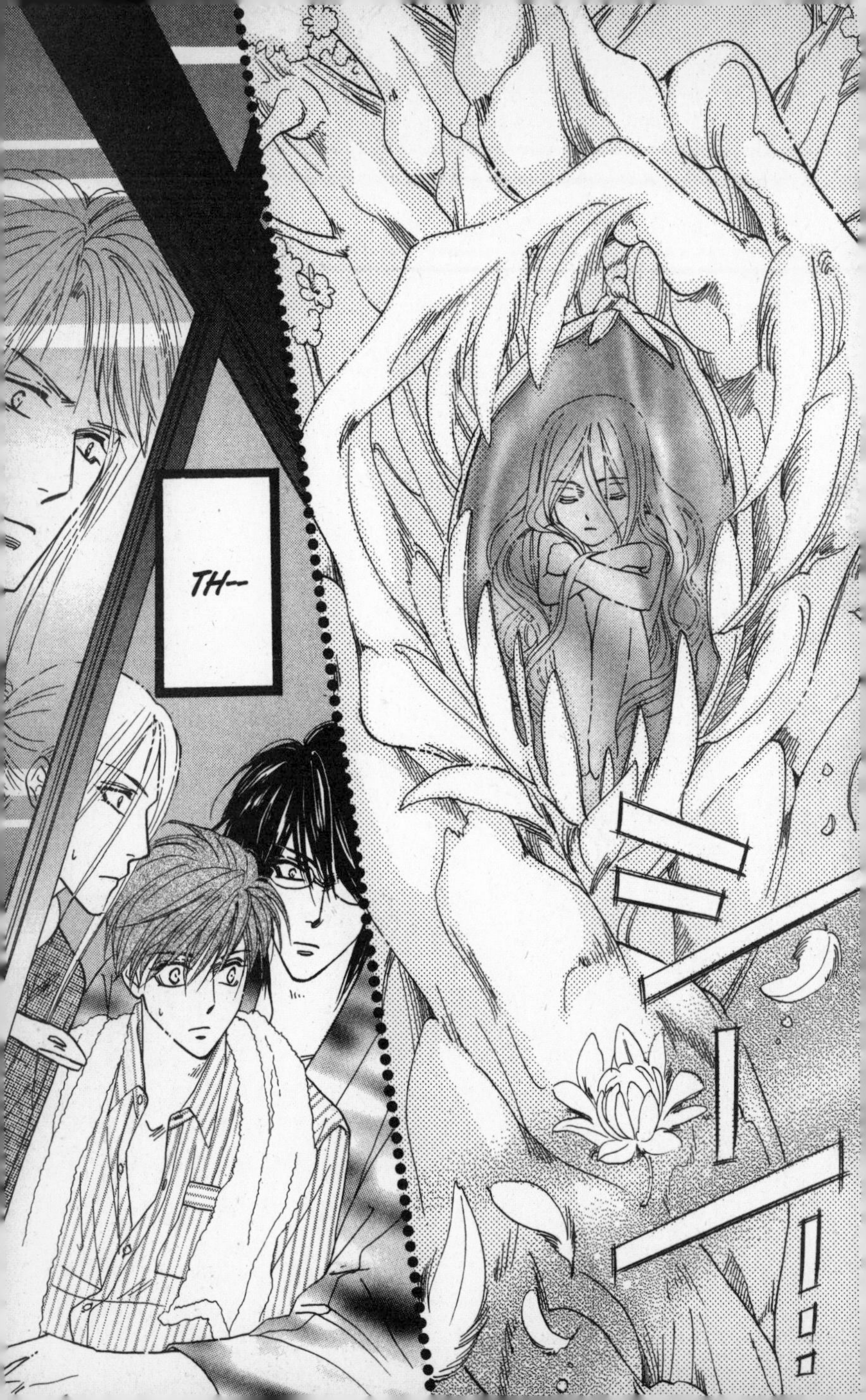
TH--

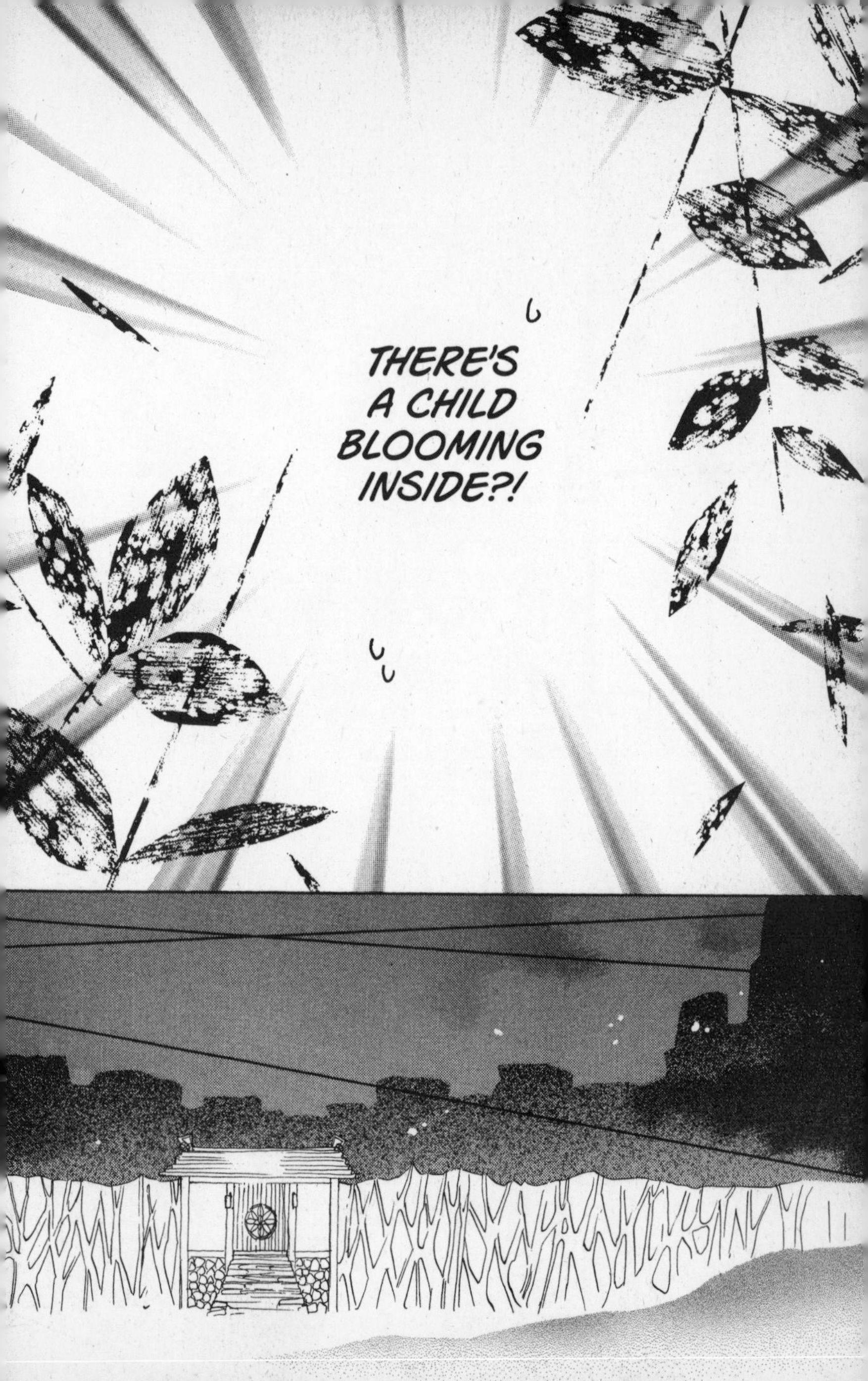
THERE'S A CHILD BLOOMING INSIDE?!

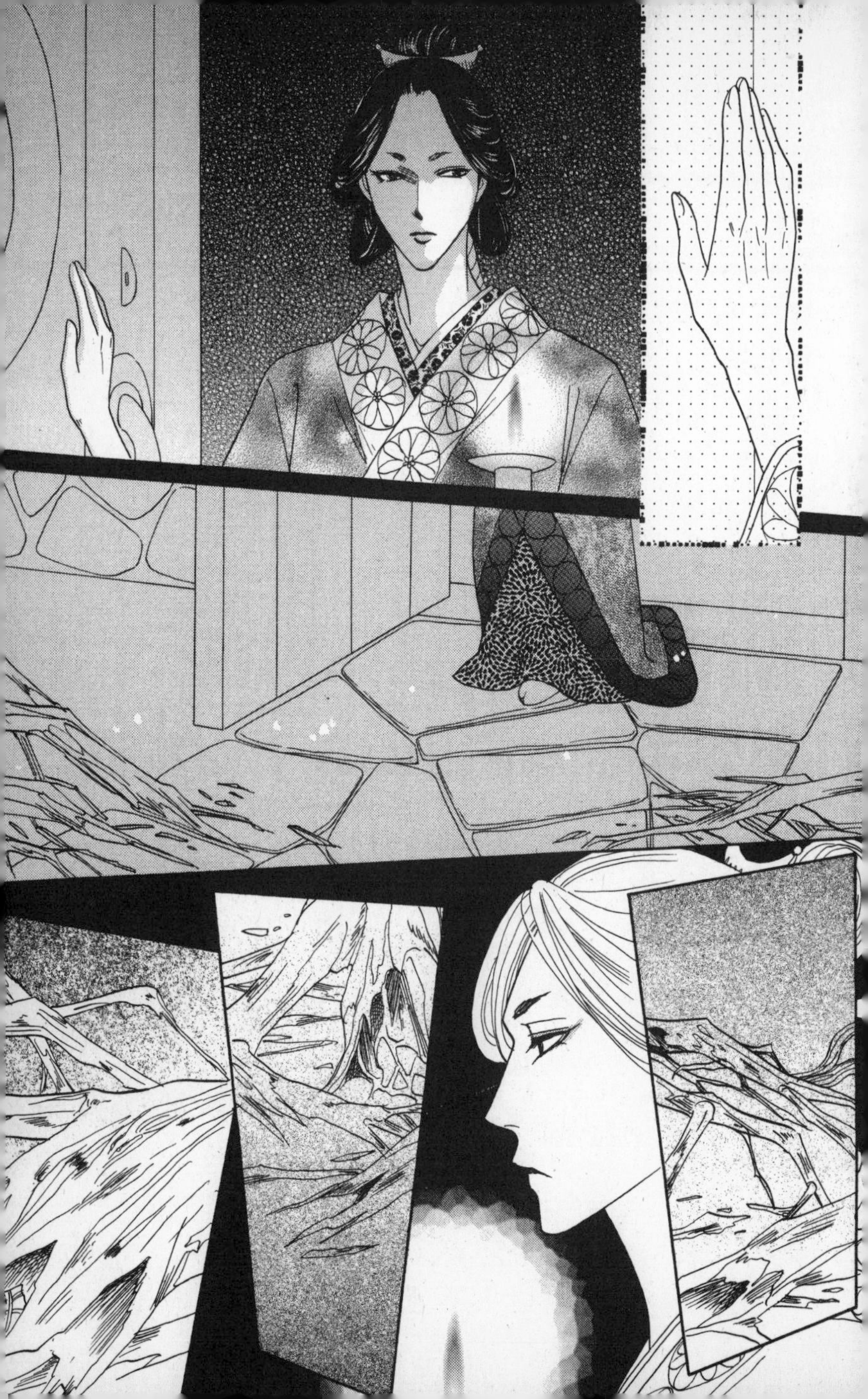

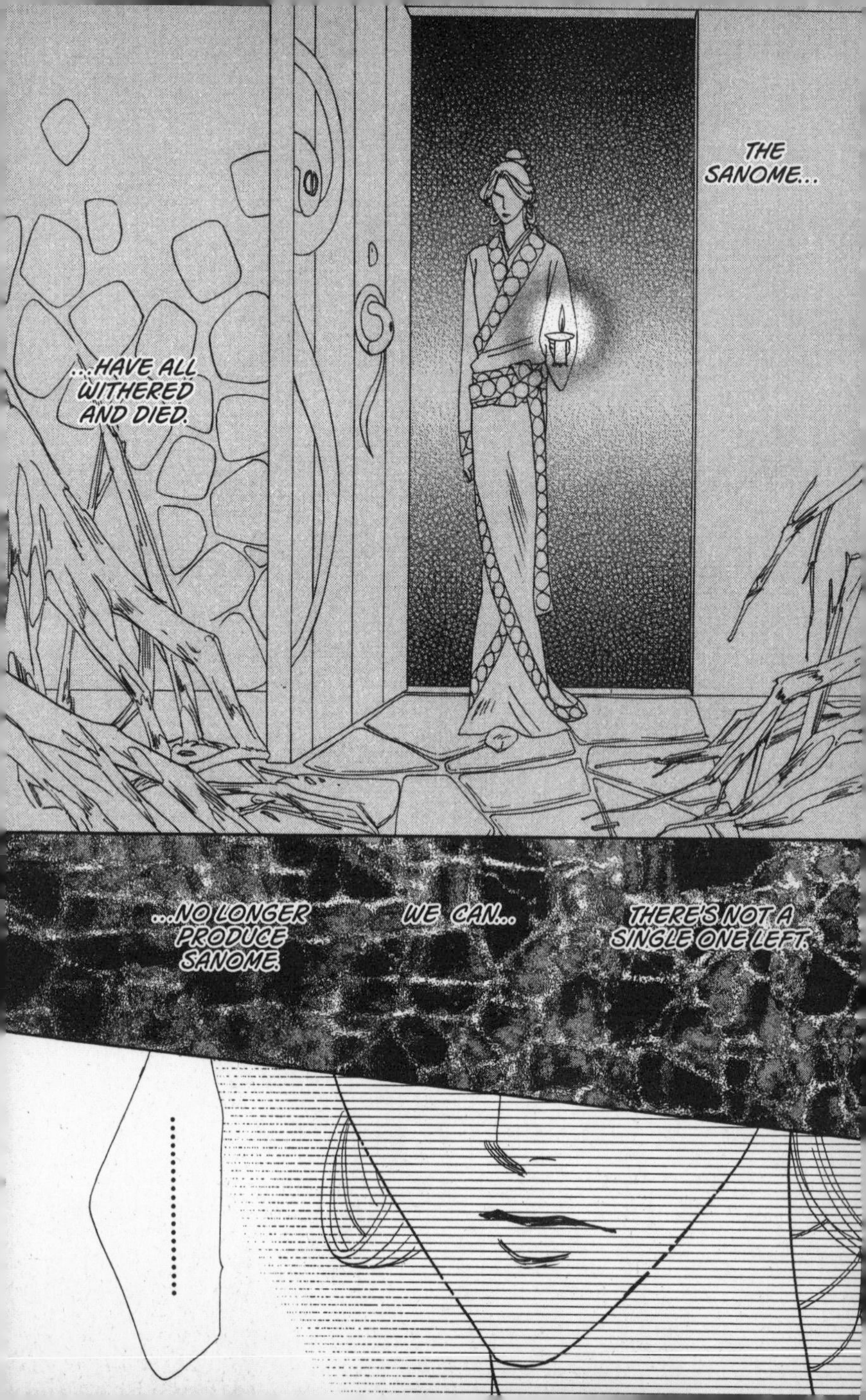
THE SANOME...
...HAVE ALL WITHERED AND DIED.
THERE'S NOT A SINGLE ONE LEFT.
WE CAN...
...NO LONGER PRODUCE SANOME.
......

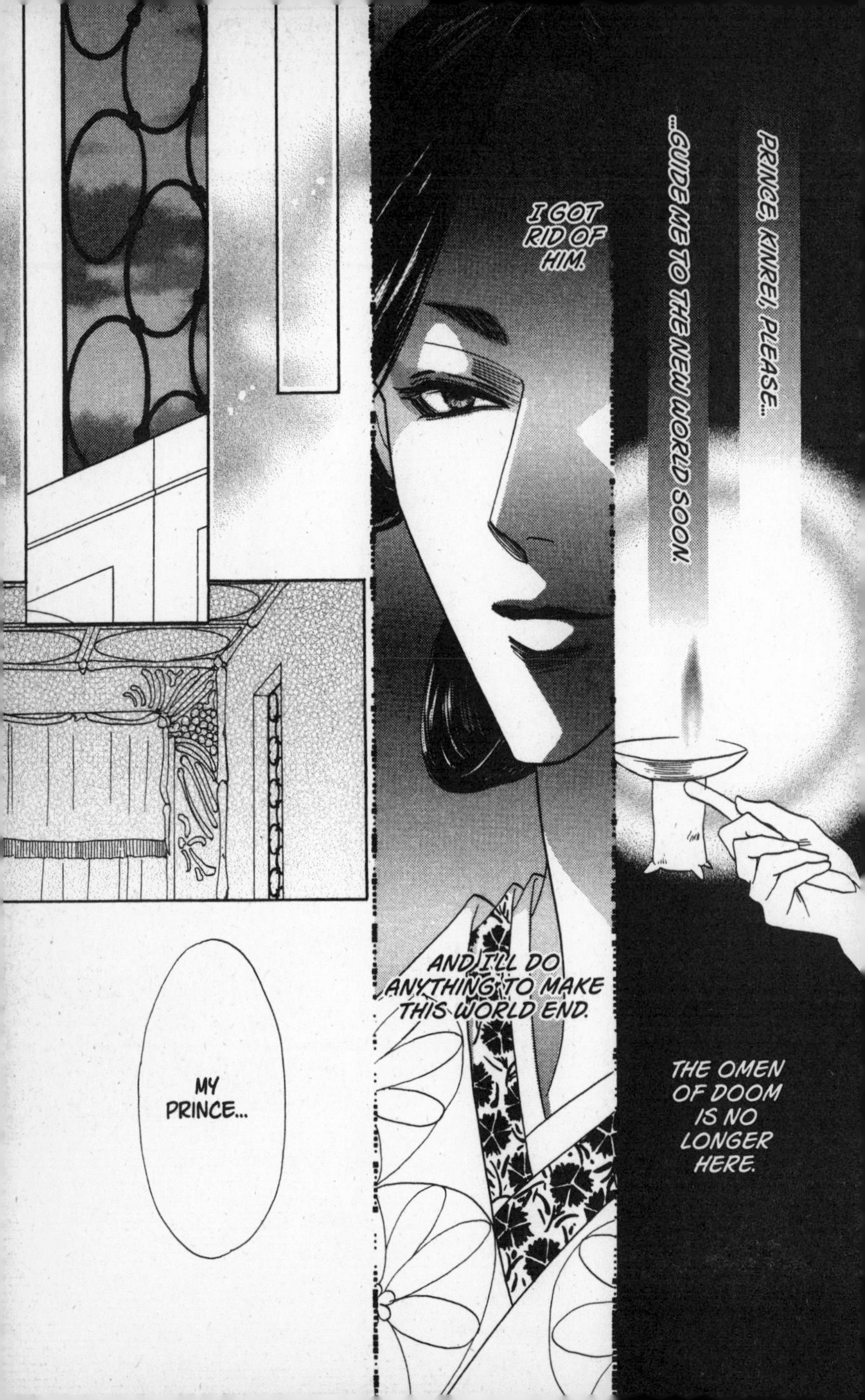
PRINCE, KINREI, PLEASE...
...GUIDE ME TO THE NEW WORLD SOON.
THE OMEN OF DOOM IS NO LONGER HERE.
I GOT RID OF HIM.
AND I'LL DO ANYTHING TO MAKE THIS WORLD END.
MY PRINCE...

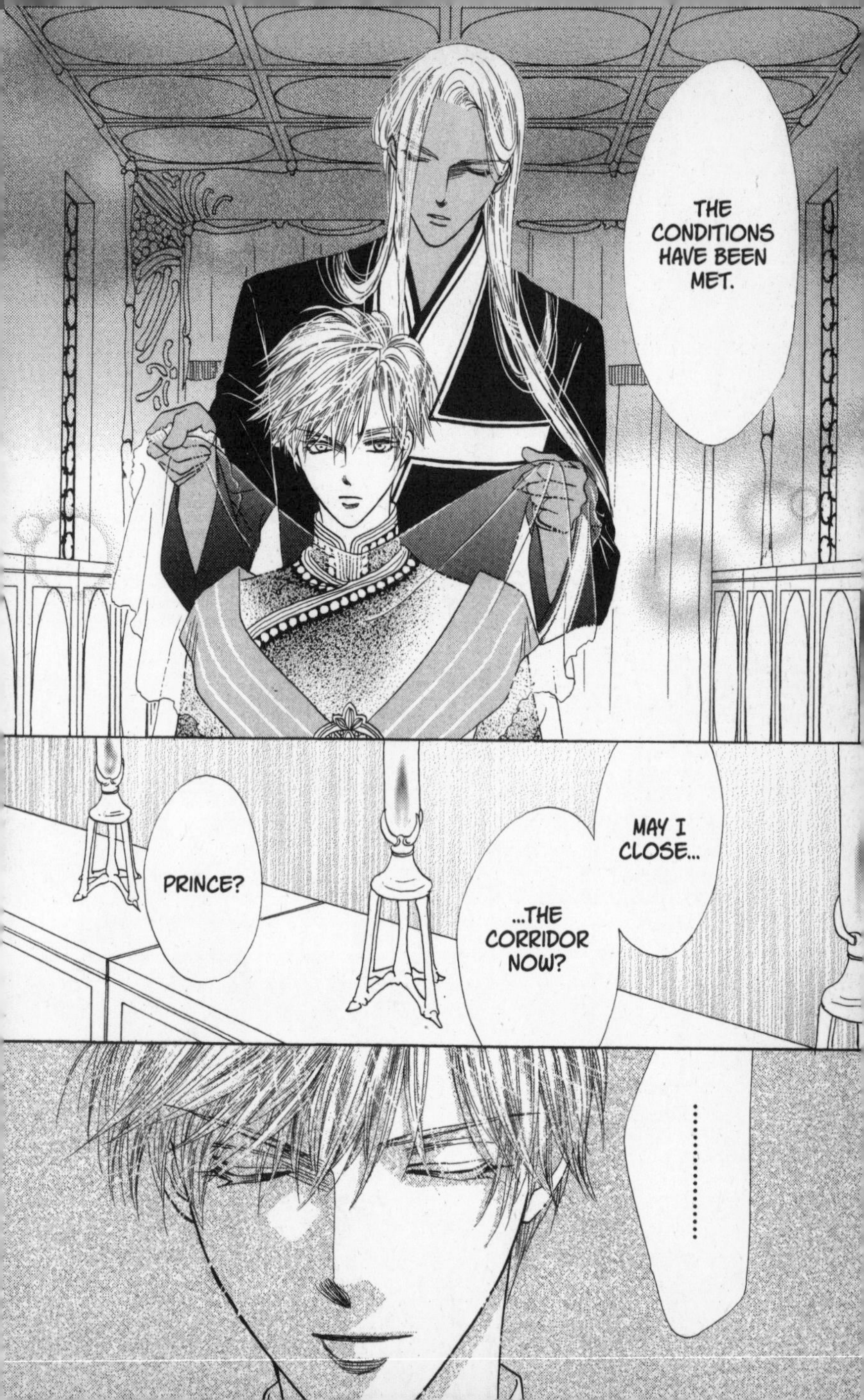
THE CONDITIONS HAVE BEEN MET.
MAY I CLOSE...
...THE CORRIDOR NOW?
PRINCE?
......

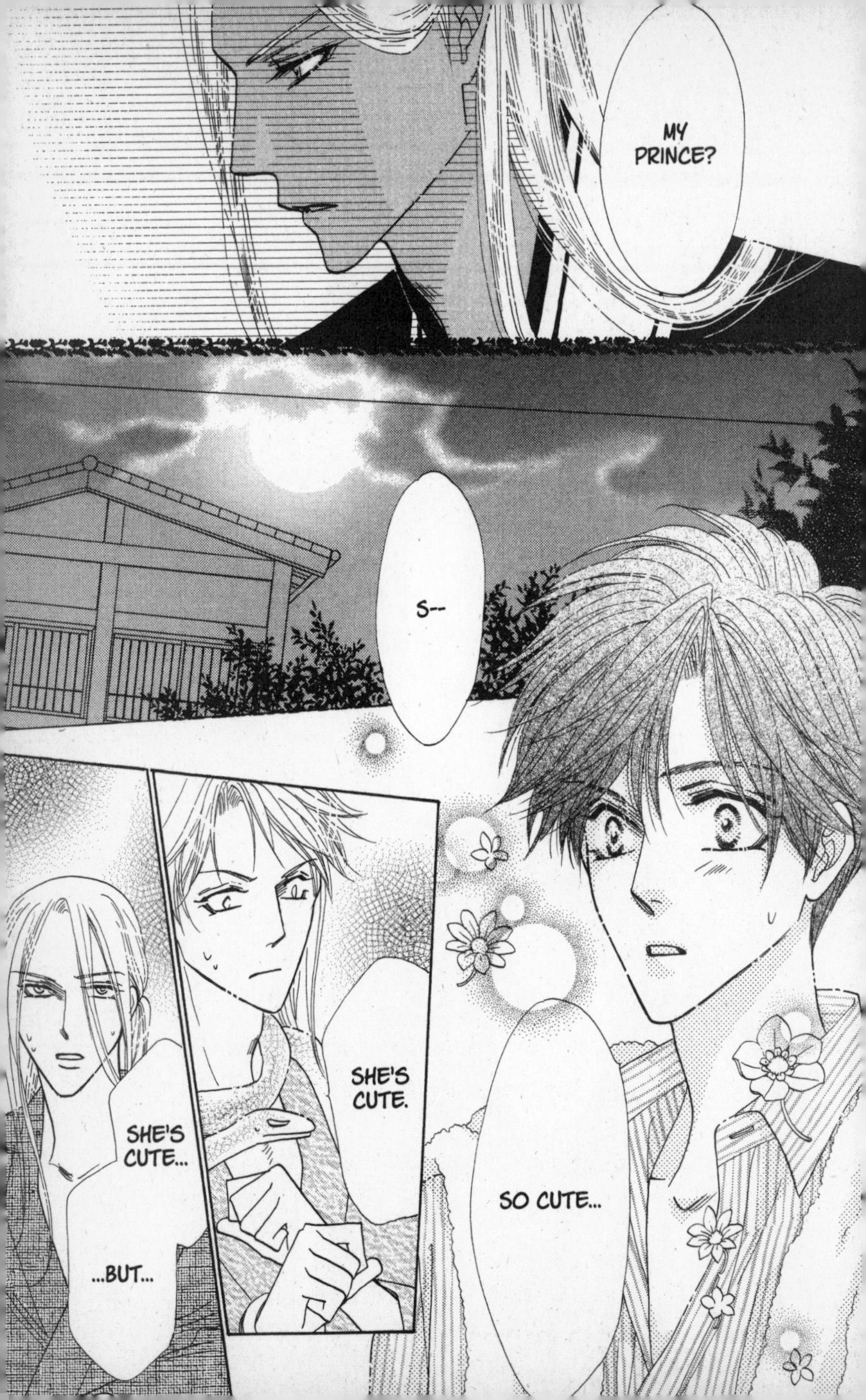
MY PRINCE?
S--
SO CUTE...
SHE'S CUTE.
SHE'S CUTE...
...BUT...

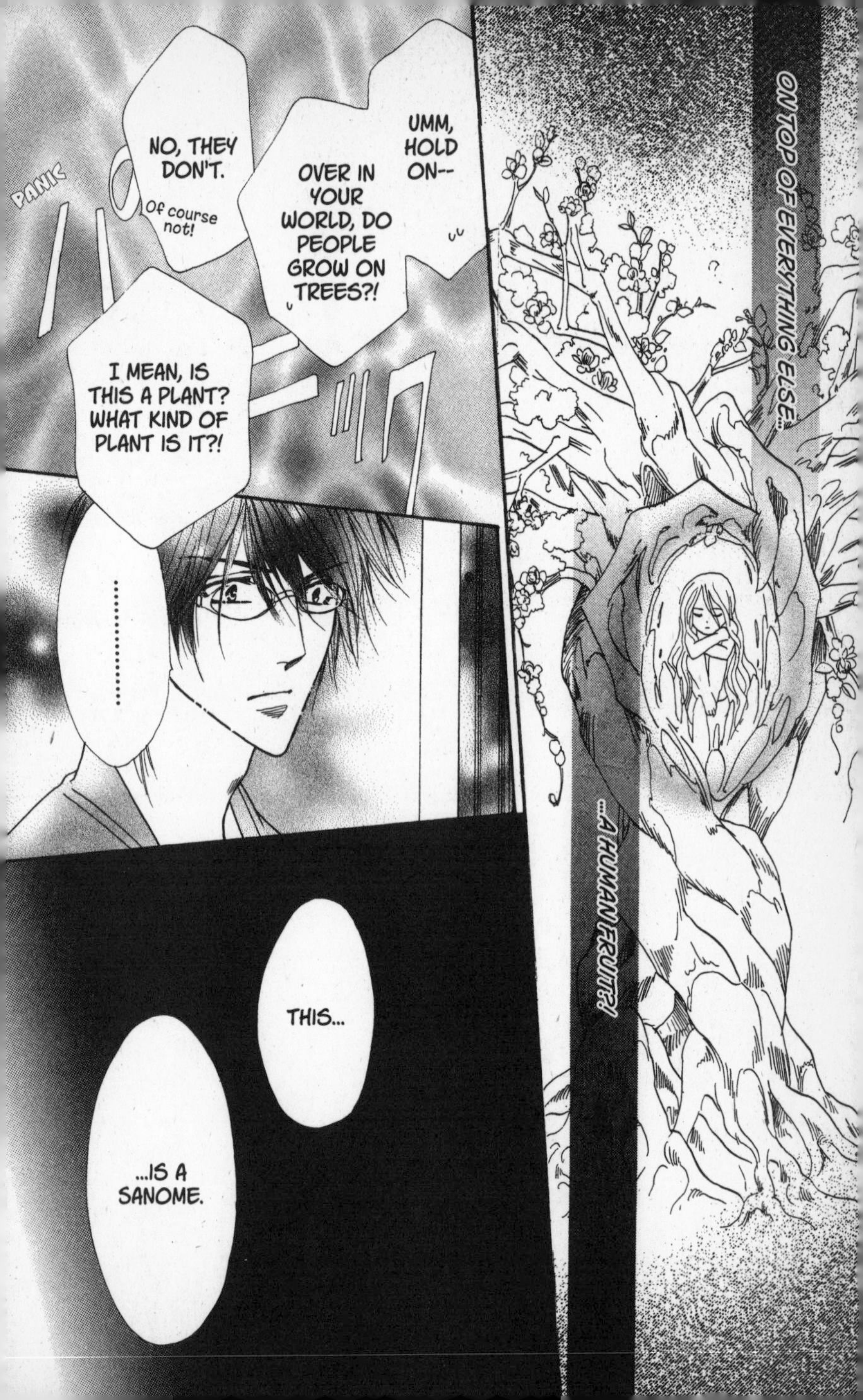
ON TOP OF EVERYTHING ELSE...
...A HUMAN FRUIT?!
UMM, HOLD ON--
OVER IN YOUR WORLD, DO PEOPLE GROW ON TREES?!
NO, THEY DON'T.
Of course not!
PANIC
I MEAN, IS THIS A PLANT? WHAT KIND OF PLANT IS IT?!
......
THIS...
...IS A SANOME.

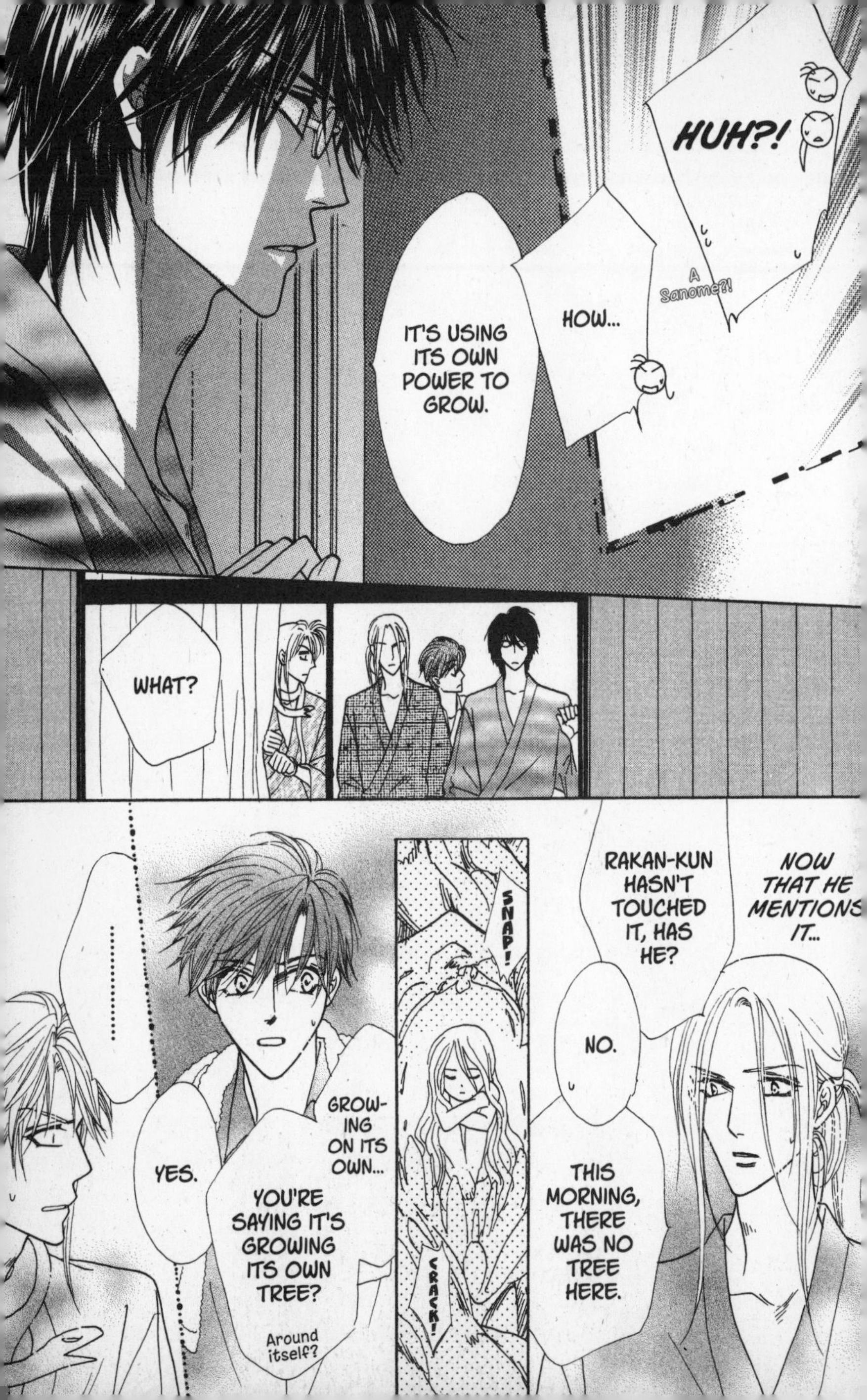
HUH?!
A Sanome?!
HOW...
IT'S USING ITS OWN POWER TO GROW.
WHAT?
NOW THAT HE MENTIONS IT...
RAKAN-KUN HASN'T TOUCHED IT, HAS HE?
NO.
THIS MORNING, THERE WAS NO TREE HERE.
SNAP!
CRACK!
......
GROWING ON ITS OWN...
YES.
YOU'RE SAYING IT'S GROWING ITS OWN TREE?
Around itself?

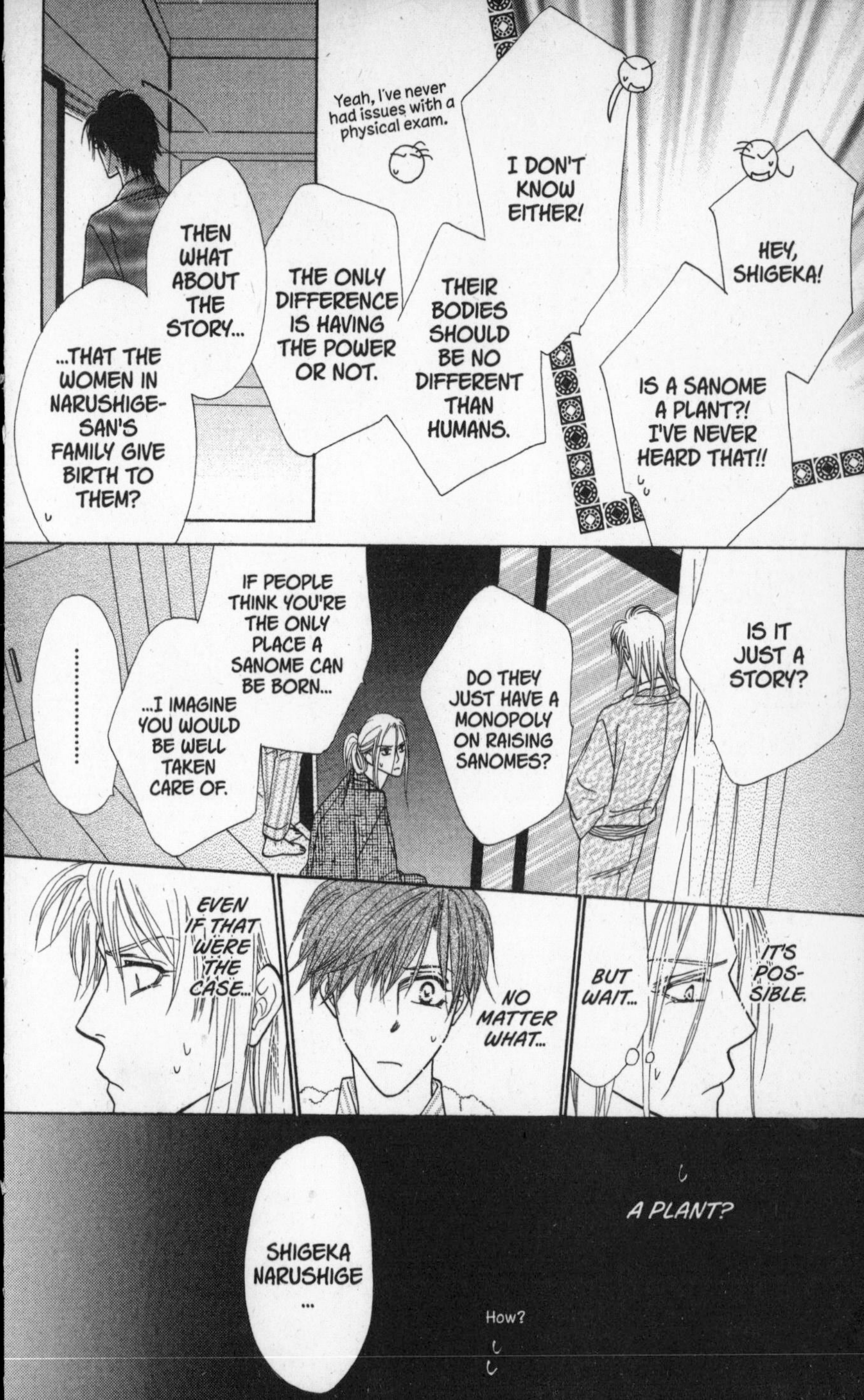
HEY, SHIGEKA!
IS A SANOME A PLANT?! I'VE NEVER HEARD THAT!!
I DON'T KNOW EITHER!
Yeah, I've never had issues with a physical exam.
THEIR BODIES SHOULD BE NO DIFFERENT THAN HUMANS.
THE ONLY DIFFERENCE IS HAVING THE POWER OR NOT.
THEN WHAT ABOUT THE STORY...
...THAT THE WOMEN IN NARUSHIGE-SAN'S FAMILY GIVE BIRTH TO THEM?
IS IT JUST A STORY?
DO THEY JUST HAVE A MONOPOLY ON RAISING SANOMES?
IF PEOPLE THINK YOU'RE THE ONLY PLACE A SANOME CAN BE BORN...
...I IMAGINE YOU WOULD BE WELL TAKEN CARE OF.
....
IT'S POS-SIBLE.
BUT WAIT...
NO MATTER WHAT...
EVEN IF THAT WERE THE CASE...
A PLANT?
How?
SHIGEKA NARUSHIGE ...

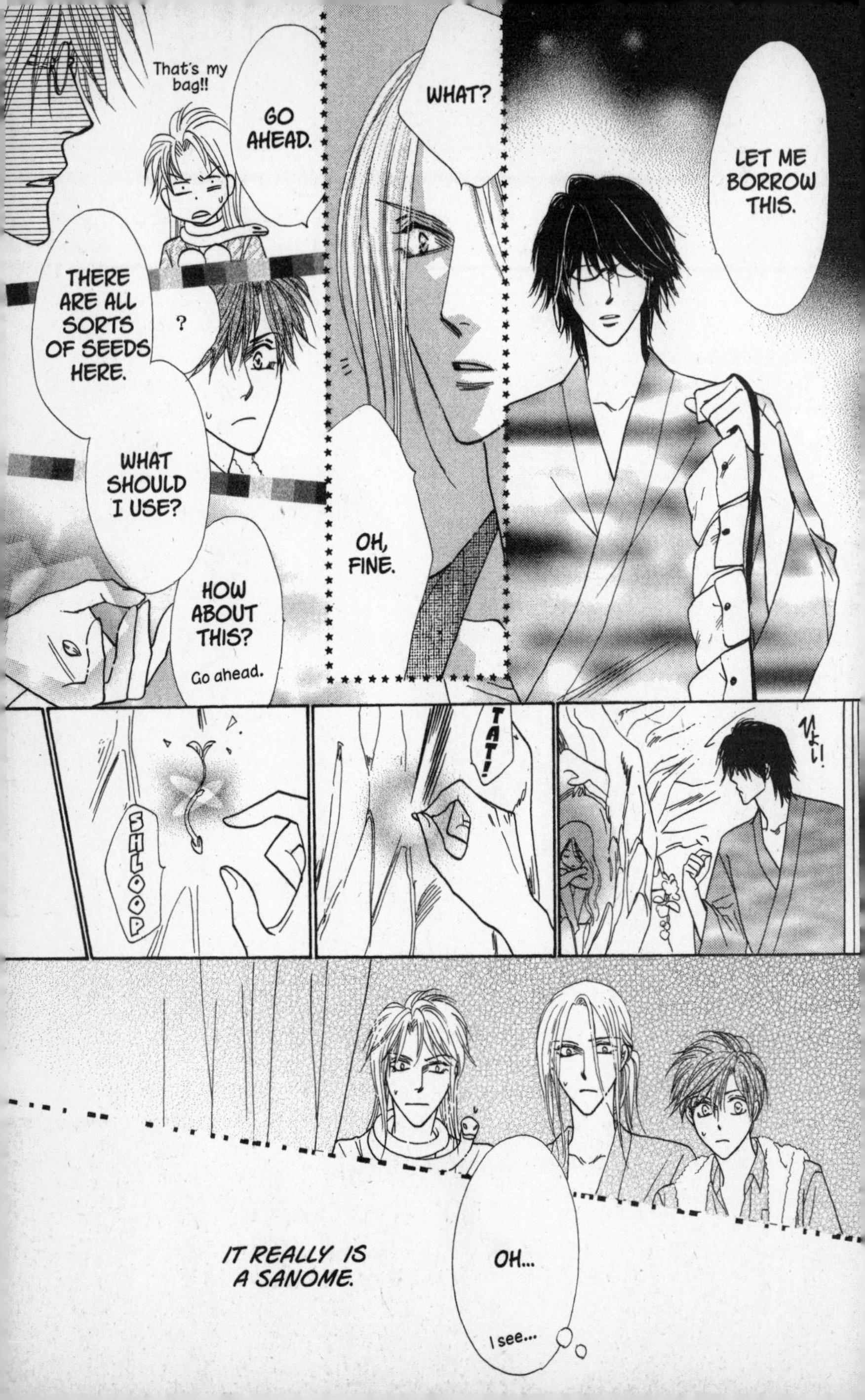
LET ME BORROW THIS.
WHAT?
OH, FINE.
GO AHEAD.
That's my bag!!
THERE ARE ALL SORTS OF SEEDS HERE.
?
WHAT SHOULD I USE?
HOW ABOUT THIS?
Go ahead.
ひょい!
TAT!
SHLOOP
OH...
I see...
IT REALLY IS A SANOME.

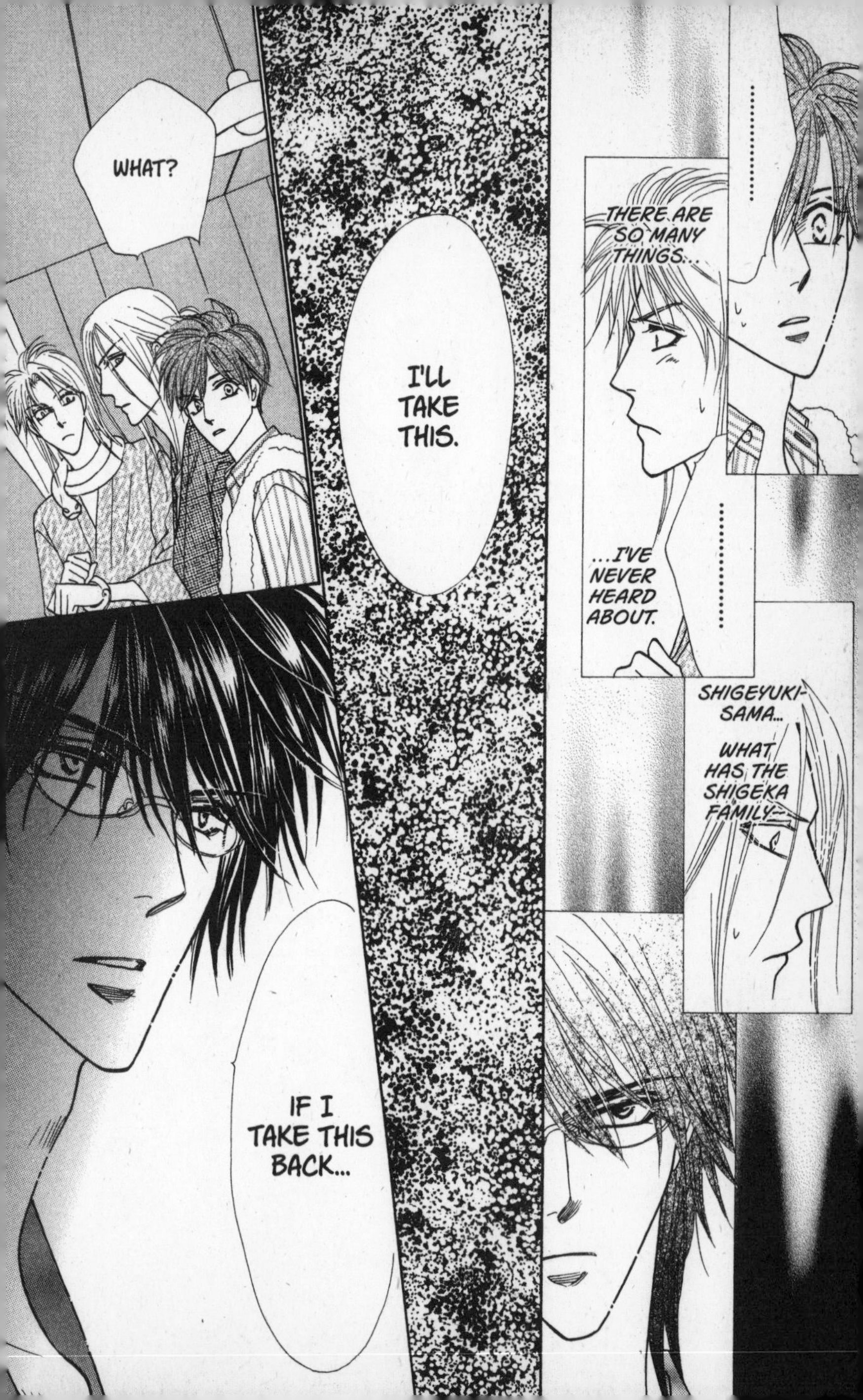
......
THERE ARE SO MANY THINGS...
...I'VE NEVER HEARD ABOUT.
......
SHIGEYUKI-SAMA...
WHAT HAS THE SHIGEKA FAMILY-
I'LL TAKE THIS.
WHAT?
IF I TAKE THIS BACK...

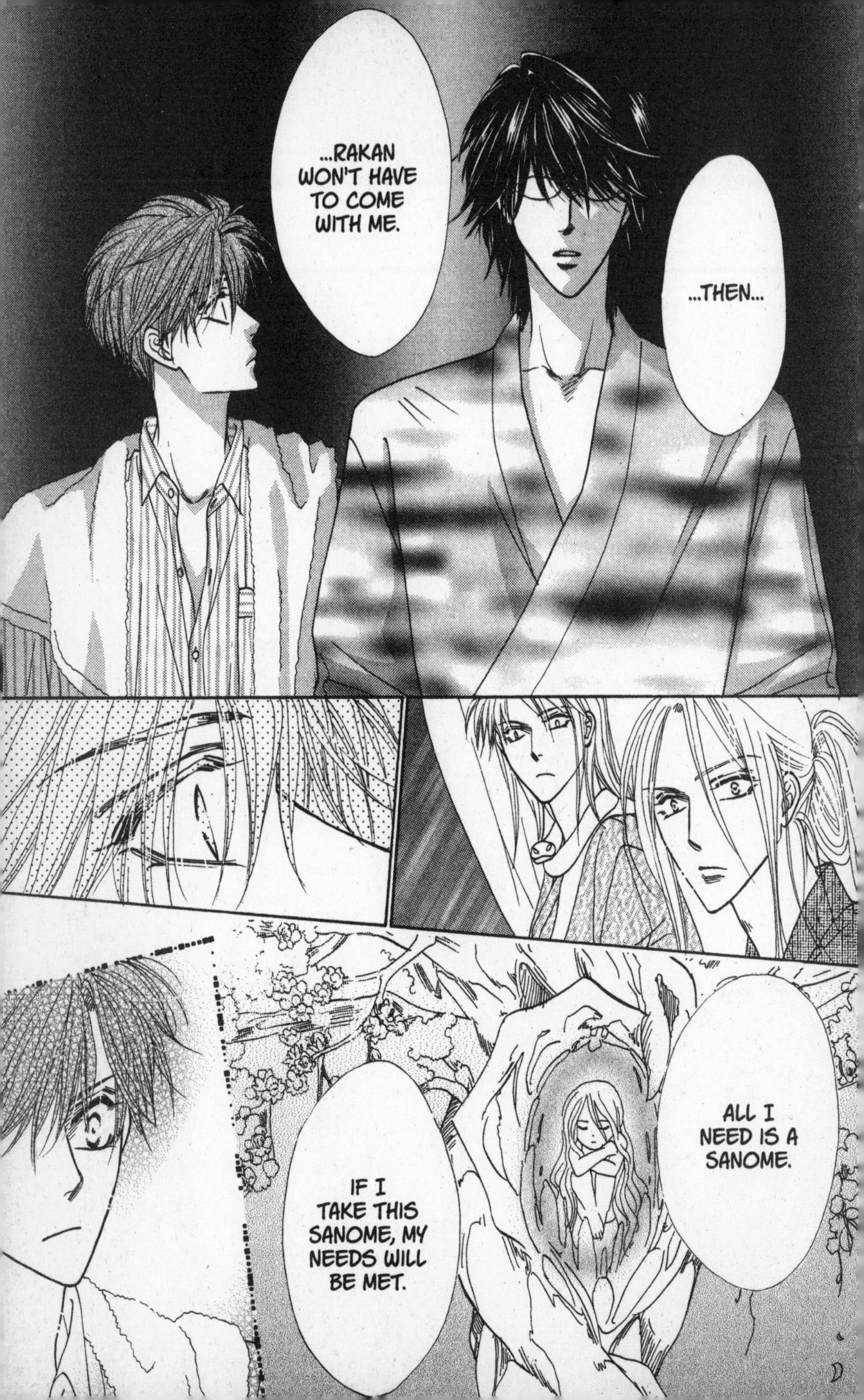
...THEN...
...RAKAN WON'T HAVE TO COME WITH ME.
ALL I NEED IS A SANOME.
IF I TAKE THIS SANOME, MY NEEDS WILL BE MET.

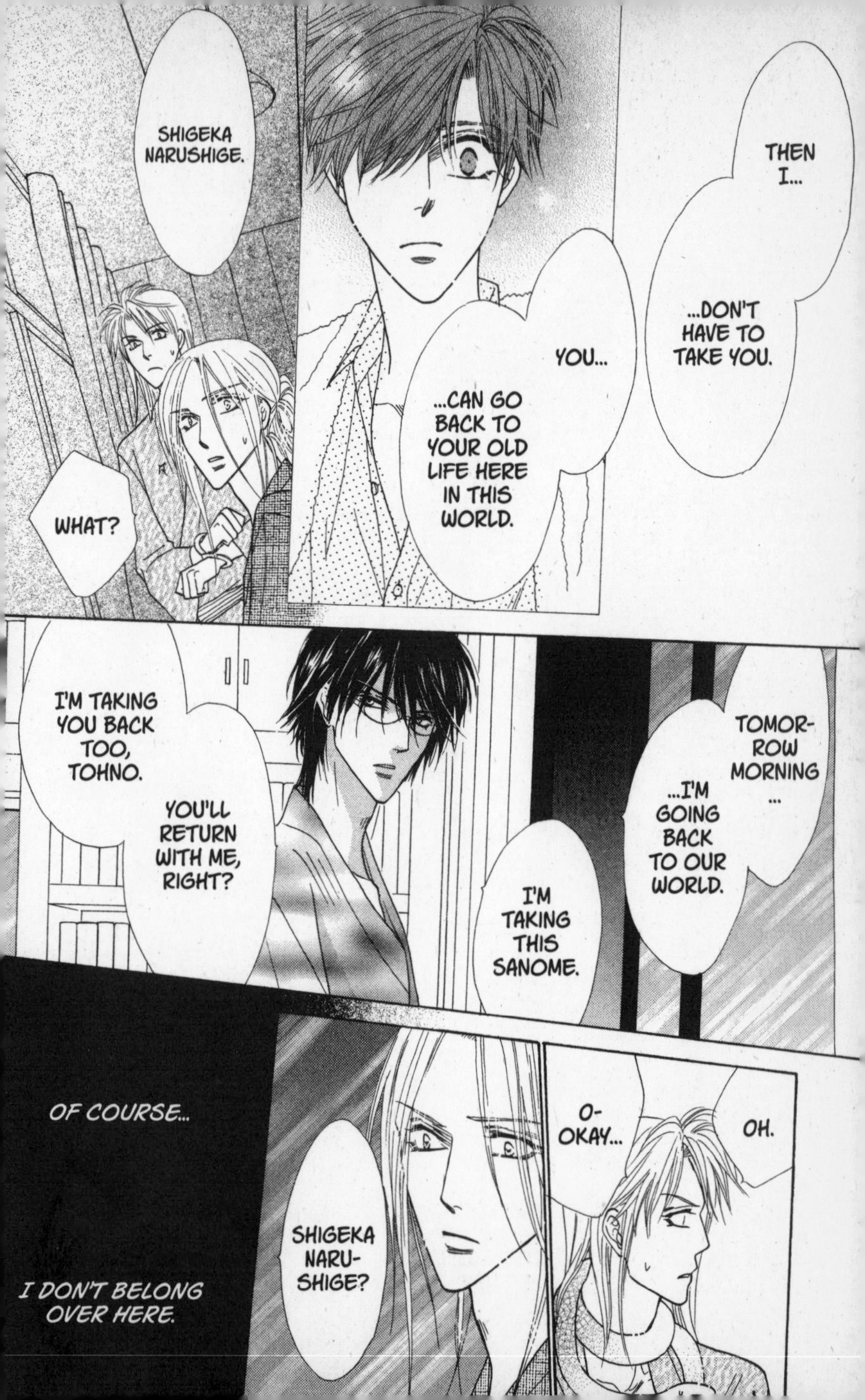
THEN I...
...DON'T HAVE TO TAKE YOU.
YOU...
...CAN GO BACK TO YOUR OLD LIFE HERE IN THIS WORLD.
SHIGEKA NARUSHIGE.
WHAT?
TOMORROW MORNING...
...I'M GOING BACK TO OUR WORLD.
I'M TAKING THIS SANOME.
I'M TAKING YOU BACK TOO, TOHNO.
YOU'LL RETURN WITH ME, RIGHT?
OH.
O-OKAY...
SHIGEKA NARUSHIGE?
OF COURSE...
I DON'T BELONG OVER HERE.

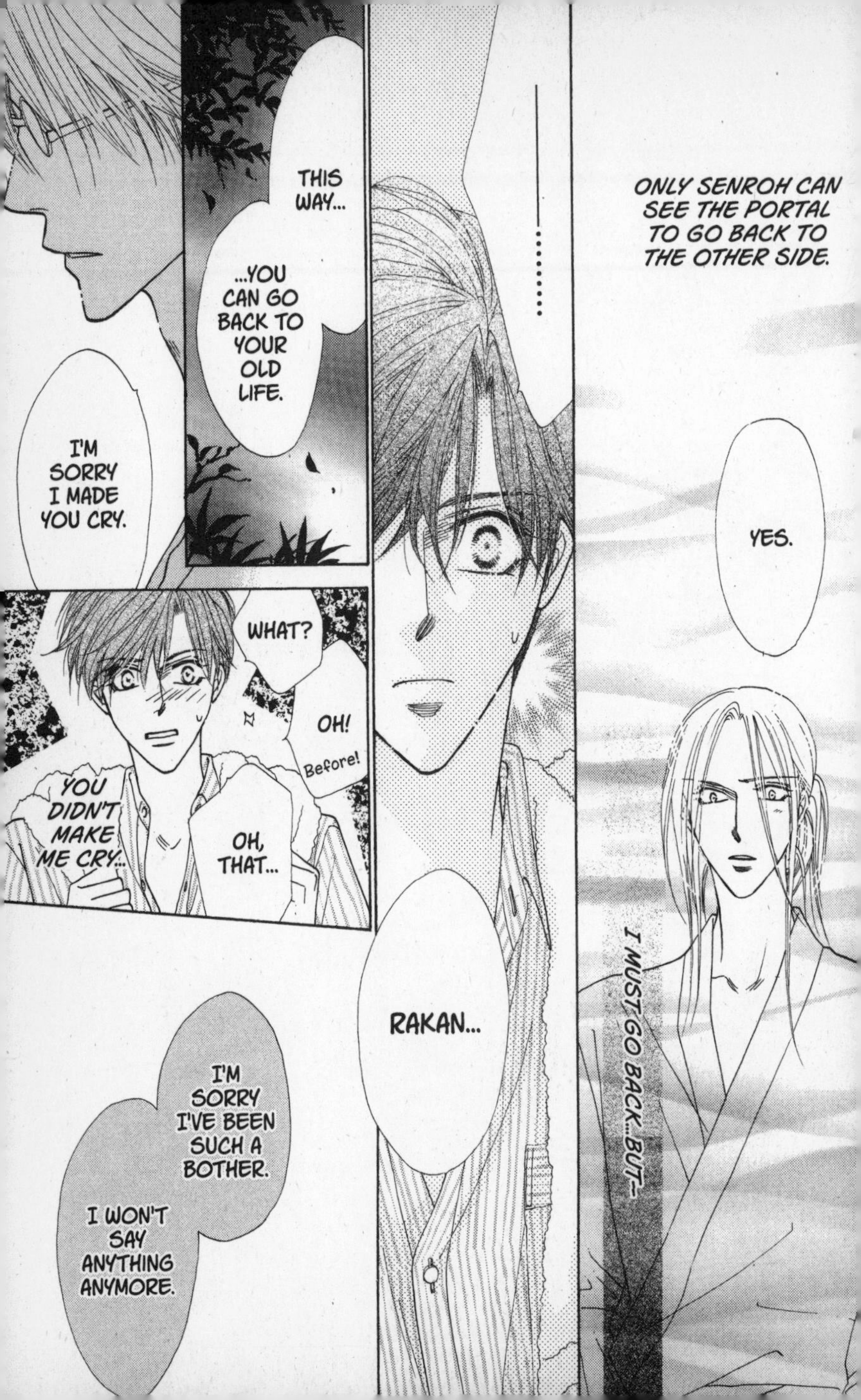
ONLY SENROH CAN SEE THE PORTAL TO GO BACK TO THE OTHER SIDE.
YES.
I MUST GO BACK...BUT–
——......
RAKAN...
THIS WAY...
...YOU CAN GO BACK TO YOUR OLD LIFE.
I'M SORRY I MADE YOU CRY.
WHAT?
OH! Before!
OH, THAT...
YOU DIDN'T MAKE ME CRY...
I'M SORRY I'VE BEEN SUCH A BOTHER.
I WON'T SAY ANYTHING ANYMORE.

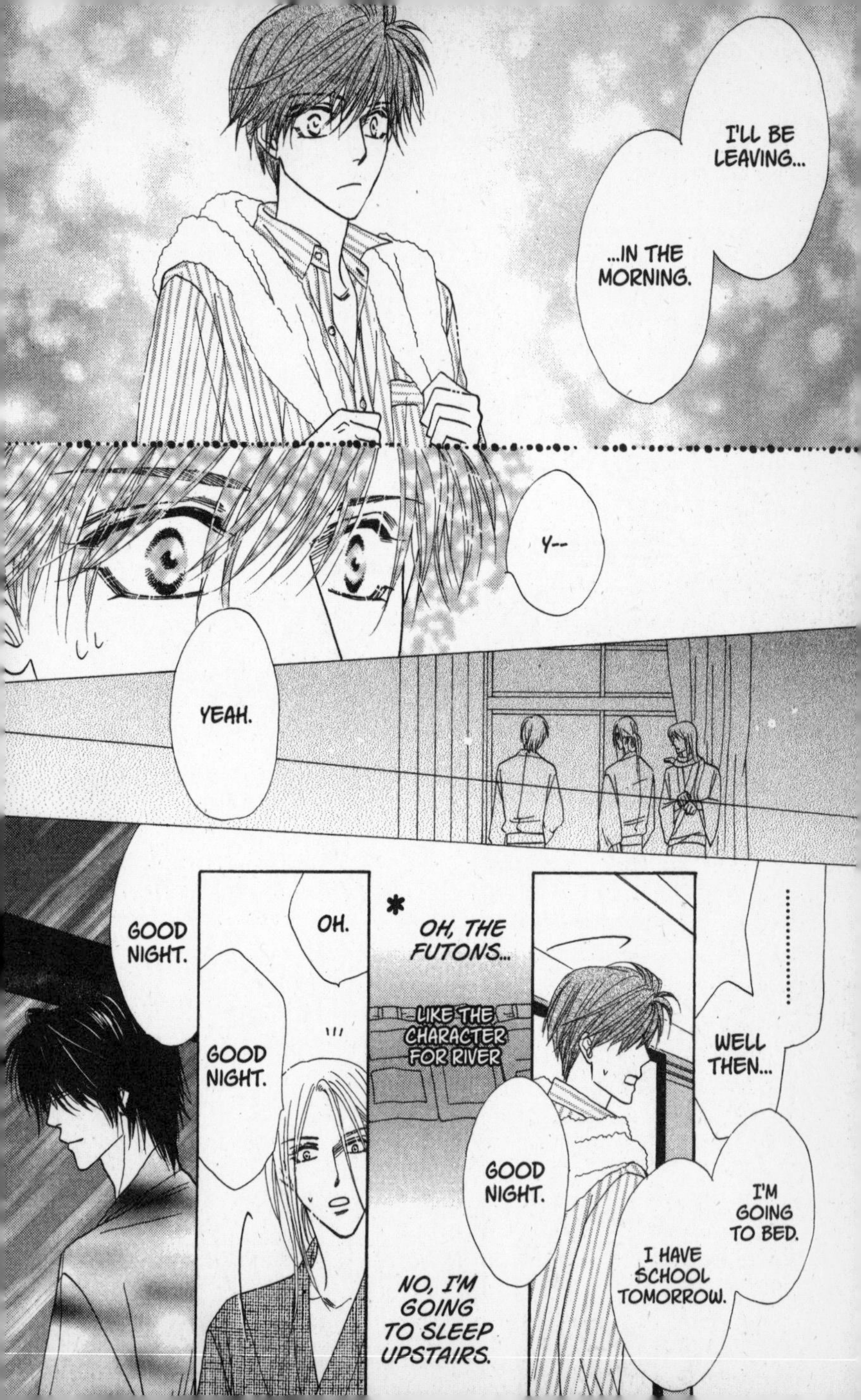
I'LL BE LEAVING...
...IN THE MORNING.
Y--
YEAH.
......
WELL THEN...
I'M GOING TO BED.
I HAVE SCHOOL TOMORROW.
GOOD NIGHT.
* OH, THE FUTONS...
LIKE THE CHARACTER FOR RIVER
NO, I'M GOING TO SLEEP UPSTAIRS.
OH.
GOOD NIGHT.
GOOD NIGHT.

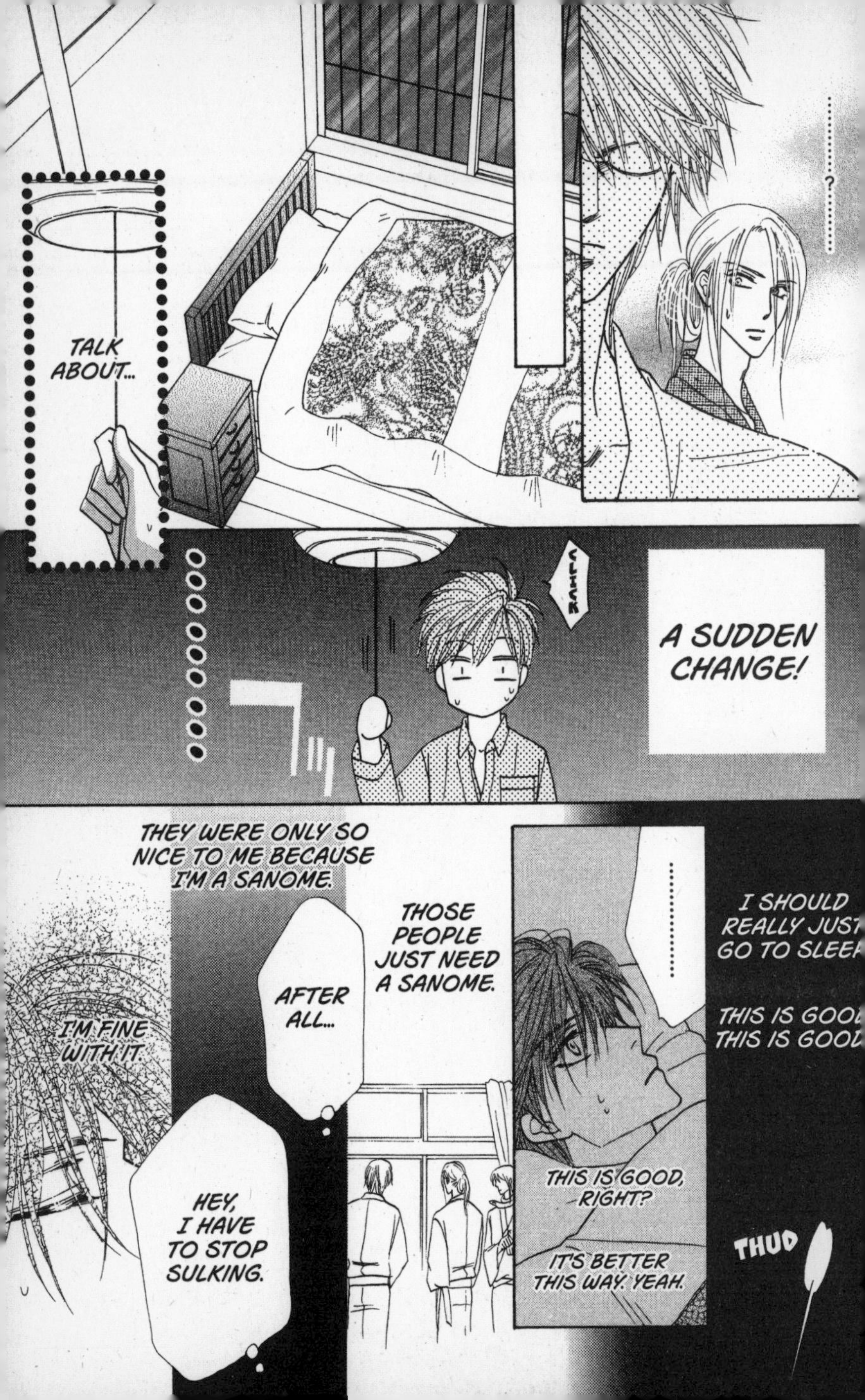

......?
TALK ABOUT...
A SUDDEN CHANGE!
CLICK
I SHOULD REALLY JUST GO TO SLEEP
THIS IS GOOD THIS IS GOOD
......
THIS IS GOOD, RIGHT?
IT'S BETTER THIS WAY. YEAH.
THUD
THOSE PEOPLE JUST NEED A SANOME.
AFTER ALL...
THEY WERE ONLY SO NICE TO ME BECAUSE I'M A SANOME.
HEY, I HAVE TO STOP SULKING.
I'M FINE WITH IT.

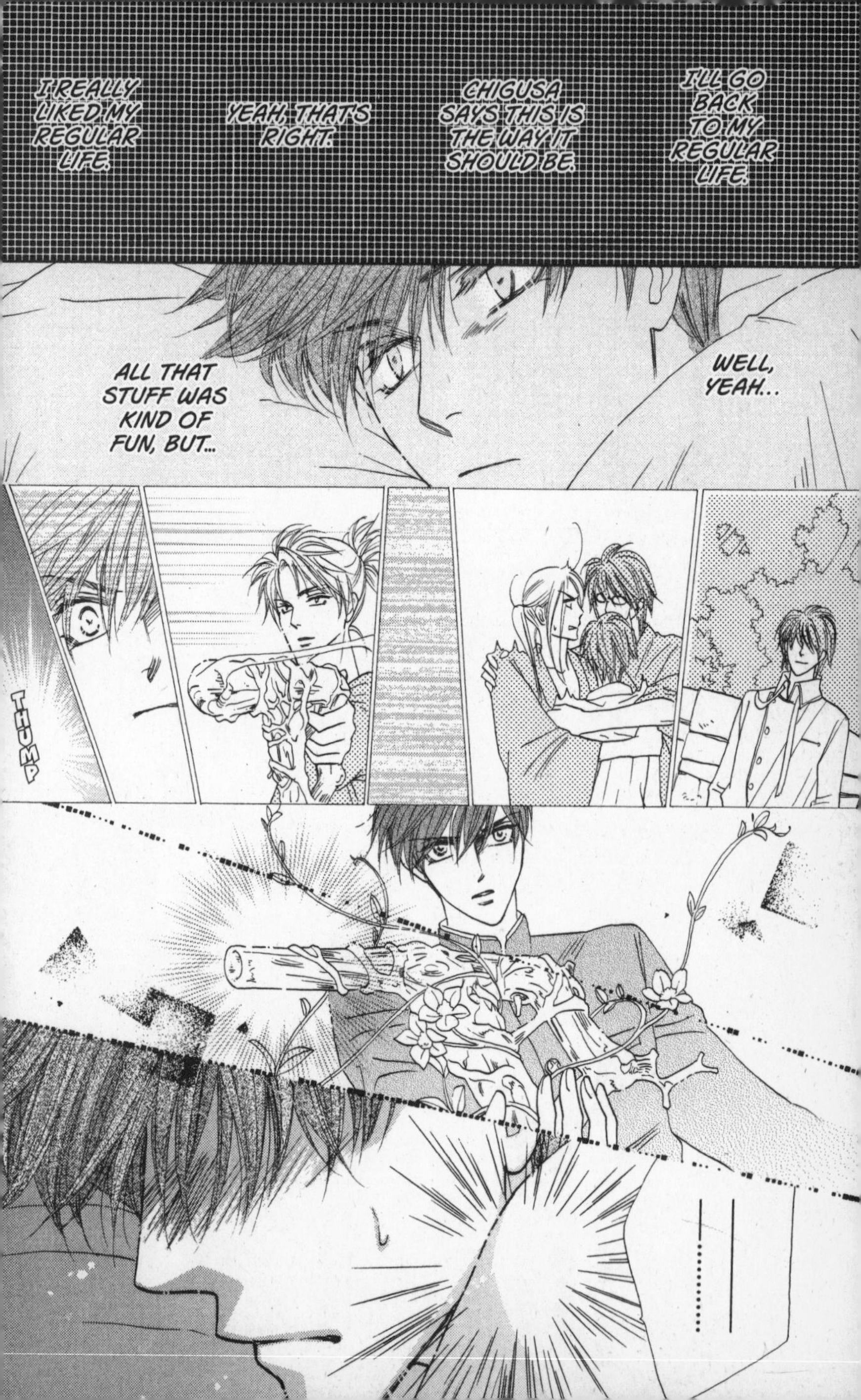
I'LL GO BACK TO MY REGULAR LIFE.
CHIGUSA SAYS THIS IS THE WAY IT SHOULD BE.
YEAH, THAT'S RIGHT.
I REALLY LIKED MY REGULAR LIFE.
WELL, YEAH...
ALL THAT STUFF WAS KIND OF FUN, BUT...
THUMP

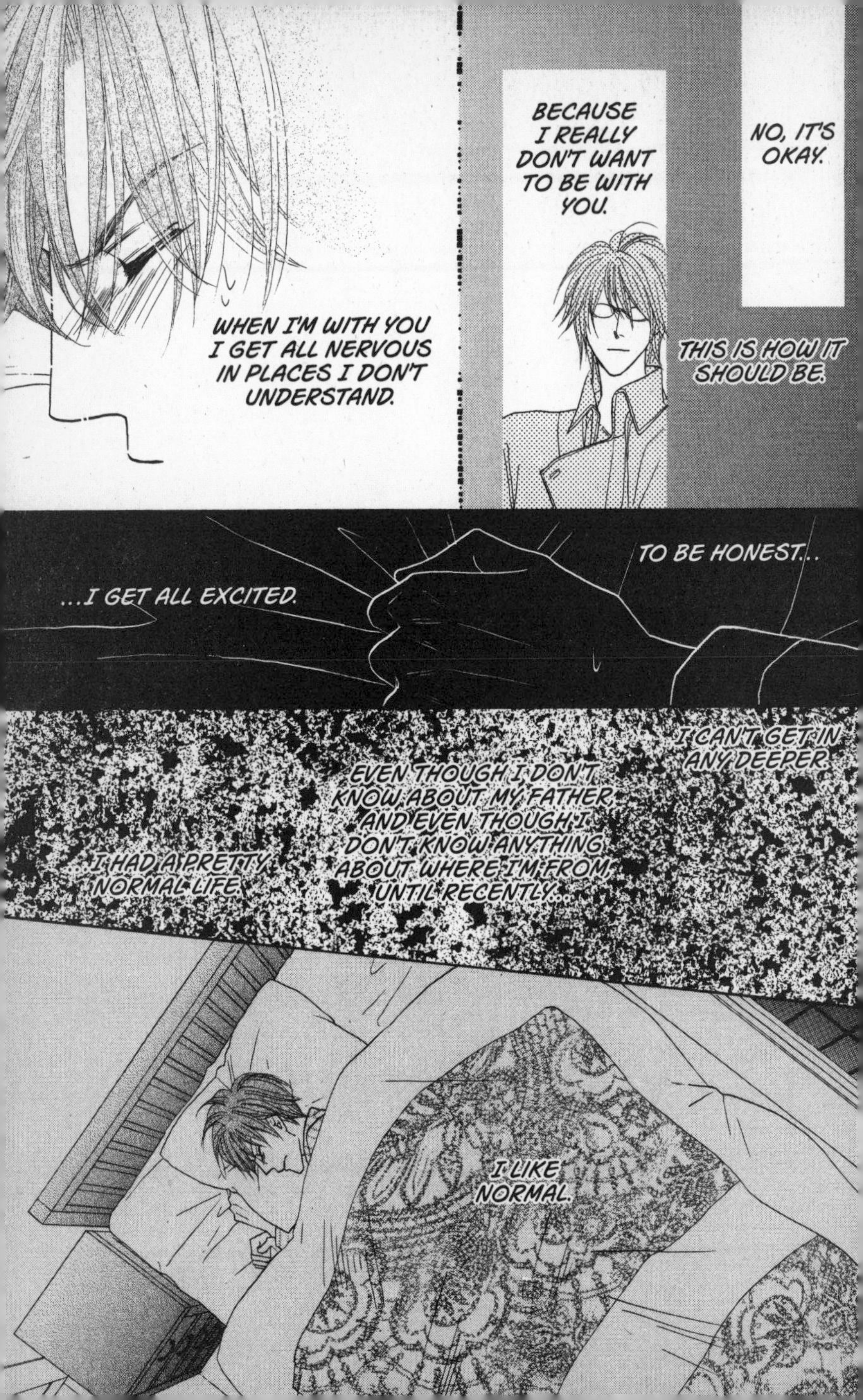
NO, IT'S OKAY.
BECAUSE I REALLY DON'T WANT TO BE WITH YOU.
THIS IS HOW IT SHOULD BE.
WHEN I'M WITH YOU I GET ALL NERVOUS IN PLACES I DON'T UNDERSTAND.
TO BE HONEST...
...I GET ALL EXCITED.
I CAN'T GET IN ANY DEEPER.
EVEN THOUGH I DON'T KNOW ABOUT MY FATHER, AND EVEN THOUGH I DON'T KNOW ANYTHING ABOUT WHERE I'M FROM, UNTIL RECENTLY...
I HAD A PRETTY NORMAL LIFE.
I LIKE NORMAL.

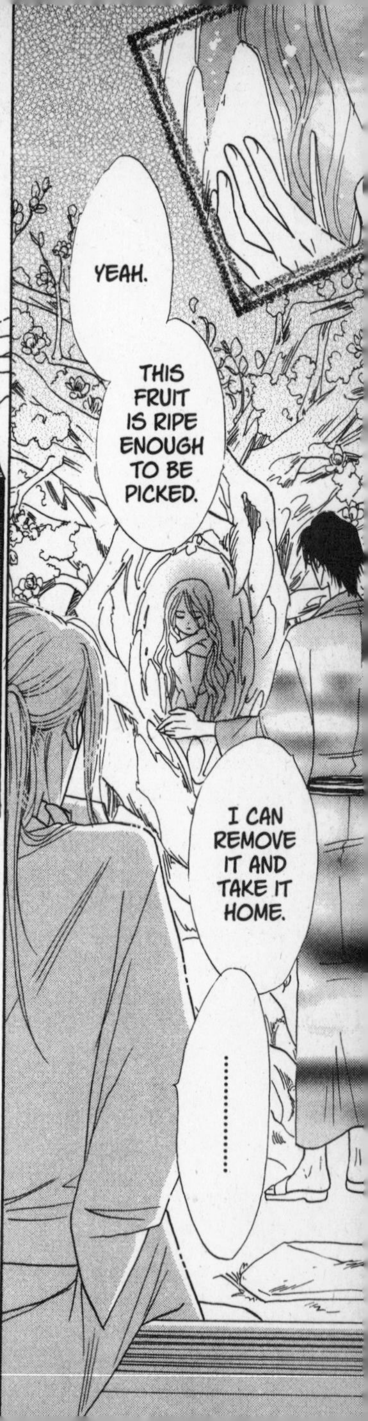
YEAH.
THIS FRUIT IS RIPE ENOUGH TO BE PICKED.
I CAN REMOVE IT AND TAKE IT HOME.
....

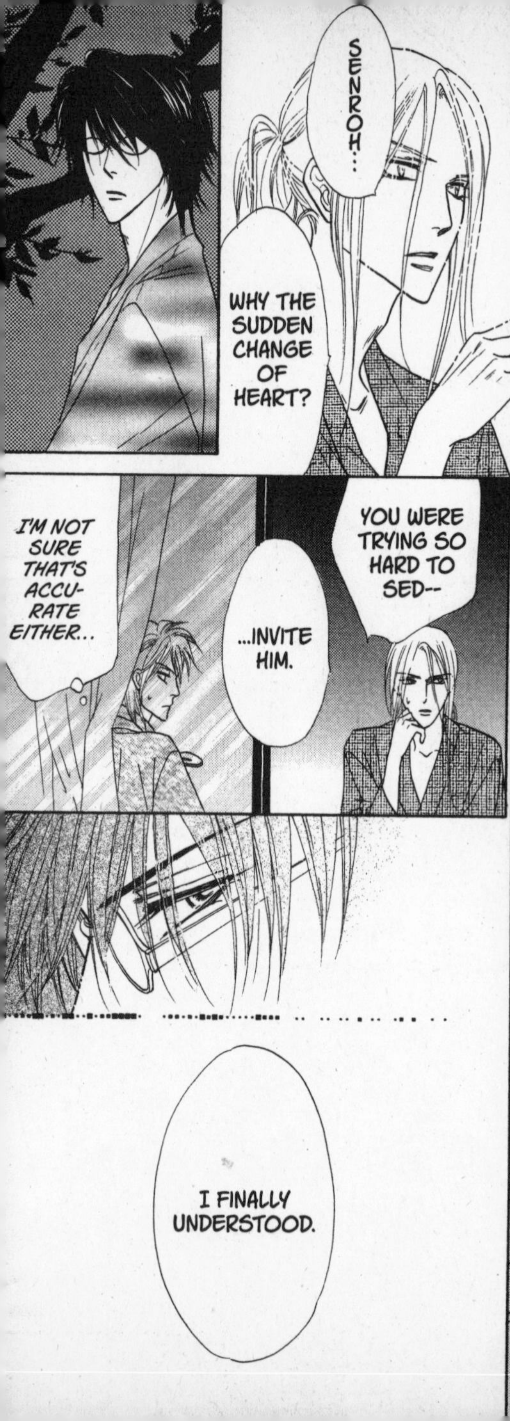
SENROH...
WHY THE SUDDEN CHANGE OF HEART?
YOU WERE TRYING SO HARD TO SED--
...INVITE HIM.
I'M NOT SURE THAT'S ACCURATE EITHER...
I FINALLY UNDERSTOOD.

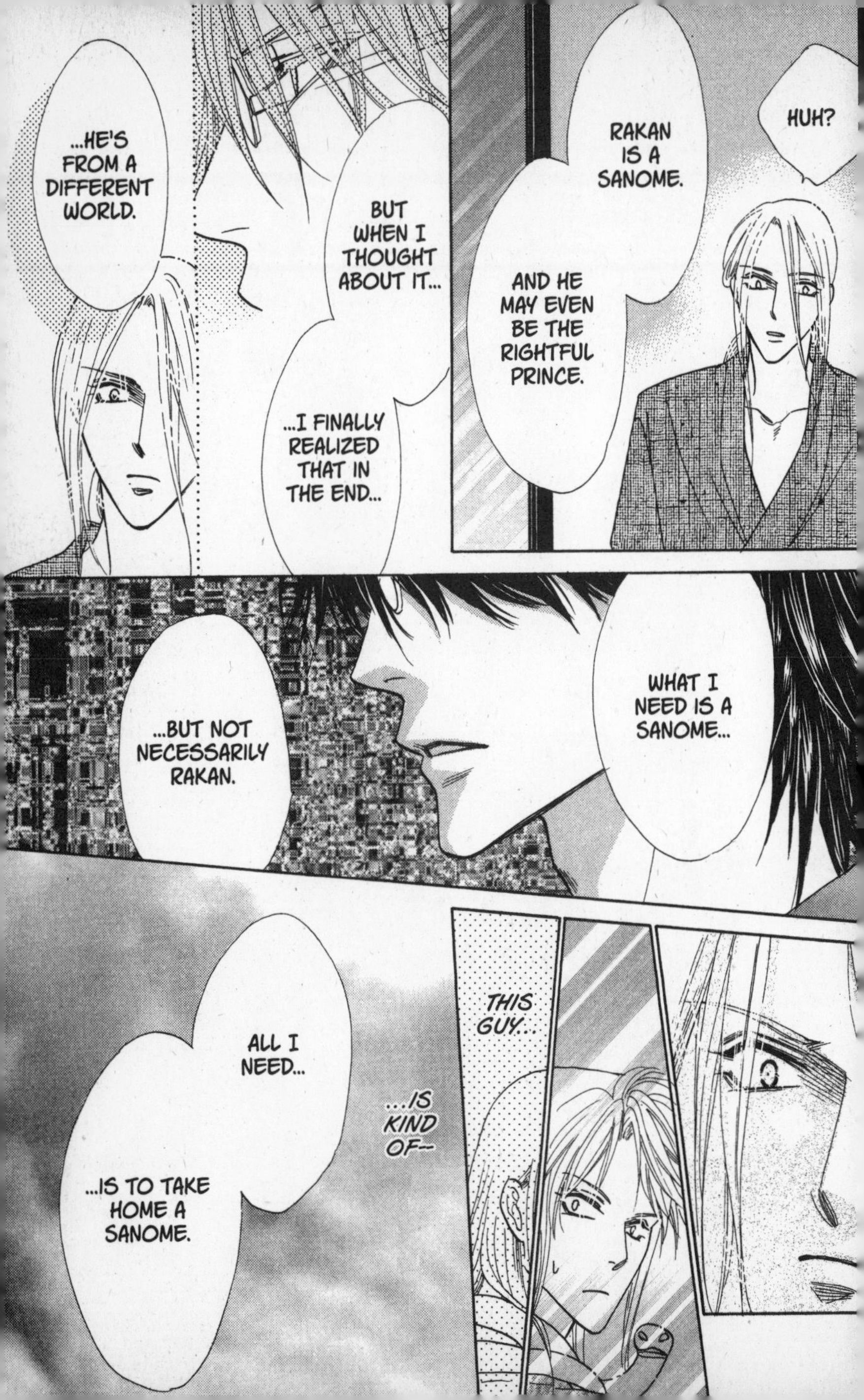
HUH?
RAKAN IS A SANOME.
AND HE MAY EVEN BE THE RIGHTFUL PRINCE.
BUT WHEN I THOUGHT ABOUT IT...
...I FINALLY REALIZED THAT IN THE END...
...HE'S FROM A DIFFERENT WORLD.
WHAT I NEED IS A SANOME...
...BUT NOT NECESSARILY RAKAN.
ALL I NEED...
...IS TO TAKE HOME A SANOME.
THIS GUY...
...IS KIND OF--

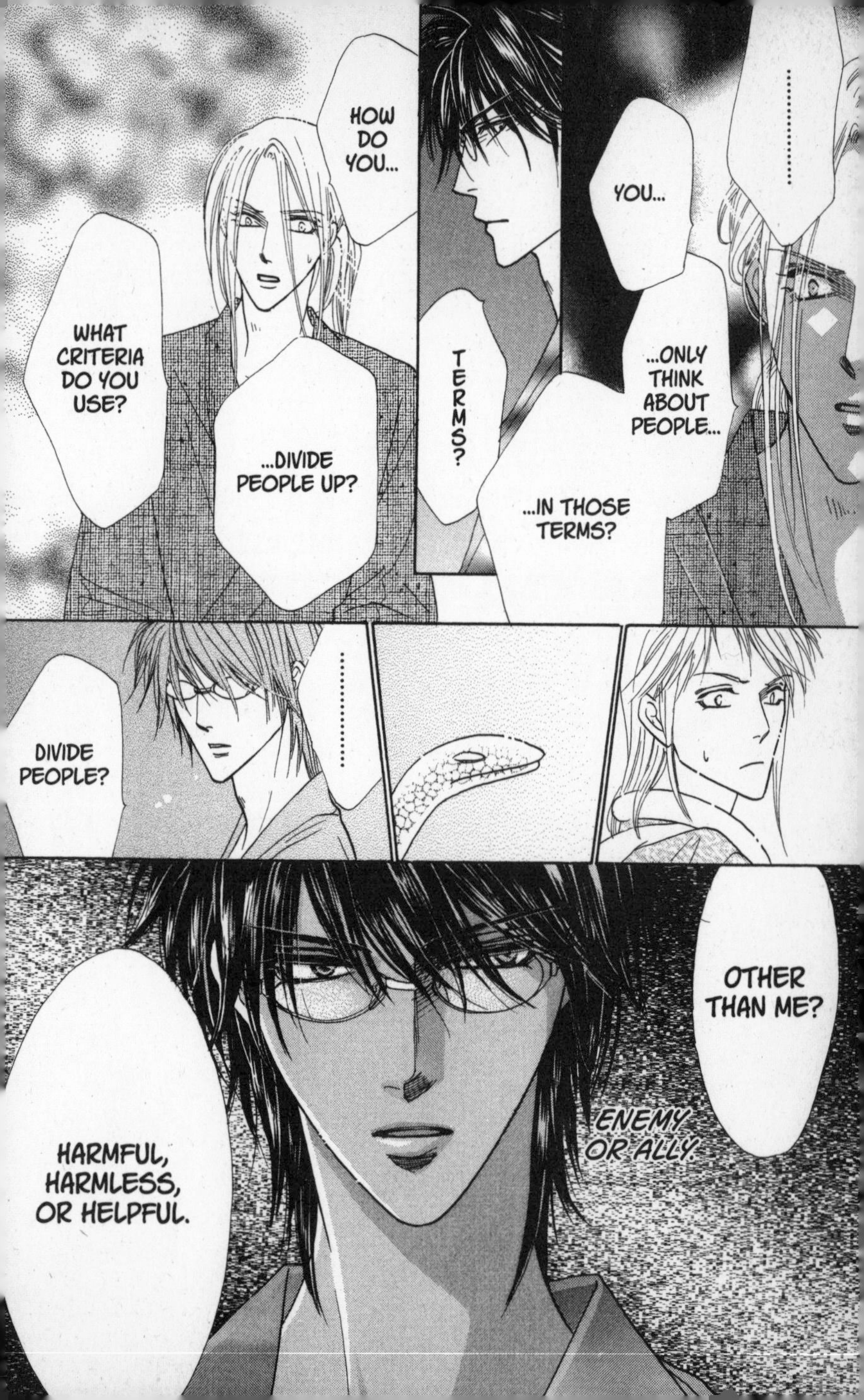
......
YOU...
...ONLY THINK ABOUT PEOPLE...
...IN THOSE TERMS?
TERMS?
HOW DO YOU...
...DIVIDE PEOPLE UP?
WHAT CRITERIA DO YOU USE?
......
DIVIDE PEOPLE?
OTHER THAN ME?
ENEMY OR ALLY.
HARMFUL, HARMLESS, OR HELPFUL.

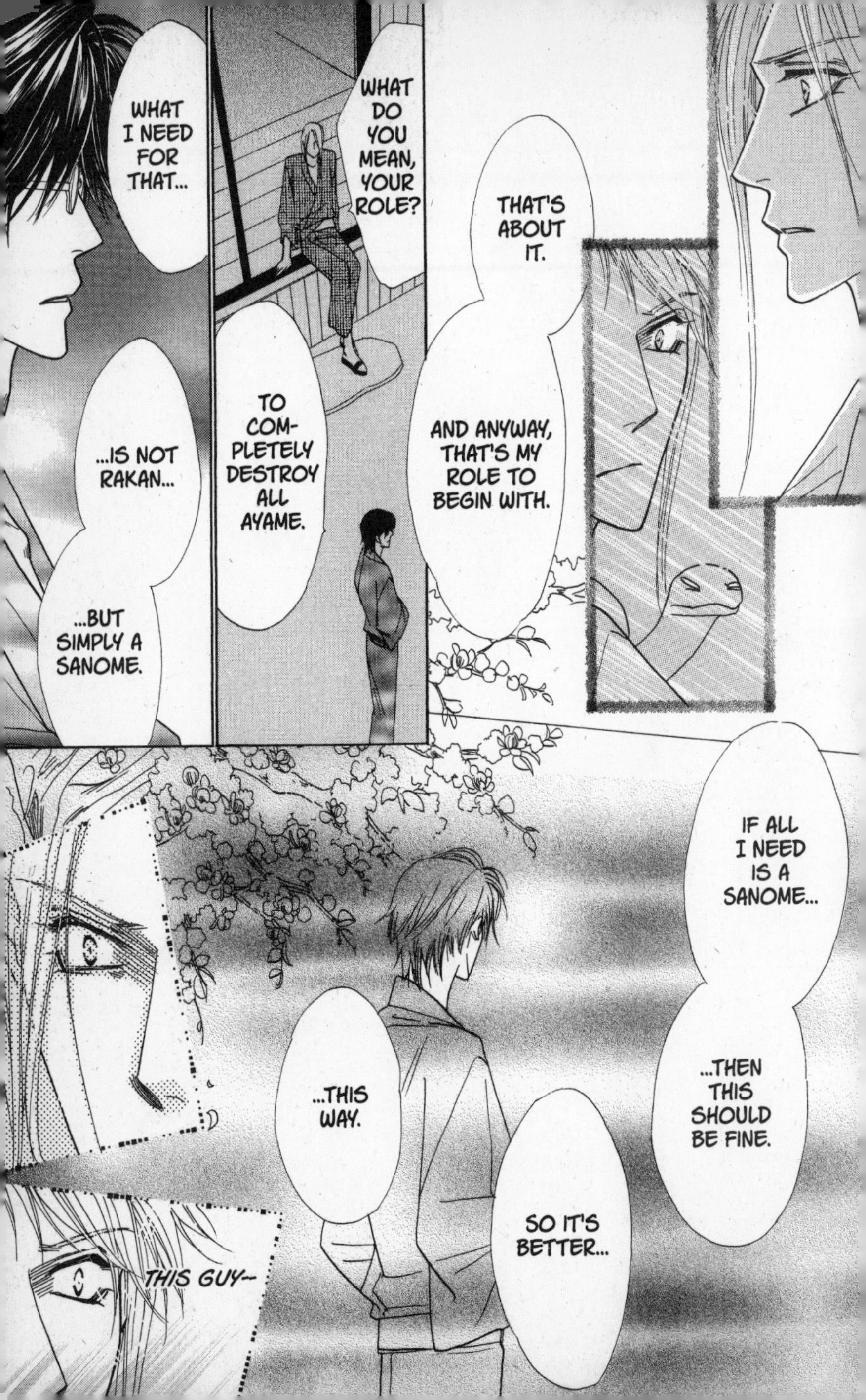
THAT'S ABOUT IT.
AND ANYWAY, THAT'S MY ROLE TO BEGIN WITH.
WHAT DO YOU MEAN, YOUR ROLE?
TO COMPLETELY DESTROY ALL AYAME.
WHAT I NEED FOR THAT...
...IS NOT RAKAN...
...BUT SIMPLY A SANOME.
IF ALL I NEED IS A SANOME...
...THEN THIS SHOULD BE FINE.
SO IT'S BETTER...
...THIS WAY.
THIS GUY--

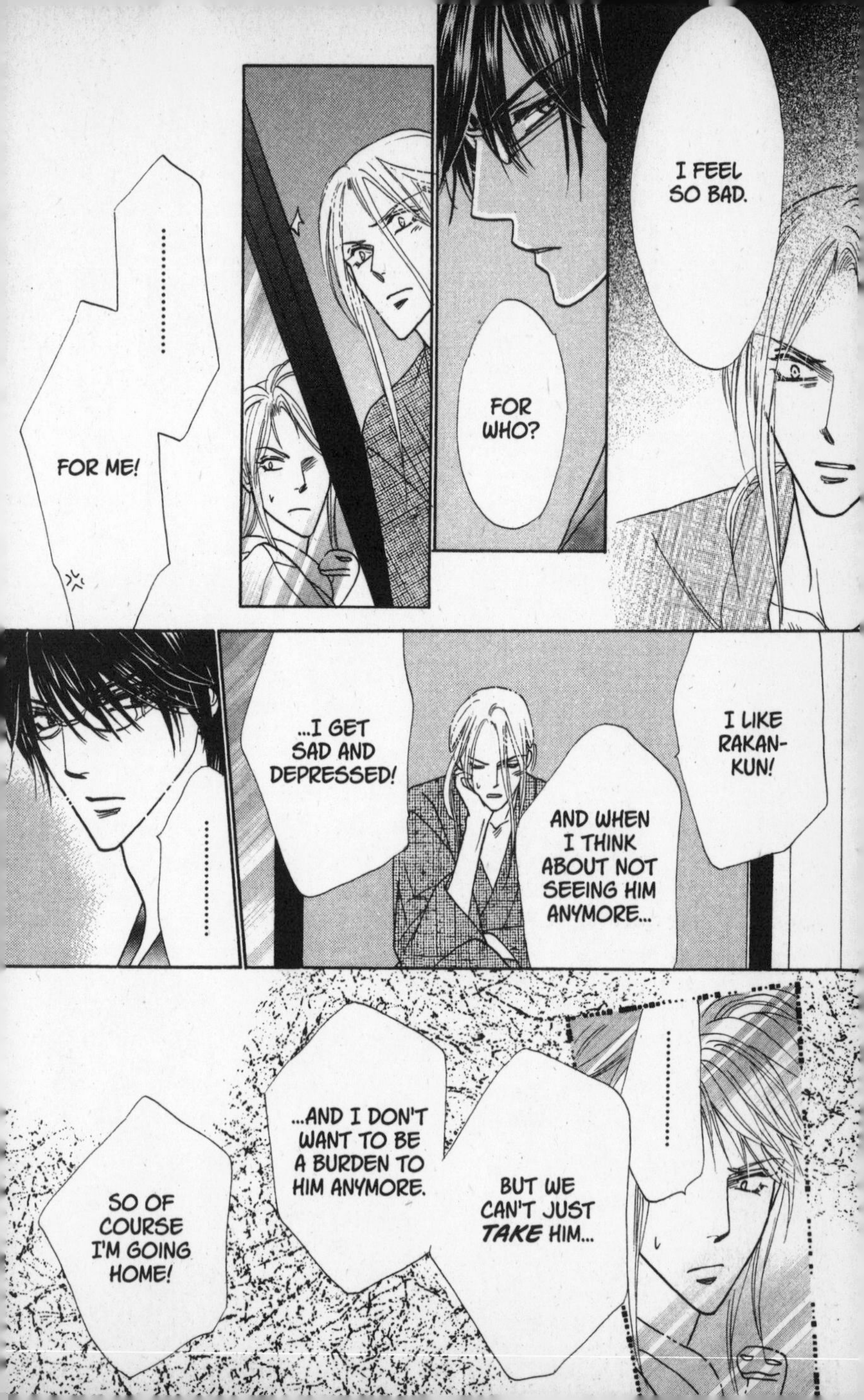
I FEEL SO BAD.
FOR WHO?
......
FOR ME!
I LIKE RAKAN-KUN!
AND WHEN I THINK ABOUT NOT SEEING HIM ANYMORE...
...I GET SAD AND DEPRESSED!
......
......
BUT WE CAN'T JUST *TAKE* HIM...
...AND I DON'T WANT TO BE A BURDEN TO HIM ANYMORE.
SO OF COURSE I'M GOING HOME!

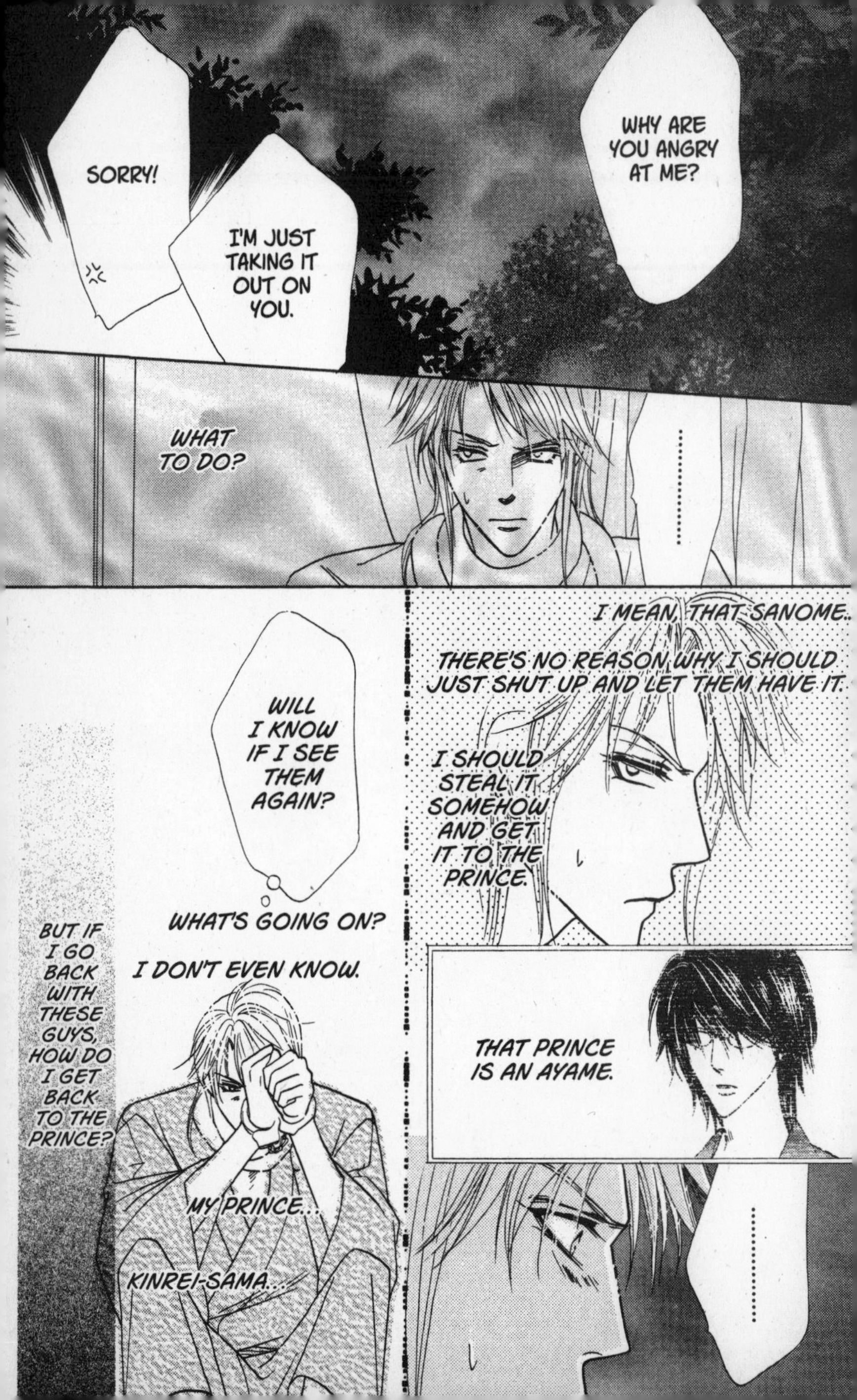

WHY ARE YOU ANGRY AT ME?
SORRY!
I'M JUST TAKING IT OUT ON YOU.
......
WHAT TO DO?
I MEAN, THAT SANOME...
THERE'S NO REASON WHY I SHOULD JUST SHUT UP AND LET THEM HAVE IT.
I SHOULD STEAL IT SOMEHOW AND GET IT TO THE PRINCE.
THAT PRINCE IS AN AYAME.
......
WILL I KNOW IF I SEE THEM AGAIN?
WHAT'S GOING ON?
I DON'T EVEN KNOW.
BUT IF I GO BACK WITH THESE GUYS, HOW DO I GET BACK TO THE PRINCE?
MY PRINCE...
KINREI-SAMA...

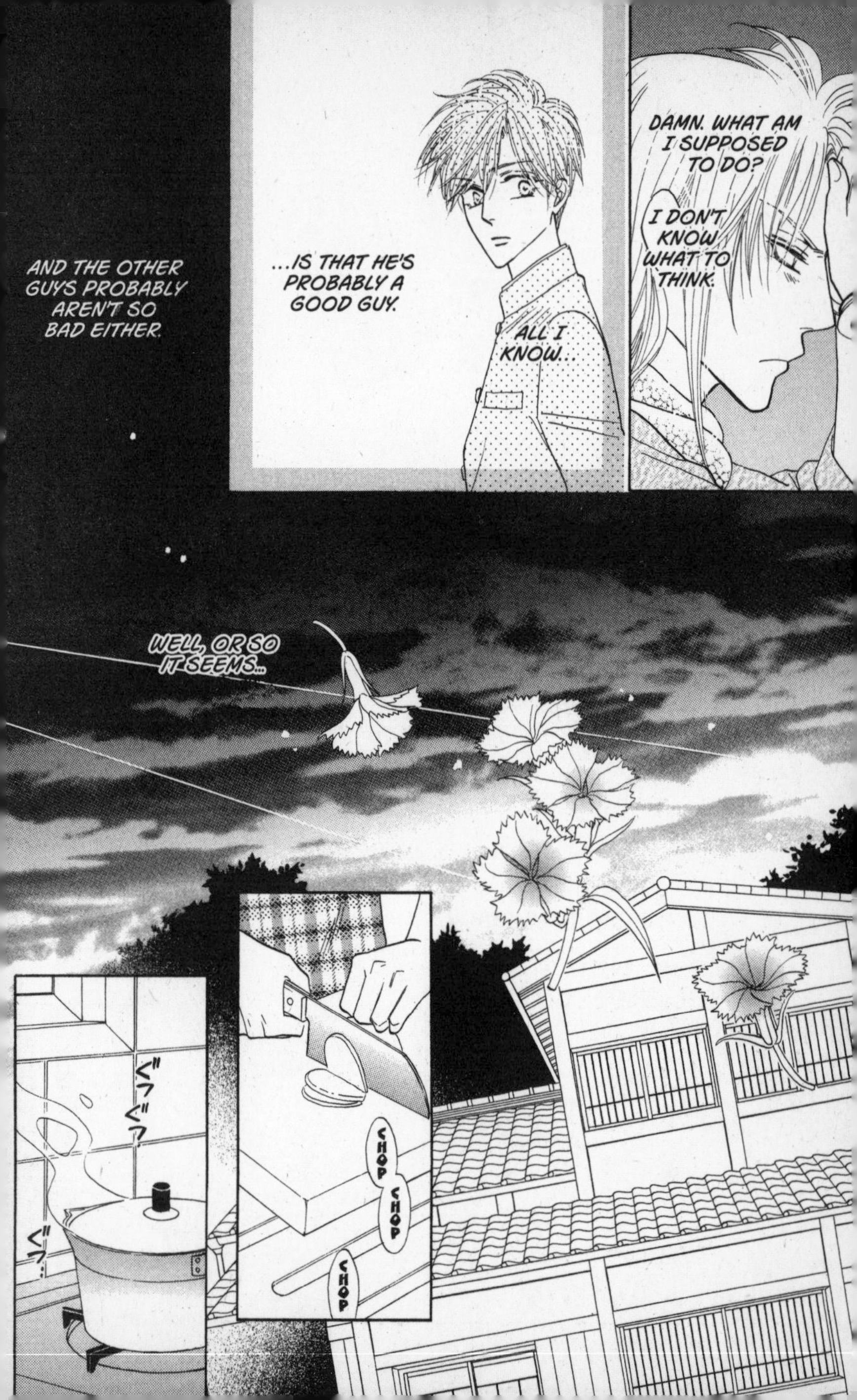
DAMN. WHAT AM I SUPPOSED TO DO?
I DON'T KNOW WHAT TO THINK.
ALL I KNOW...
...IS THAT HE'S PROBABLY A GOOD GUY.
AND THE OTHER GUYS PROBABLY AREN'T SO BAD EITHER.
WELL, OR SO IT SEEMS...
CHOP
CHOP
CHOP

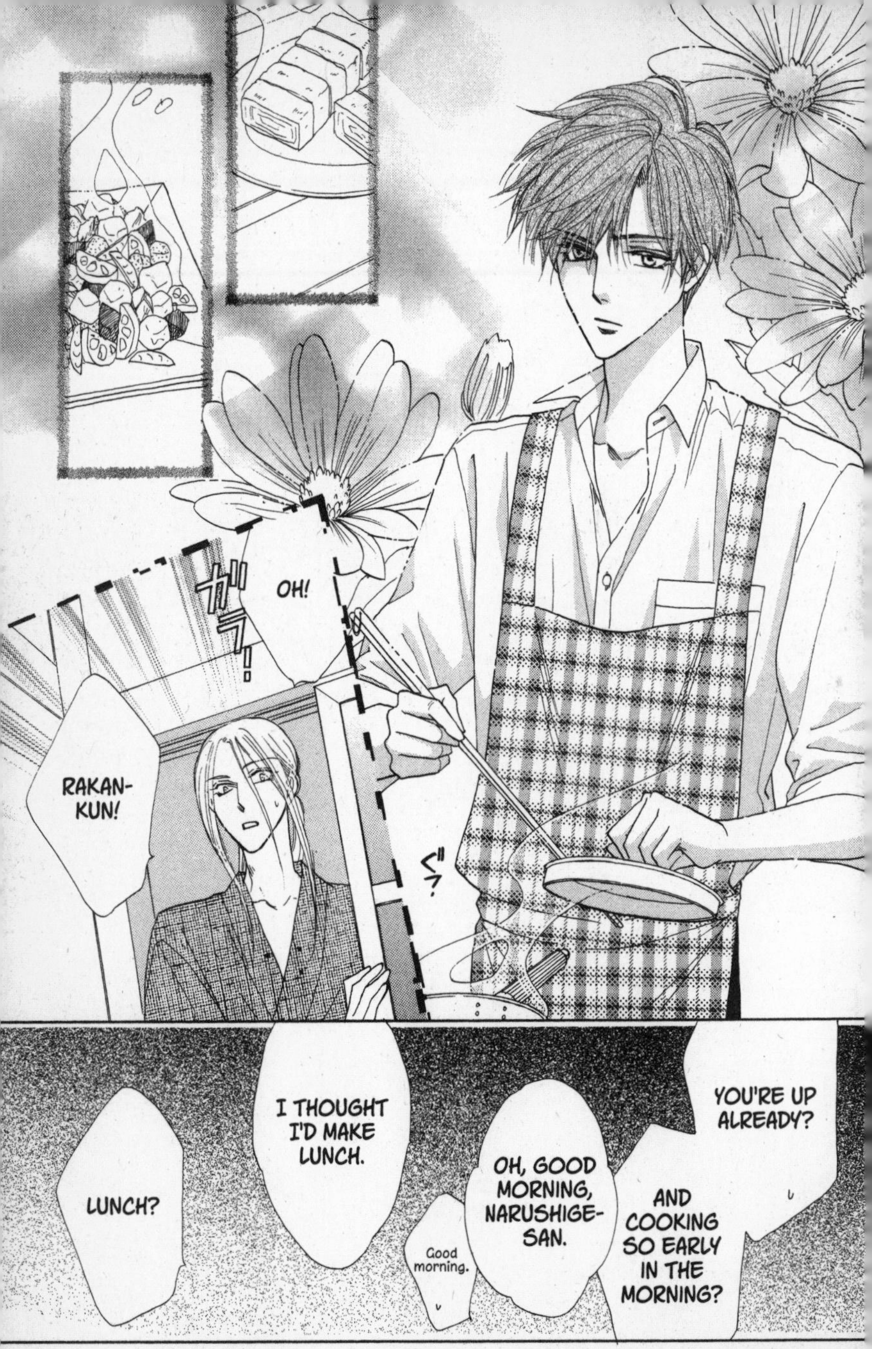
OH!
ガラ!
RAKAN-KUN!
ぐ
YOU'RE UP ALREADY?
AND COOKING SO EARLY IN THE MORNING?
OH, GOOD MORNING, NARUSHIGE-SAN.
Good morning.
I THOUGHT I'D MAKE LUNCH.
LUNCH?

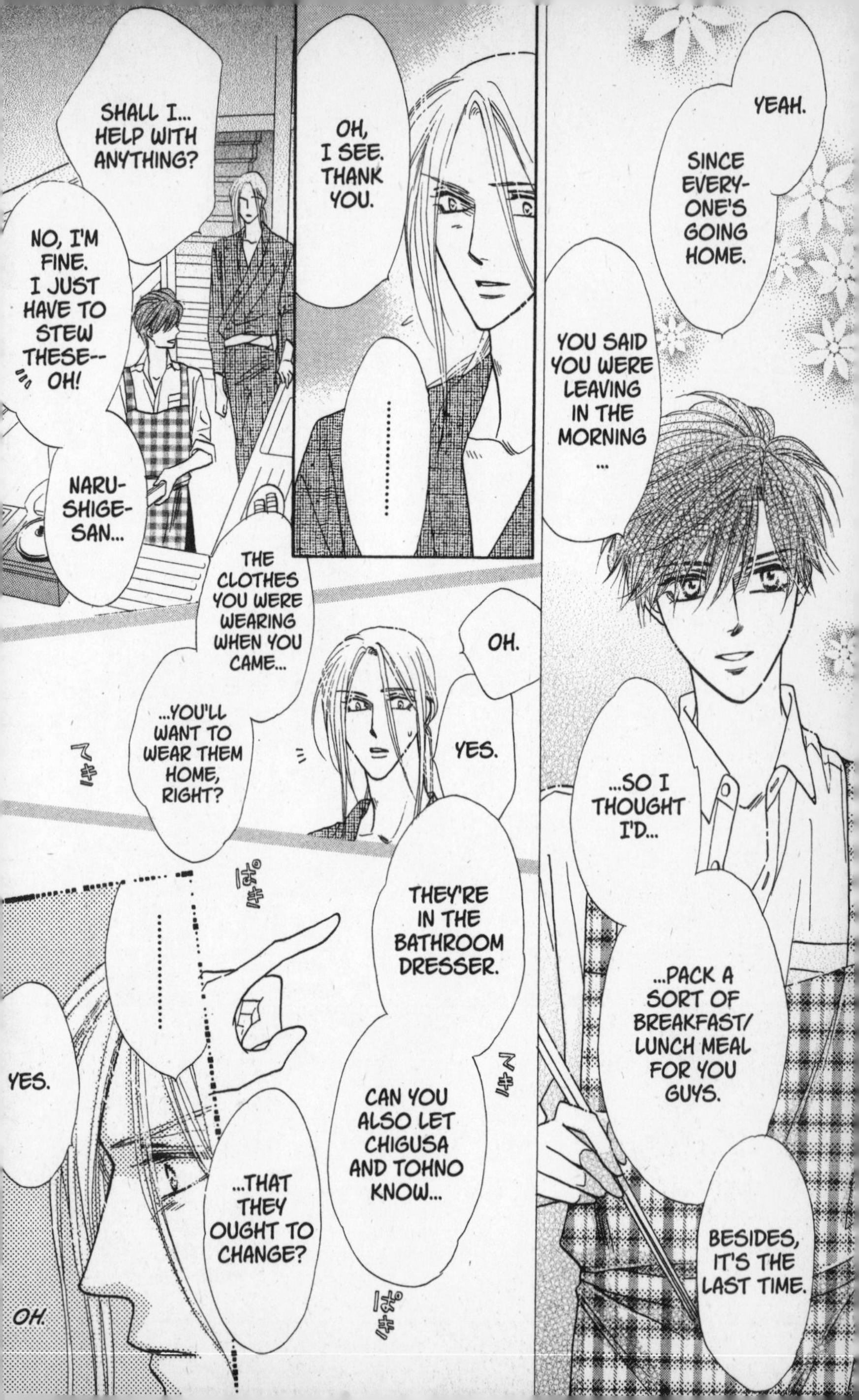
YEAH.
SINCE EVERY-ONE'S GOING HOME.
YOU SAID YOU WERE LEAVING IN THE MORNING ...
...SO I THOUGHT I'D...
...PACK A SORT OF BREAKFAST/ LUNCH MEAL FOR YOU GUYS.
BESIDES, IT'S THE LAST TIME.
OH, I SEE. THANK YOU.
......
SHALL I... HELP WITH ANYTHING?
NO, I'M FINE. I JUST HAVE TO STEW THESE-- OH!
NARU-SHIGE-SAN...
OH.
YES.
THE CLOTHES YOU WERE WEARING WHEN YOU CAME...
...YOU'LL WANT TO WEAR THEM HOME, RIGHT?
THEY'RE IN THE BATHROOM DRESSER.
CAN YOU ALSO LET CHIGUSA AND TOHNO KNOW...
...THAT THEY OUGHT TO CHANGE?
......
YES.
OH.

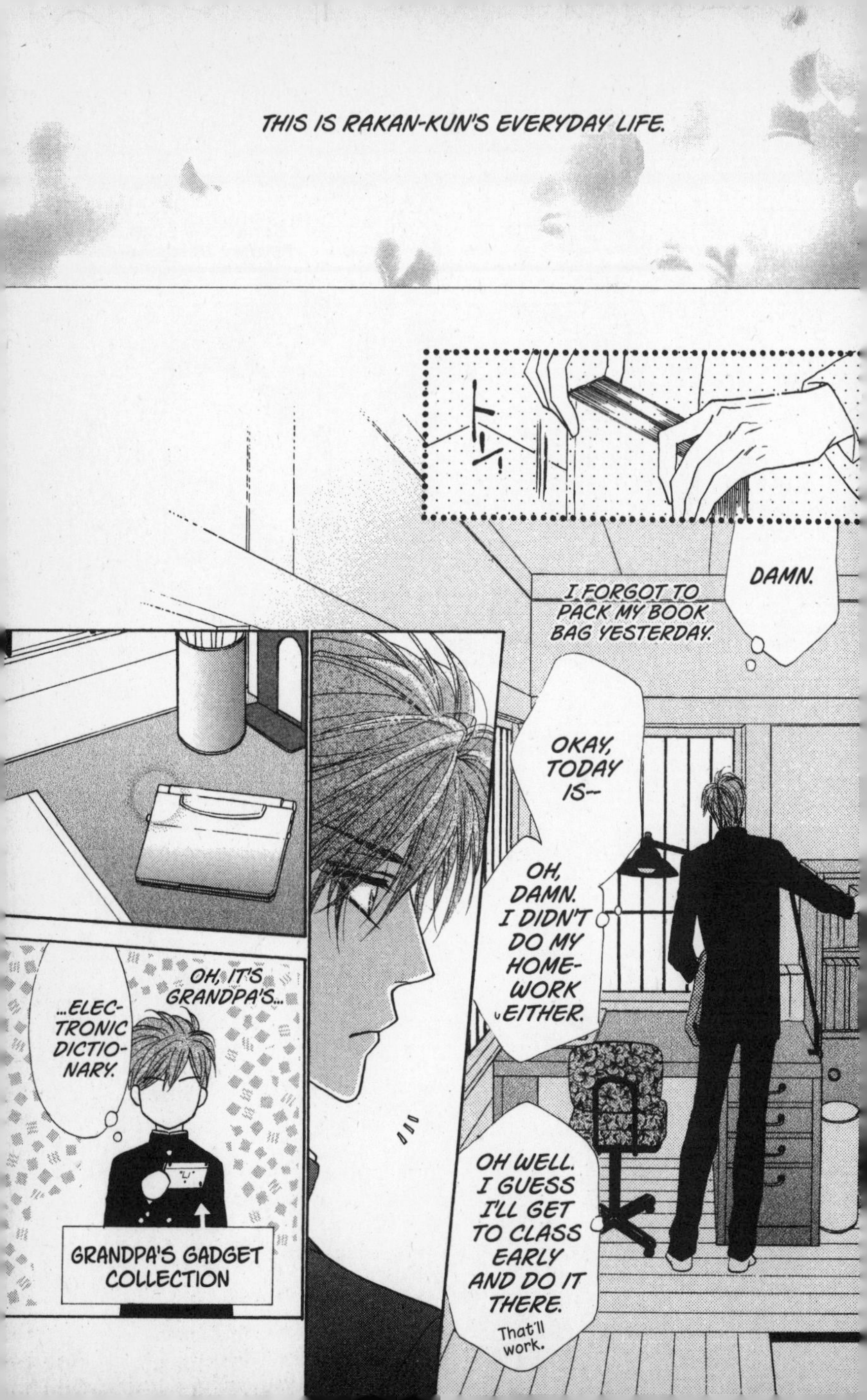
THIS IS RAKAN-KUN'S EVERYDAY LIFE.
DAMN.
I FORGOT TO PACK MY BOOK BAG YESTERDAY.
OKAY, TODAY IS--
OH, DAMN. I DIDN'T DO MY HOMEWORK EITHER.
OH WELL. I GUESS I'LL GET TO CLASS EARLY AND DO IT THERE.
That'll work.
OH, IT'S GRANDPA'S...
...ELECTRONIC DICTIONARY.
GRANDPA'S GADGET COLLECTION

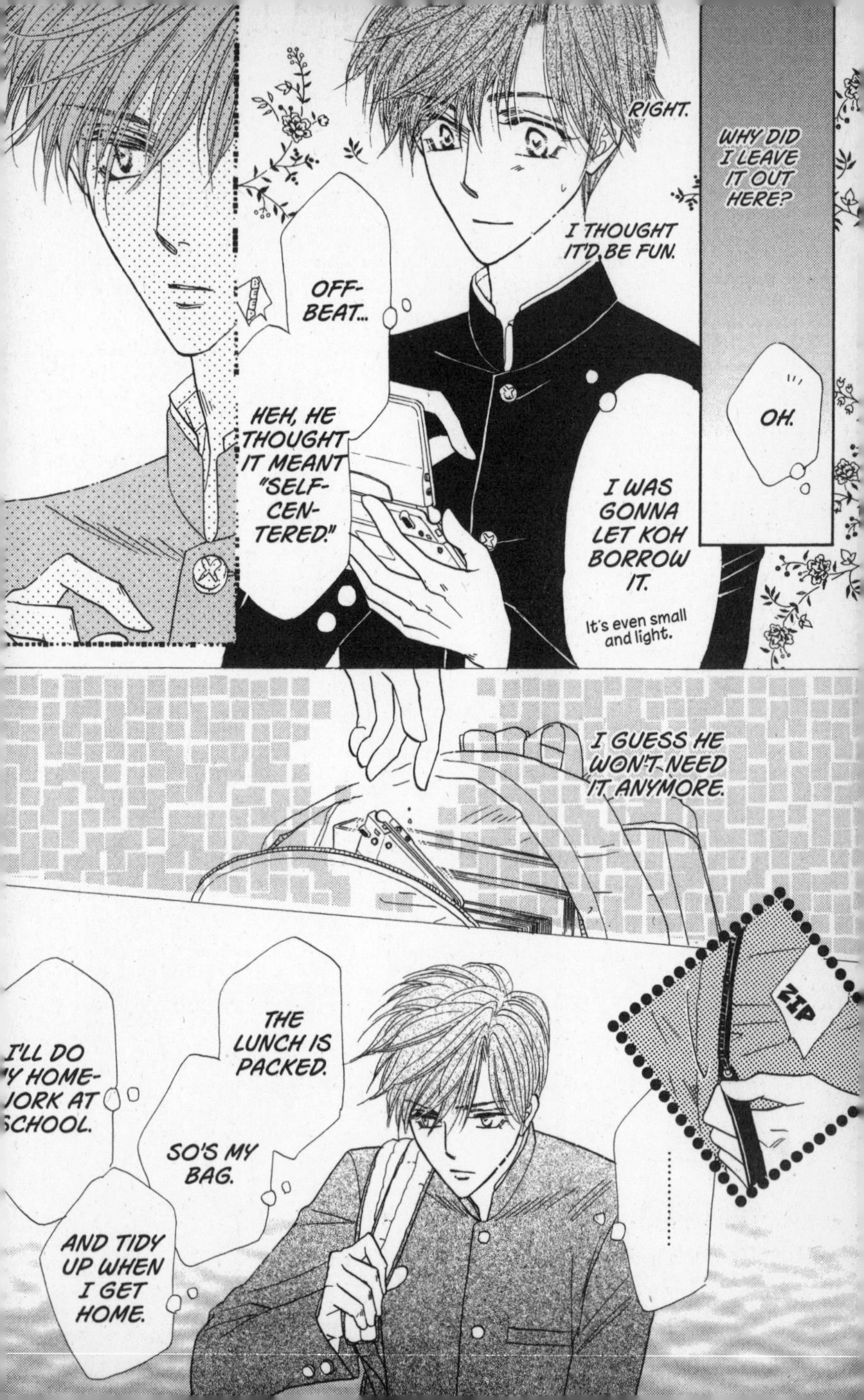
WHY DID I LEAVE IT OUT HERE?
OH.
RIGHT.
I THOUGHT IT'D BE FUN.
I WAS GONNA LET KOH BORROW IT.
It's even small and light.
OFF-BEAT...
BEEP
HEH, HE THOUGHT IT MEANT "SELF-CENTERED."
I GUESS HE WON'T NEED IT ANYMORE.
ZIP
......
THE LUNCH IS PACKED.
SO'S MY BAG.
I'LL DO 'Y HOME- 'ORK AT 'CHOOL.
AND TIDY UP WHEN I GET HOME.

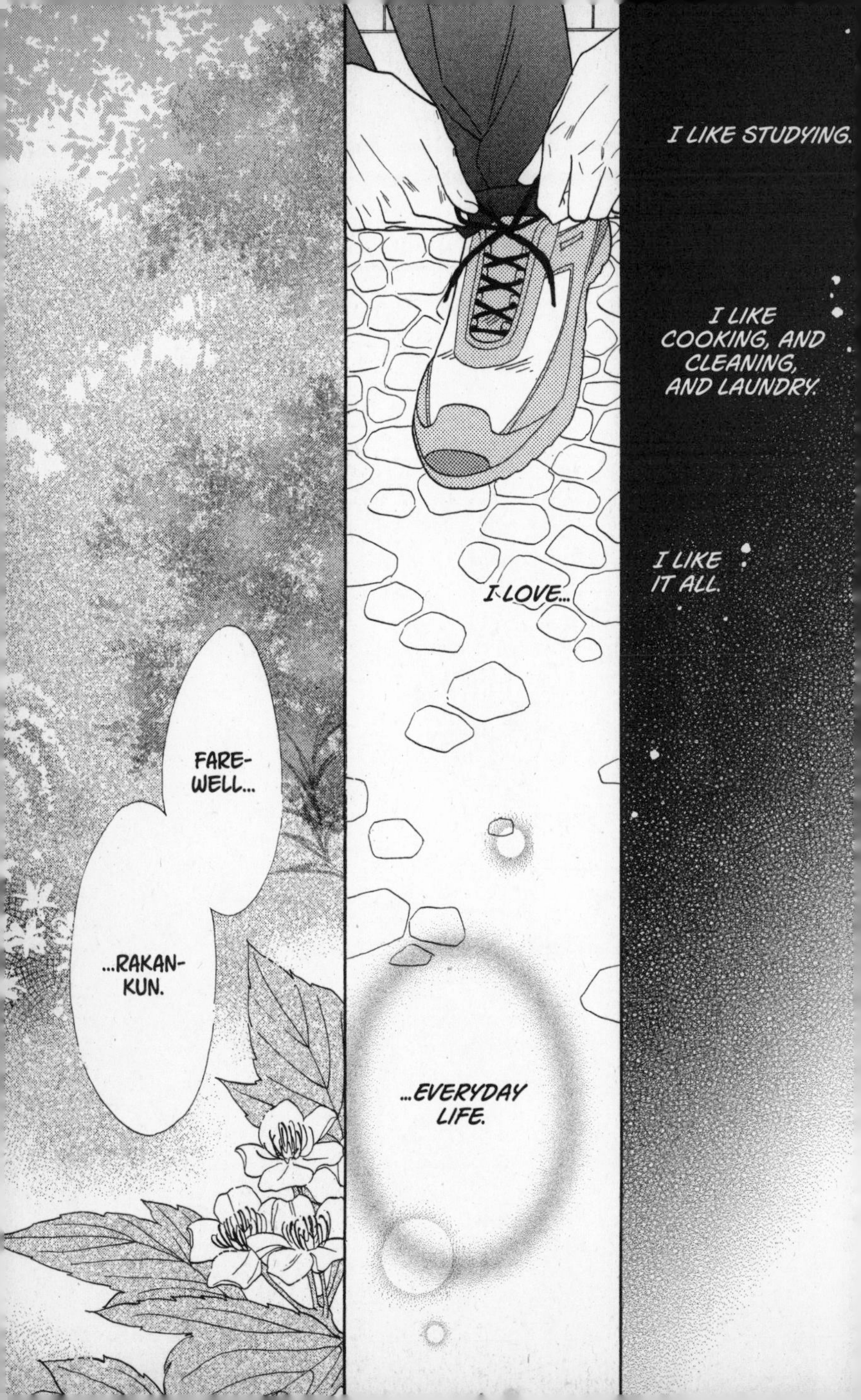
I LIKE STUDYING.
I LIKE COOKING, AND CLEANING, AND LAUNDRY.
I LIKE IT ALL.
I LOVE...
...EVERYDAY LIFE.
FARE-WELL...
...RAKAN-KUN.

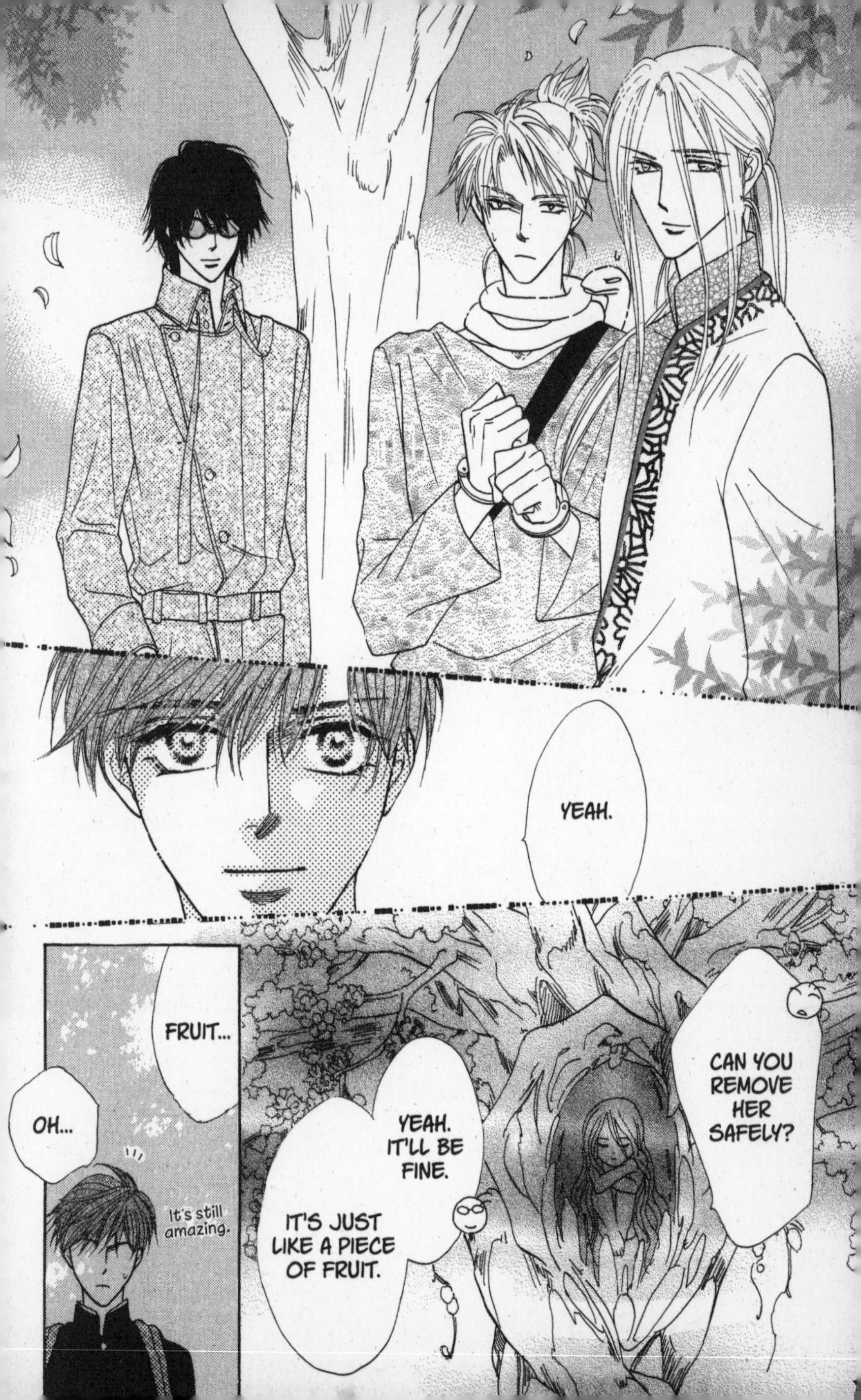
YEAH.
CAN YOU REMOVE HER SAFELY?
YEAH. IT'LL BE FINE.
IT'S JUST LIKE A PIECE OF FRUIT.
FRUIT...
OH...
It's still amazing.

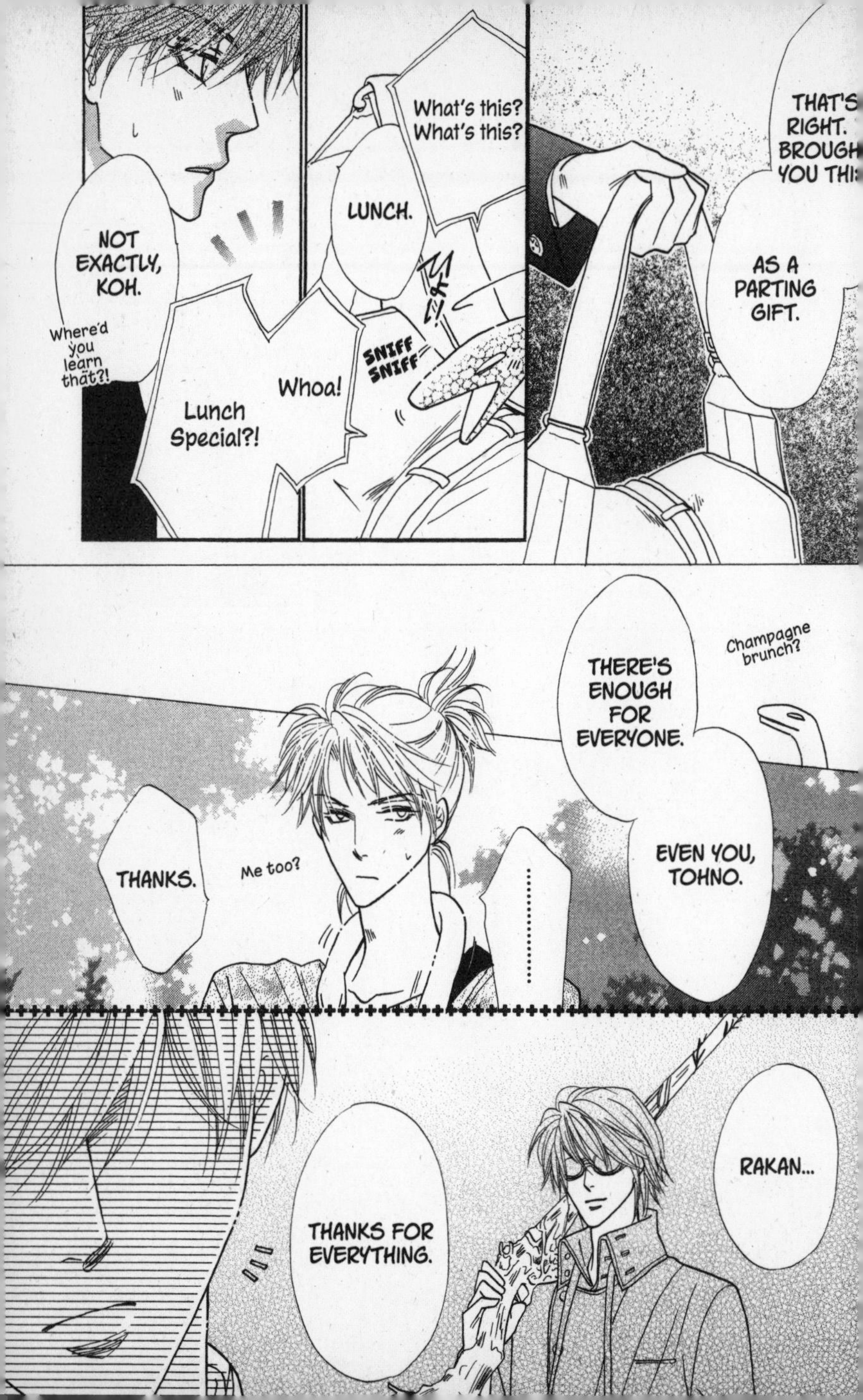
THAT'S RIGHT. BROUGH YOU THI
AS A PARTING GIFT.
What's this? What's this?
LUNCH.
SNIFF SNIFF
Whoa!
Lunch Special?!
NOT EXACTLY, KOH.
Where'd you learn that?!
Champagne brunch?
THERE'S ENOUGH FOR EVERYONE.
EVEN YOU, TOHNO.
......
Me too?
THANKS.
RAKAN...
THANKS FOR EVERYTHING.

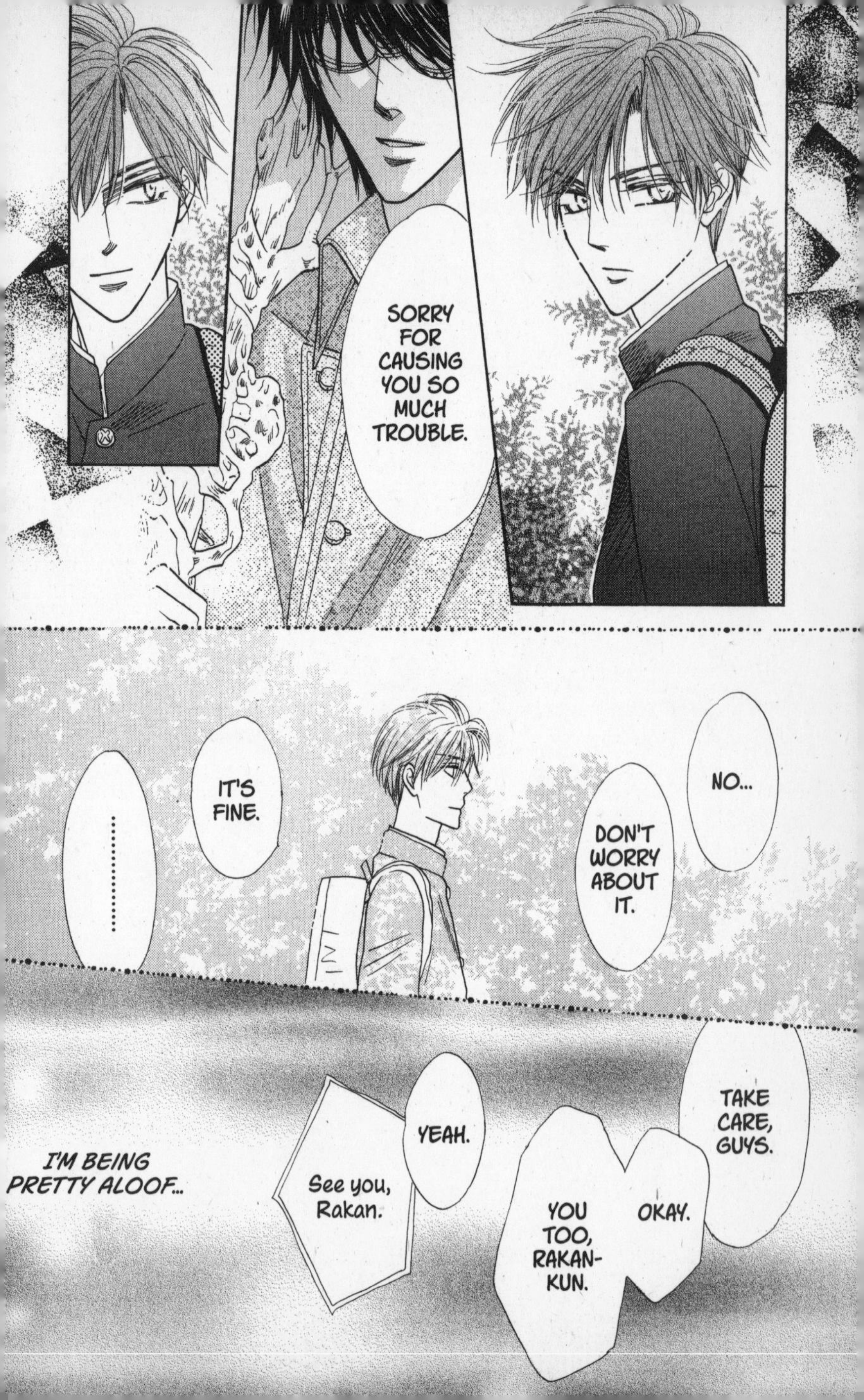
SORRY FOR CAUSING YOU SO MUCH TROUBLE.
NO...
DON'T WORRY ABOUT IT.
IT'S FINE.
......
TAKE CARE, GUYS.
OKAY.
YOU TOO, RAKAN-KUN.
YEAH.
See you, Rakan.
I'M BEING PRETTY ALOOF...

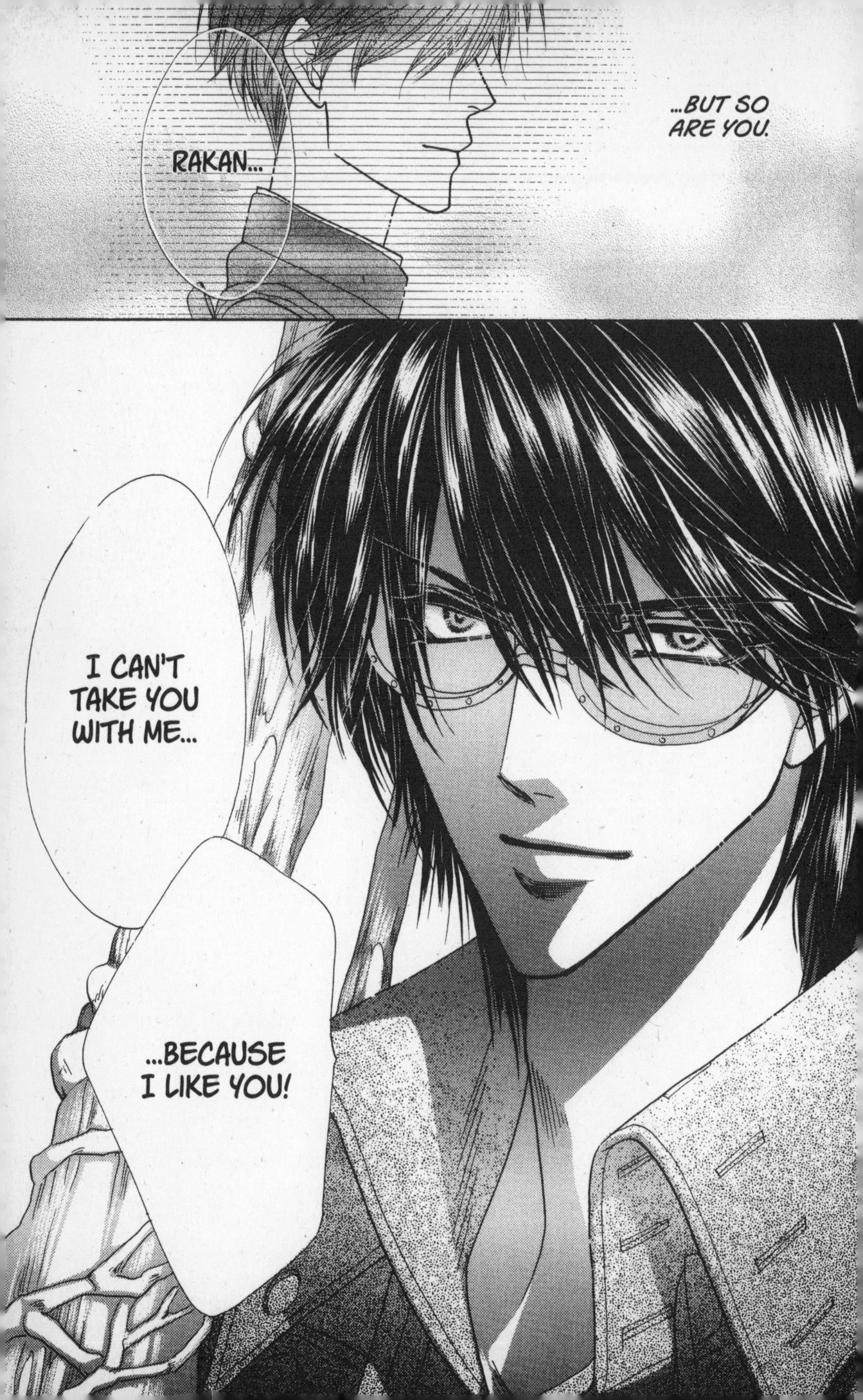
...BUT SO ARE YOU.
RAKAN...
I CAN'T TAKE YOU WITH ME...
...BECAUSE I LIKE YOU!

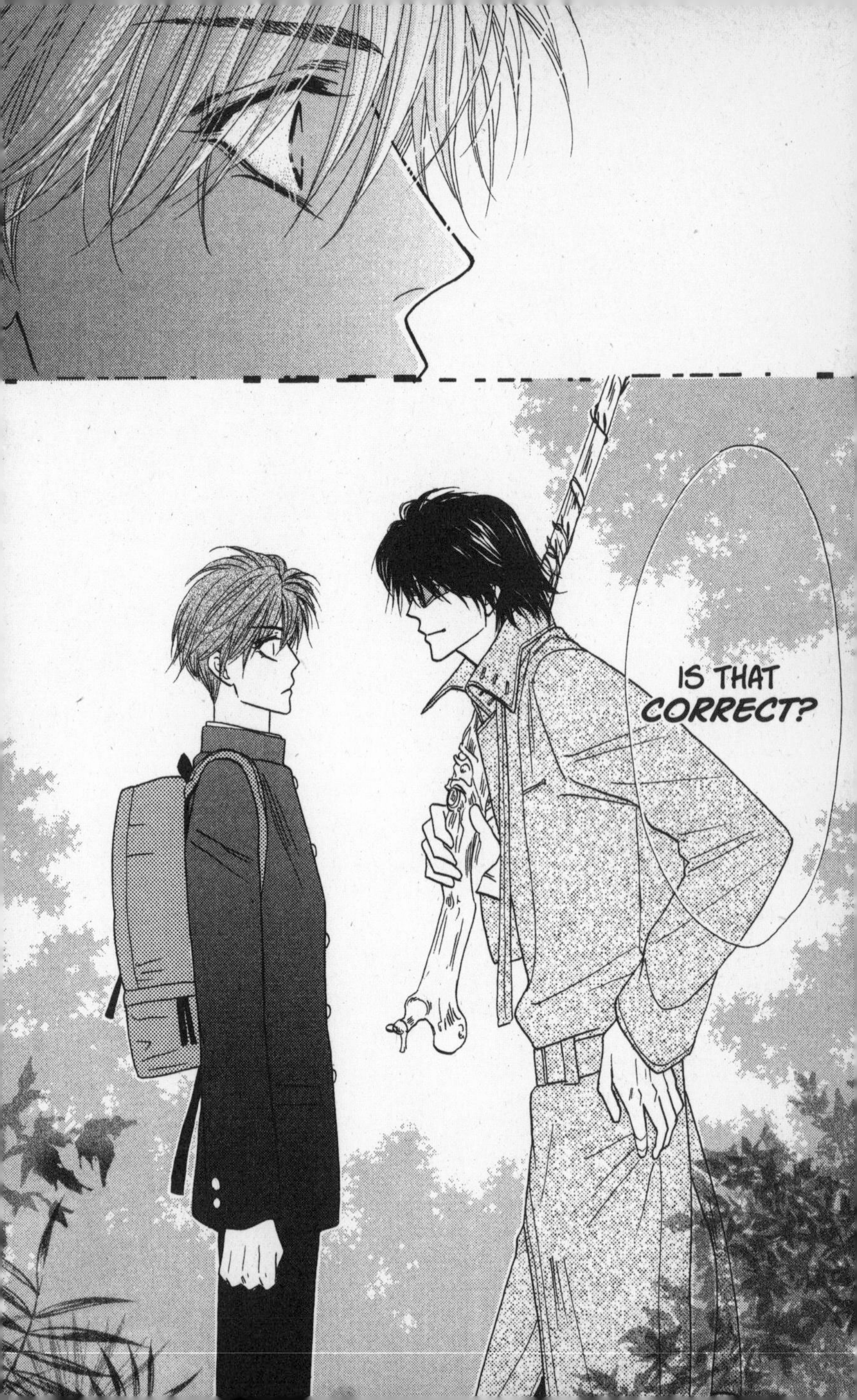
IS THAT CORRECT?

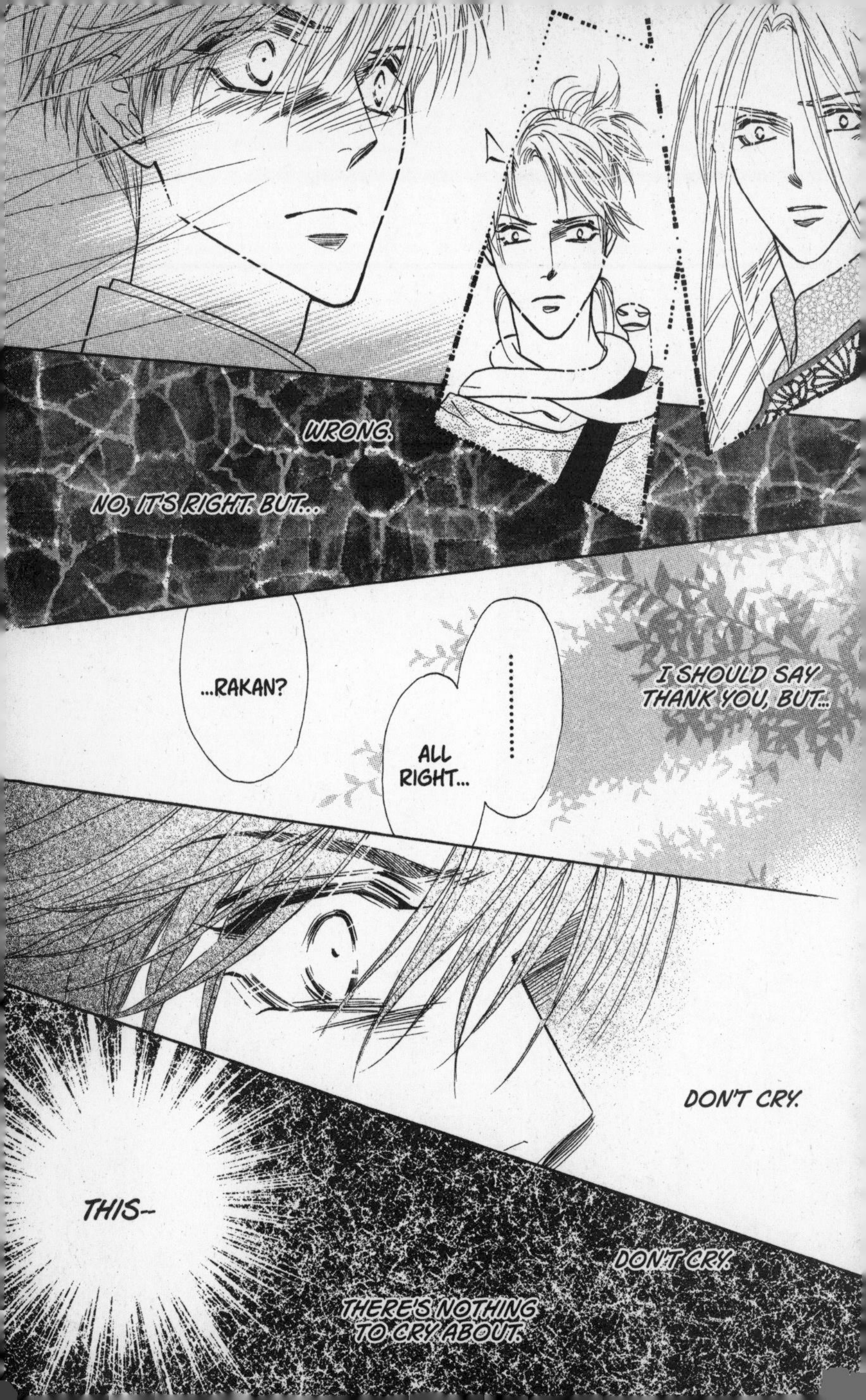
WRONG.
NO, IT'S RIGHT. BUT...
I SHOULD SAY THANK YOU, BUT...
......
ALL RIGHT...
...RAKAN?
DON'T CRY.
THIS--
DON'T CRY.
THERE'S NOTHING TO CRY ABOUT.

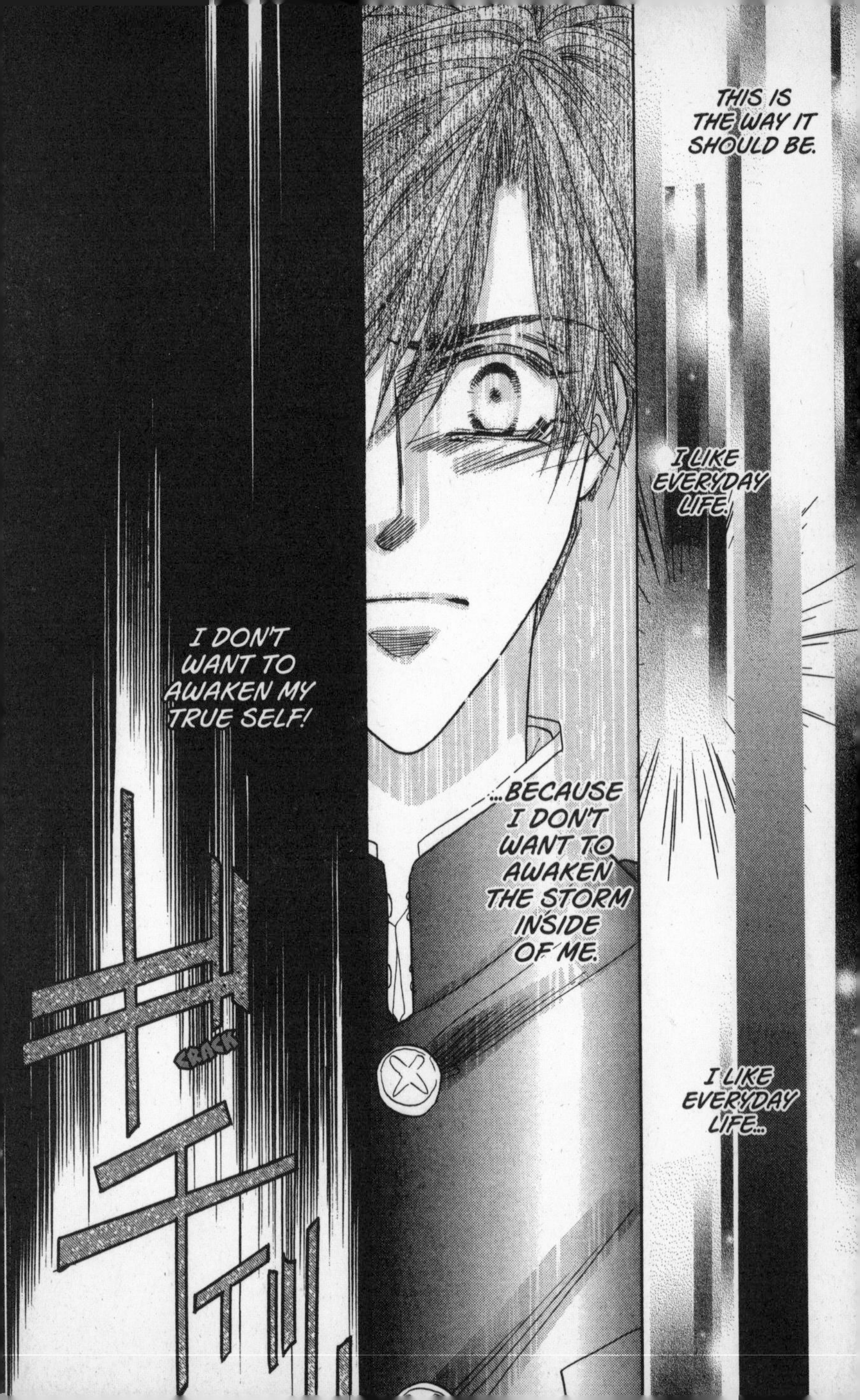
THIS IS THE WAY IT SHOULD BE.
I LIKE EVERYDAY LIFE!
I LIKE EVERYDAY LIFE...
...BECAUSE I DON'T WANT TO AWAKEN THE STORM INSIDE OF ME.
I DON'T WANT TO AWAKEN MY TRUE SELF!
CRACK

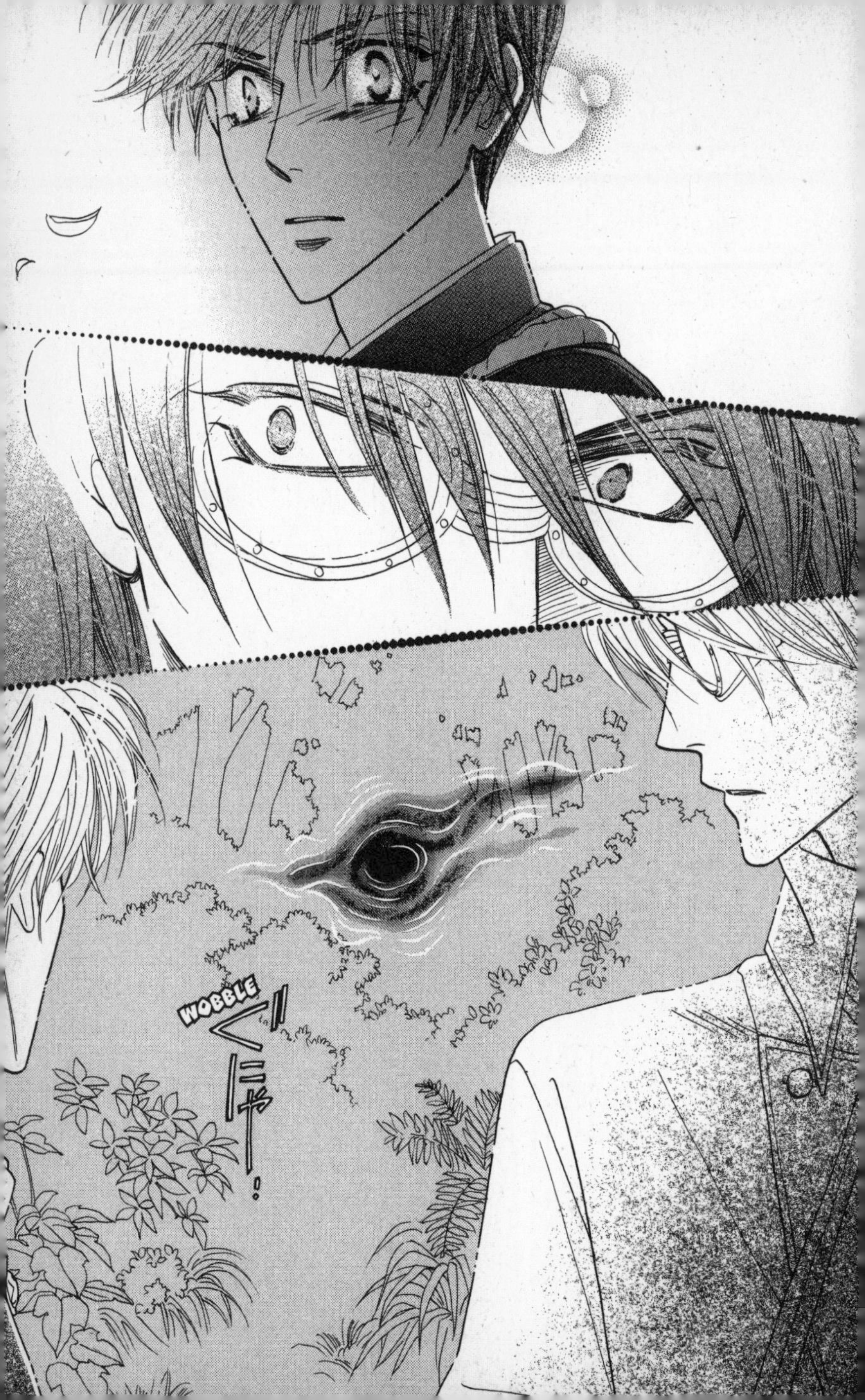
WOBBLE
ぐにゃ!

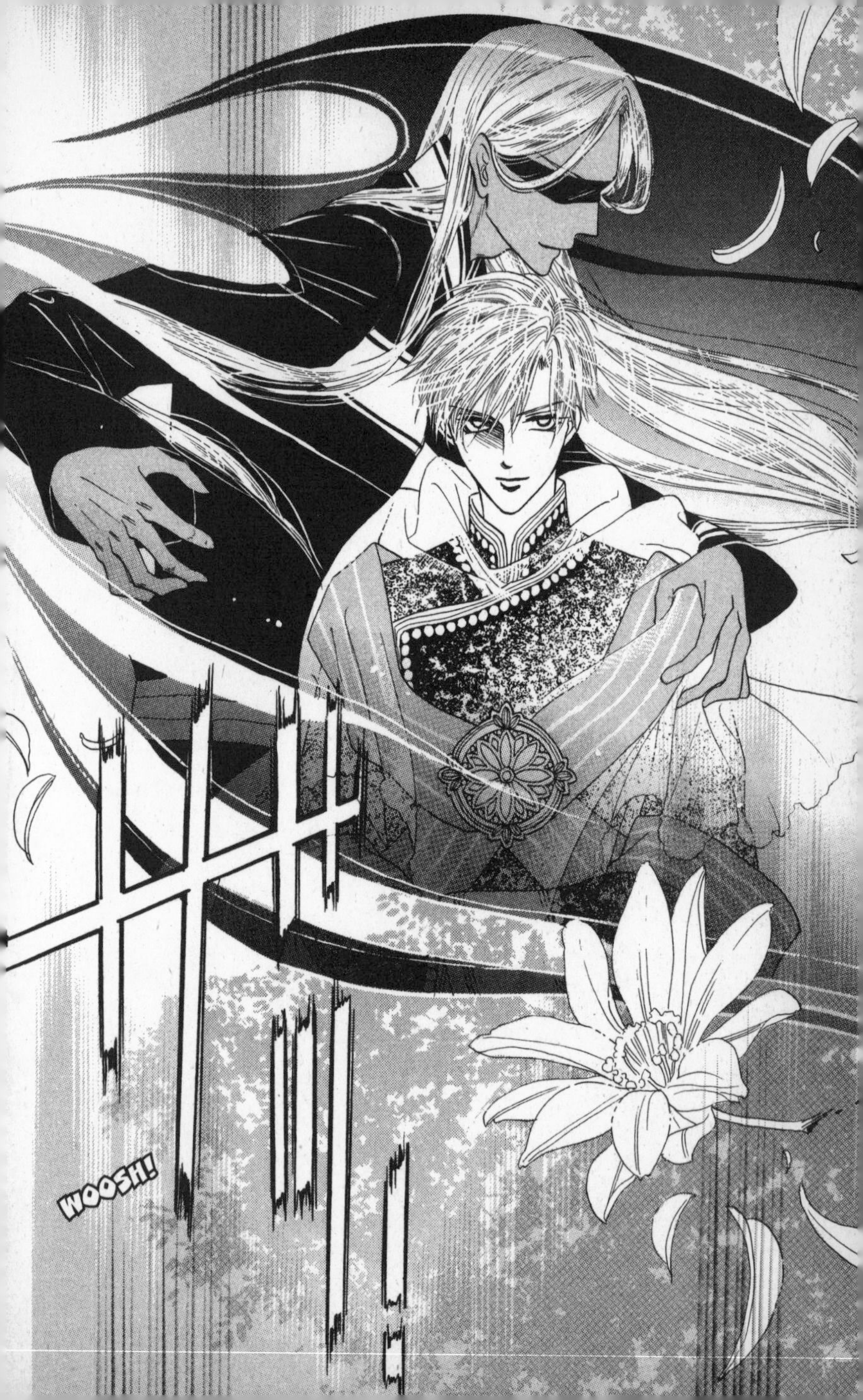
WOOSH!

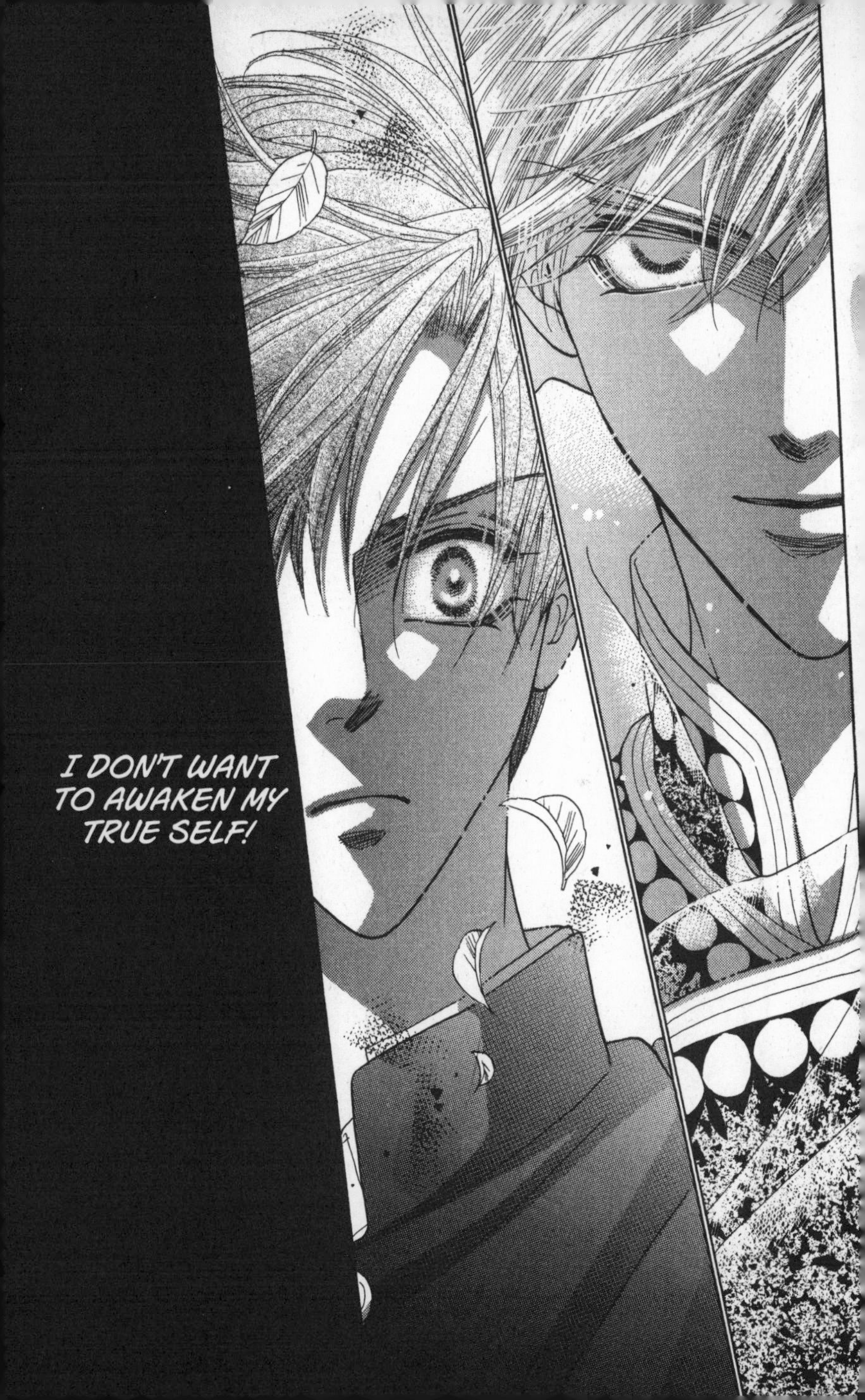
I DON'T WANT TO AWAKEN MY TRUE SELF!

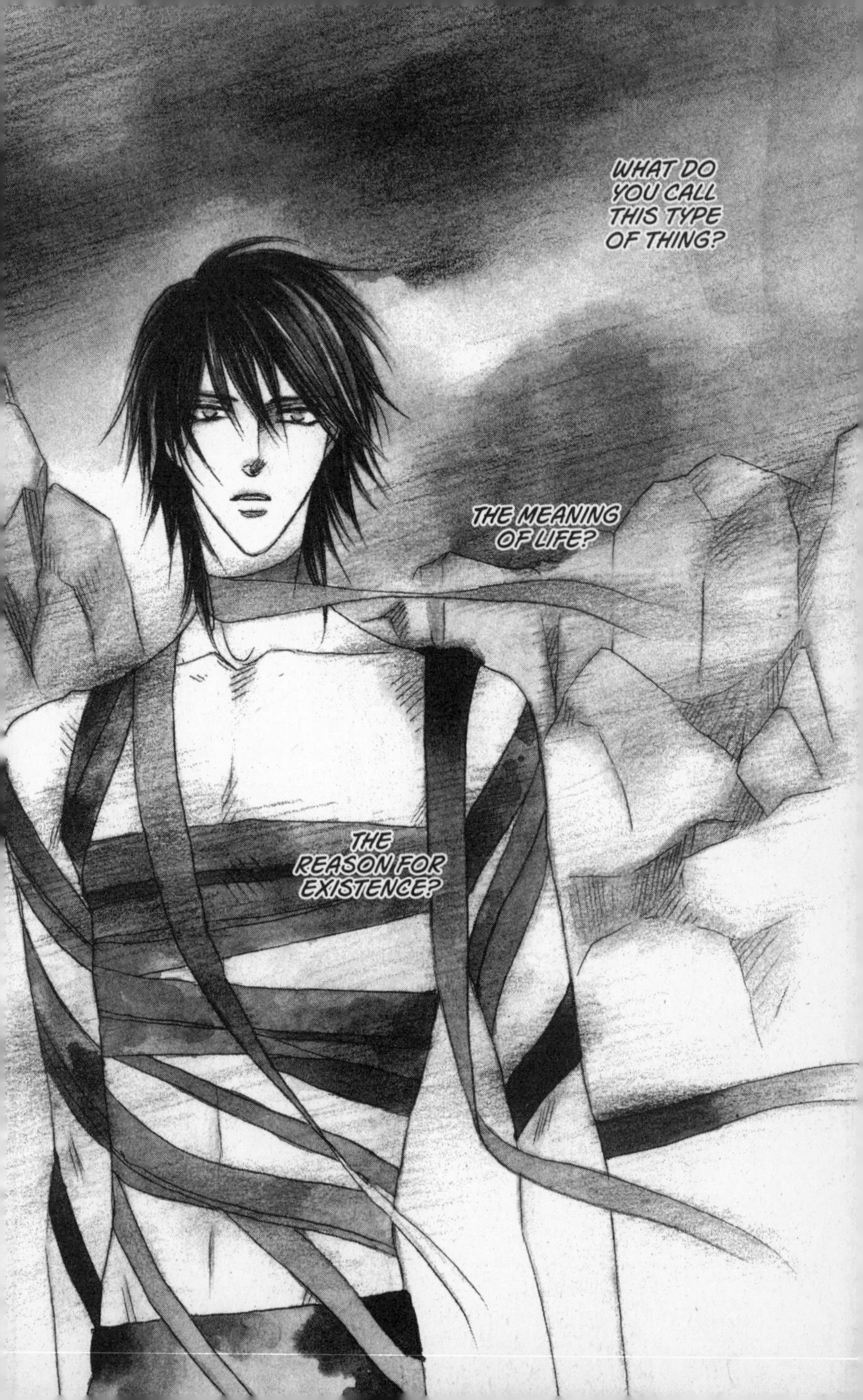
WHAT DO YOU CALL THIS TYPE OF THING?
THE MEANING OF LIFE?
THE REASON FOR EXISTENCE?

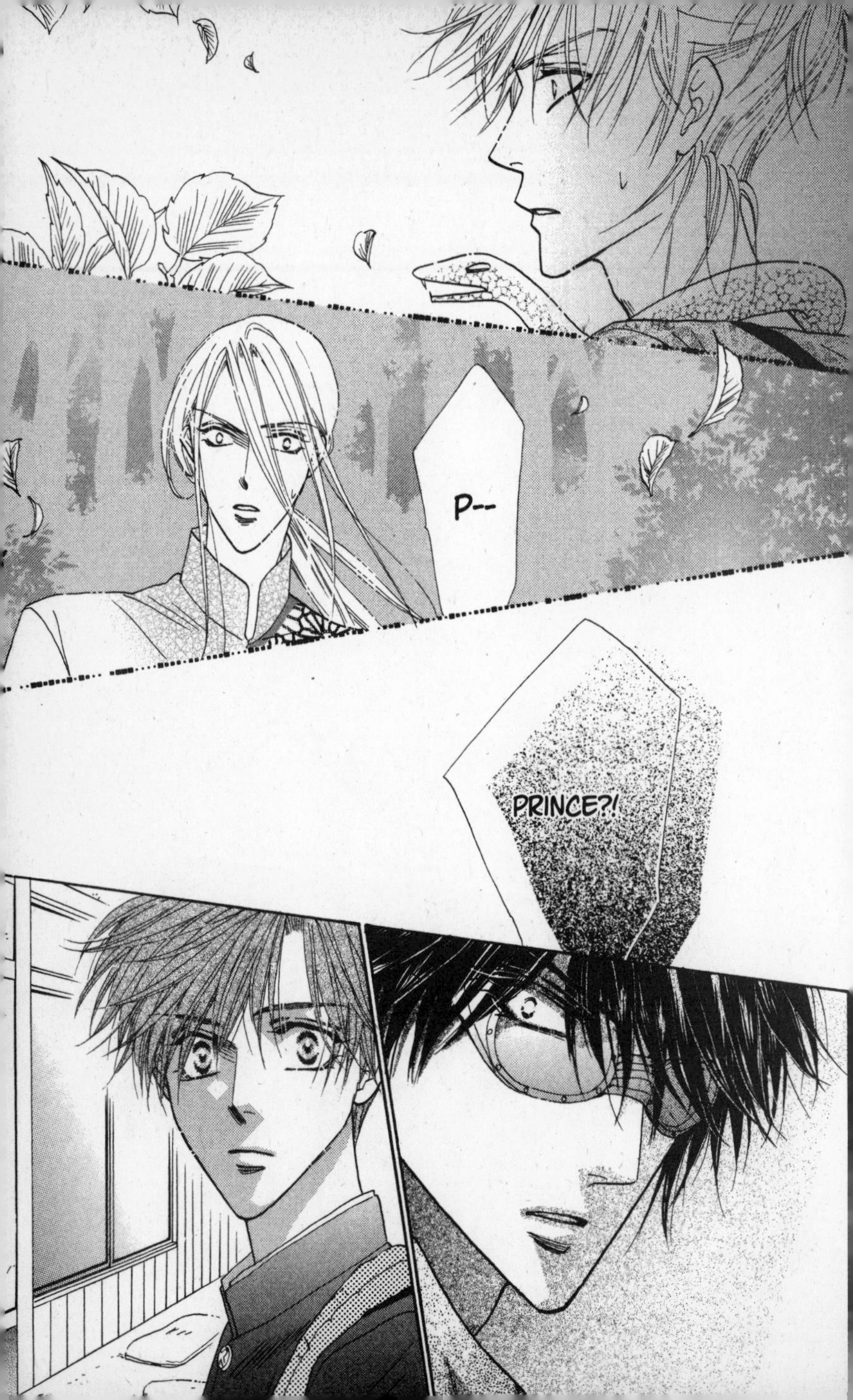
P--
PRINCE?!

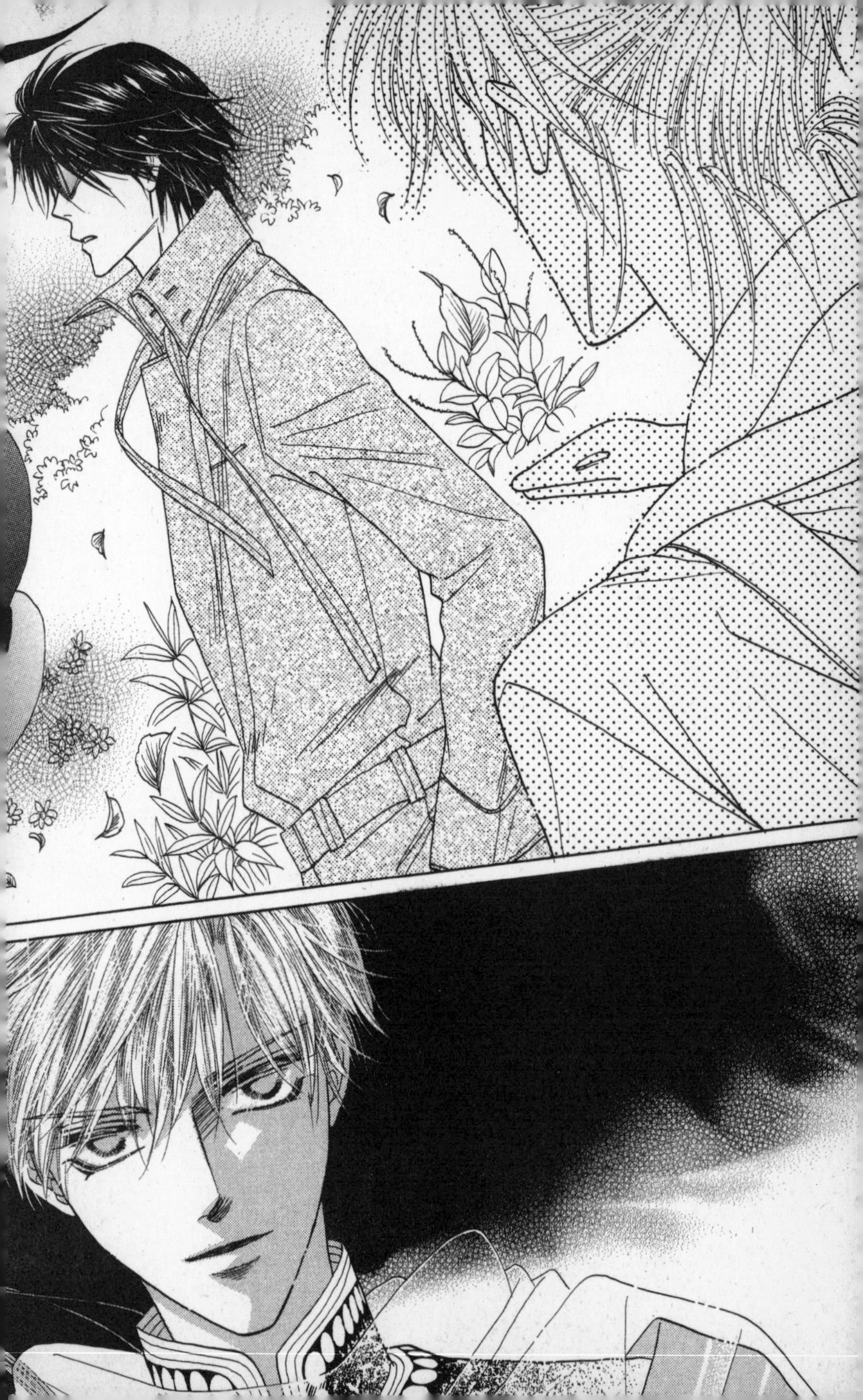

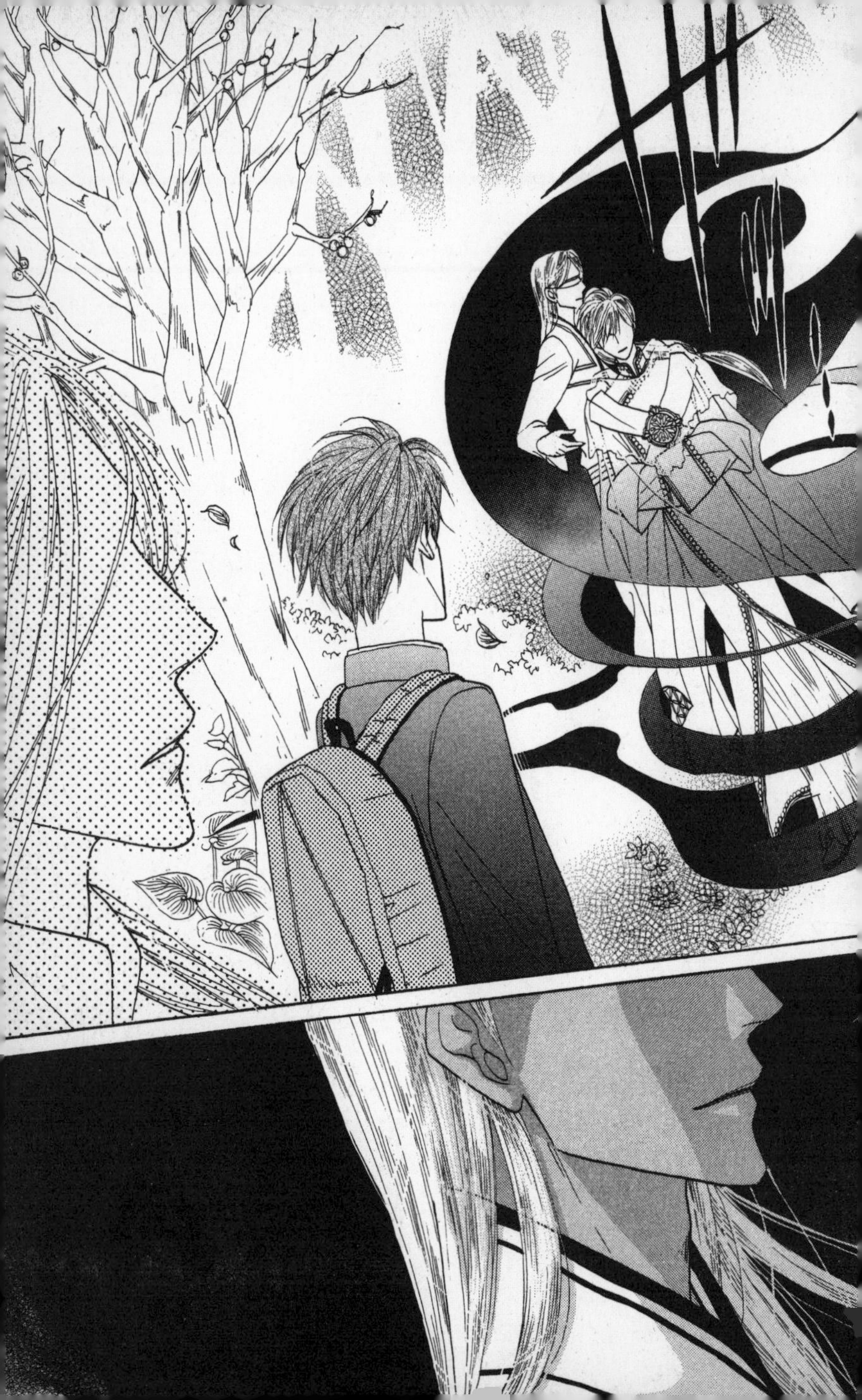

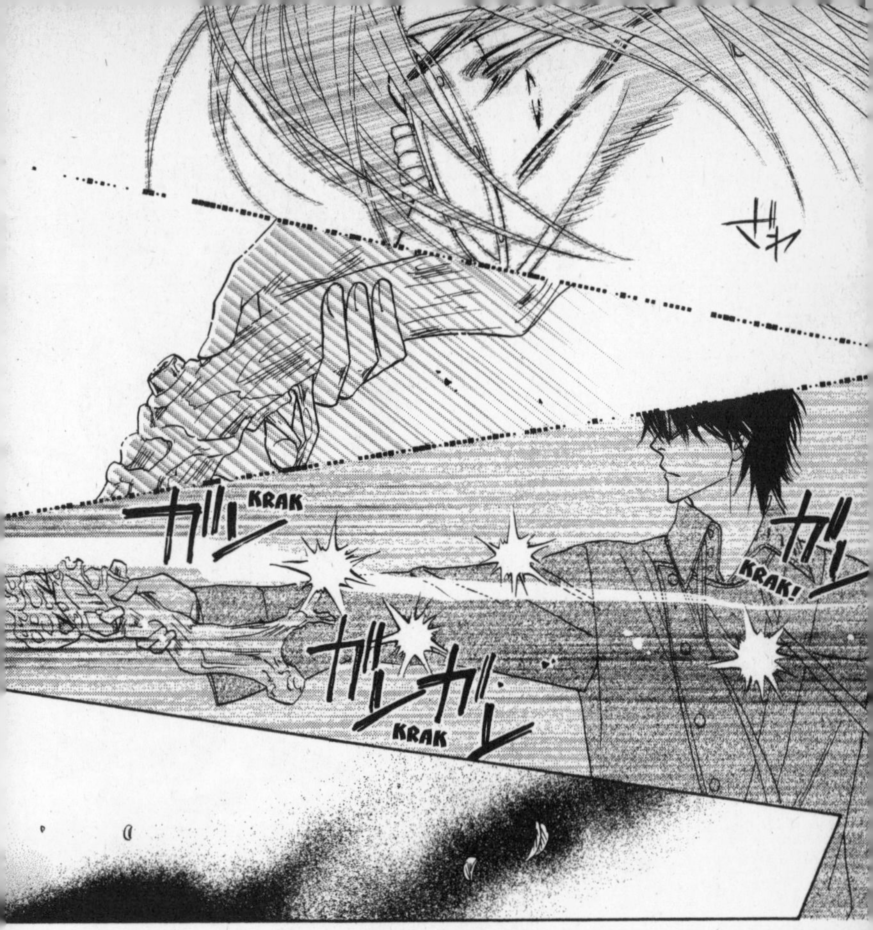
ざわ
ガリ
KRAK!
ガン
KRAK
ガリガリ
KRAK

Switch All On

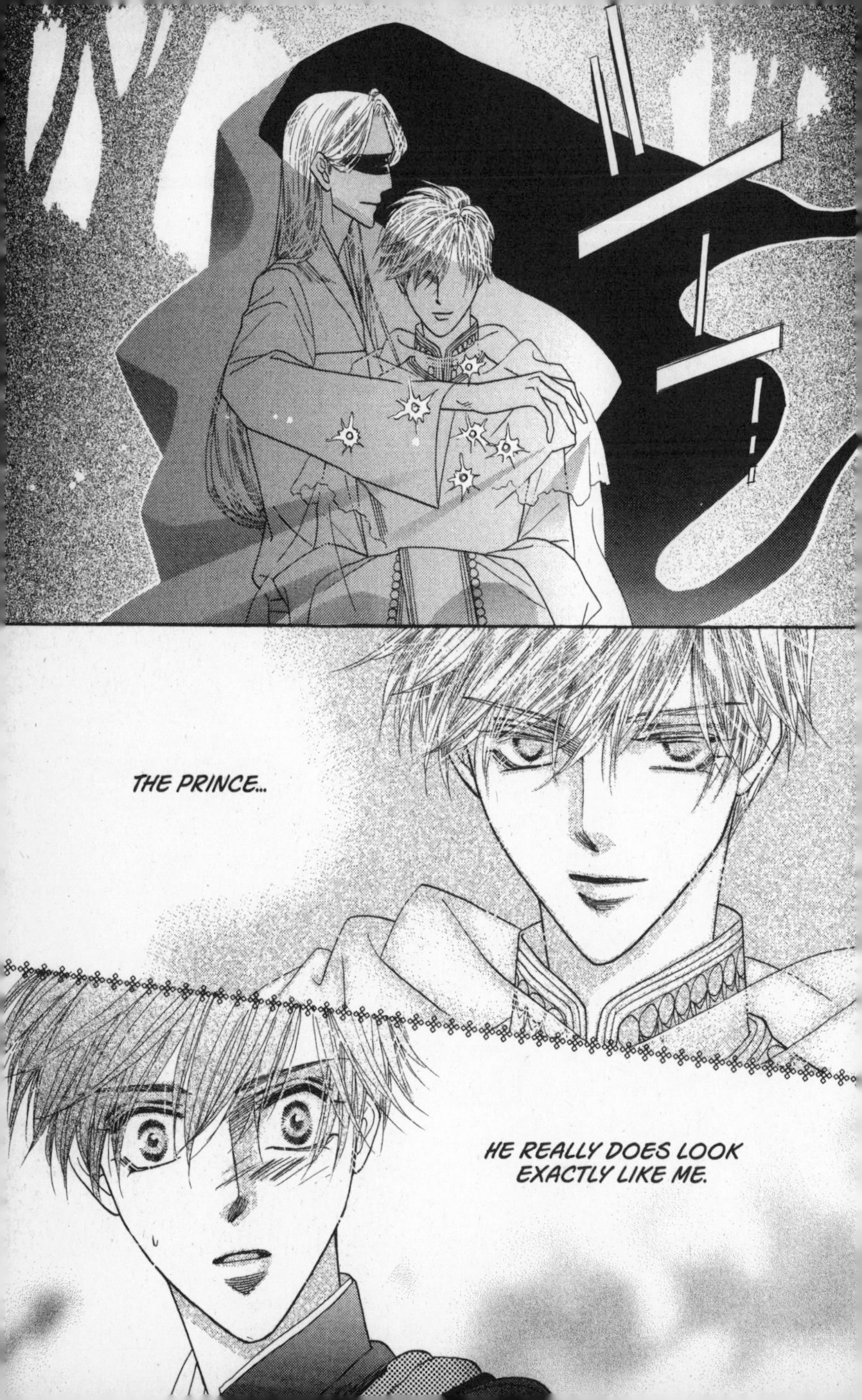
THE PRINCE...
HE REALLY DOES LOOK EXACTLY LIKE ME.

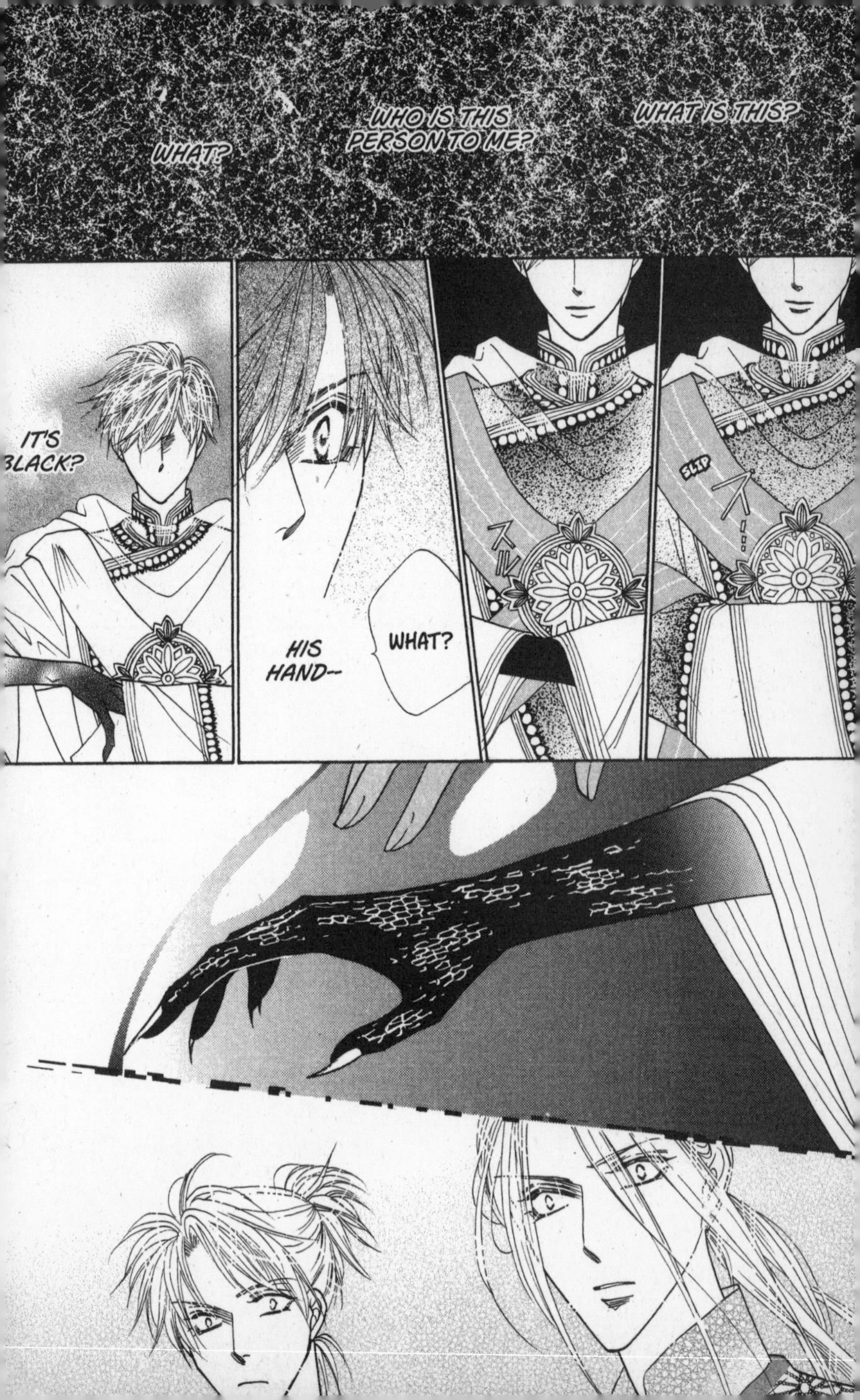
WHAT IS THIS?
WHO IS THIS PERSON TO ME?
WHAT?
SLIP
WHAT?
HIS HAND--
IT'S BLACK?

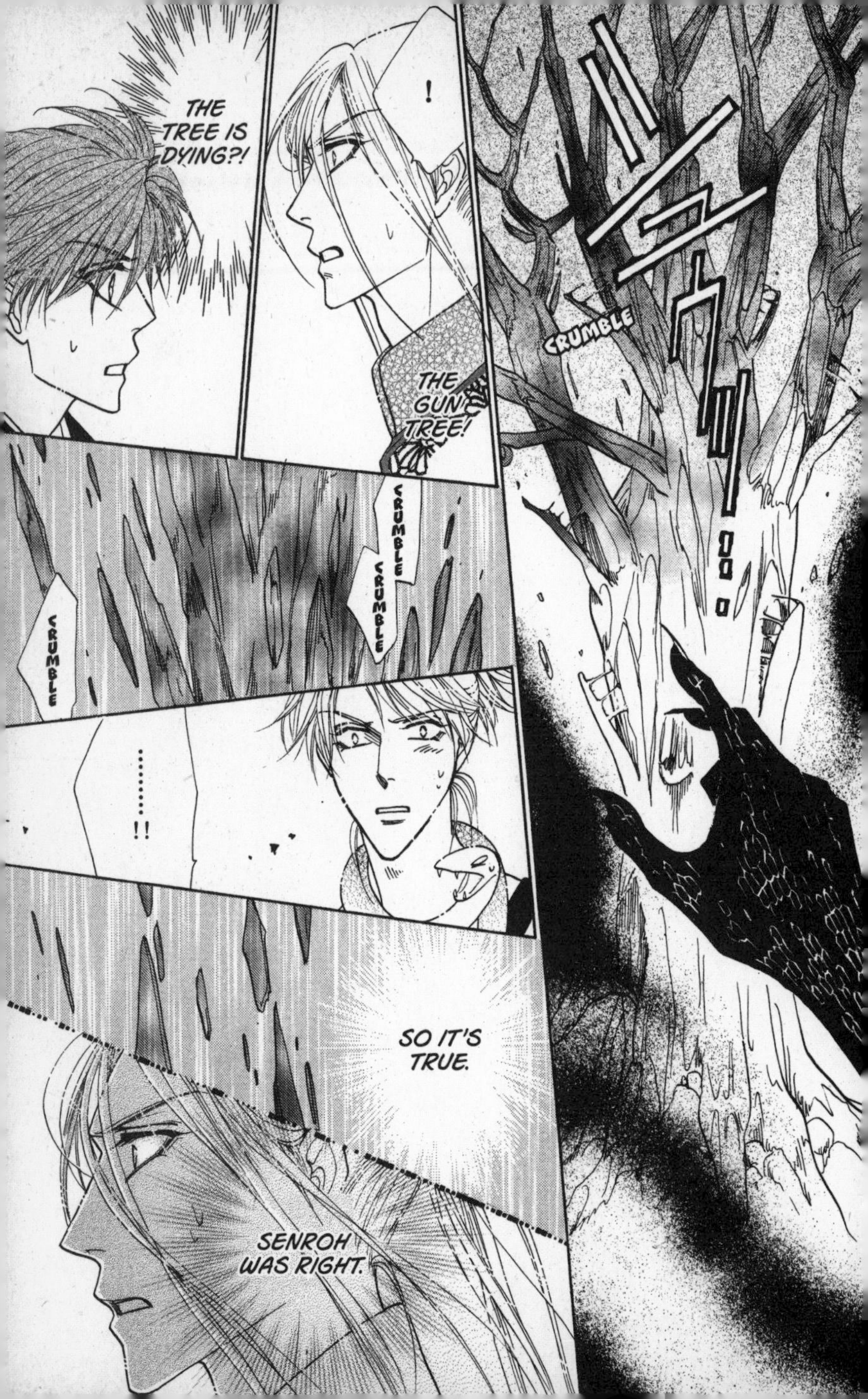
CRUMBLE
!
THE GUN TREE!
THE TREE IS DYING?!
CRUMBLE CRUMBLE
CRUMBLE
......!!
SO IT'S TRUE.
SENROH WAS RIGHT.

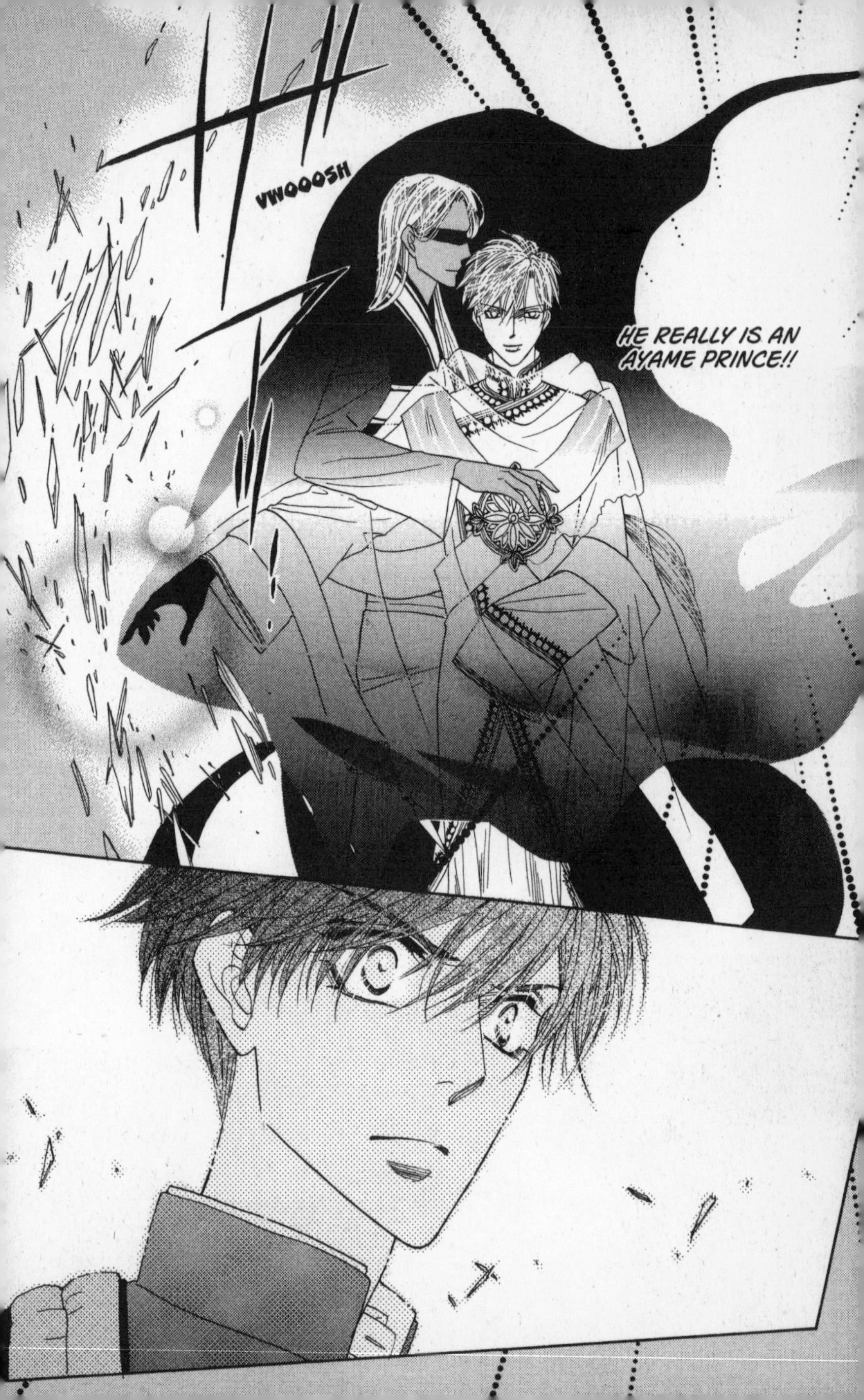
VWOOOSH
HE REALLY IS AN AYAME PRINCE!!

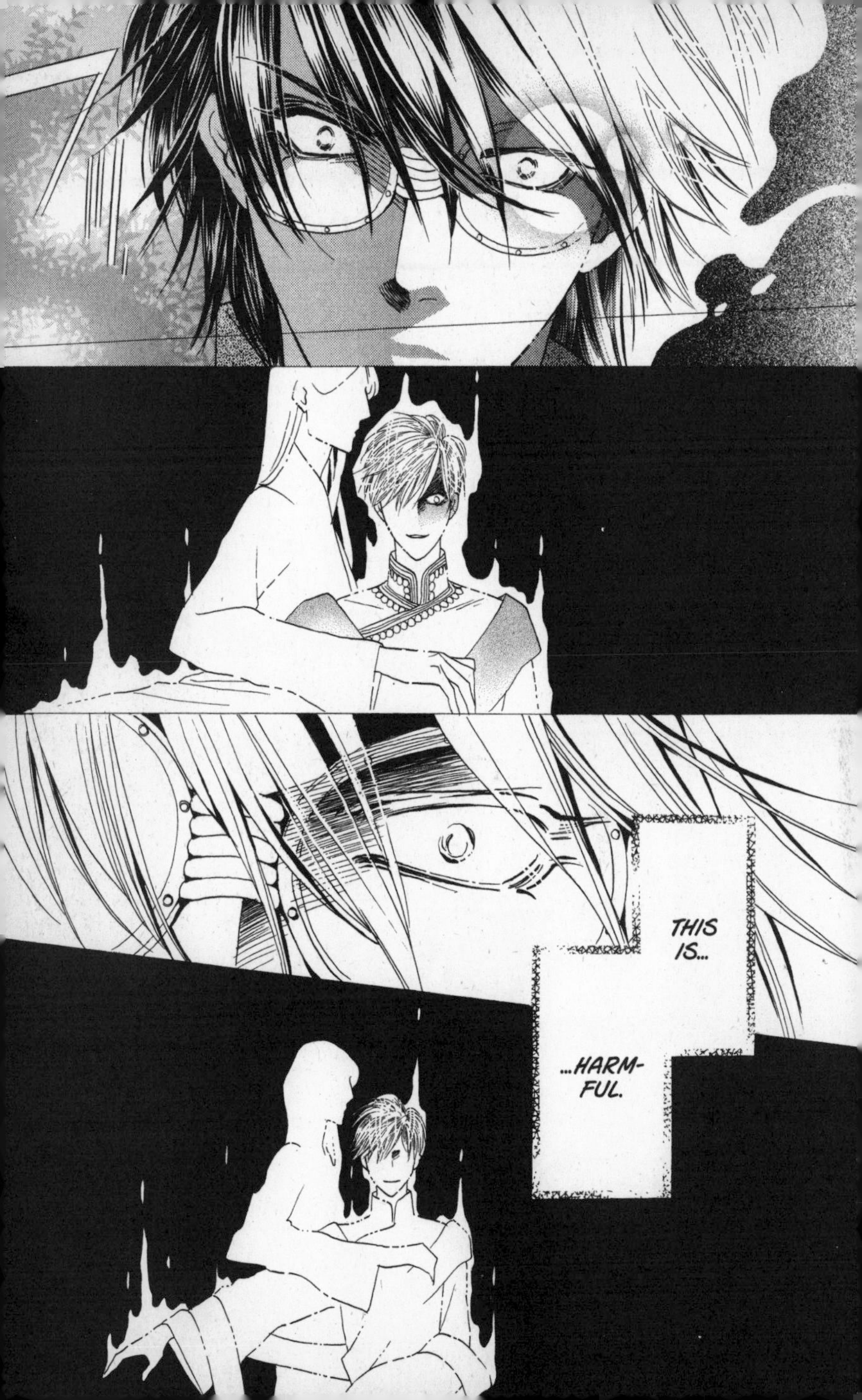
THIS IS...
...HARM-FUL.

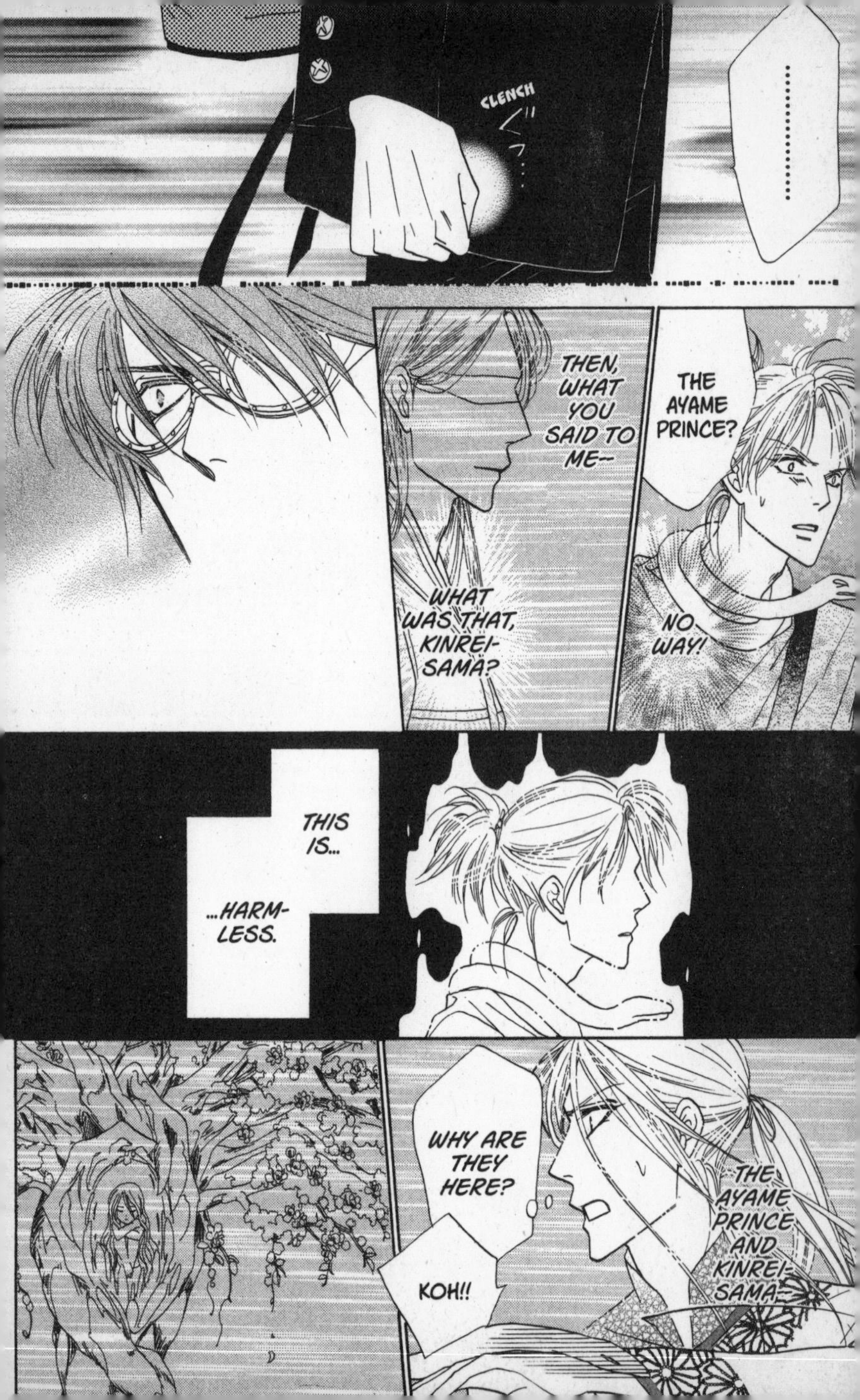
……
CLENCH
THE AYAME PRINCE?
NO WAY!
THEN, WHAT YOU SAID TO ME--
WHAT WAS THAT, KINREI-SAMA?
THIS IS...
...HARMLESS.
THE AYAME PRINCE AND KINREI-SAMA--
WHY ARE THEY HERE?
KOH!!

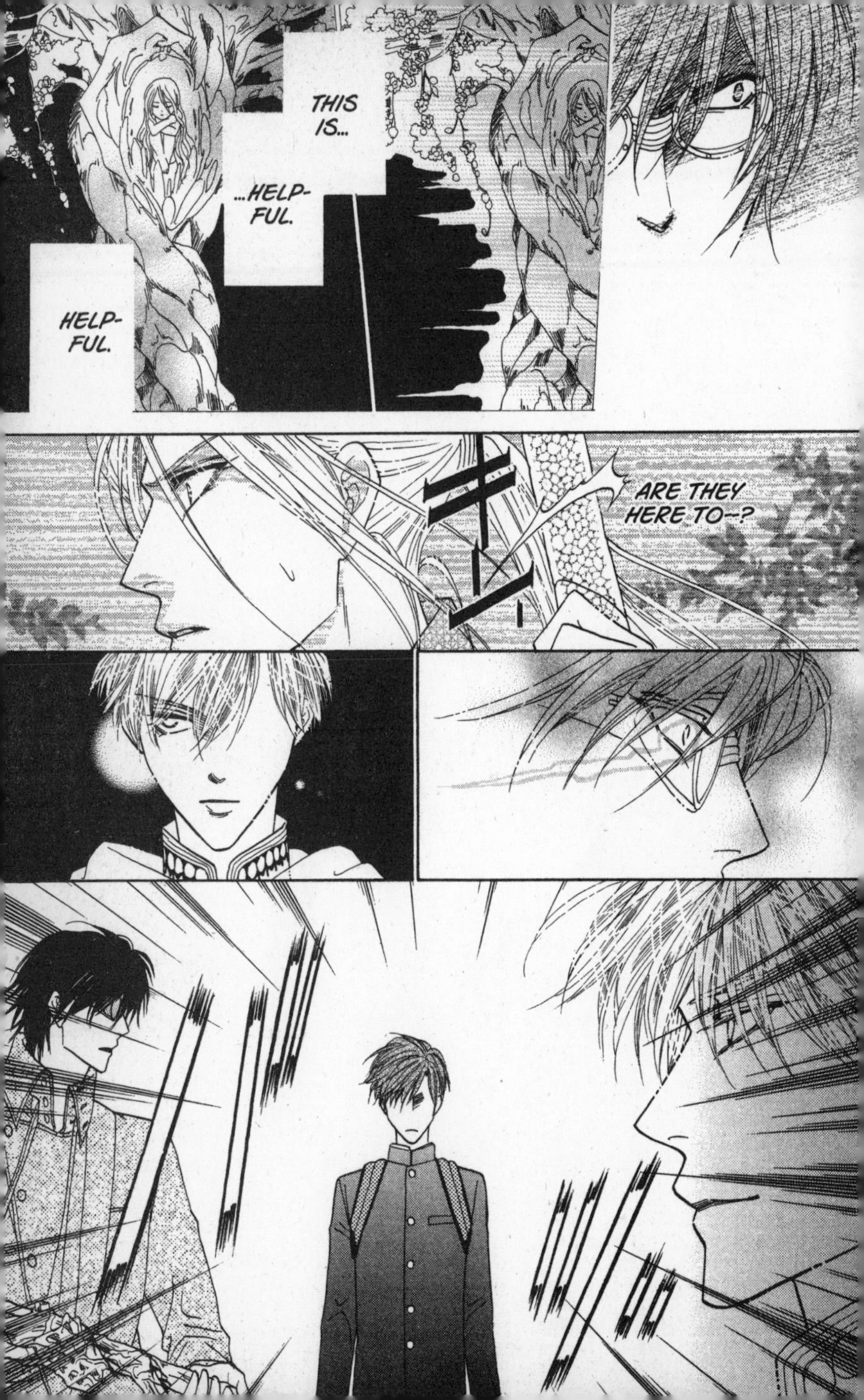
THIS IS...
...HELP-FUL.
HELP-FUL.
ARE THEY HERE TO--?

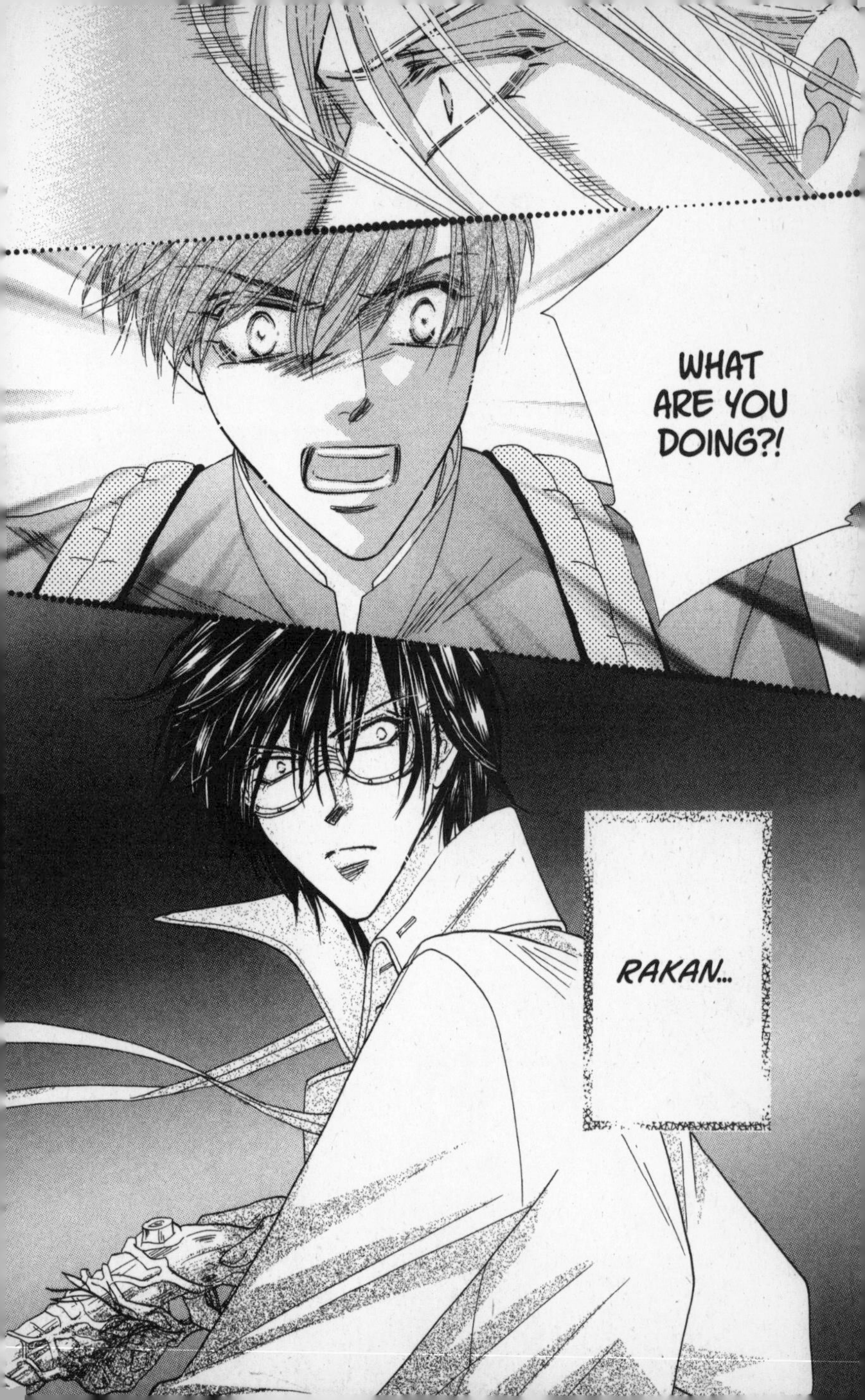
WHAT ARE YOU DOING?!
RAKAN...

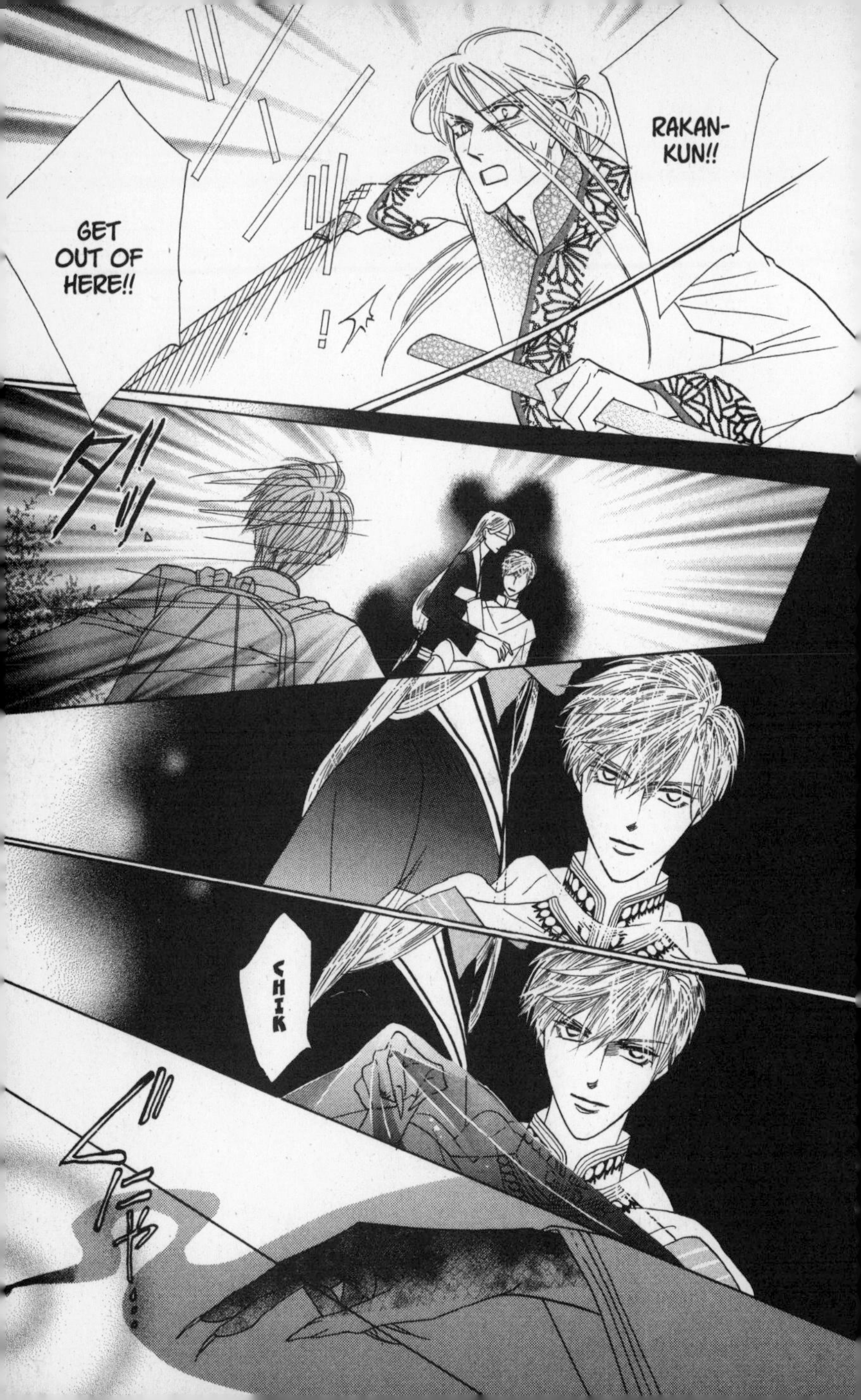
RAKAN-KUN!!
GET OUT OF HERE!!
ダッ
CHIK

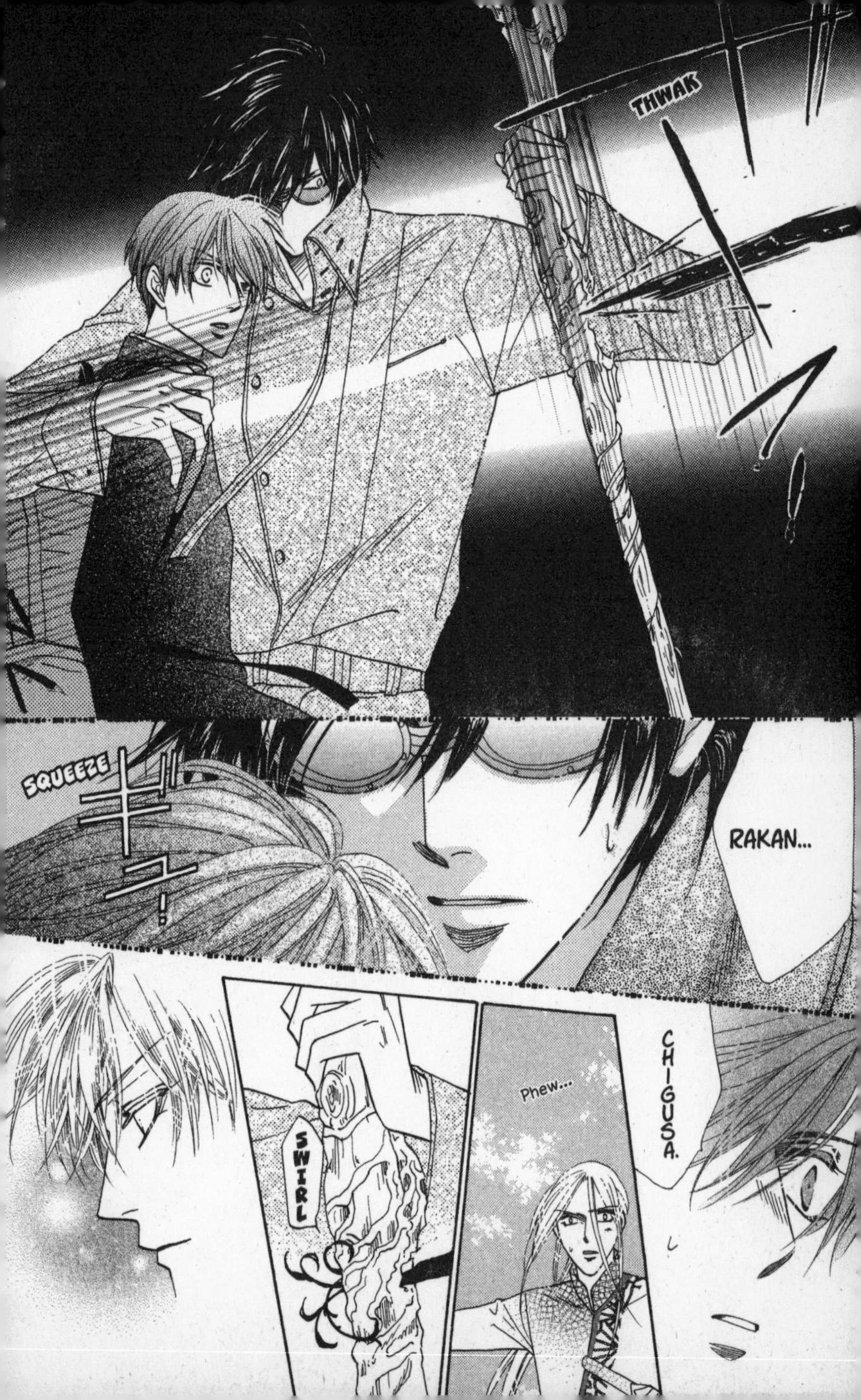
THWAK
RAKAN...
SQUEEZE
CHIGUSA.
Phew...
SWIRL

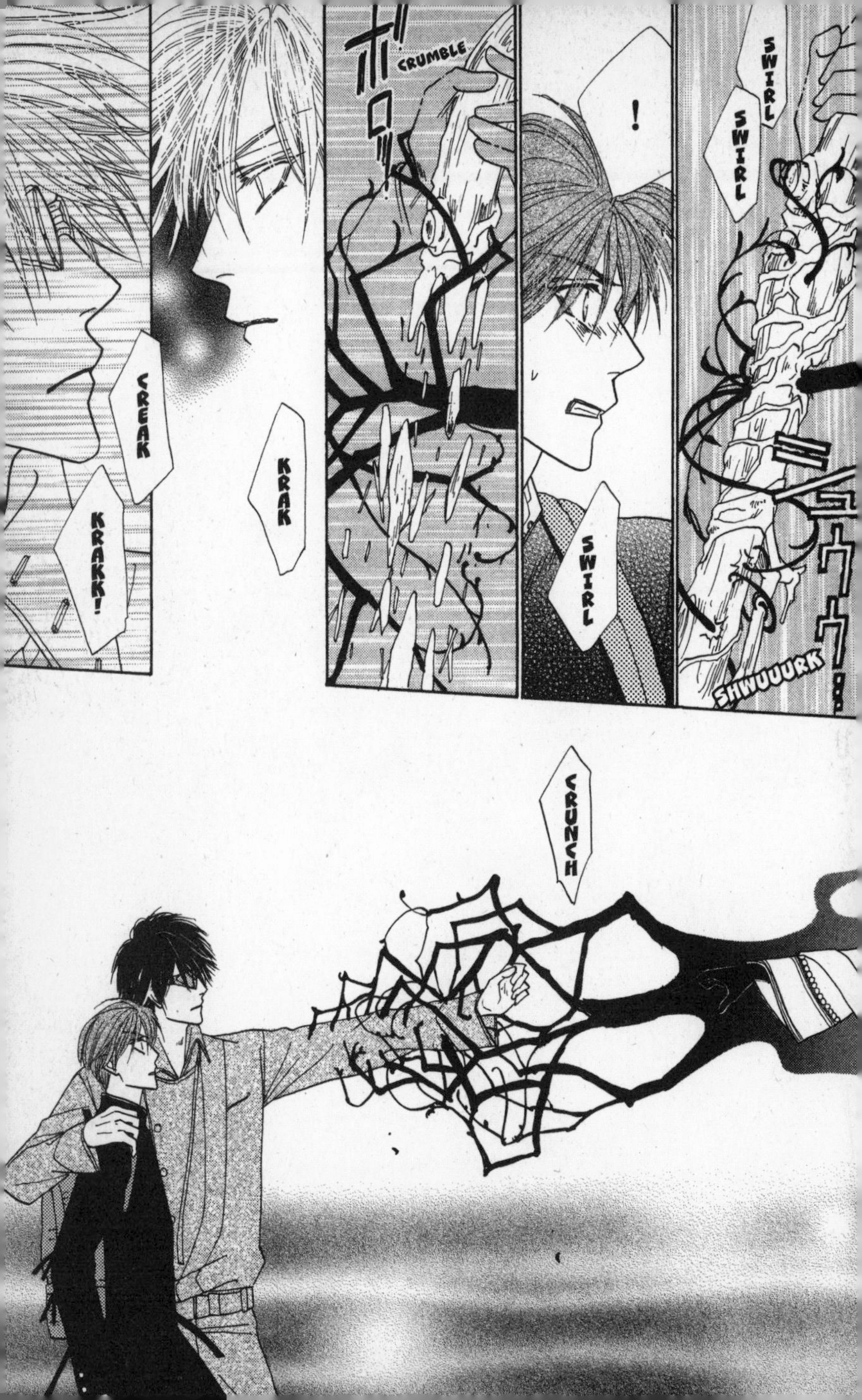
SWIRL
SWIRL
SHWUUURK
!
SWIRL
CRUMBLE
KRAK
CREAK
KRAKK!
CRUNCH

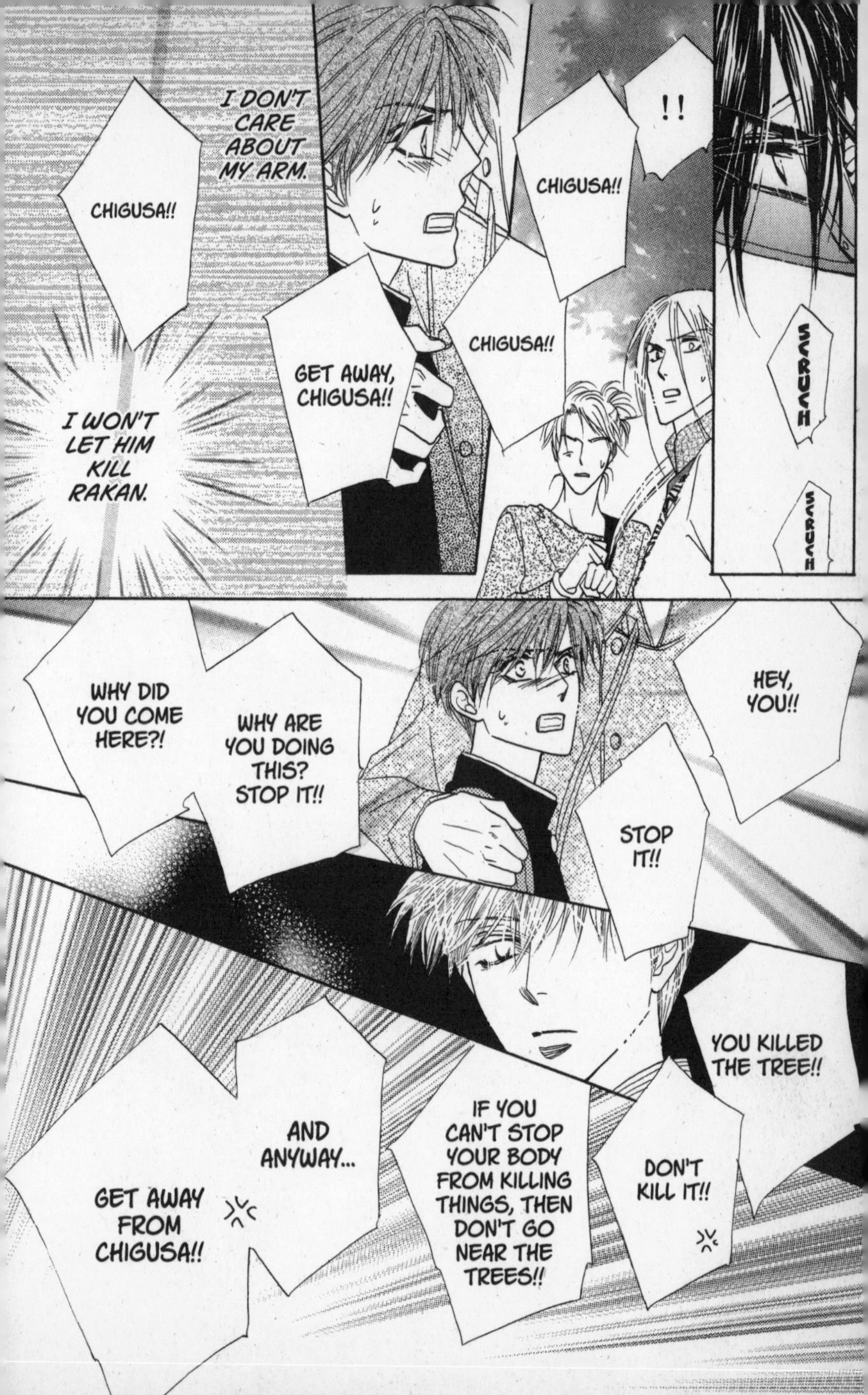
SCRUCH
SCRUCH
!!
CHIGUSA!!
I DON'T CARE ABOUT MY ARM.
CHIGUSA!!
GET AWAY, CHIGUSA!!
CHIGUSA!!
I WON'T LET HIM KILL RAKAN.
HEY, YOU!!
STOP IT!!
WHY ARE YOU DOING THIS? STOP IT!!
WHY DID YOU COME HERE?!
YOU KILLED THE TREE!!
DON'T KILL IT!!
IF YOU CAN'T STOP YOUR BODY FROM KILLING THINGS, THEN DON'T GO NEAR THE TREES!!
AND ANYWAY...
GET AWAY FROM CHIGUSA!!

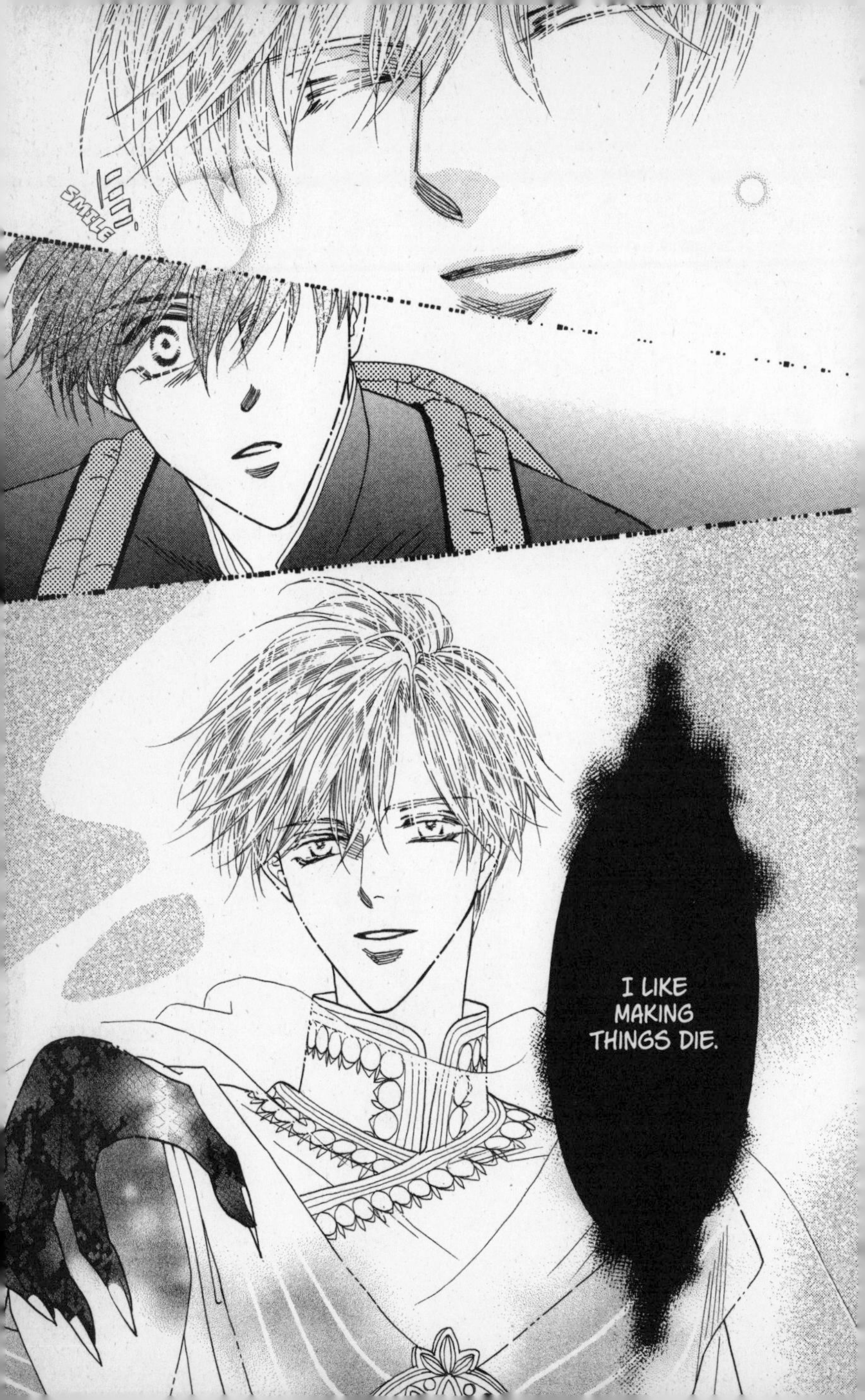
SMILE
I LIKE MAKING THINGS DIE.

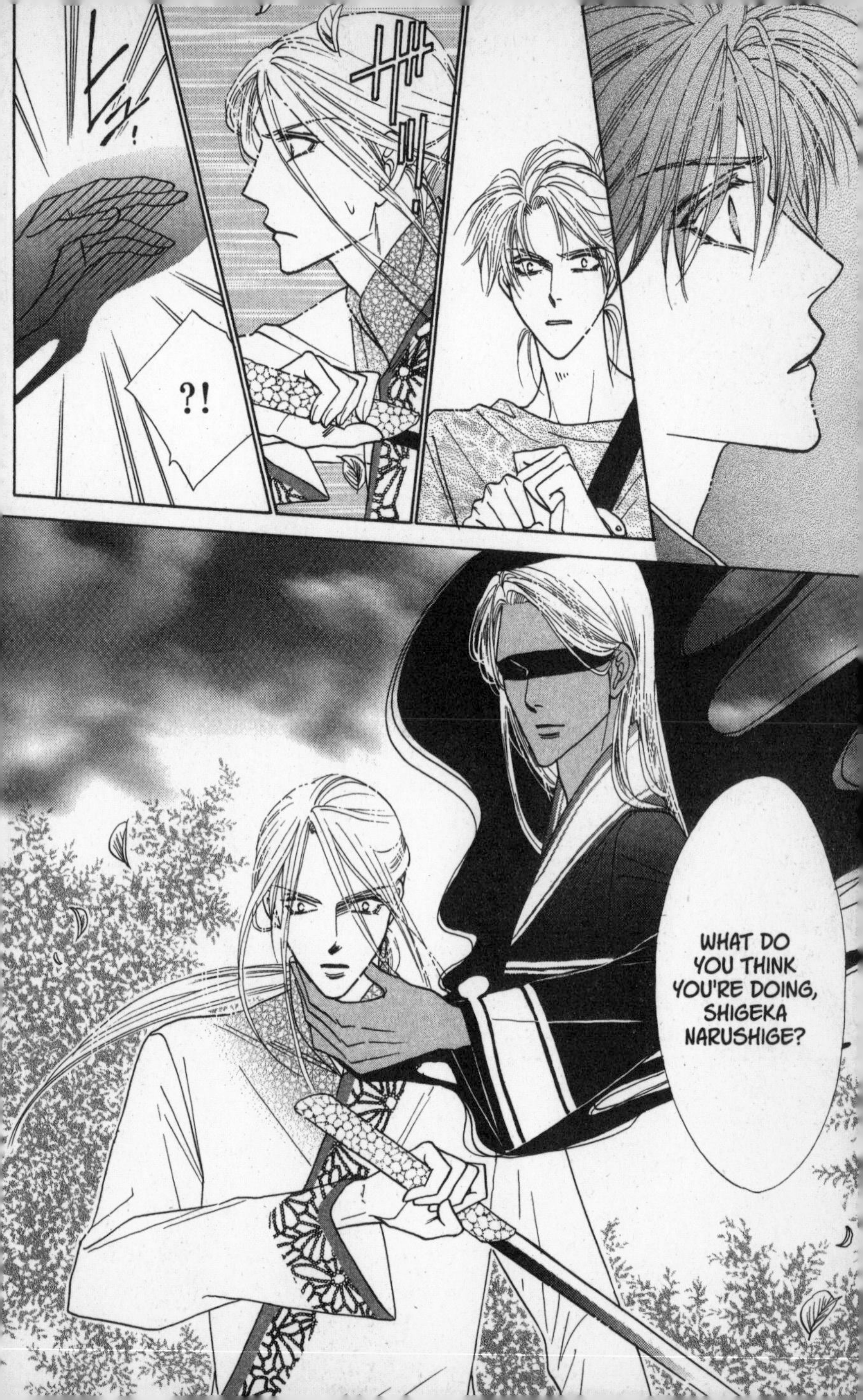
?!
WHAT DO YOU THINK YOU'RE DOING, SHIGEKA NARUSHIGE?

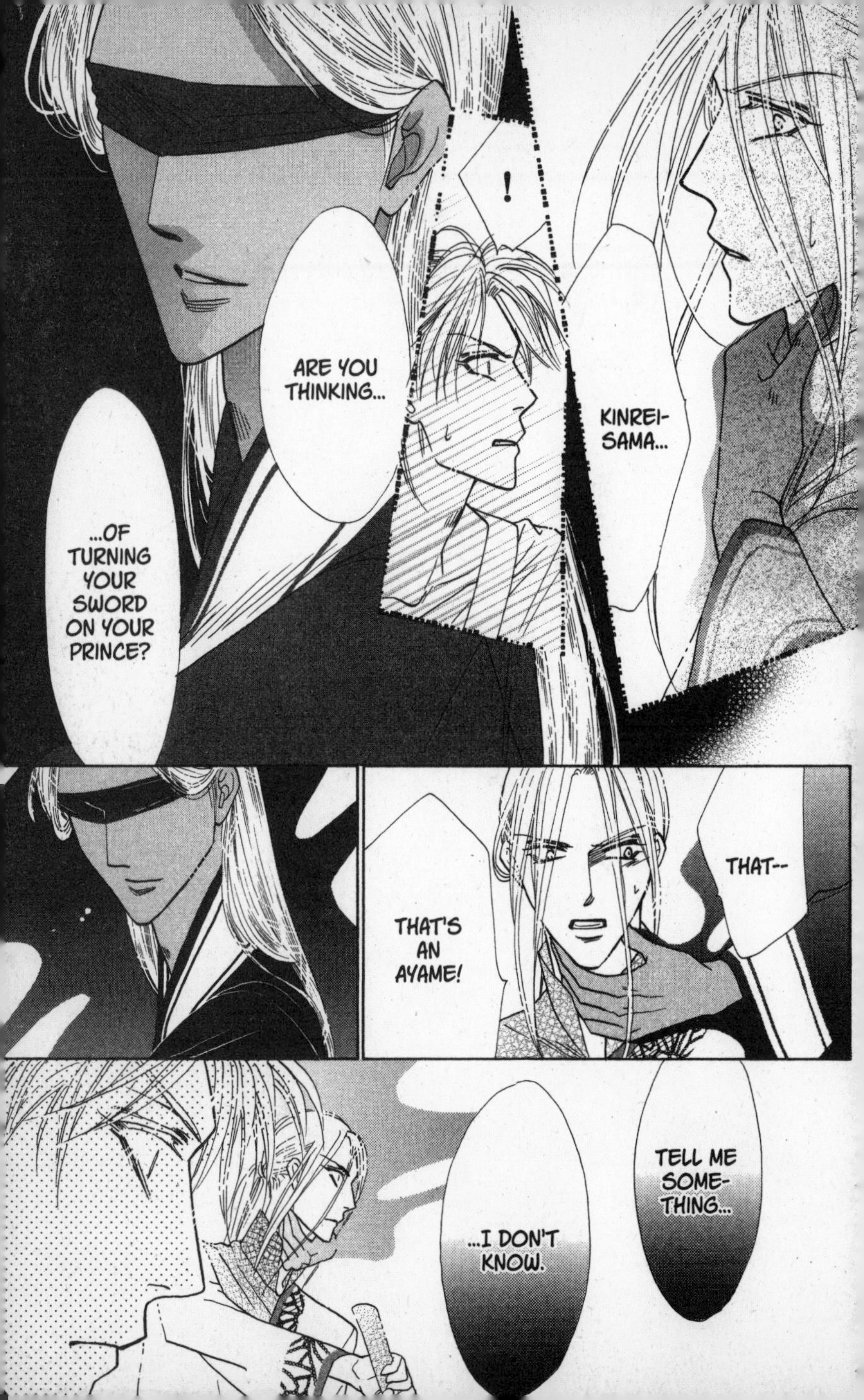
KINREI-SAMA...
!
ARE YOU THINKING...
...OF TURNING YOUR SWORD ON YOUR PRINCE?
THAT--
THAT'S AN AYAME!
TELL ME SOMETHING...
...I DON'T KNOW.

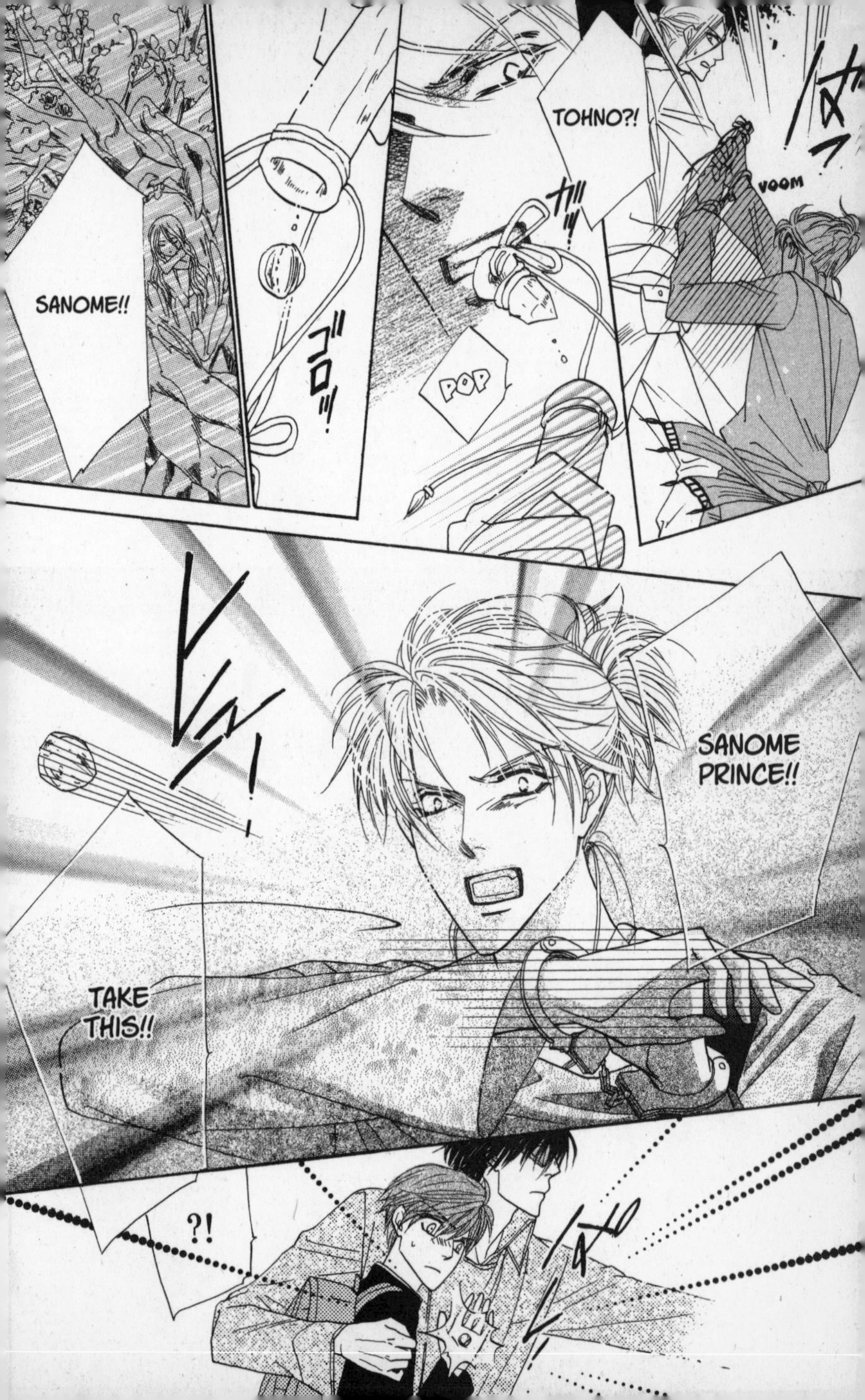
TOHNO?!
VOOM
POP
SANOME!!
SANOME PRINCE!!
TAKE THIS!!
?!

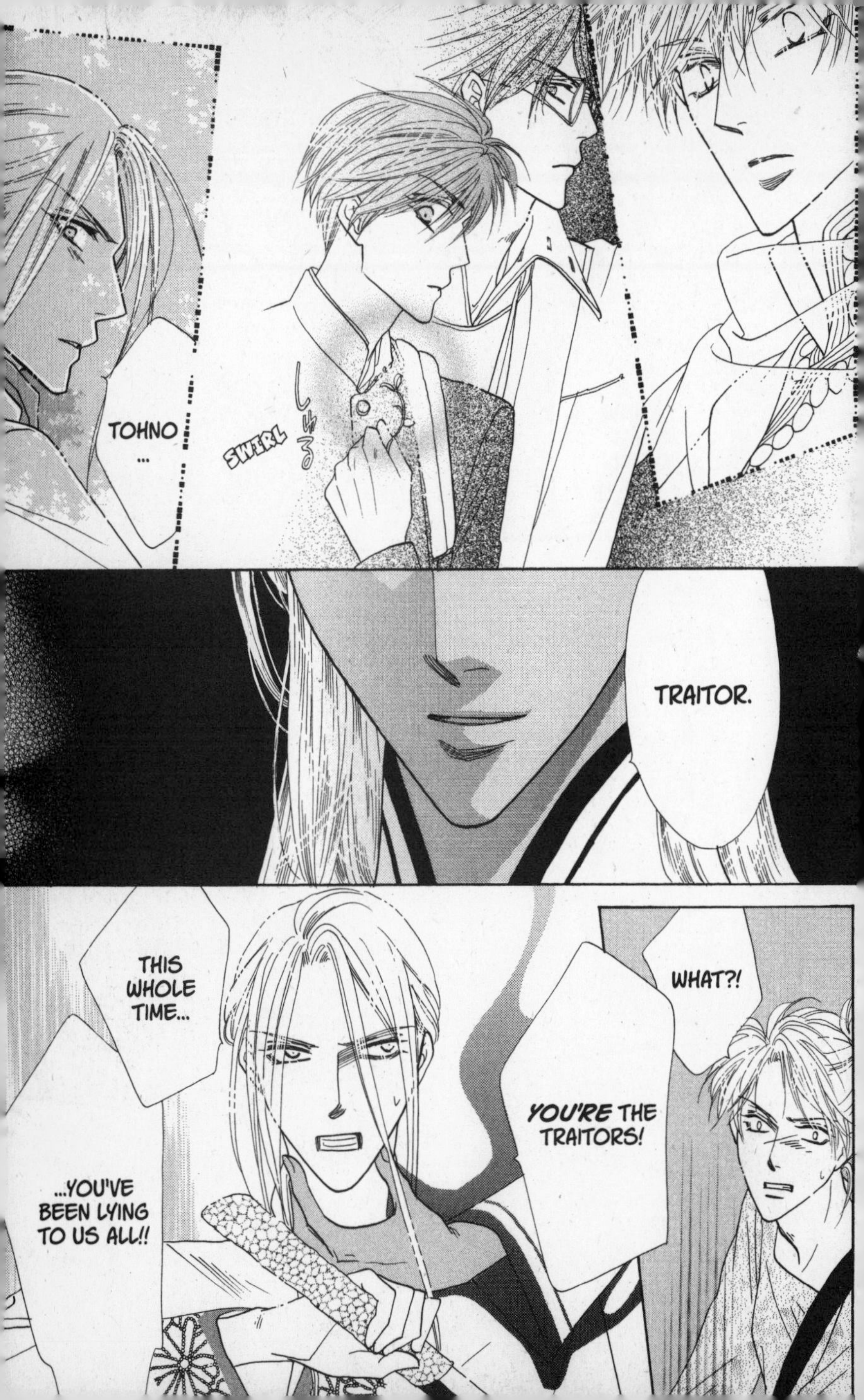
SWIRL
しゅる
TOHNO ...
TRAITOR.
WHAT?!
YOU'RE THE TRAITORS!
THIS WHOLE TIME...
...YOU'VE BEEN LYING TO US ALL!!

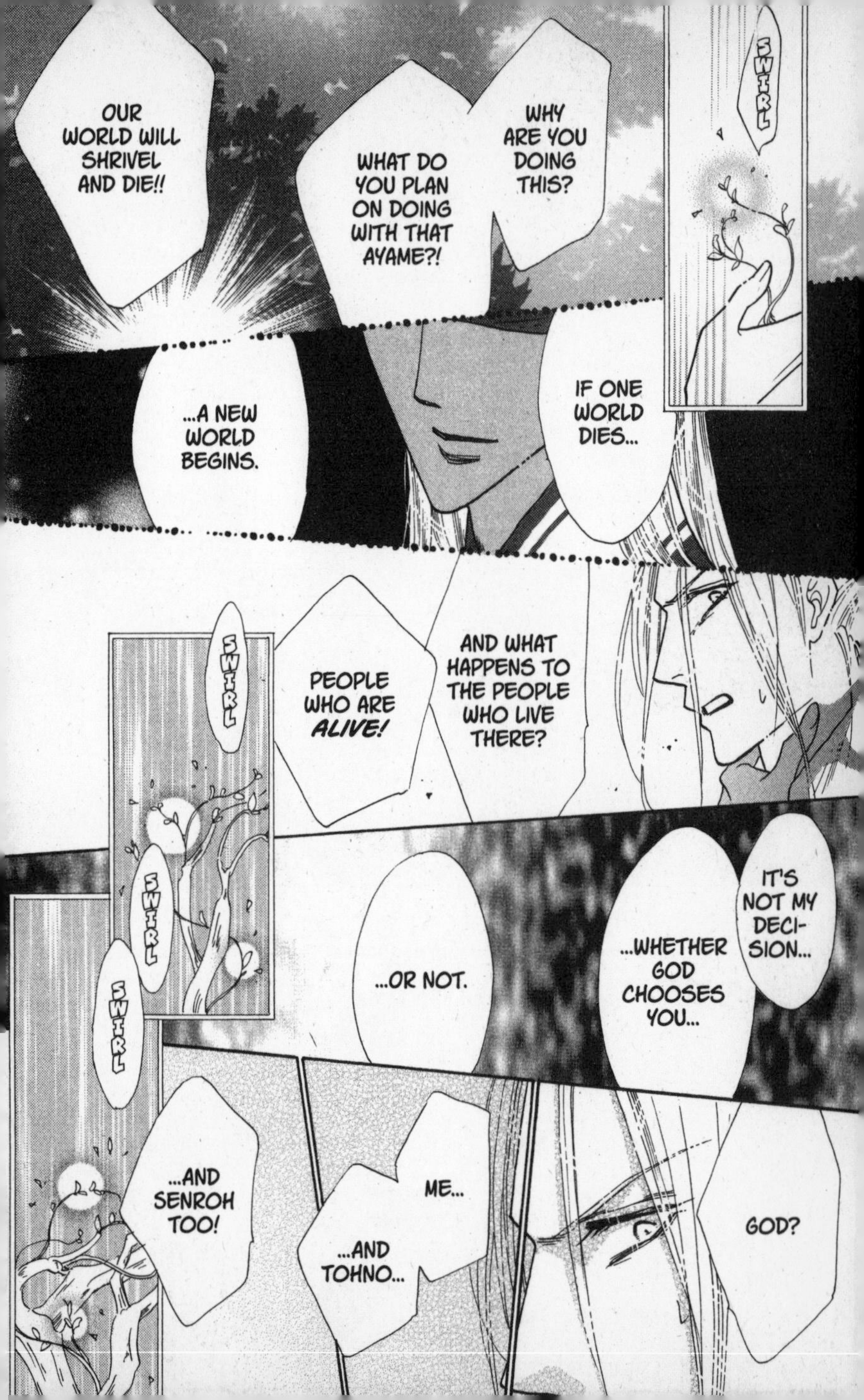
SWIRL
WHY ARE YOU DOING THIS?
WHAT DO YOU PLAN ON DOING WITH THAT AYAME?!
OUR WORLD WILL SHRIVEL AND DIE!!
IF ONE WORLD DIES...
...A NEW WORLD BEGINS.
AND WHAT HAPPENS TO THE PEOPLE WHO LIVE THERE?
PEOPLE WHO ARE *ALIVE!*
SWIRL
IT'S NOT MY DECI-SION...
...WHETHER GOD CHOOSES YOU...
...OR NOT.
SWIRL
SWIRL
GOD?
ME...
...AND TOHNO...
...AND SENROH TOO!

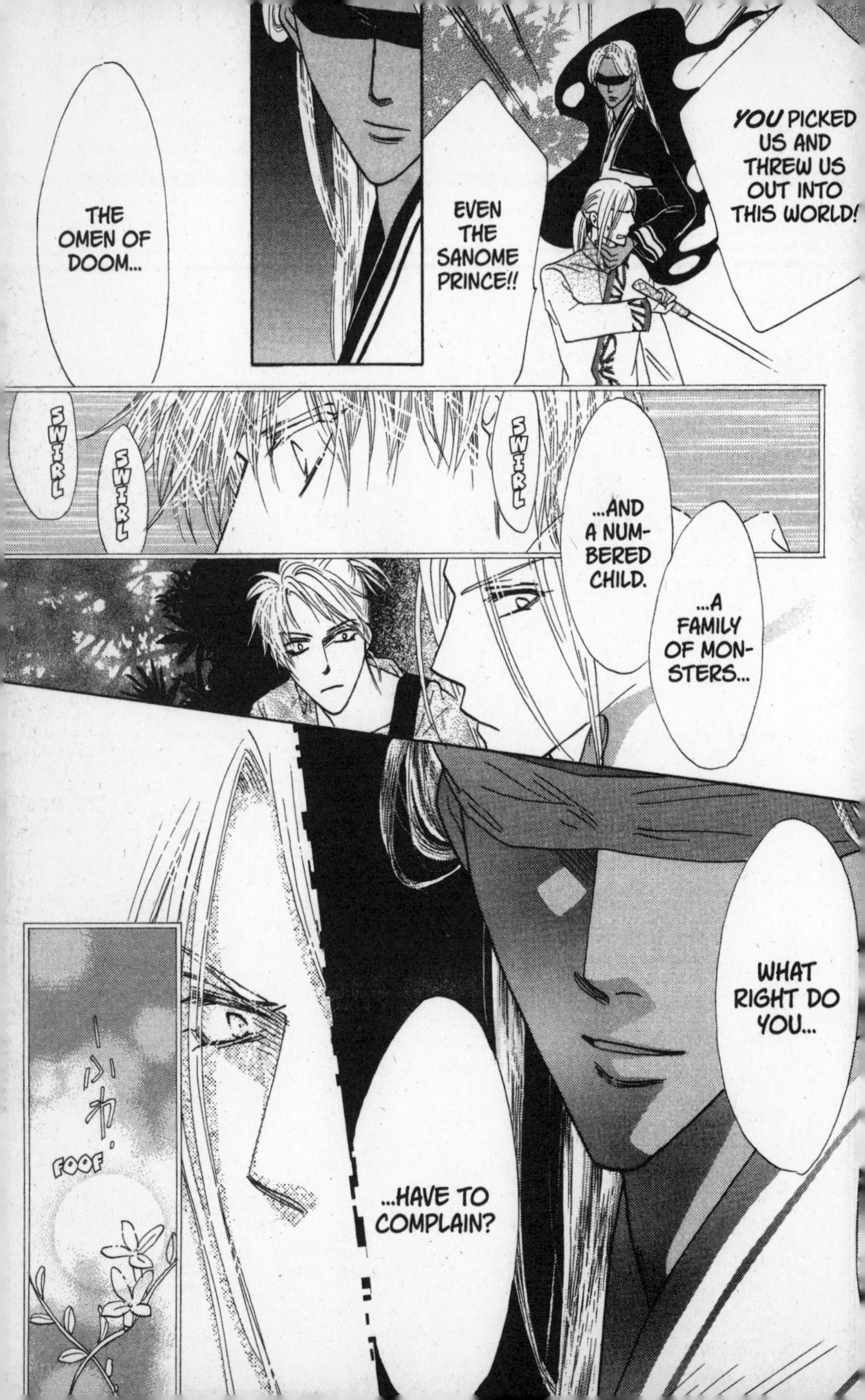
YOU PICKED US AND THREW US OUT INTO THIS WORLD!
EVEN THE SANOME PRINCE!!
THE OMEN OF DOOM...
SWIRL
SWIRL
SWIRL
...A FAMILY OF MON-STERS...
...AND A NUM-BERED CHILD.
WHAT RIGHT DO YOU...
...HAVE TO COMPLAIN?
ふわ
FOOF

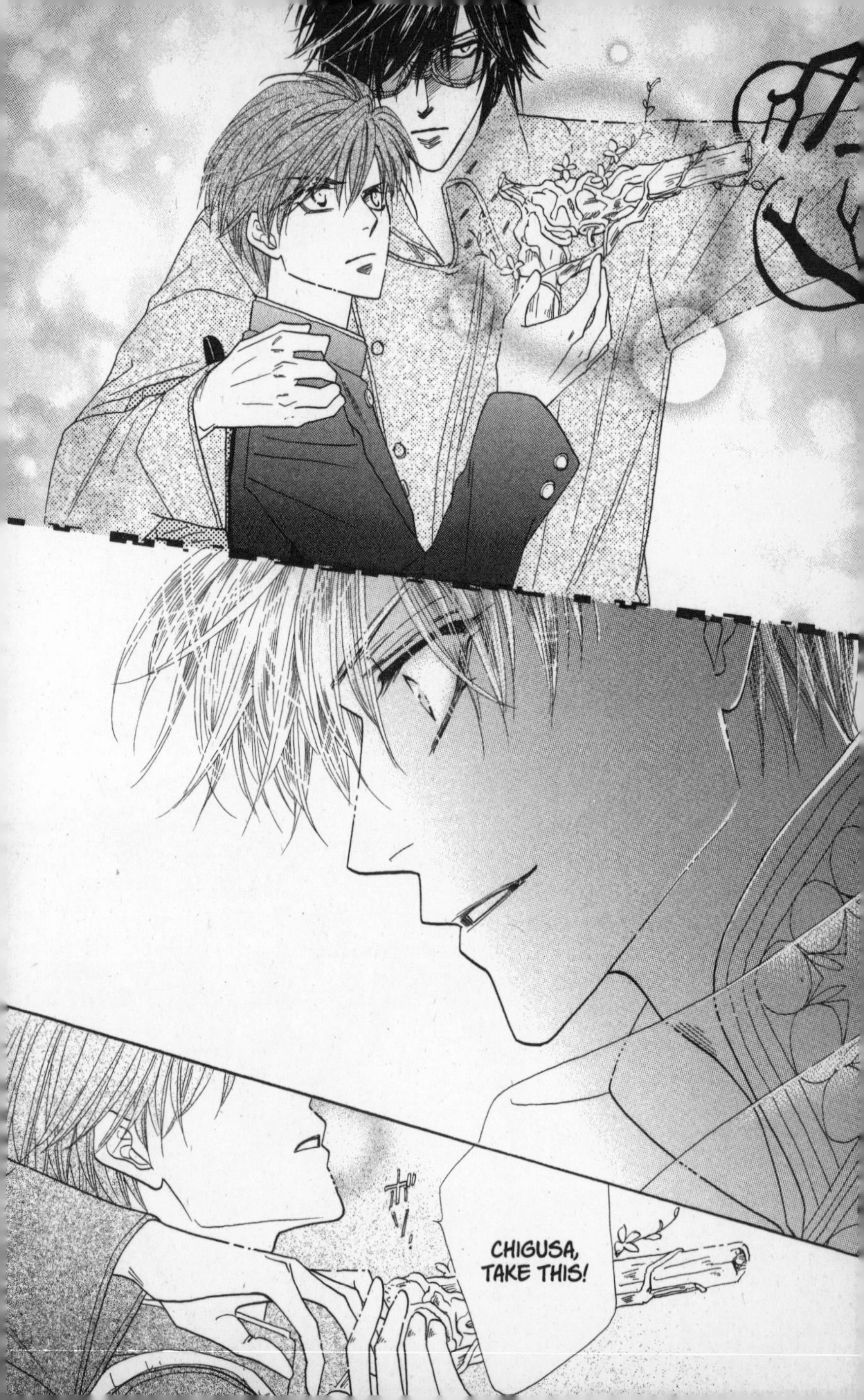
CHIGUSA, TAKE THIS!

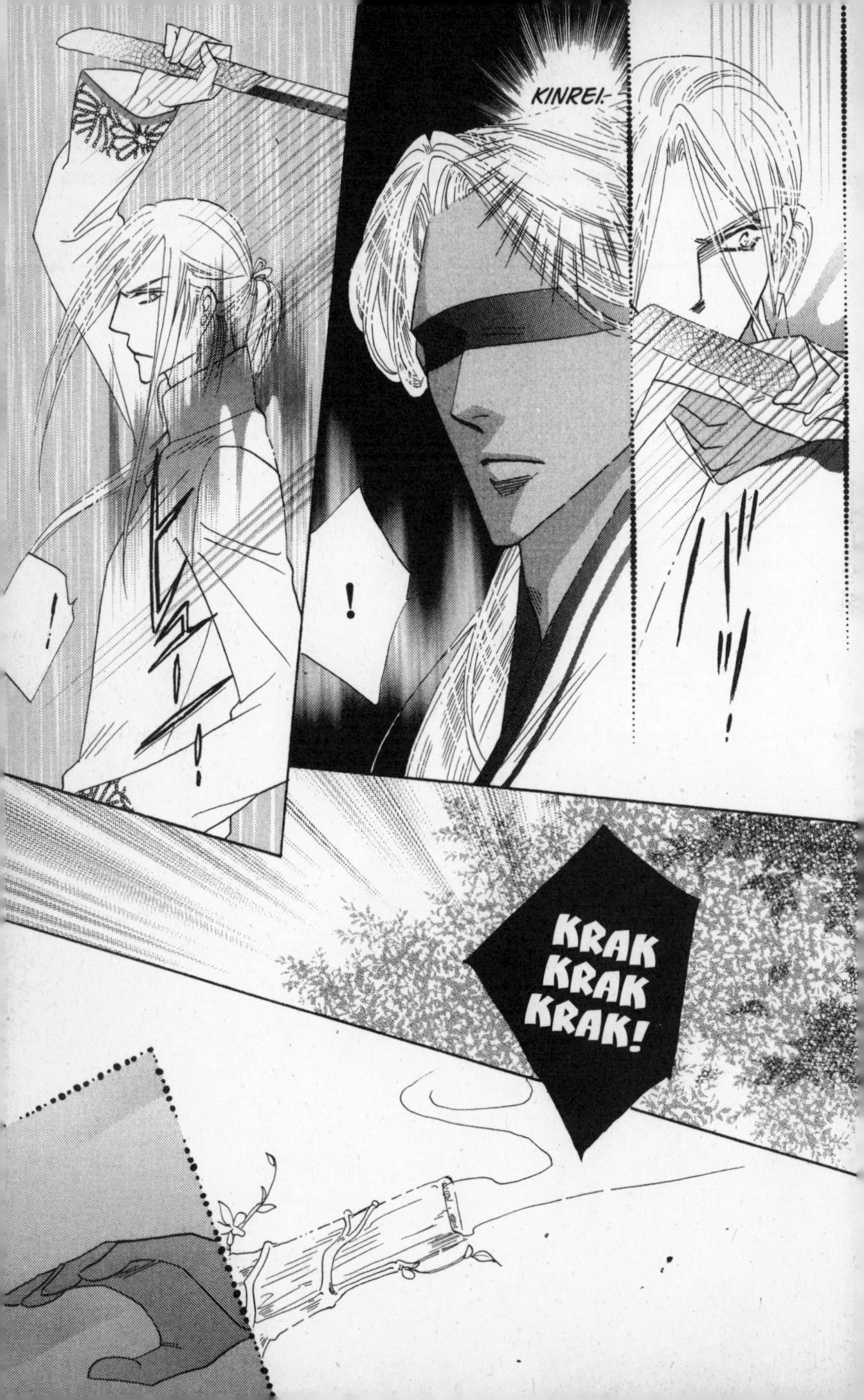
KINREI-
!
KRAK KRAK KRAK!

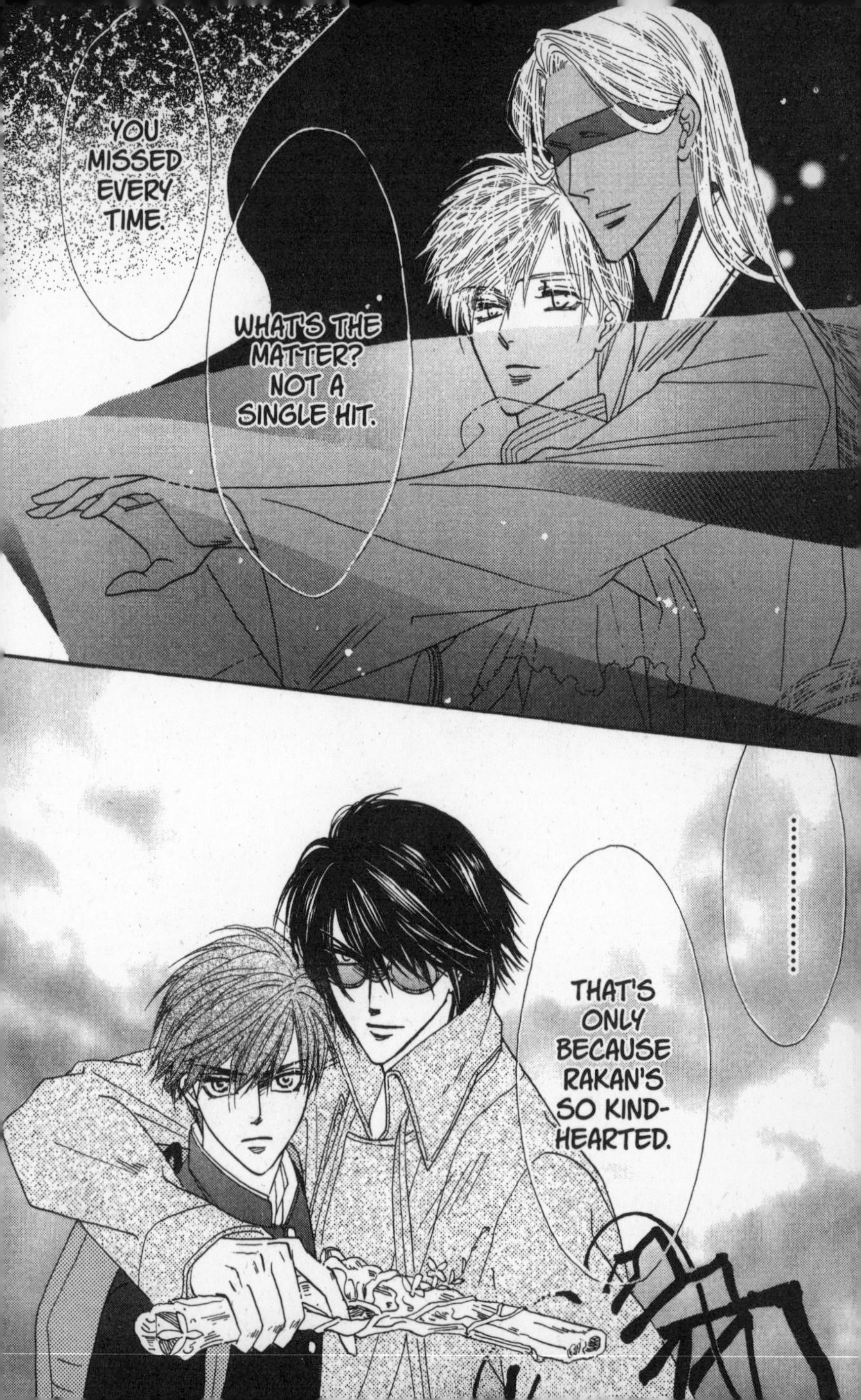
WHAT'S THE MATTER? NOT A SINGLE HIT.
YOU MISSED EVERY TIME.
......
THAT'S ONLY BECAUSE RAKAN'S SO KIND-HEARTED.

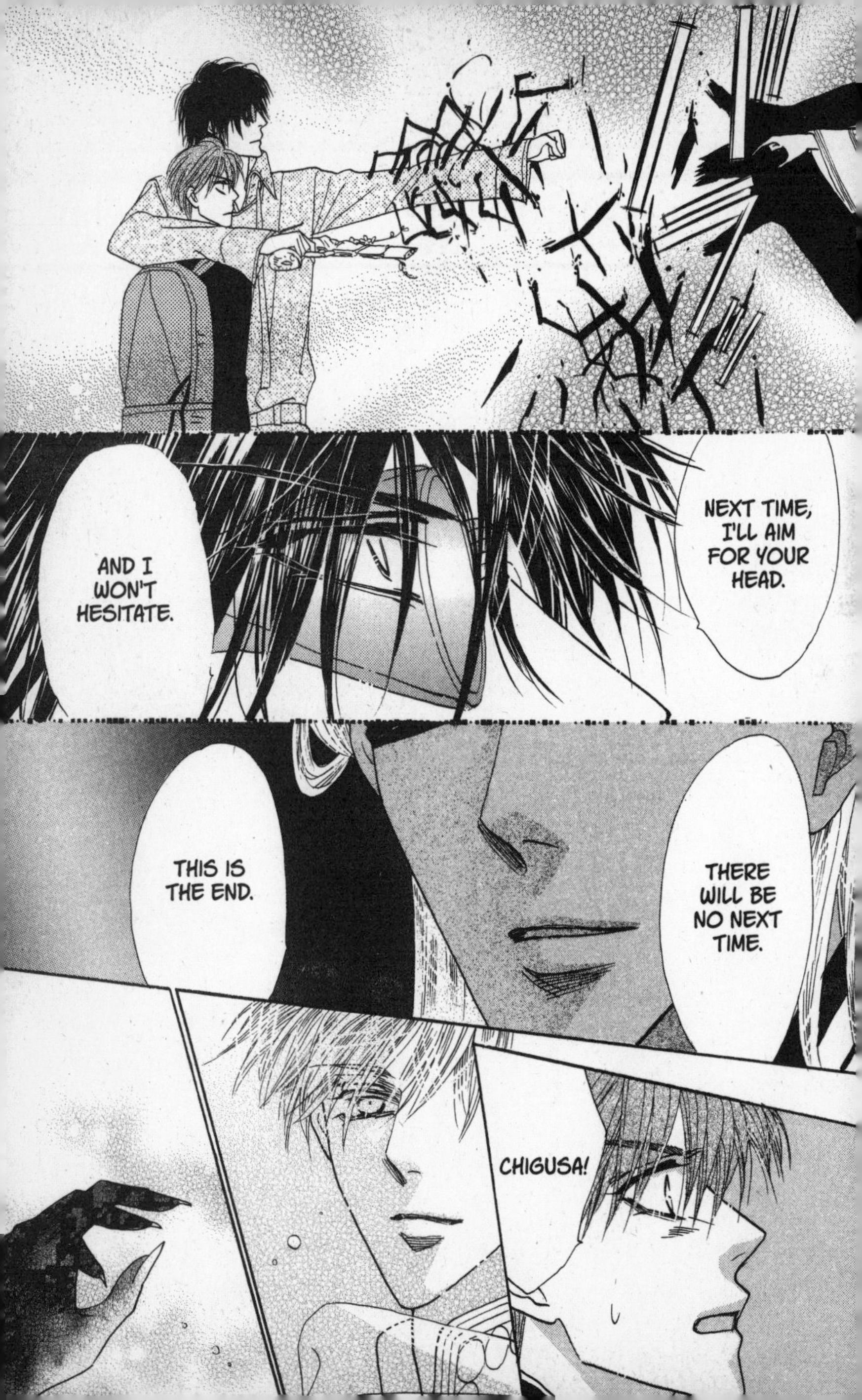
NEXT TIME, I'LL AIM FOR YOUR HEAD.
AND I WON'T HESITATE.
THERE WILL BE NO NEXT TIME.
THIS IS THE END.
CHIGUSA!

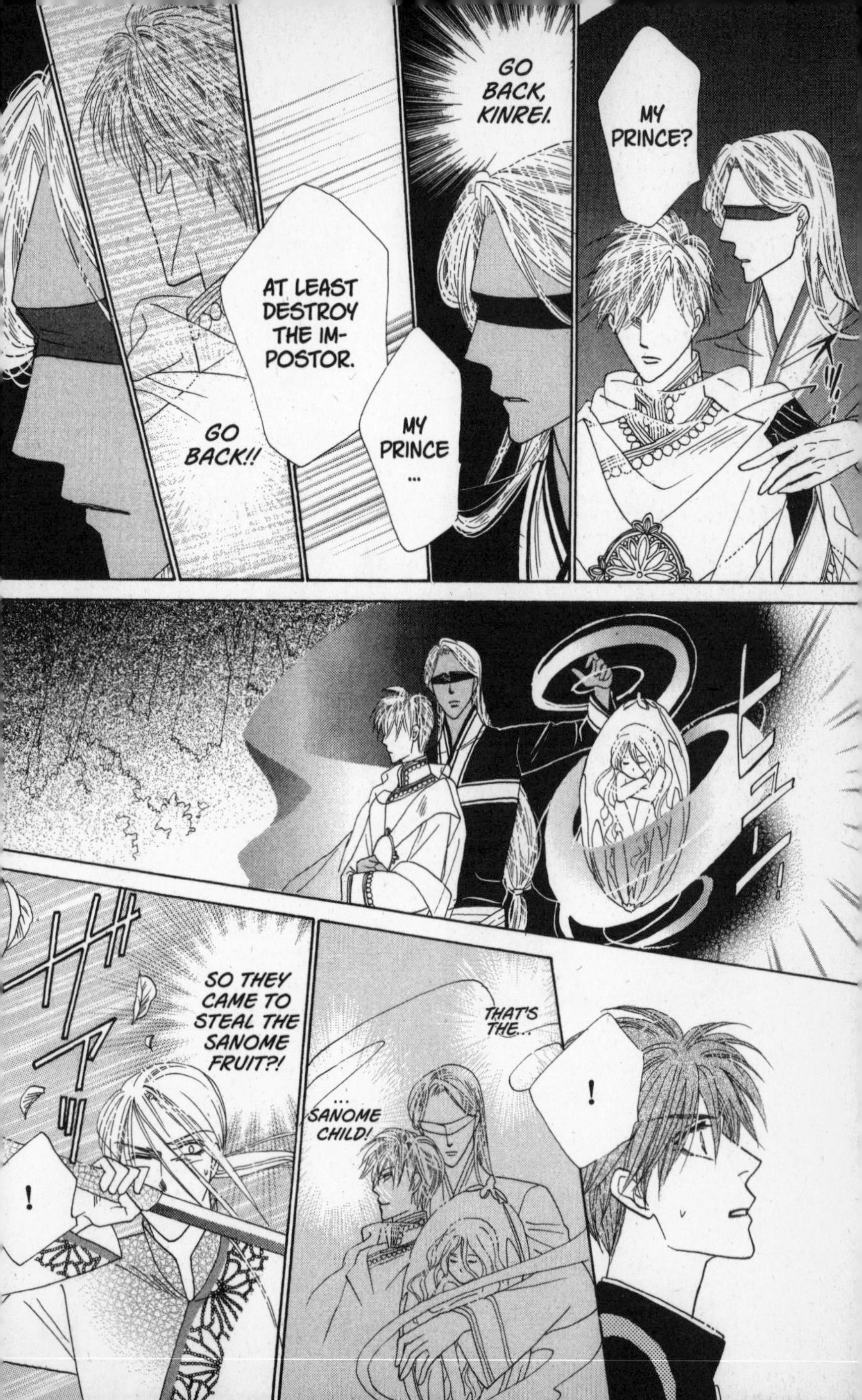
MY PRINCE?
GO BACK, KINREI.
MY PRINCE ...
AT LEAST DESTROY THE IM-POSTOR.
GO BACK!!
!
THAT'S THE...
... SANOME CHILD!
SO THEY CAME TO STEAL THE SANOME FRUIT?!
!

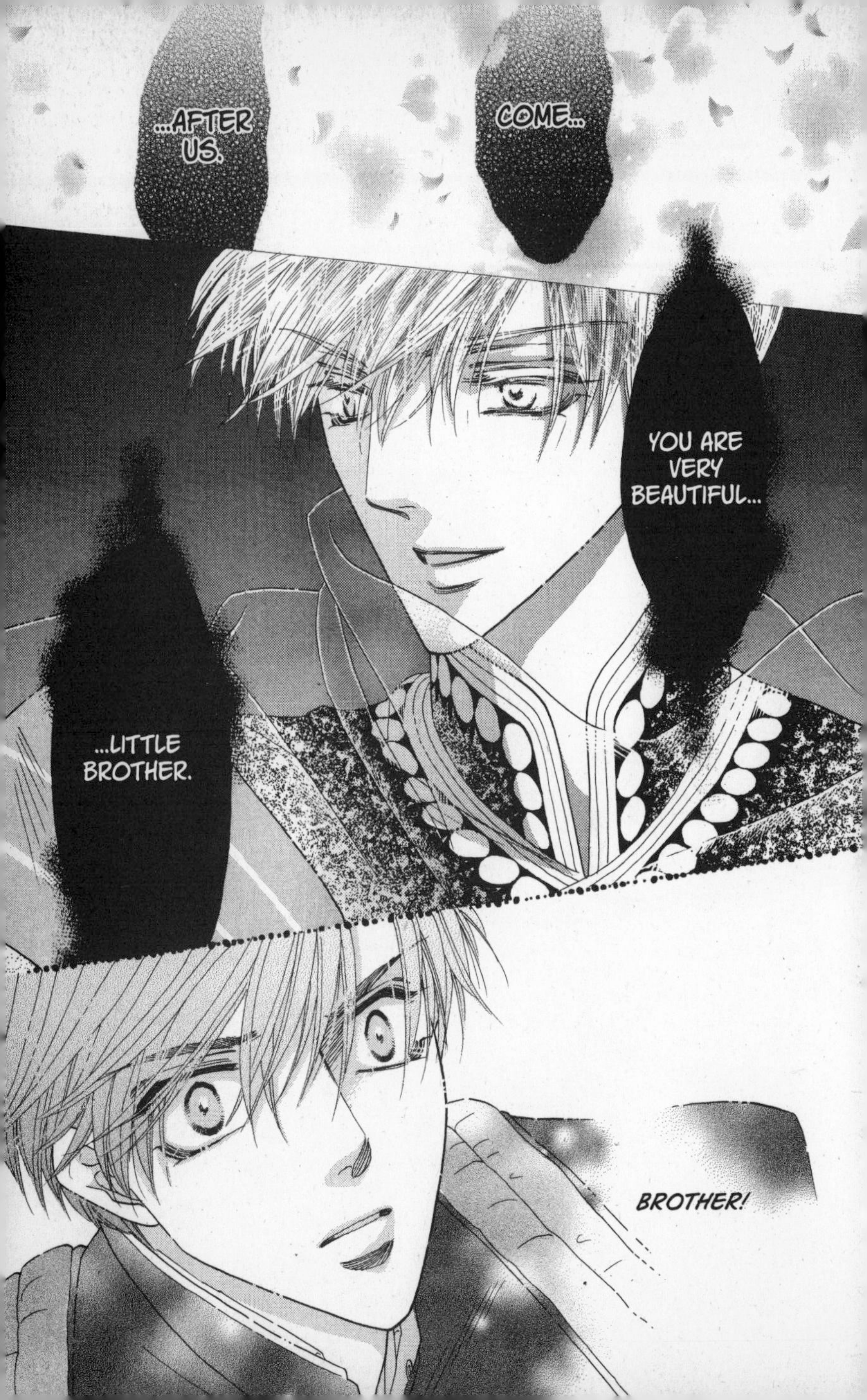
COME...
...AFTER US.
YOU ARE VERY BEAUTIFUL...
...LITTLE BROTHER.
BROTHER!

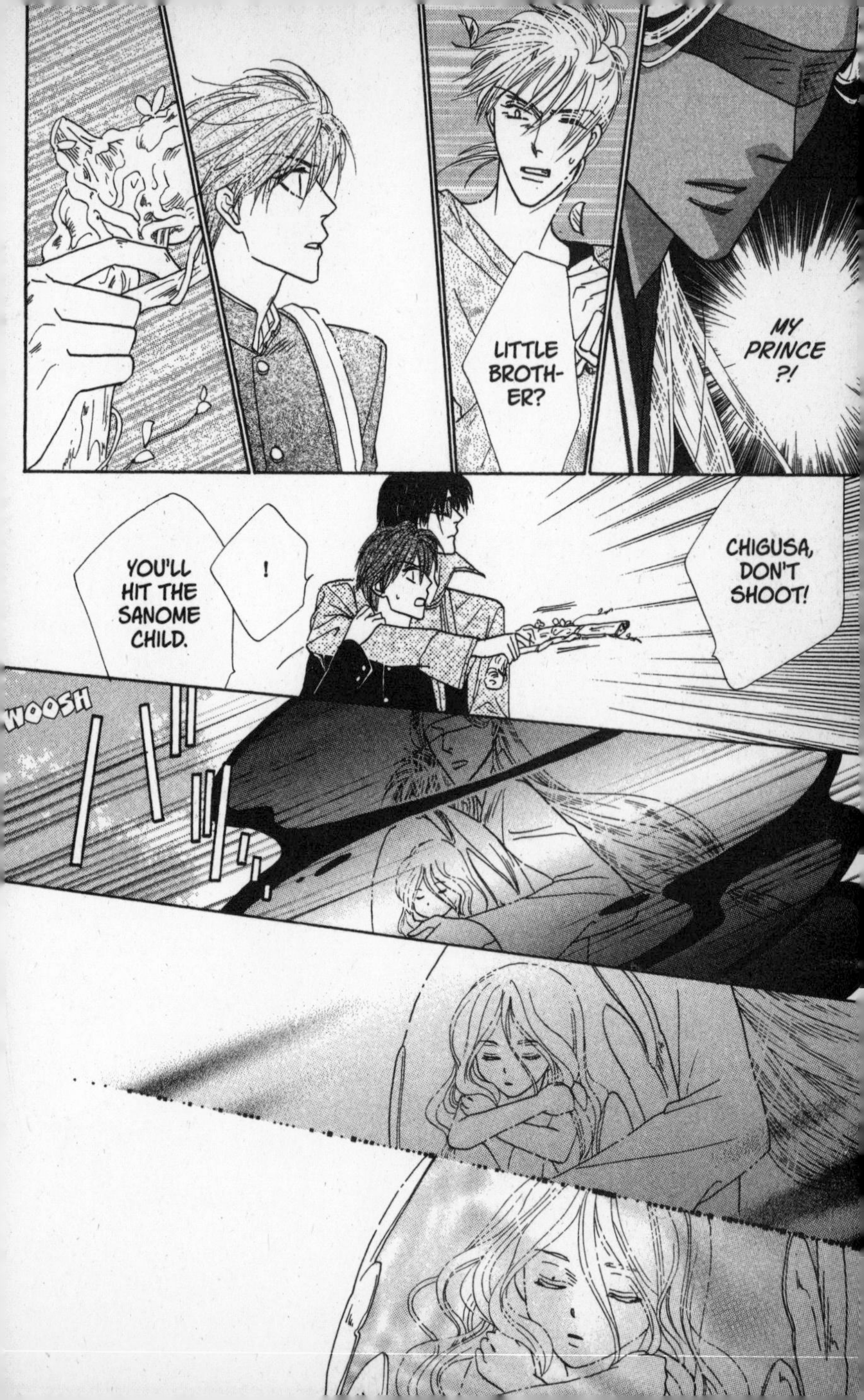
MY PRINCE ?!
LITTLE BROTH-ER?
CHIGUSA, DON'T SHOOT!
!
YOU'LL HIT THE SANOME CHILD.
WOOSH

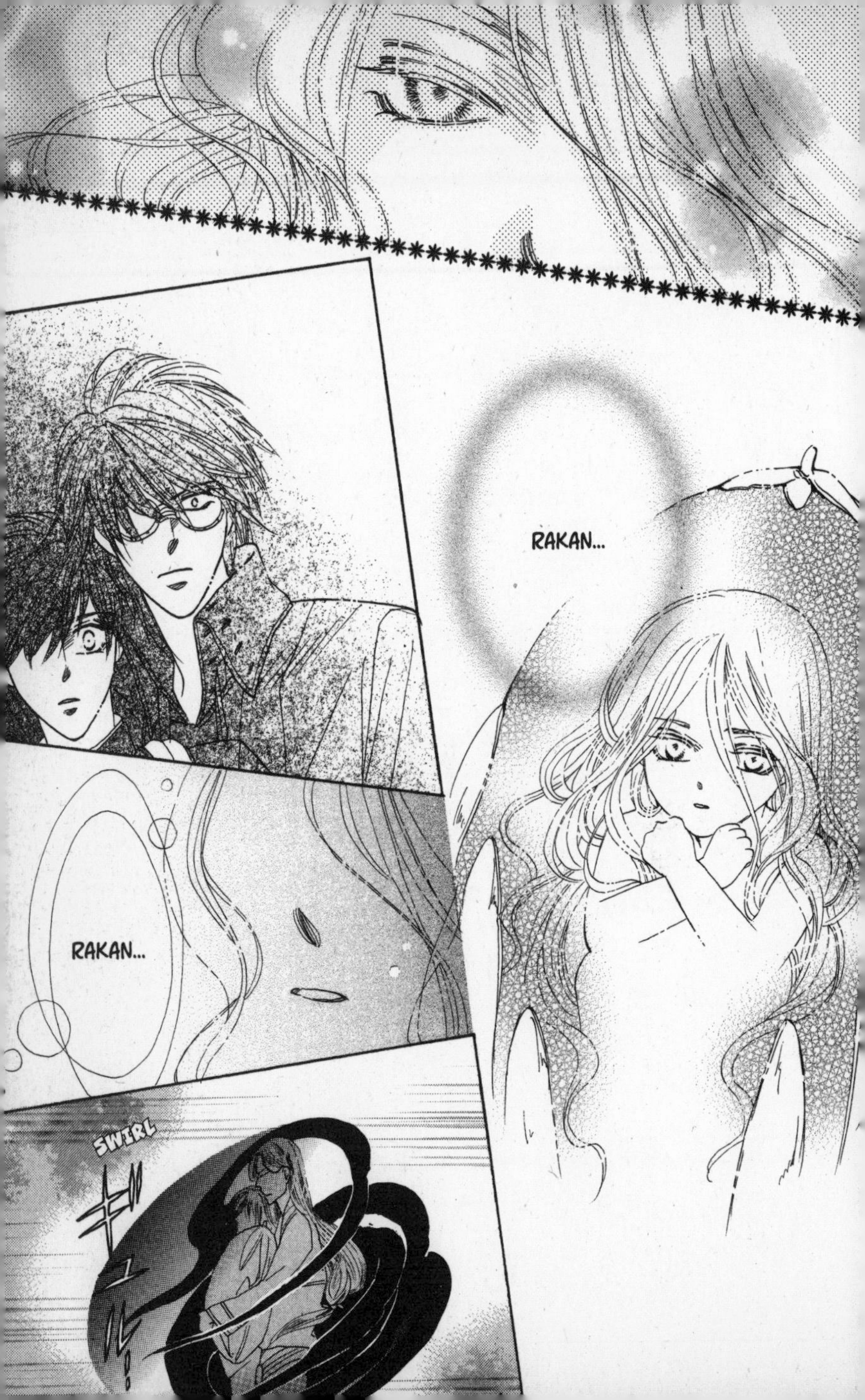
RAKAN...
RAKAN...
SWIRL

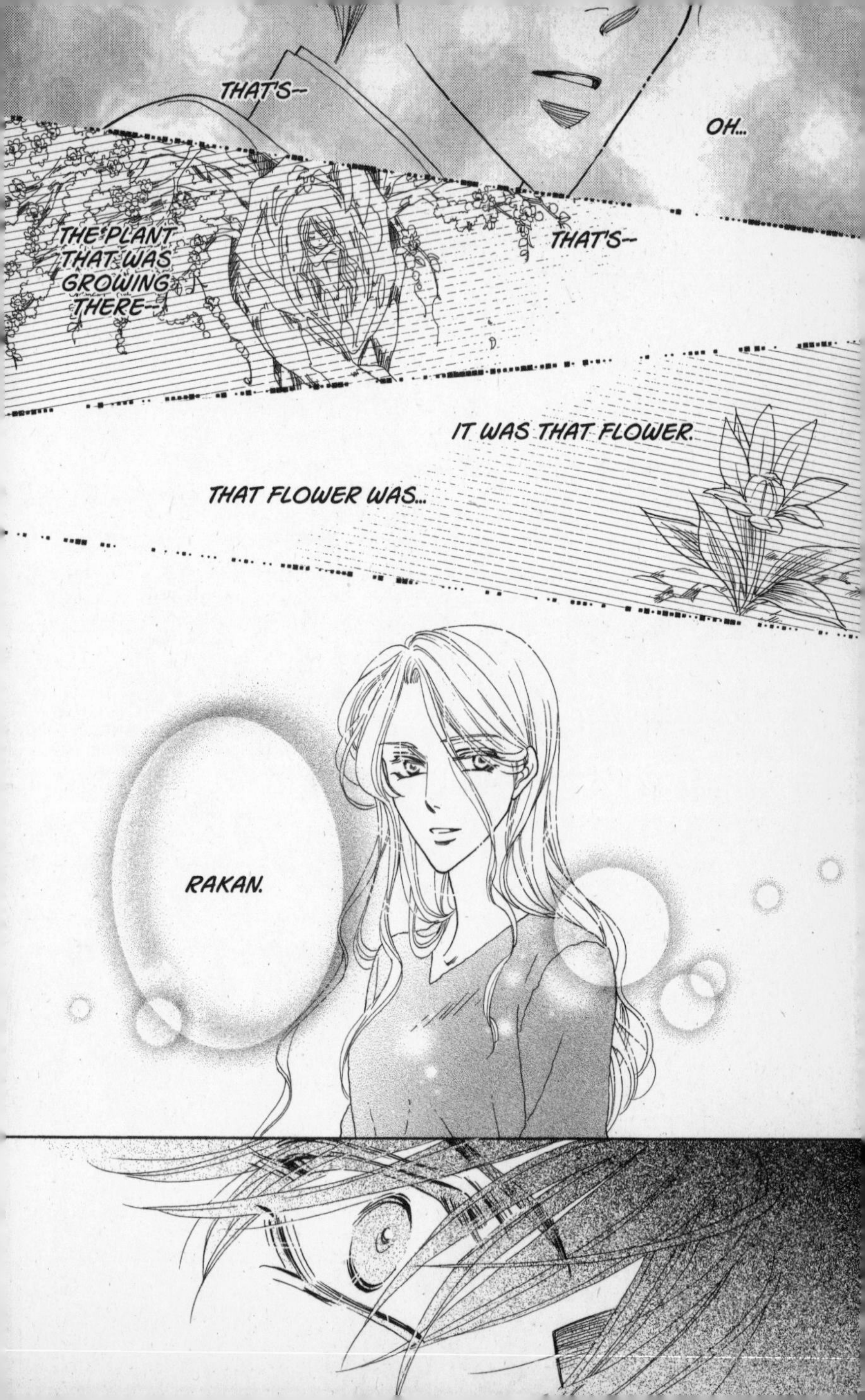
OH...
THAT'S--
THAT'S--
THE PLANT THAT WAS GROWING THERE--
IT WAS THAT FLOWER.
THAT FLOWER WAS...
RAKAN.

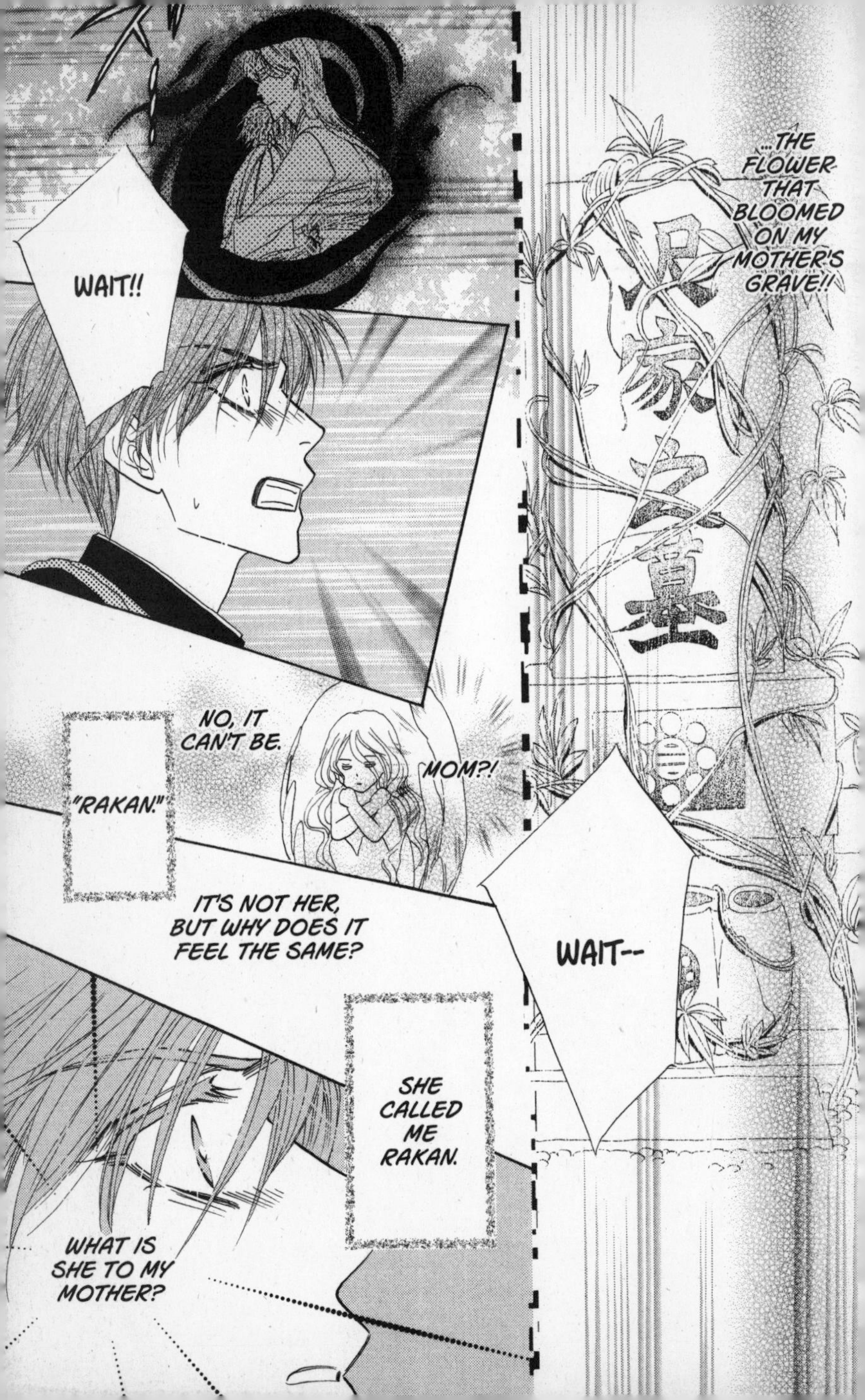
...THE FLOWER THAT BLOOMED ON MY MOTHER'S GRAVE!!
WAIT--
WAIT!!
MOM?!
NO, IT CAN'T BE.
"RAKAN."
IT'S NOT HER, BUT WHY DOES IT FEEL THE SAME?
SHE CALLED ME RAKAN.
WHAT IS SHE TO MY MOTHER?

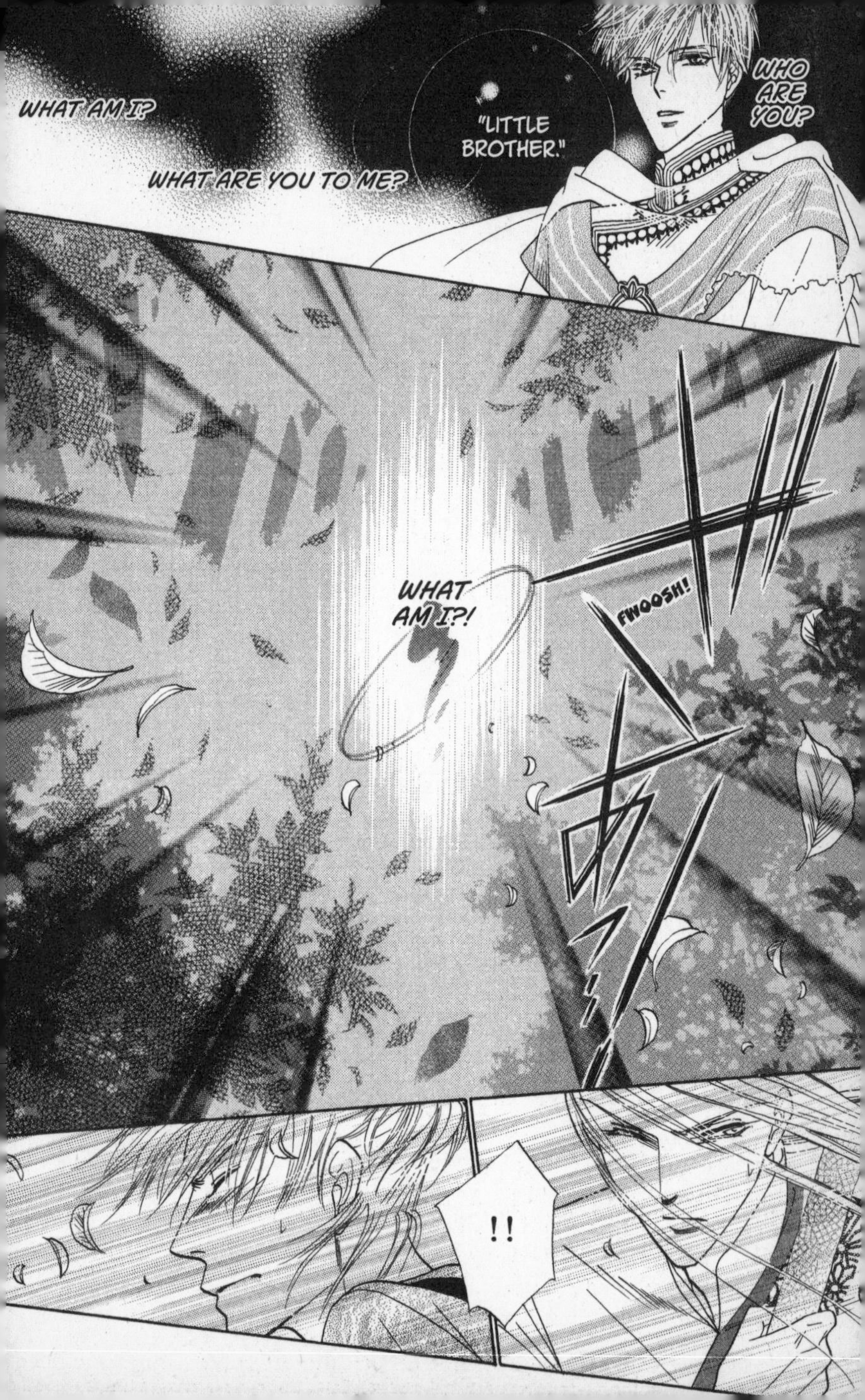
WHO ARE YOU?
"LITTLE BROTHER."
WHAT AM I?
WHAT ARE YOU TO ME?
FWOOSH!
WHAT AM I?!
!!

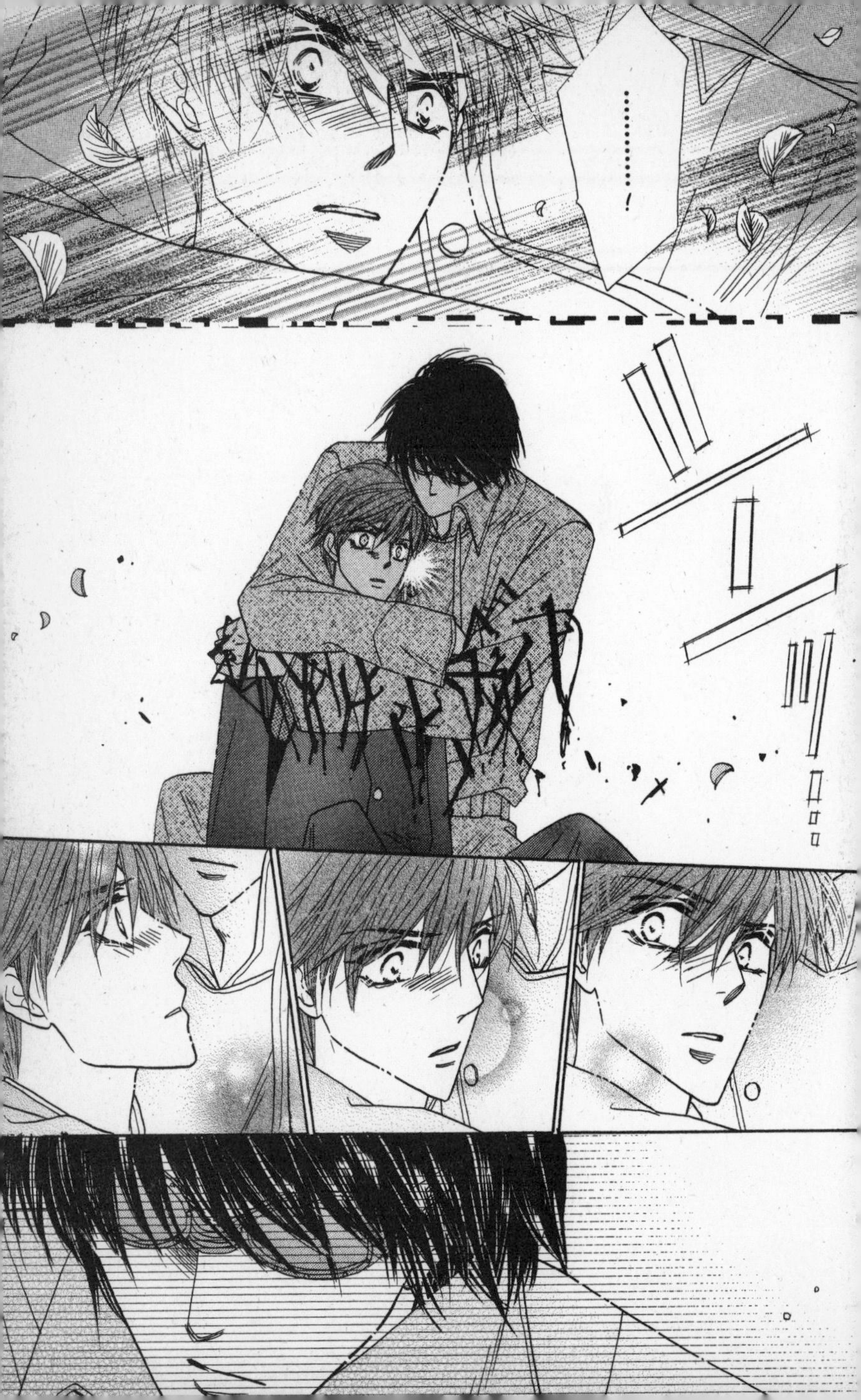
......!

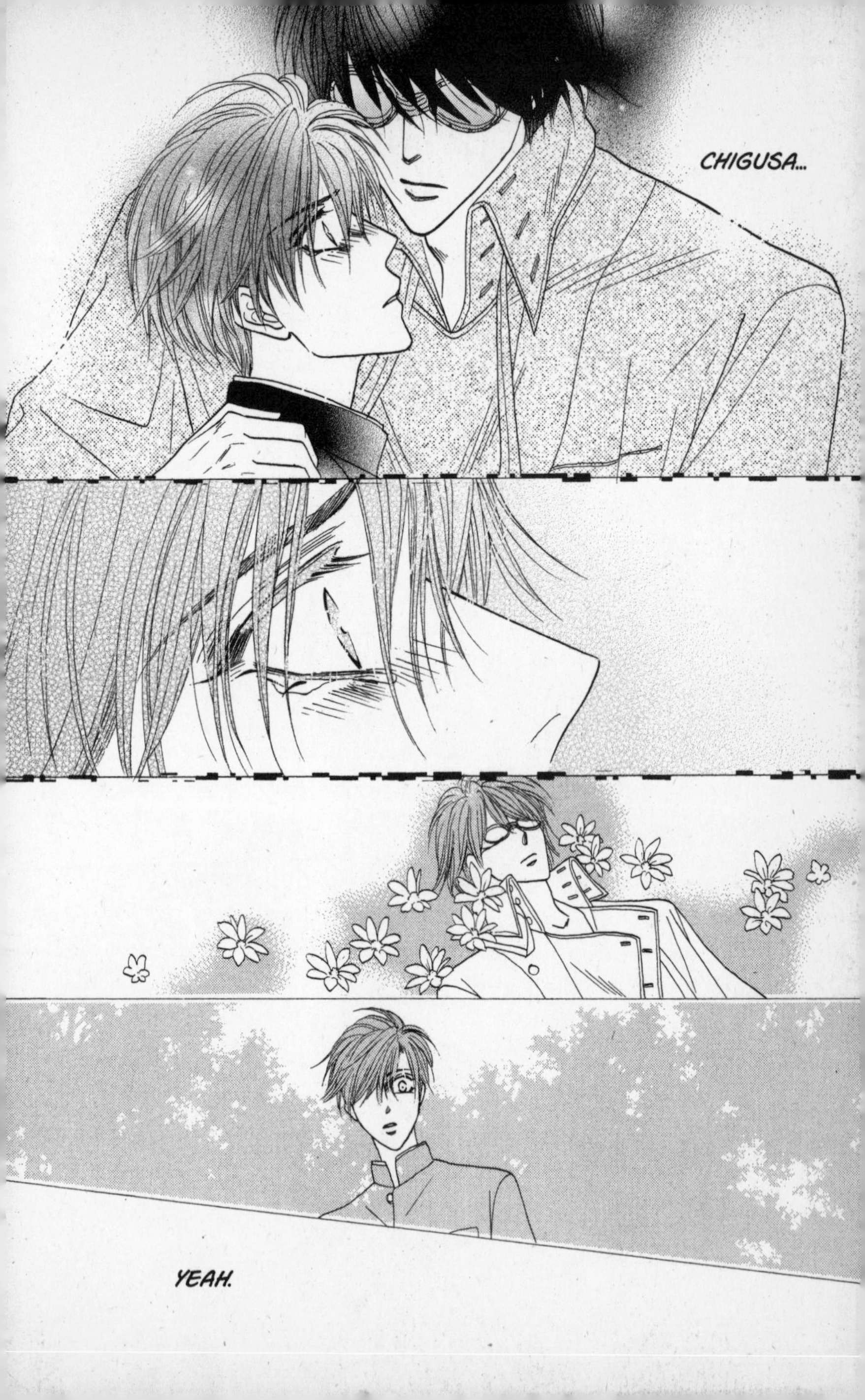
CHIGUSA...
YEAH.

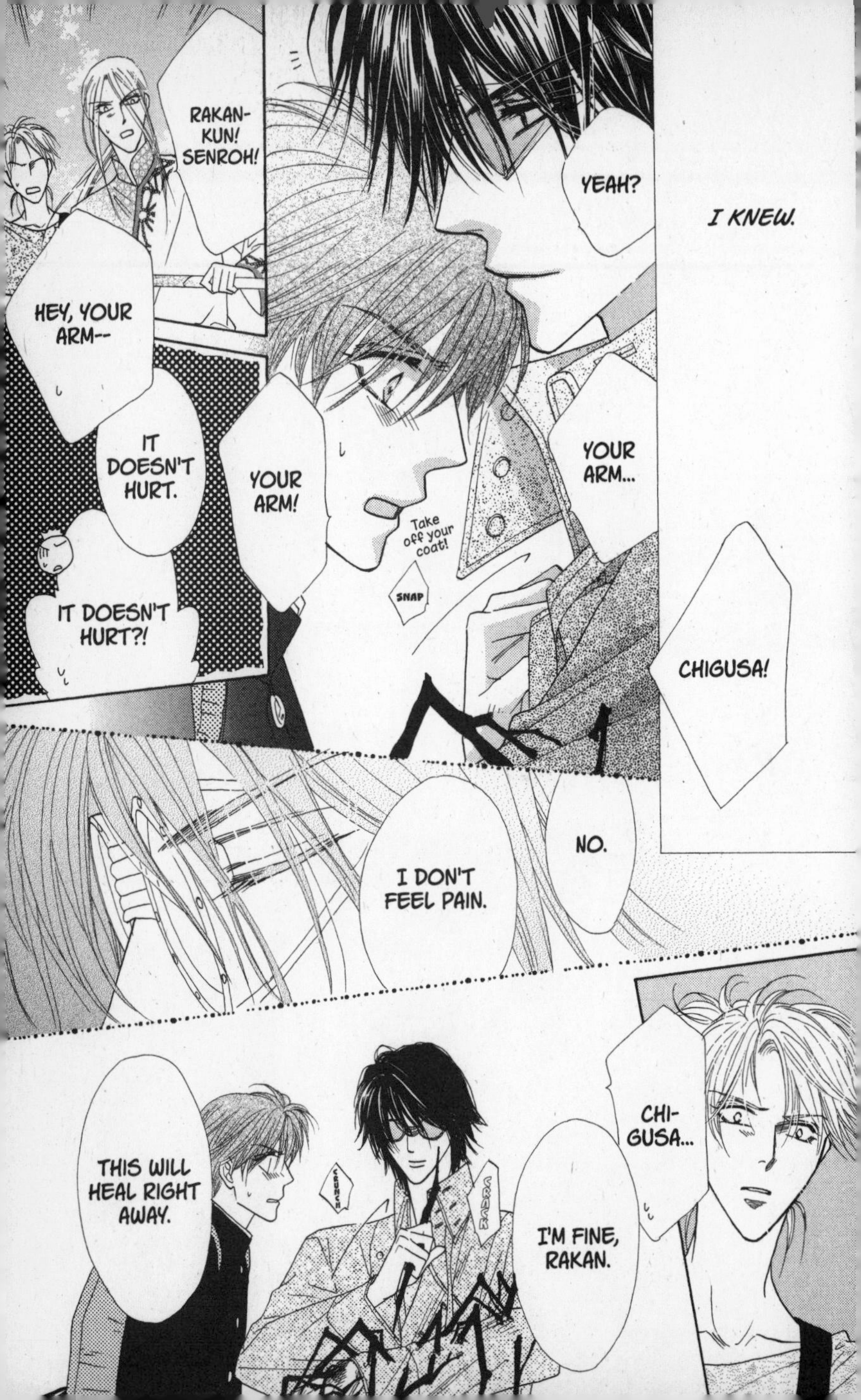
I KNEW.
CHIGUSA!
YEAH?
YOUR ARM...
YOUR ARM!
Take off your coat!
SNAP
RAKAN-KUN! SENROH!
HEY, YOUR ARM--
IT DOESN'T HURT.
IT DOESN'T HURT?!
NO.
I DON'T FEEL PAIN.
CHI-GUSA...
I'M FINE, RAKAN.
CRACK
CRUNCH
THIS WILL HEAL RIGHT AWAY.

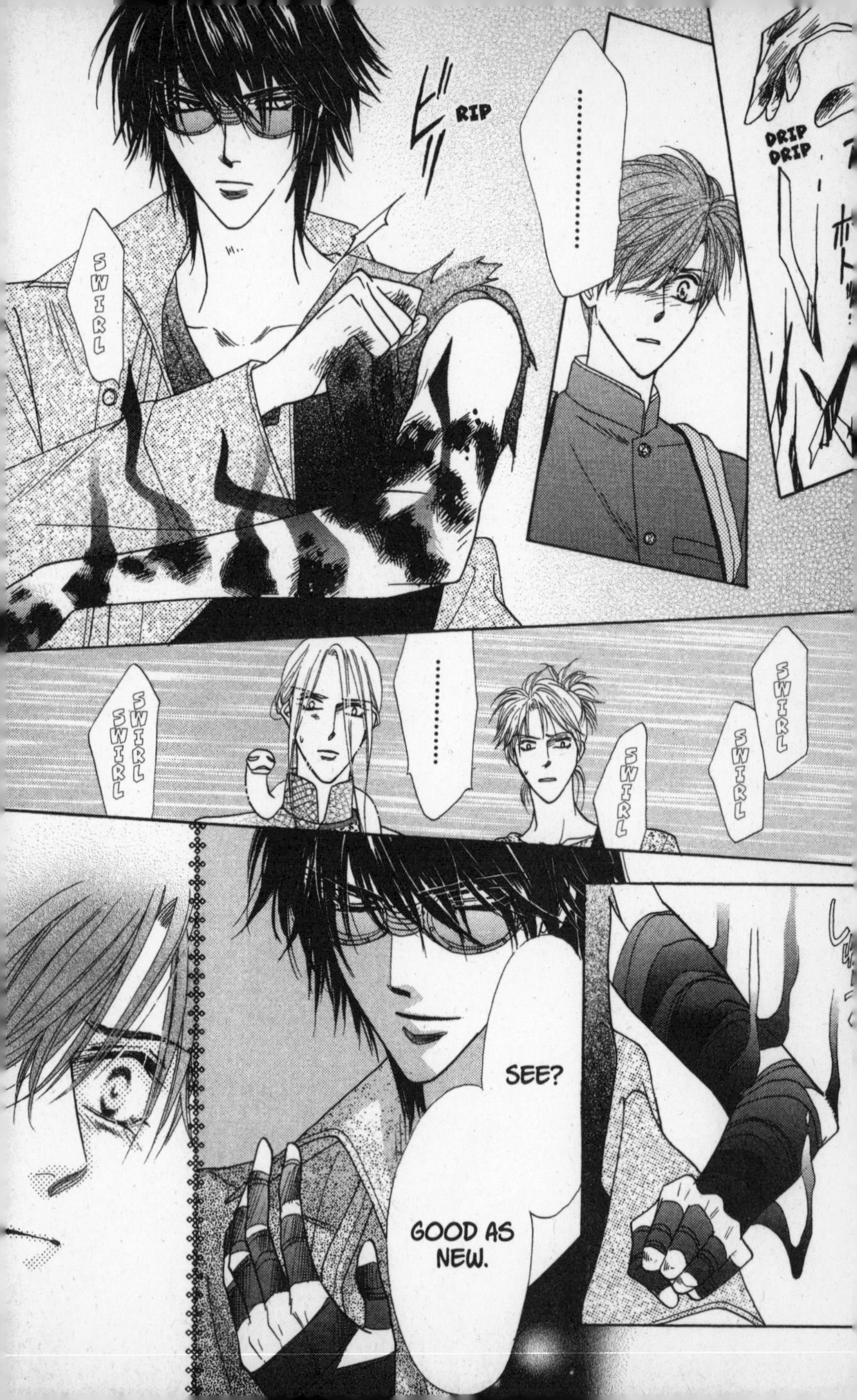
DRIP DRIP
......
RIP
SWIRL
SWIRL
SWIRL
SWIRL
......
SWIRL SWIRL
SEE?
GOOD AS NEW.

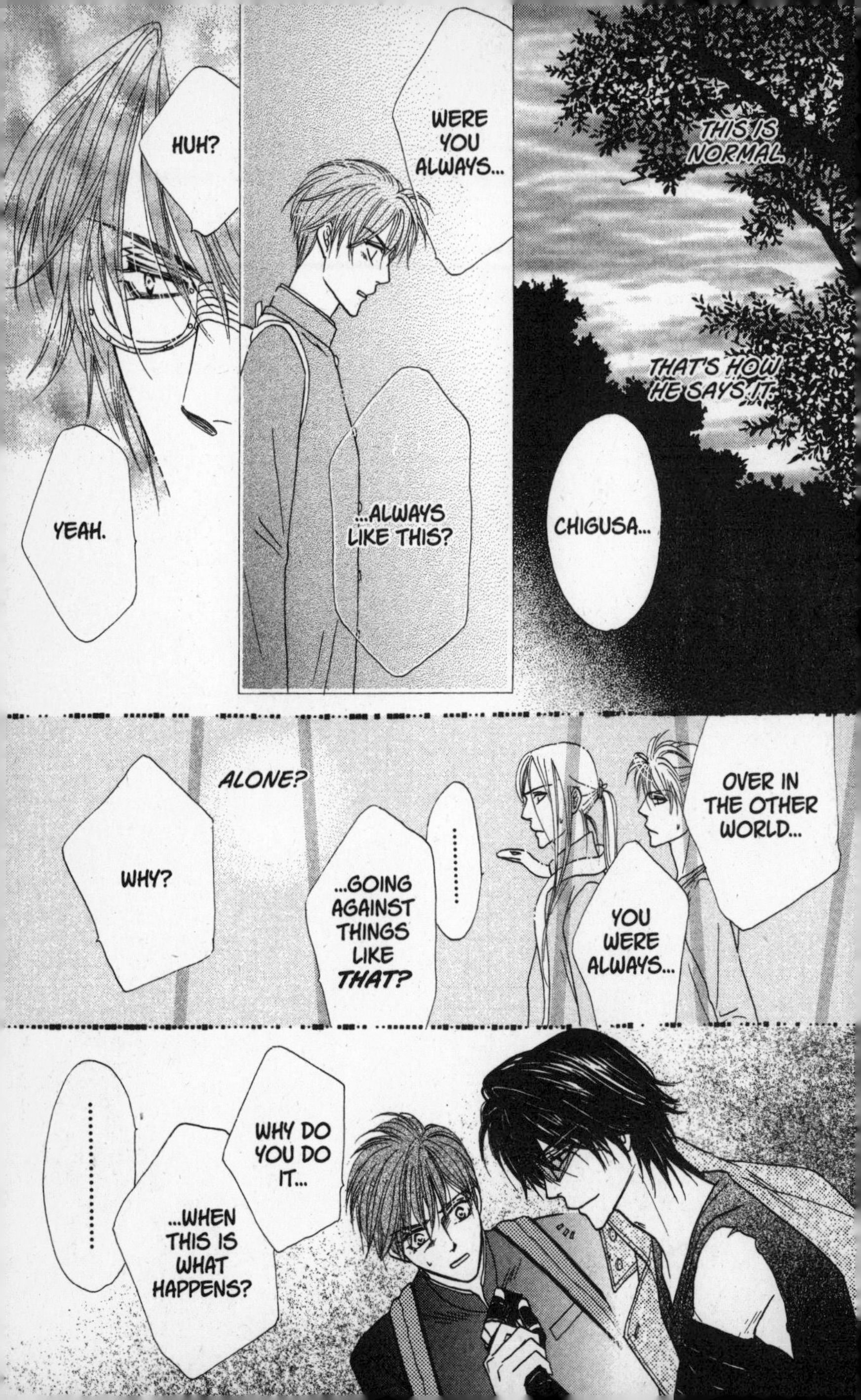
THIS IS NORMAL.
THAT'S HOW HE SAYS IT.
CHIGUSA...
WERE YOU ALWAYS...
...ALWAYS LIKE THIS?
HUH?
YEAH.
OVER IN THE OTHER WORLD...
YOU WERE ALWAYS...
......
...GOING AGAINST THINGS LIKE *THAT?*
ALONE?
WHY?
WHY DO YOU DO IT...
...WHEN THIS IS WHAT HAPPENS?
......

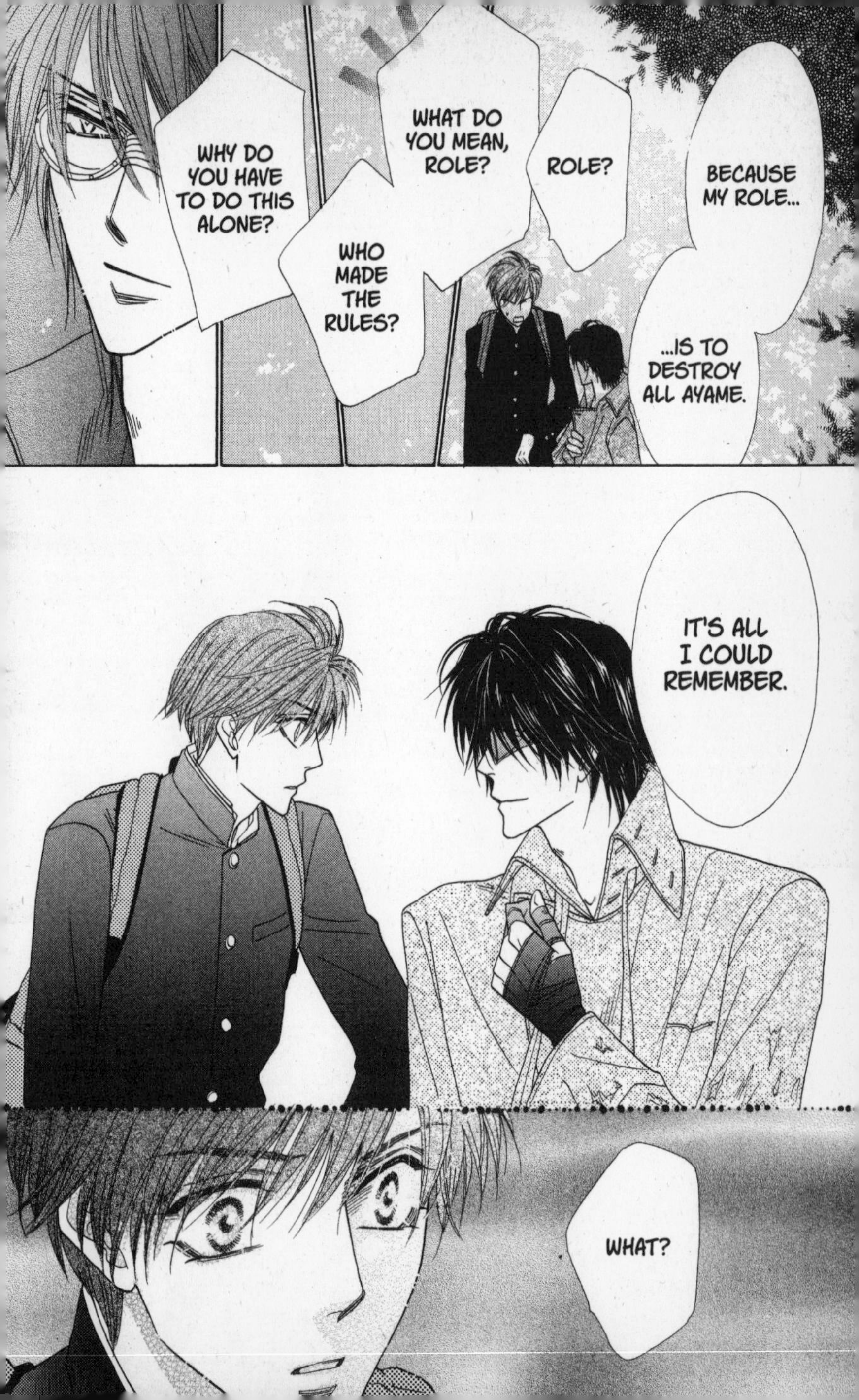
BECAUSE MY ROLE...
...IS TO DESTROY ALL AYAME.
ROLE?
WHAT DO YOU MEAN, ROLE?
WHO MADE THE RULES?
WHY DO YOU HAVE TO DO THIS ALONE?
IT'S ALL I COULD REMEMBER.
WHAT?

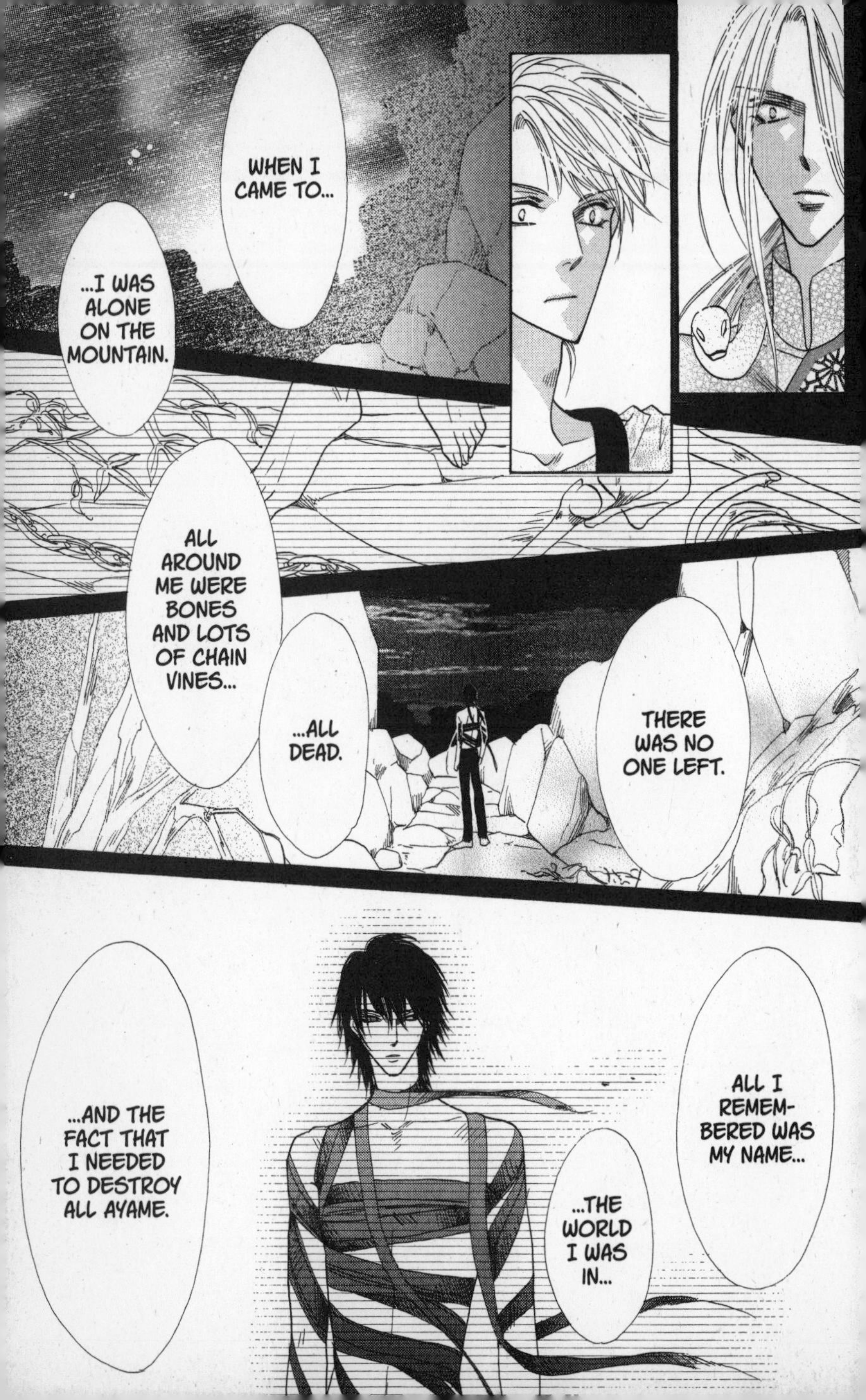
WHEN I CAME TO...
...I WAS ALONE ON THE MOUNTAIN.
ALL AROUND ME WERE BONES AND LOTS OF CHAIN VINES...
...ALL DEAD.
THERE WAS NO ONE LEFT.
ALL I REMEMBERED WAS MY NAME...
...THE WORLD I WAS IN...
...AND THE FACT THAT I NEEDED TO DESTROY ALL AYAME.

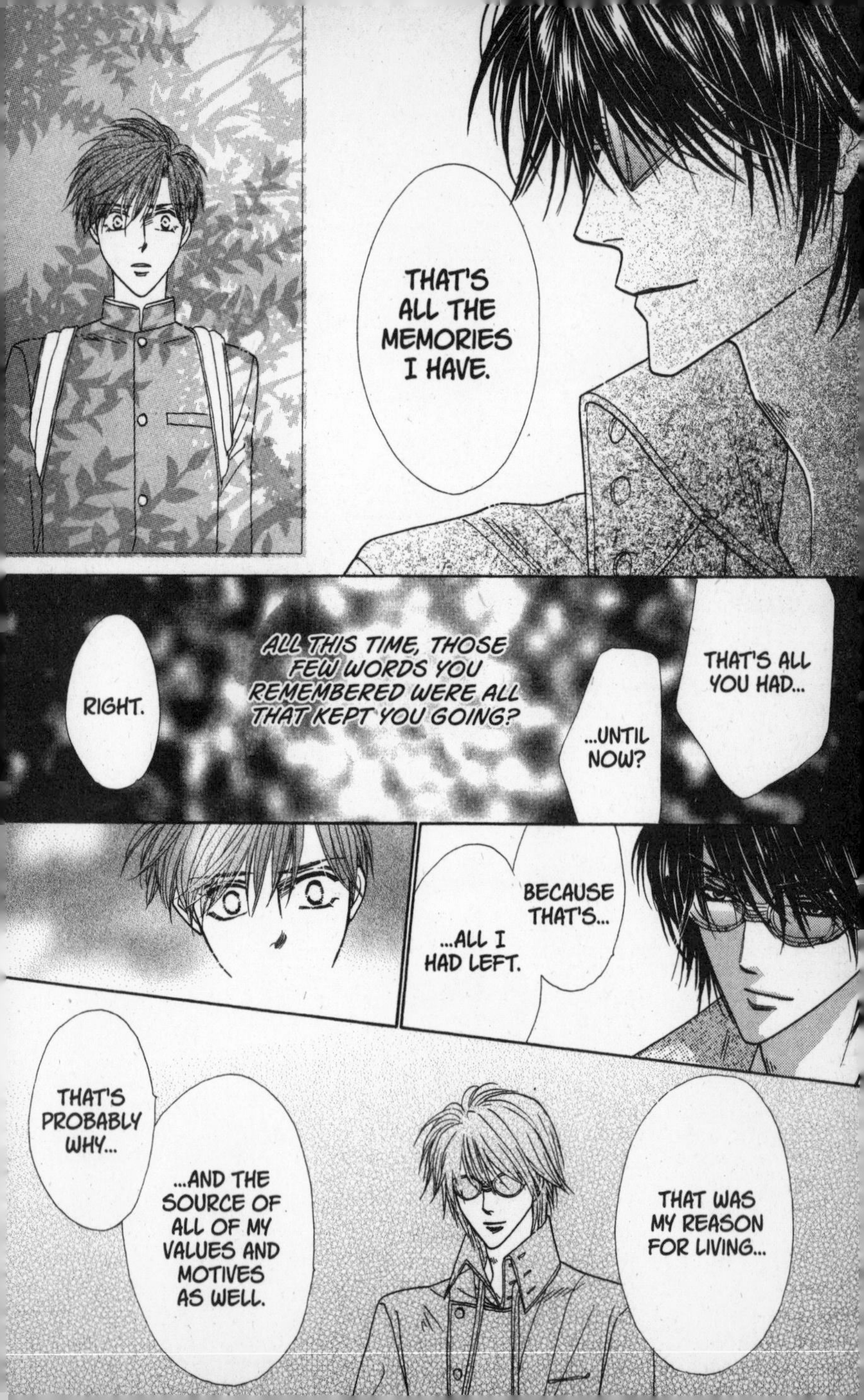
THAT'S ALL THE MEMORIES I HAVE.
THAT'S ALL YOU HAD...
...UNTIL NOW?
ALL THIS TIME, THOSE FEW WORDS YOU REMEMBERED WERE ALL THAT KEPT YOU GOING?
RIGHT.
BECAUSE THAT'S...
...ALL I HAD LEFT.
THAT WAS MY REASON FOR LIVING...
THAT'S PROBABLY WHY...
...AND THE SOURCE OF ALL OF MY VALUES AND MOTIVES AS WELL.

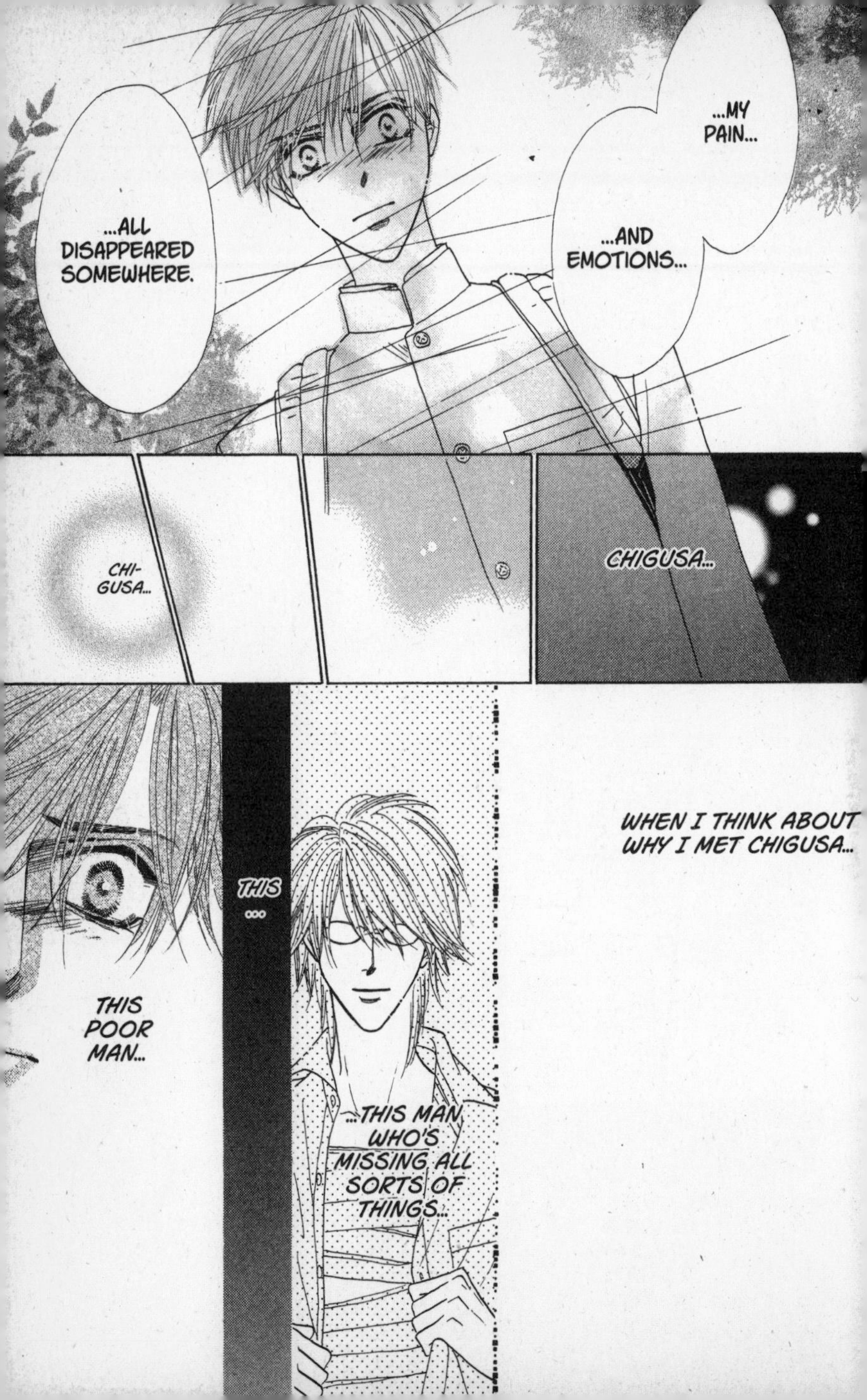

...MY PAIN...
...AND EMOTIONS...
...ALL DISAPPEARED SOMEWHERE.
CHIGUSA...
CHI-GUSA...
WHEN I THINK ABOUT WHY I MET CHIGUSA...
...THIS MAN WHO'S MISSING ALL SORTS OF THINGS...
THIS ...
THIS POOR MAN...

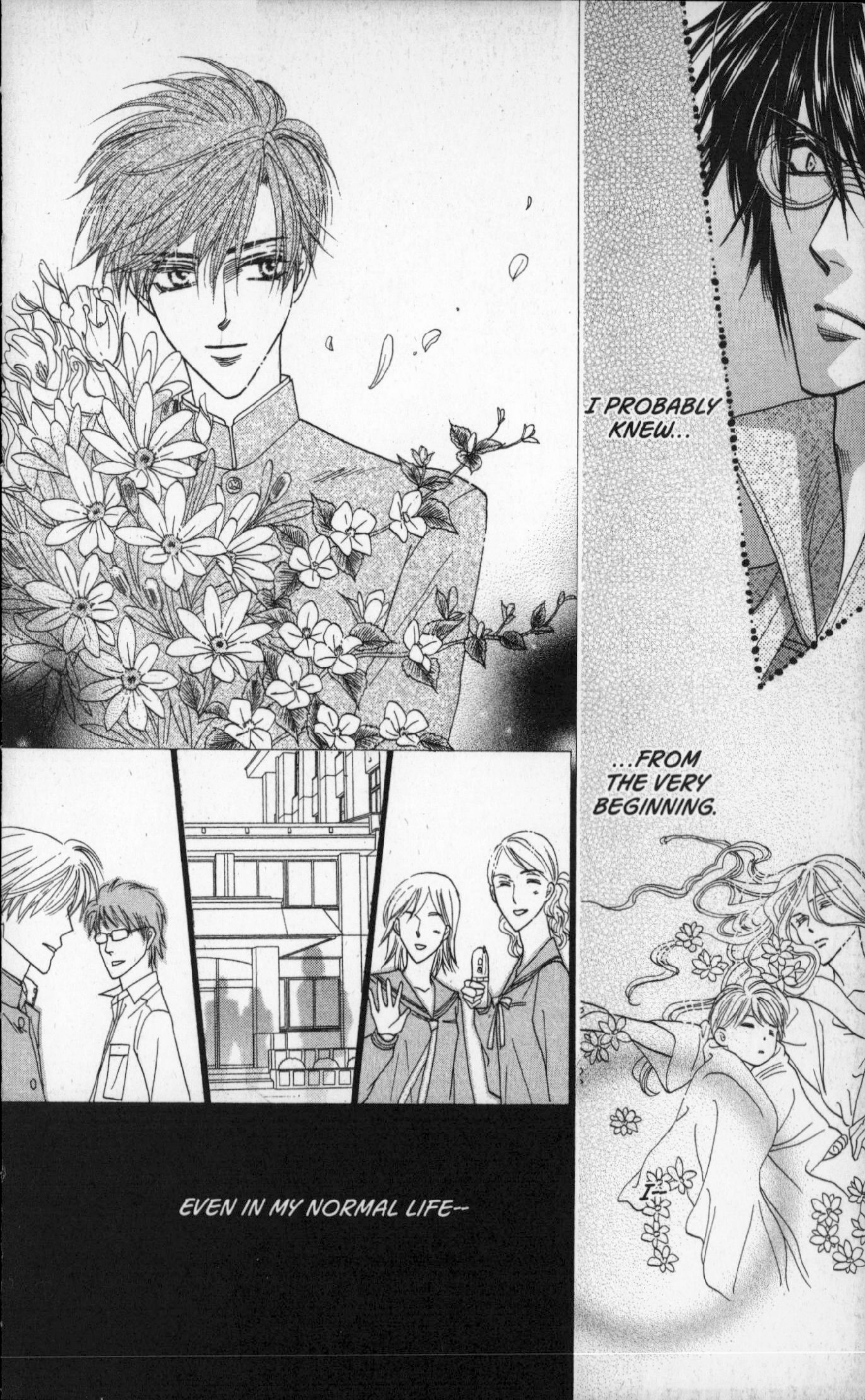
I PROBABLY KNEW...
...FROM THE VERY BEGINNING.
I--
EVEN IN MY NORMAL LIFE--

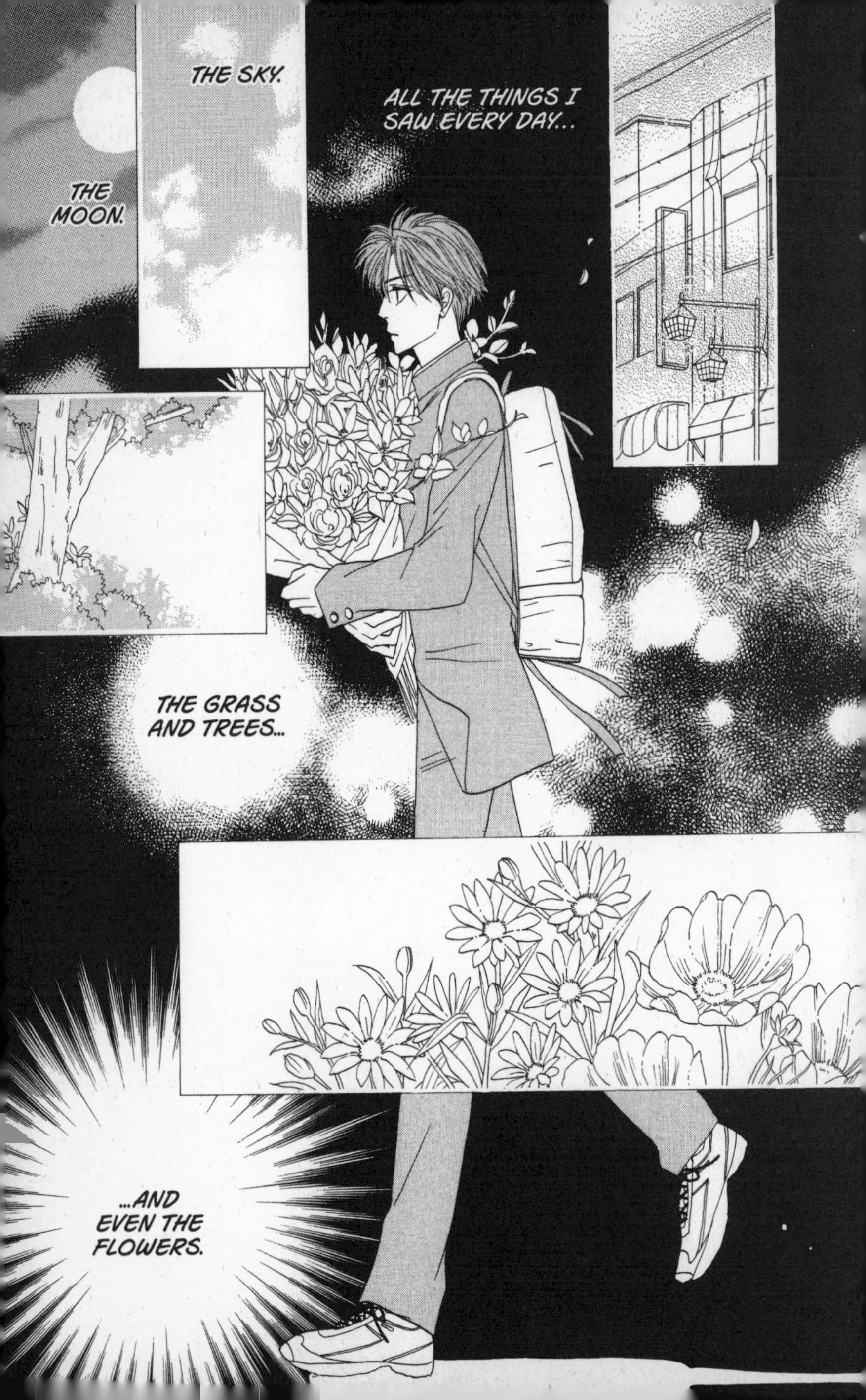
ALL THE THINGS I SAW EVERY DAY...
THE SKY.
THE MOON.
THE GRASS AND TREES...
...AND EVEN THE FLOWERS.

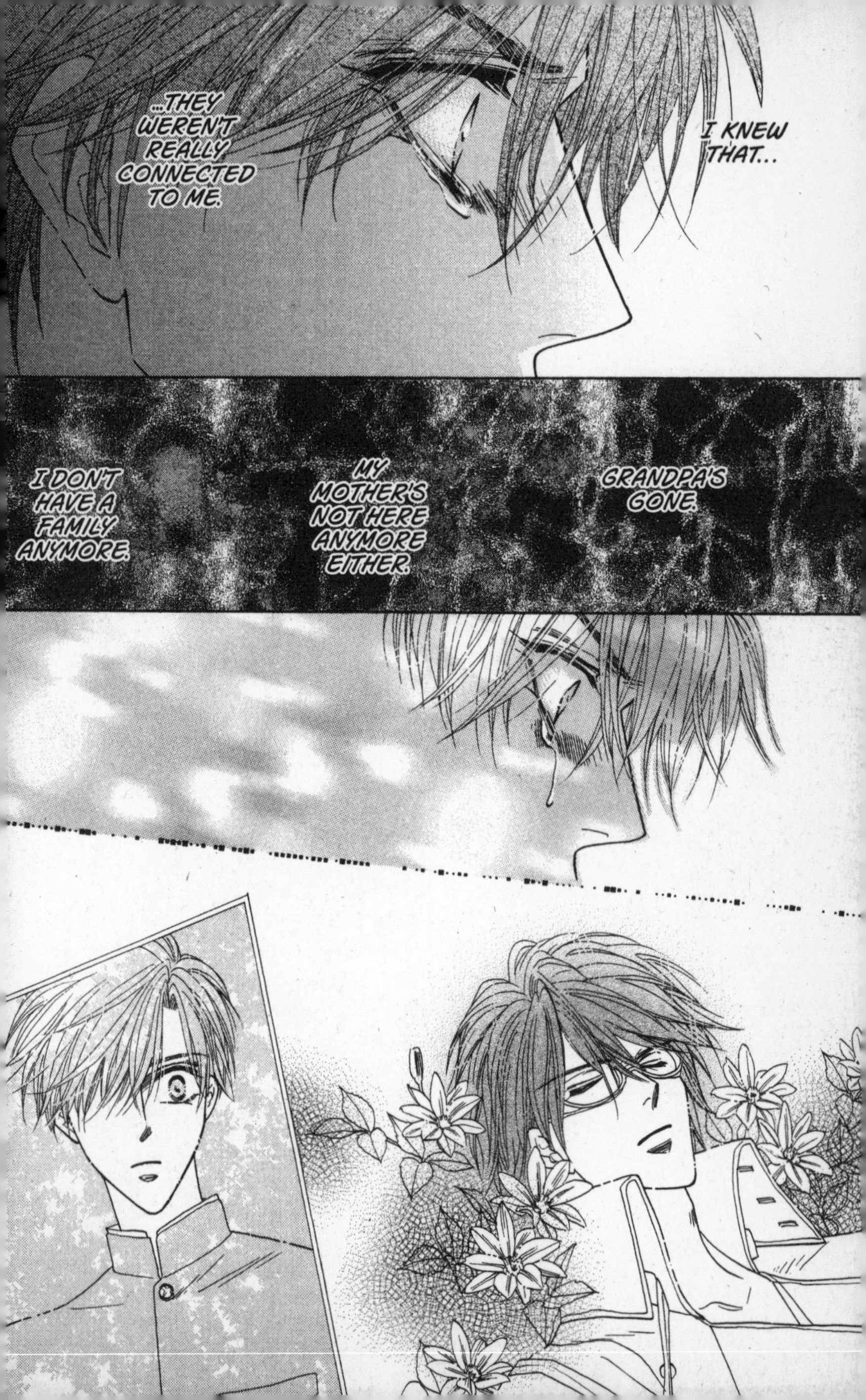
I KNEW THAT...
...THEY WEREN'T REALLY CONNECTED TO ME.
GRANDPA'S GONE.
MY MOTHER'S NOT HERE ANYMORE EITHER.
I DON'T HAVE A FAMILY ANYMORE.

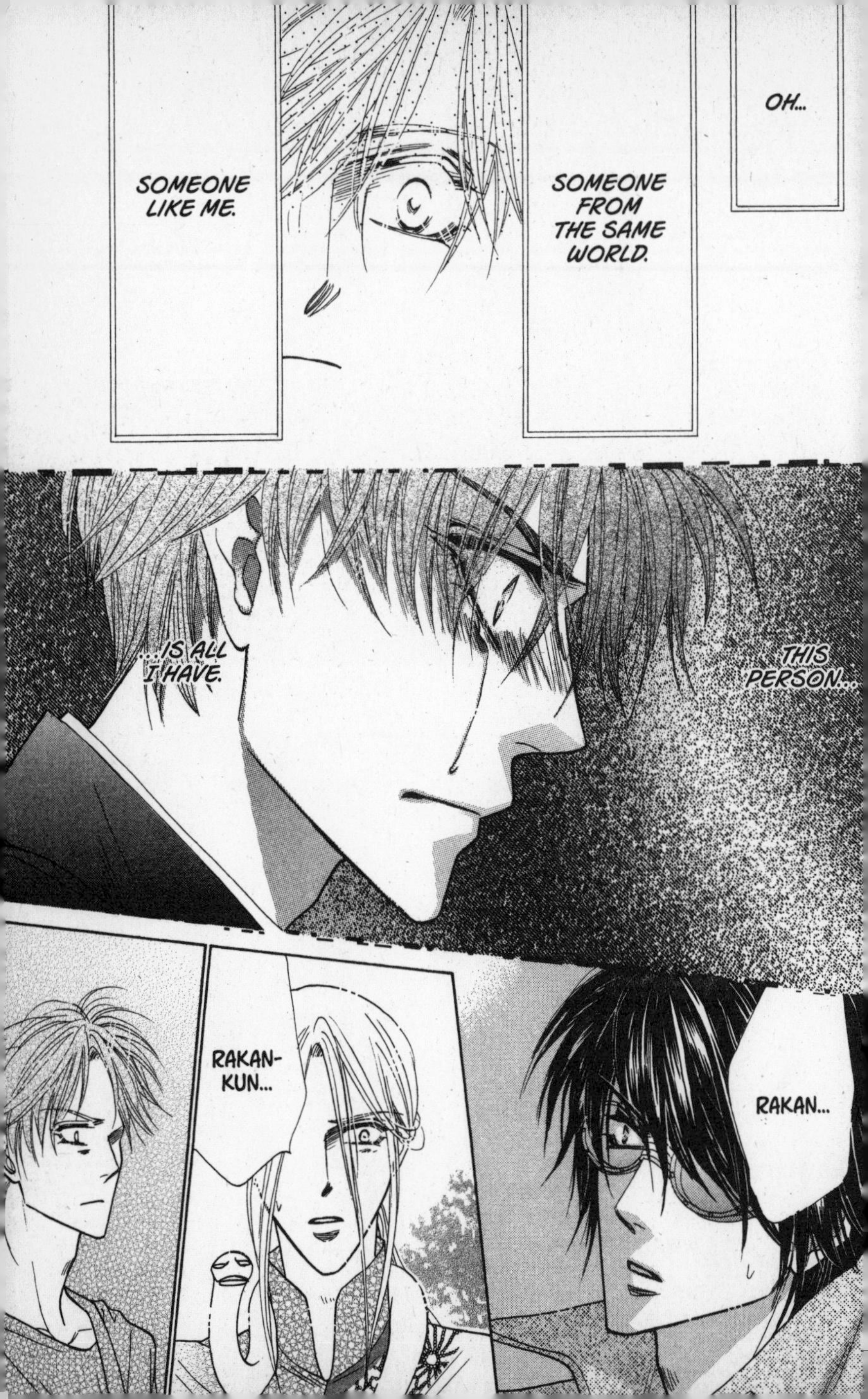
OH...
SOMEONE FROM THE SAME WORLD.
SOMEONE LIKE ME.
THIS PERSON...
...IS ALL I HAVE.
RAKAN...
RAKAN-KUN...

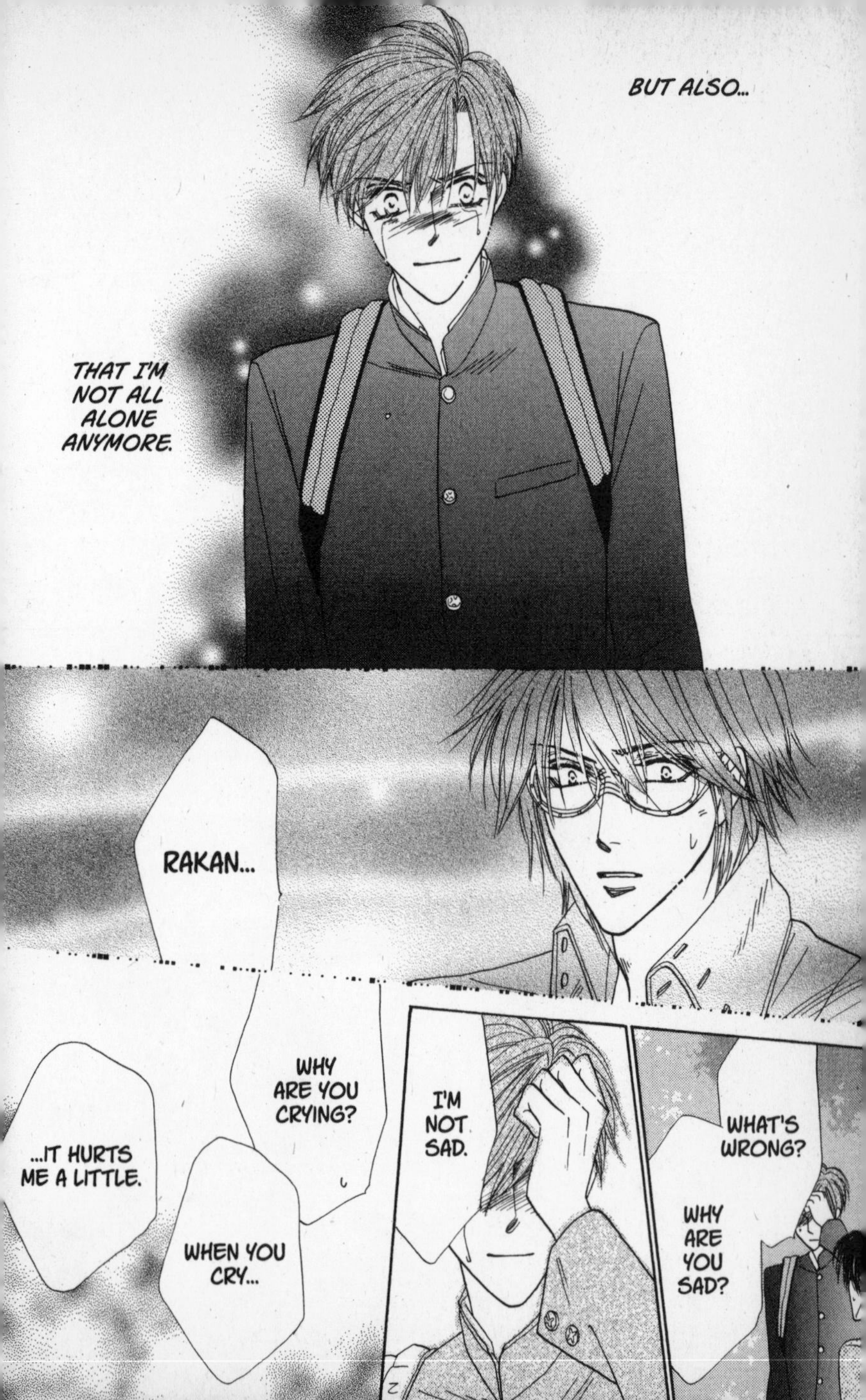
BUT ALSO...
THAT I'M NOT ALL ALONE ANYMORE.
RAKAN...
WHAT'S WRONG?
WHY ARE YOU SAD?
I'M NOT SAD.
WHY ARE YOU CRYING?
WHEN YOU CRY...
...IT HURTS ME A LITTLE.

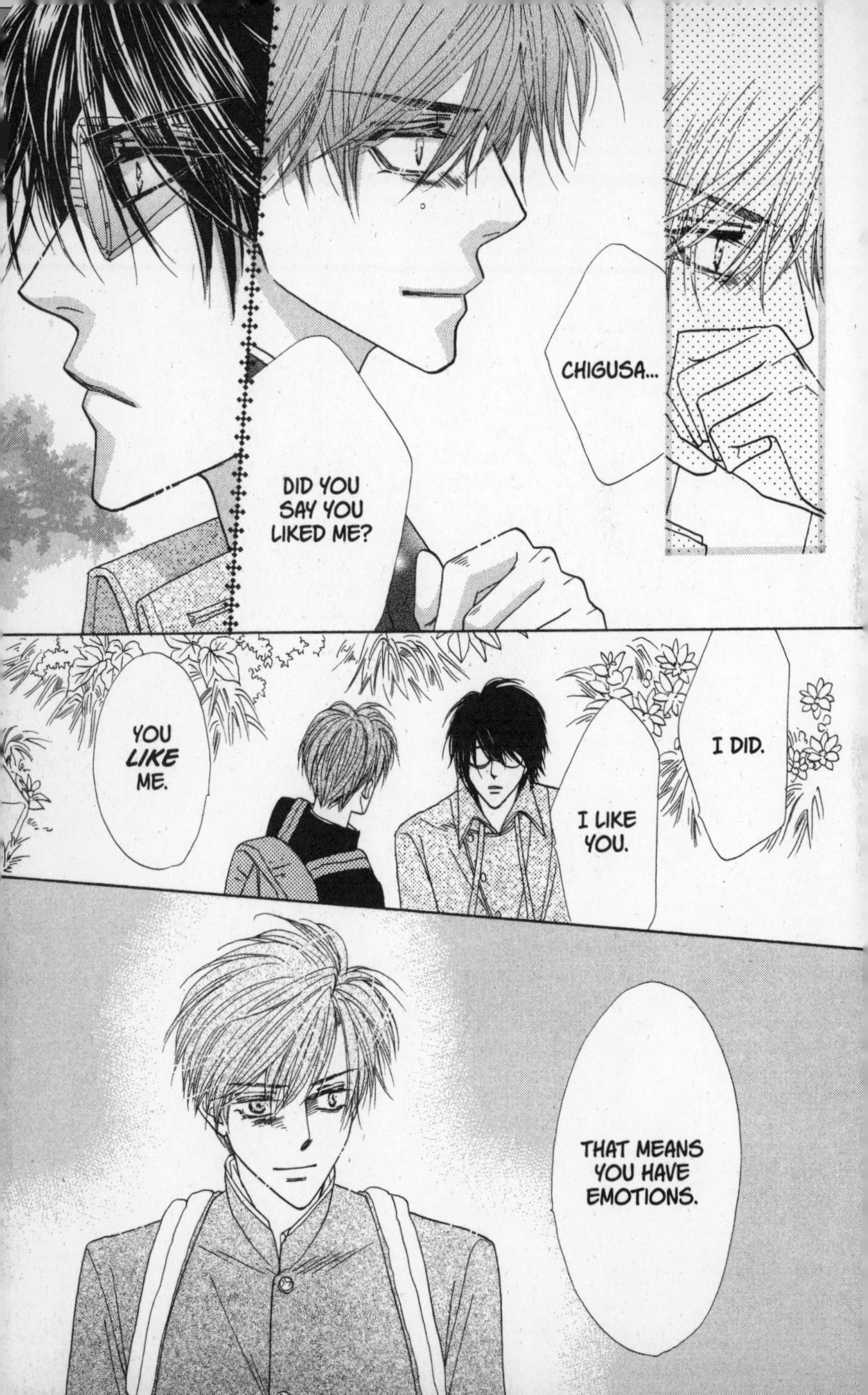
CHIGUSA...
DID YOU SAY YOU LIKED ME?
I DID.
I LIKE YOU.
YOU *LIKE* ME.
THAT MEANS YOU HAVE EMOTIONS.

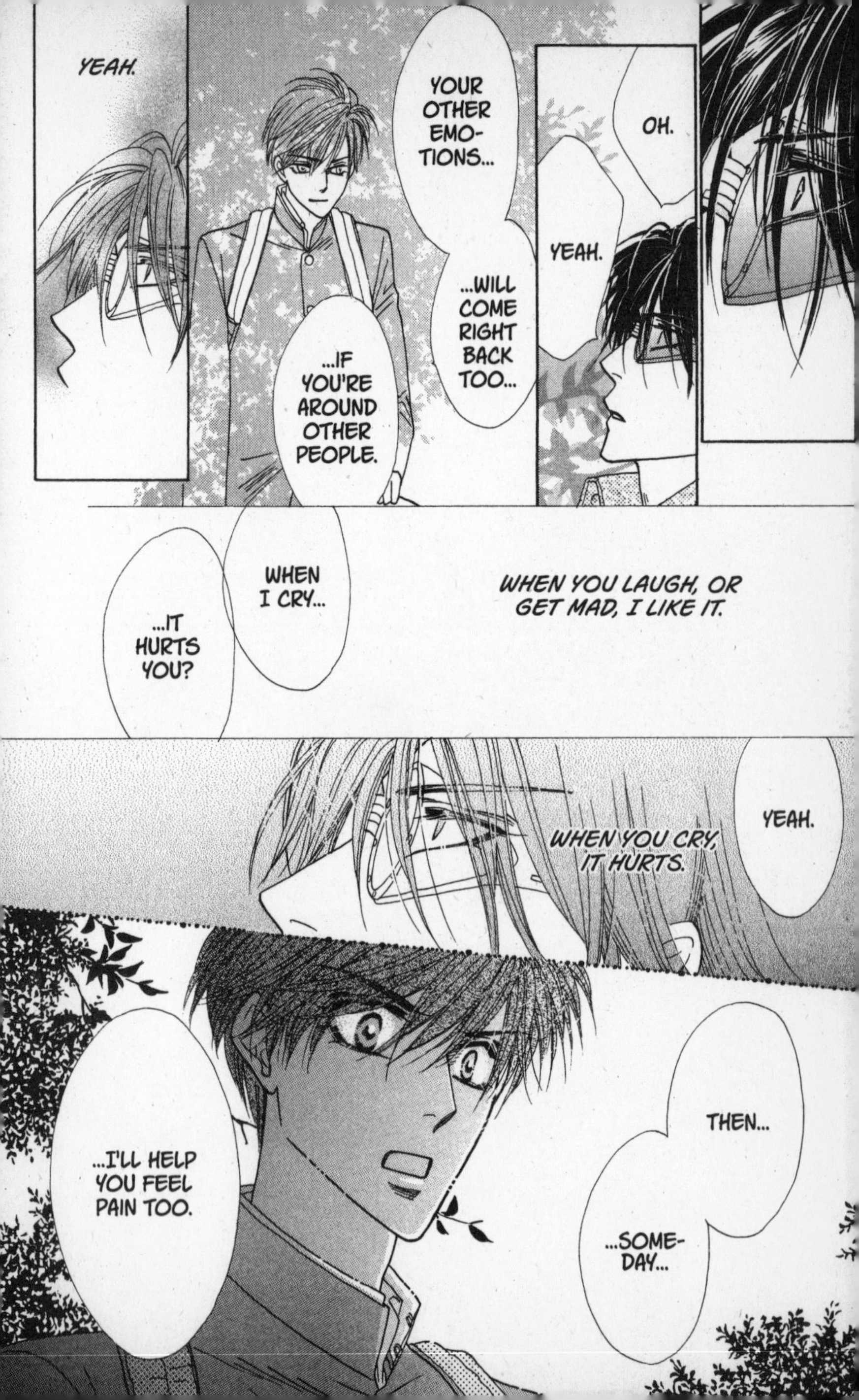
OH.
YEAH.
YOUR OTHER EMO-TIONS...
...WILL COME RIGHT BACK TOO...
...IF YOU'RE AROUND OTHER PEOPLE.
YEAH.
WHEN YOU LAUGH, OR GET MAD, I LIKE IT.
WHEN I CRY...
...IT HURTS YOU?
YEAH.
WHEN YOU CRY, IT HURTS.
THEN...
...SOME-DAY...
...I'LL HELP YOU FEEL PAIN TOO.

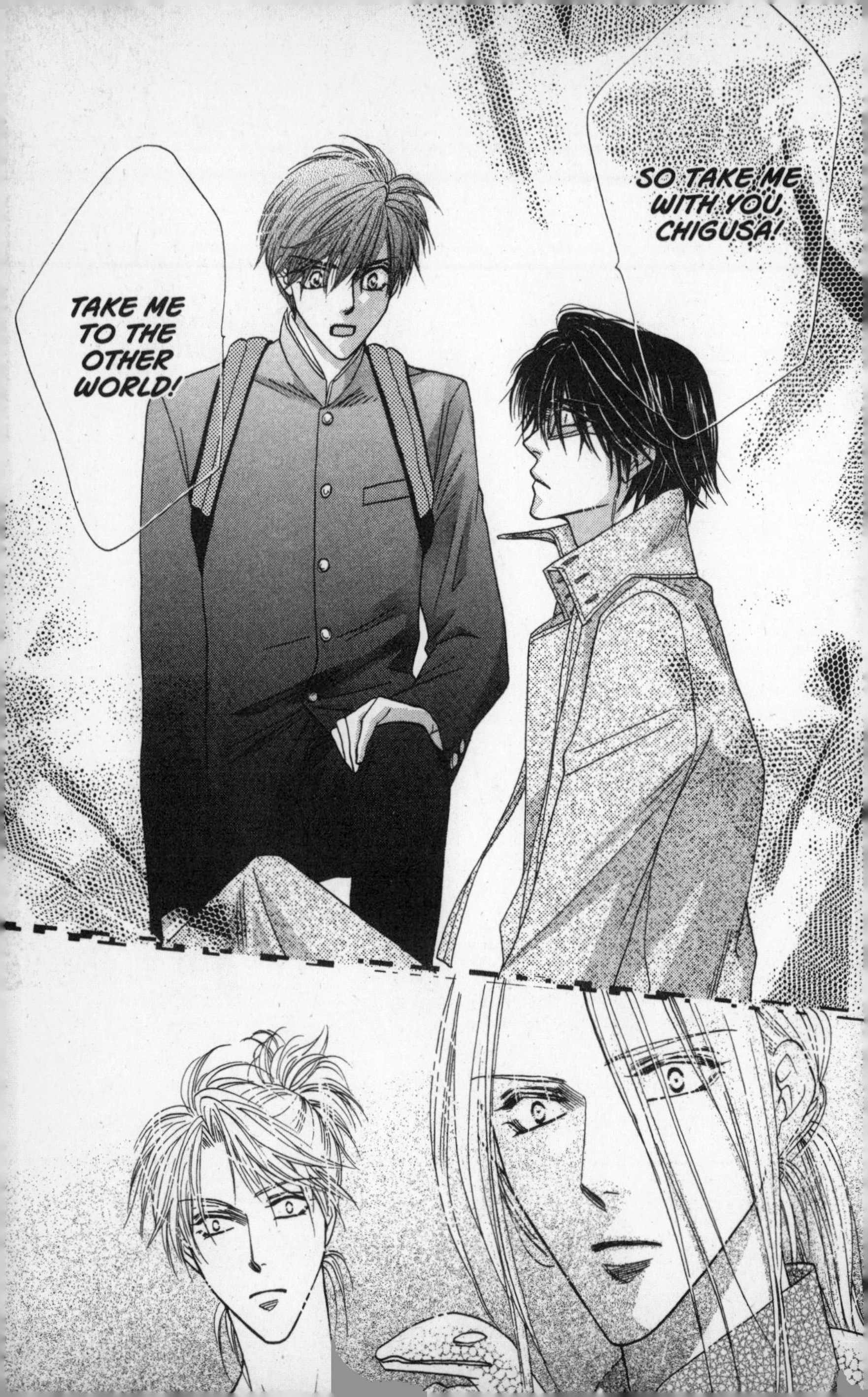
SO TAKE ME WITH YOU, CHIGUSA!
TAKE ME TO THE OTHER WORLD!

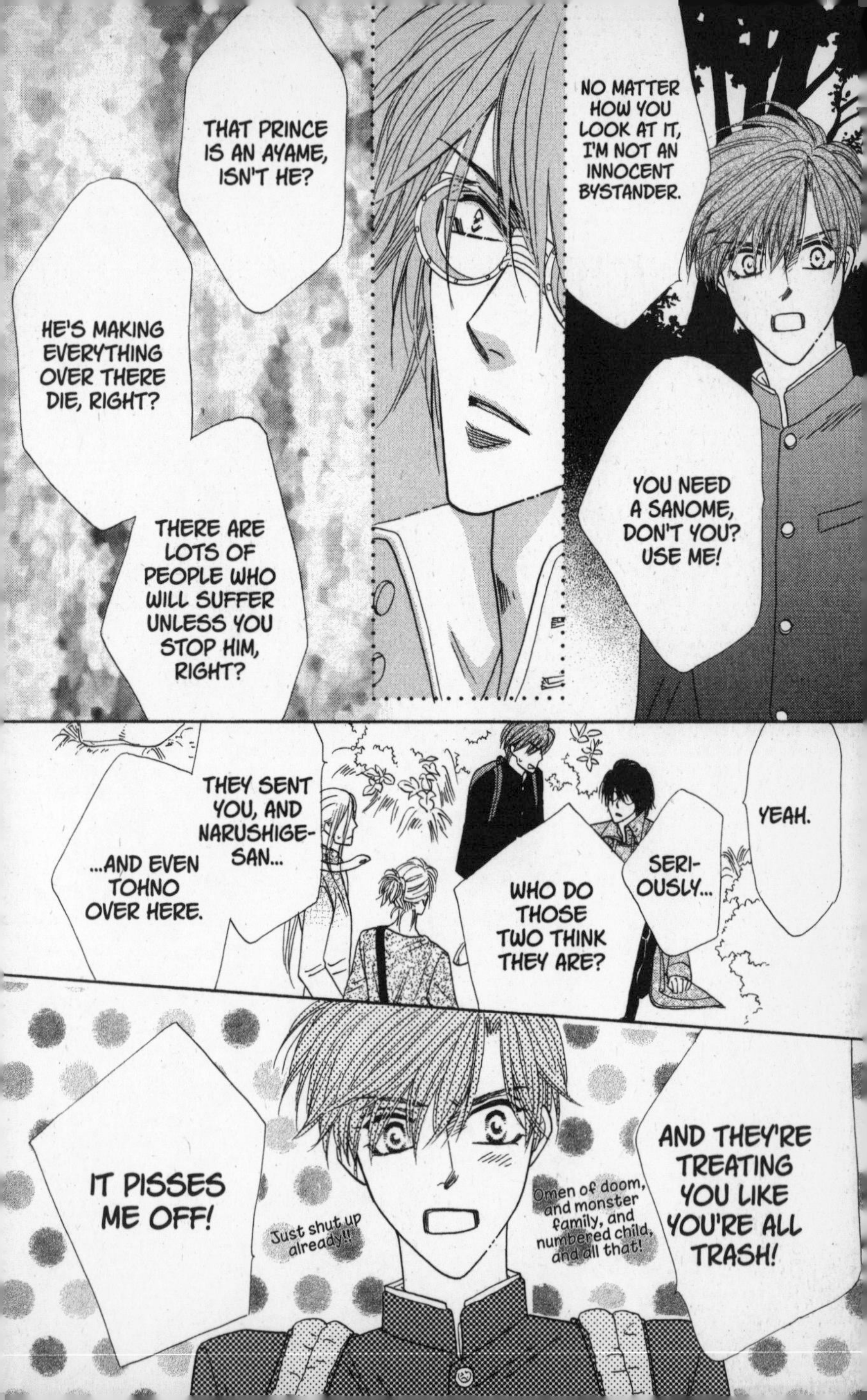
NO MATTER HOW YOU LOOK AT IT, I'M NOT AN INNOCENT BYSTANDER.
YOU NEED A SANOME, DON'T YOU? USE ME!
THAT PRINCE IS AN AYAME, ISN'T HE?
HE'S MAKING EVERYTHING OVER THERE DIE, RIGHT?
THERE ARE LOTS OF PEOPLE WHO WILL SUFFER UNLESS YOU STOP HIM, RIGHT?
YEAH.
SERI-OUSLY...
WHO DO THOSE TWO THINK THEY ARE?
THEY SENT YOU, AND NARUSHIGE-SAN...
...AND EVEN TOHNO OVER HERE.
AND THEY'RE TREATING YOU LIKE YOU'RE ALL TRASH!
Omen of doom, and monster family, and numbered child, and all that!
Just shut up already!!
IT PISSES ME OFF!

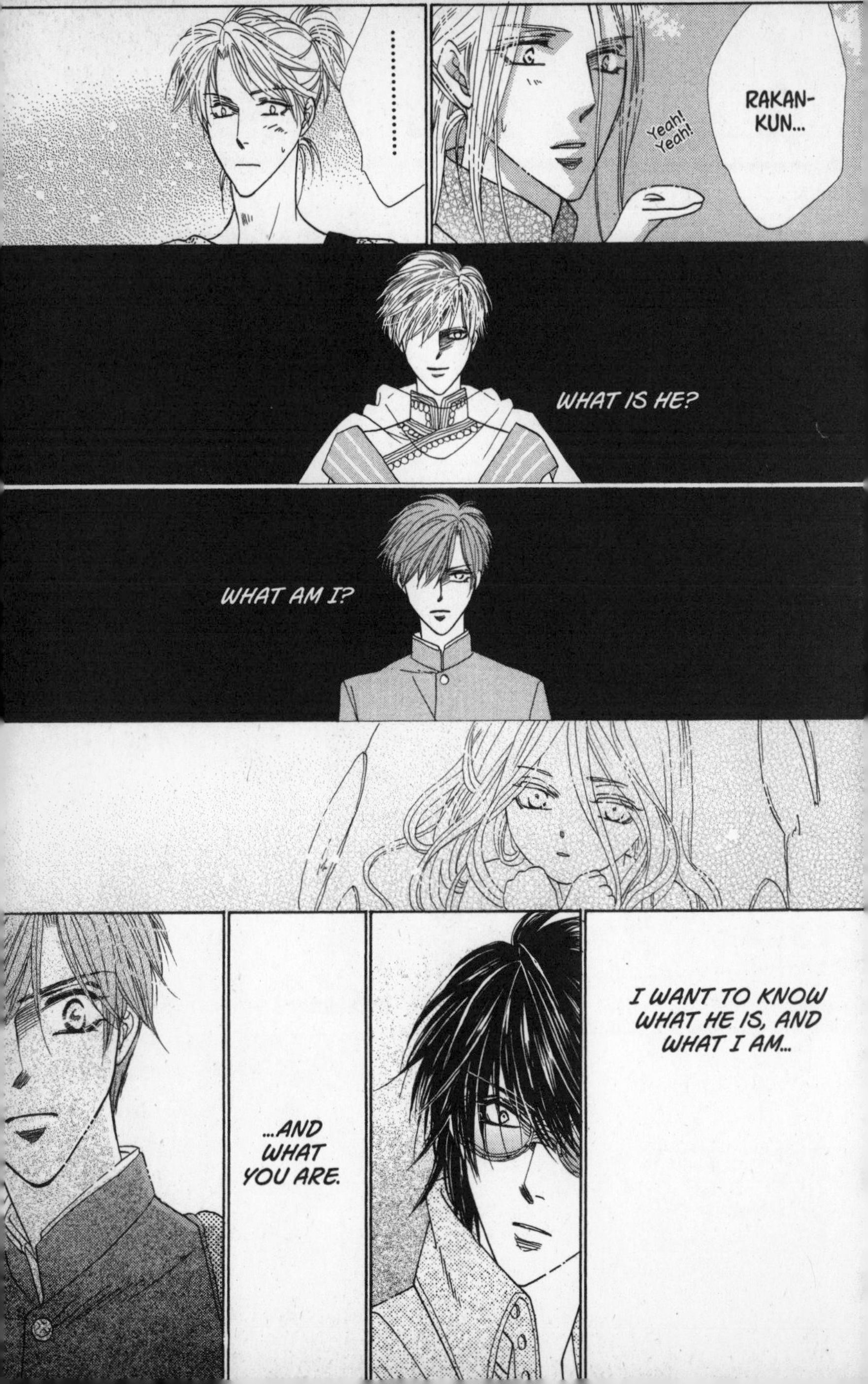
RAKAN-KUN...
Yeah! Yeah!
......
WHAT IS HE?
WHAT AM I?
I WANT TO KNOW WHAT HE IS, AND WHAT I AM...
...AND WHAT YOU ARE.

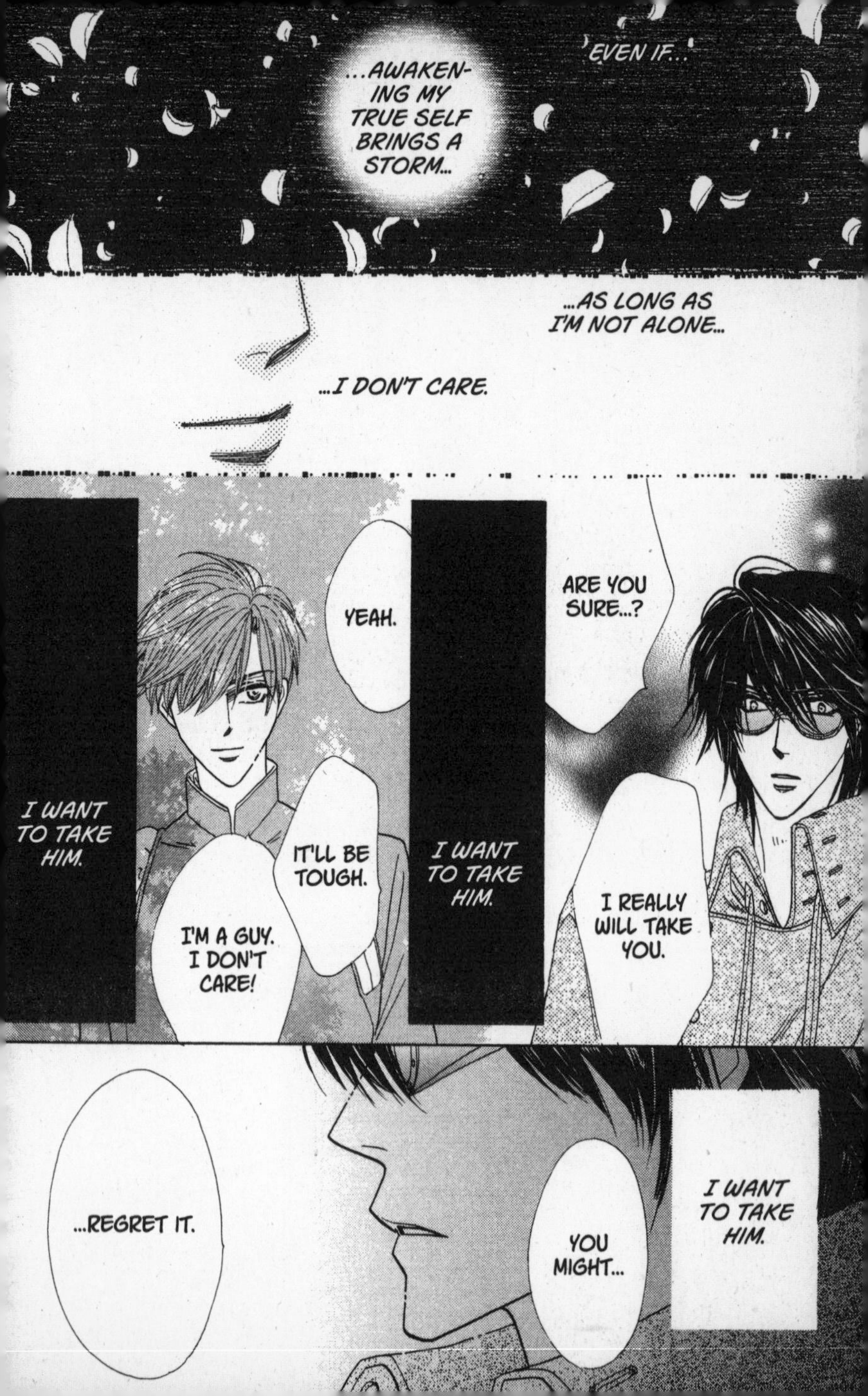
EVEN IF...
...AWAKEN-ING MY TRUE SELF BRINGS A STORM...
...AS LONG AS I'M NOT ALONE...
...I DON'T CARE.
ARE YOU SURE...?
I REALLY WILL TAKE YOU.
I WANT TO TAKE HIM.
YEAH.
IT'LL BE TOUGH.
I'M A GUY. I DON'T CARE!
I WANT TO TAKE HIM.
I WANT TO TAKE HIM.
YOU MIGHT...
...REGRET IT.

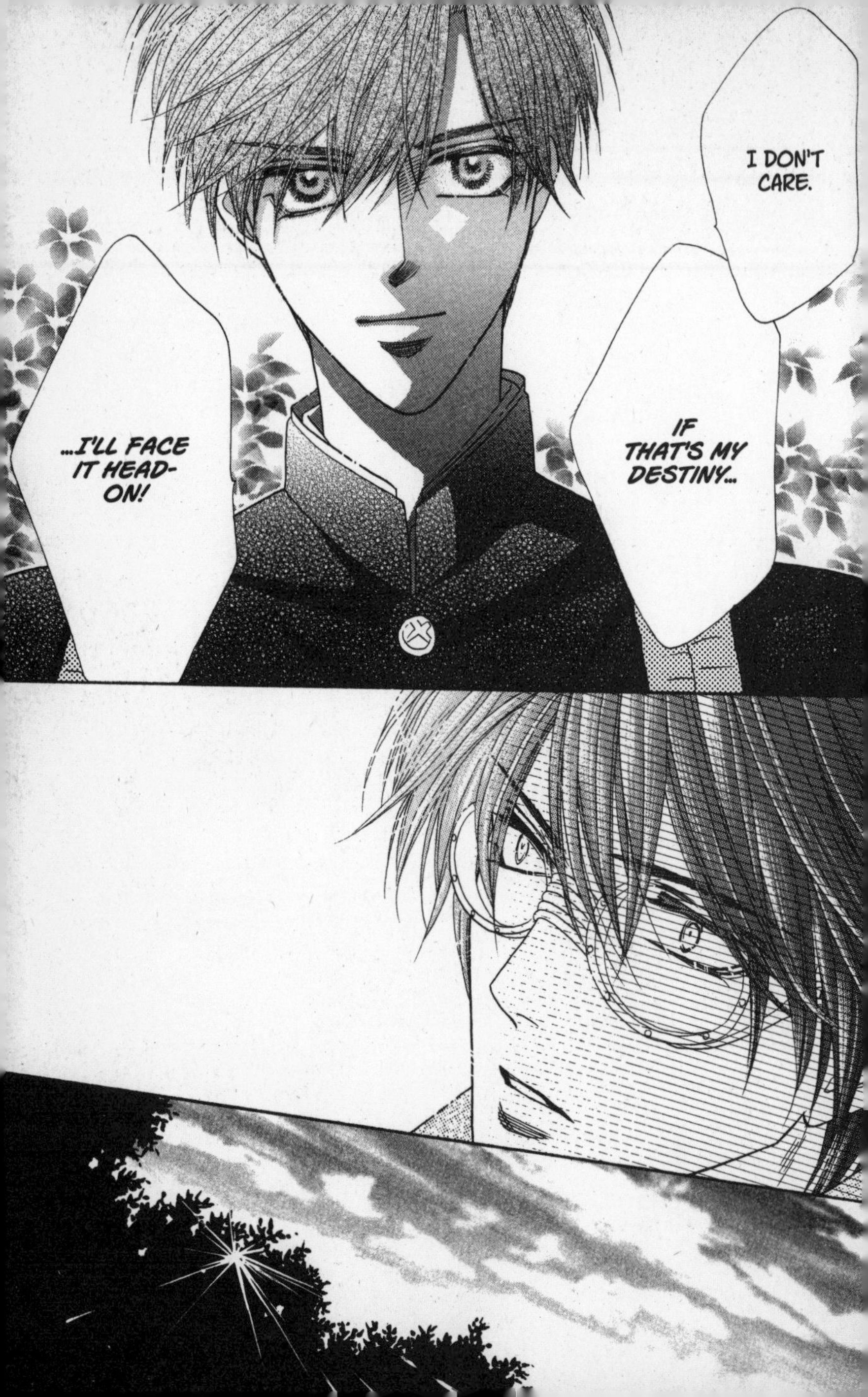
I DON'T CARE.
IF THAT'S MY DESTINY...
...I'LL FACE IT HEAD-ON!

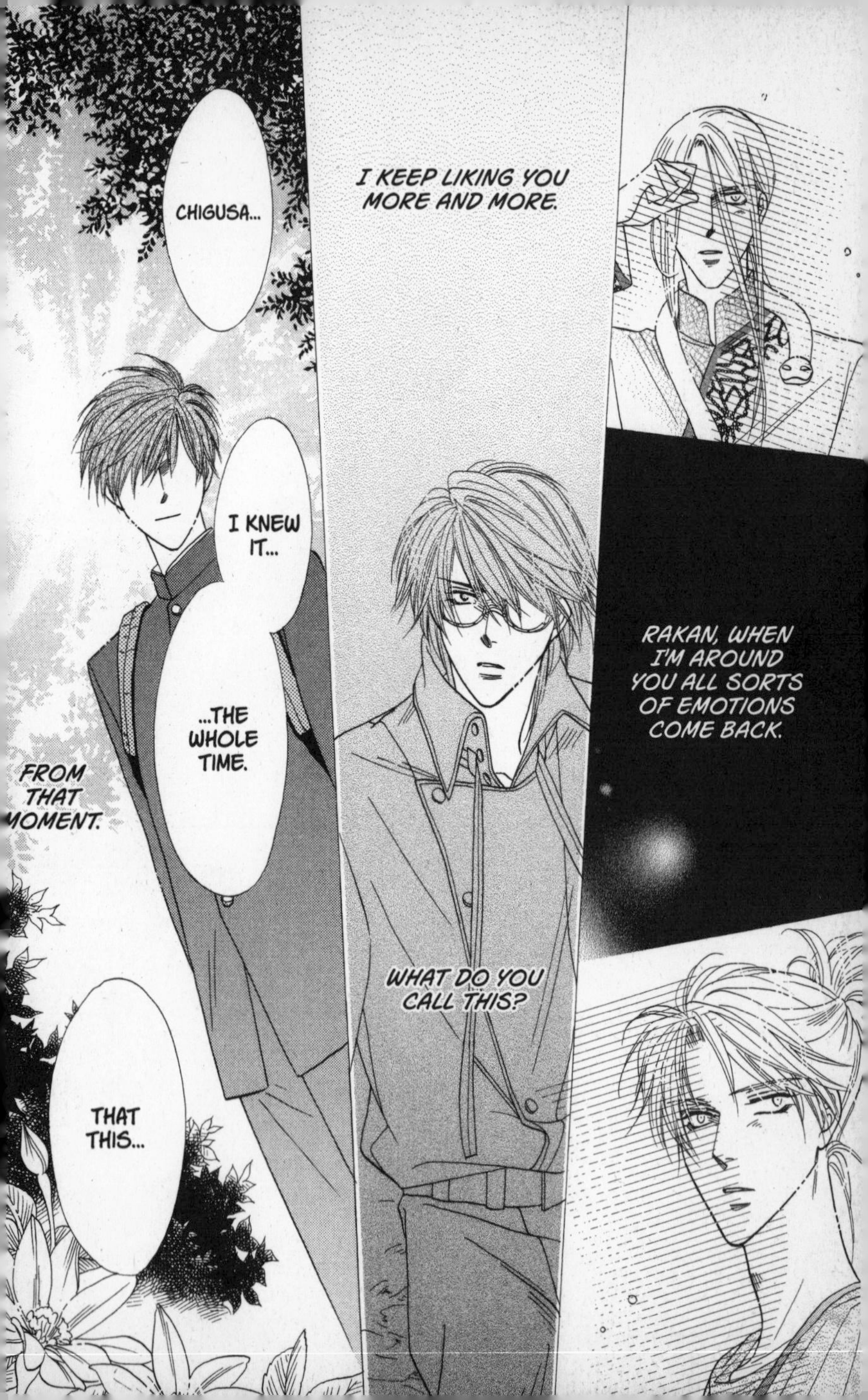
RAKAN, WHEN I'M AROUND YOU ALL SORTS OF EMOTIONS COME BACK.
I KEEP LIKING YOU MORE AND MORE.
WHAT DO YOU CALL THIS?
CHIGUSA...
I KNEW IT...
...THE WHOLE TIME.
FROM THAT MOMENT.
THAT THIS...

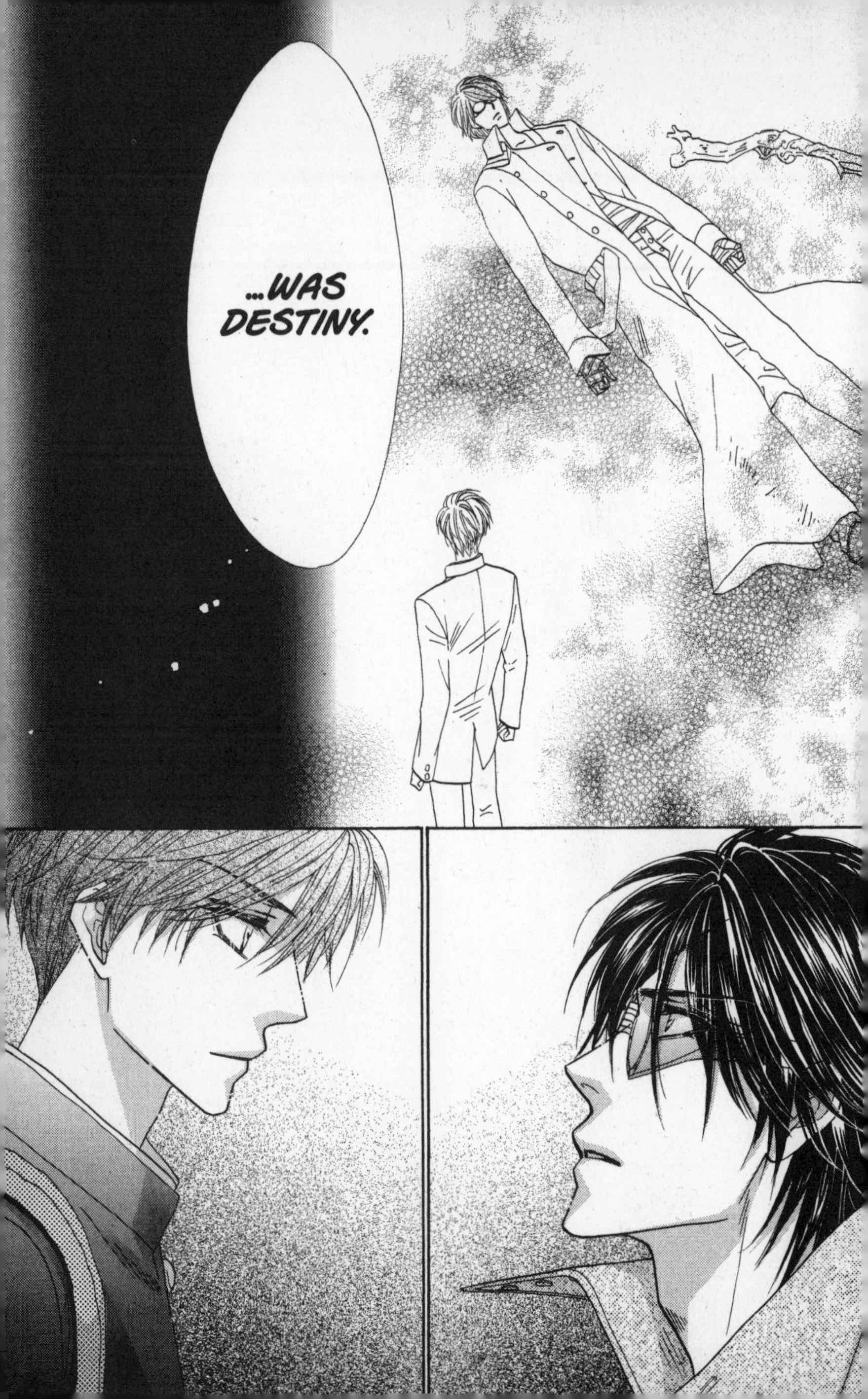
...WAS DESTINY.

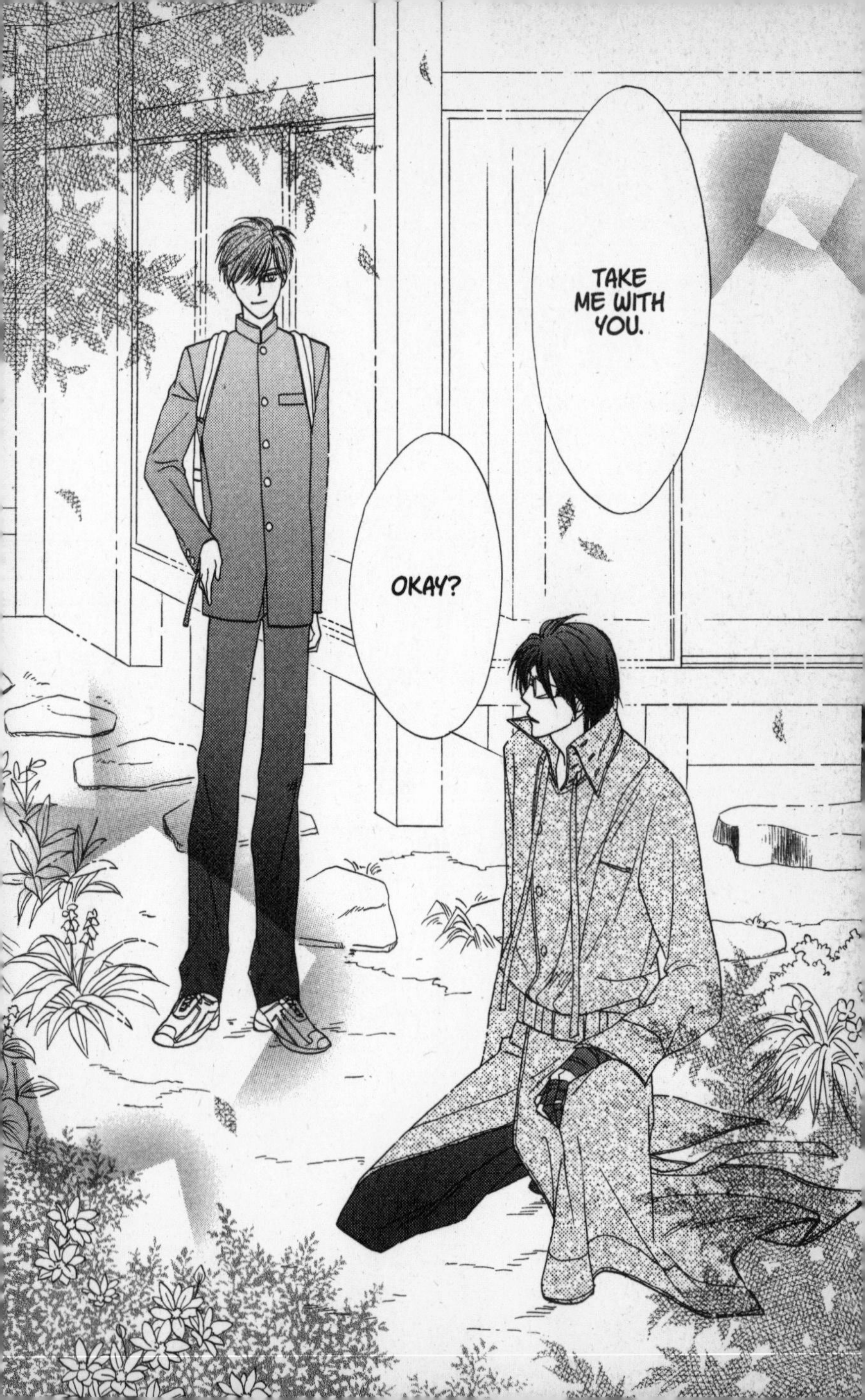
TAKE ME WITH YOU.
OKAY?

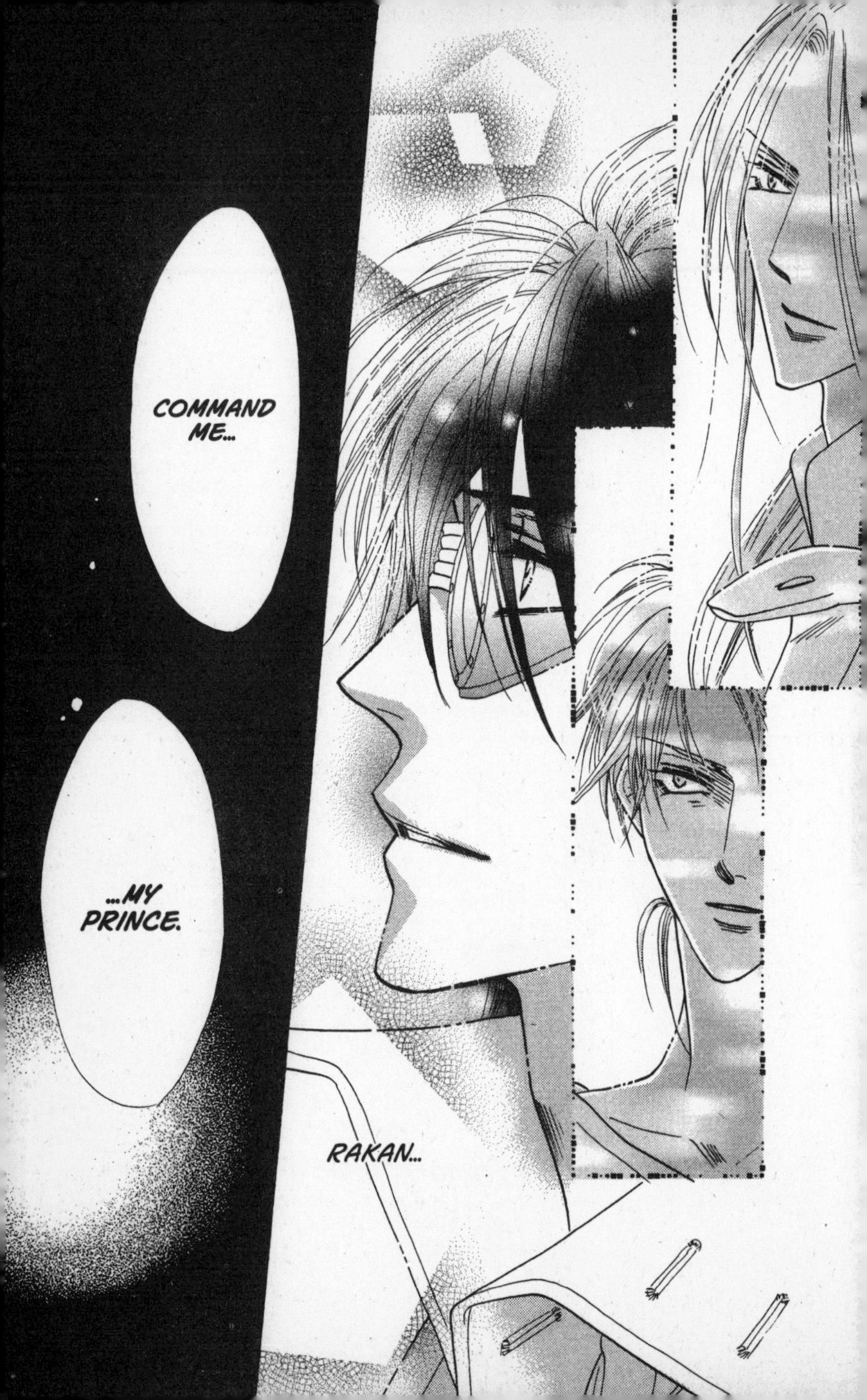
RAKAN...
COMMAND ME...
...MY PRINCE.

♣ I'm pretty used to this series now. Finally. I plan to have the foundation laid by about volume 5 (Sorry, I'm slow). By the way, I've been told that the characters this series are channeling the ones from the previous series, *Koori no Mamono*. Blood=Chigusa and Ishuca=Rakan. In my mind though, it's more like: Kauzel=Chigusa (How's that?) and Blood+Ishuca=Rakan. The details are different, but at least as far as the main flow of the character, that's how it goes.

✳ I can't write shonen manga (the mood I go for is entirely different), but I'd really like to draw a hero. Well, then this'll be more like a shonen manga. I'll be careful on that point so you'll still enjoy reading it, but anyway, I appreciate your continued support. Hey, I should've said that in volume 1.

♥ Oh, I'm also enjoying all your letters and emails. ✉ For those of you who always write me letters, thank you. ✉ Oh, in March and April there were quite a few elementary and junior high school girls who wrote, "I'm on spring break, so I'd thought I'd write a letter." It warmed my heart. ✉ Oh, and thank you to those of you who wrote me from overseas. ✉ I'm happy that the feeling translates into other languages.

Well, I'll stop here for now. See you in the next volume. ✉

Shiho Sugihara--2004, the season of the cicada

Double Cast

UMM, CHI-GUSA...
CALLING ME "MY PRINCE"...
What will people say?
I'M NOT REALLY SURE IT'S A GOOD IDEA.
NO, IT'S OKAY.
IT'S JUST SHORT FOR...
"IN MY MIND...
...YOU'RE THE REAL PRINCE."
SEE?
OH, RIGHT.
I guess it's okay then.
Right.
Yeah.
It's not okay, Rakan-kun.
How is that okay?
WHICH ONE?
WHICH ONE IS THIS MANGA'S SPACE CADET!!

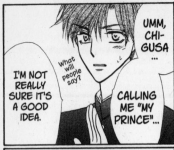

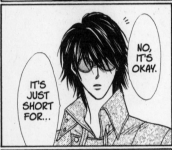

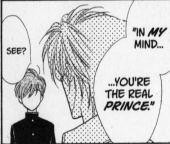

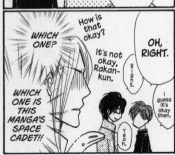

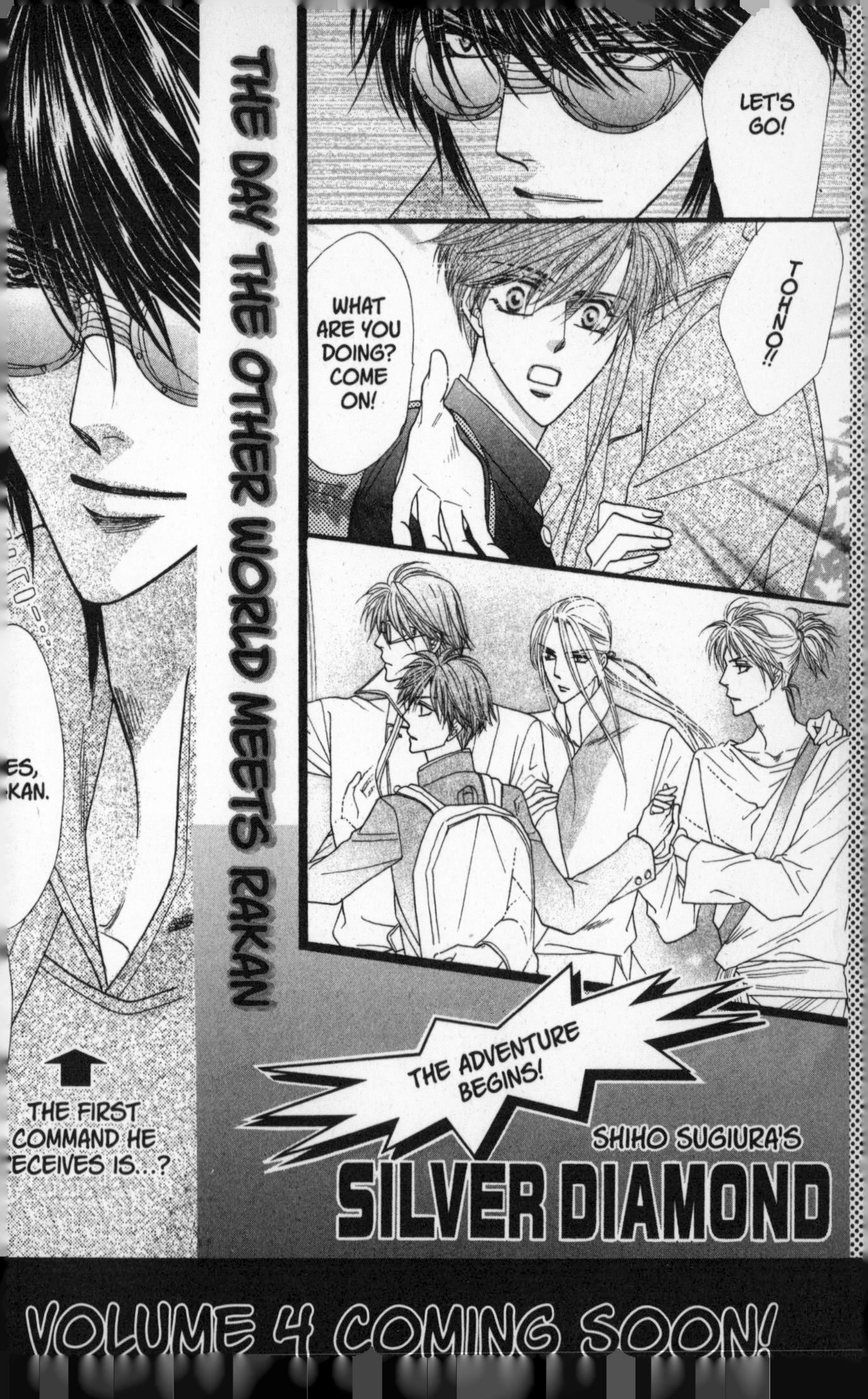
LET'S GO!
TOHNO!!
WHAT ARE YOU DOING? COME ON!
THE ADVENTURE BEGINS!
SHIHO SUGIURA'S
SILVER DIAMOND
THE DAY THE OTHER WORLD MEETS RAKAN
THE FIRST COMMAND HE ECEIVES IS...?

VOLUME 4 COMING SOON!

Inside the World of...
SILVER DIAMOND

THIS SECTION HAS BEEN CREATED TO EXPLAIN AND ANALYZE THE COMPLICATED WORLD THAT IS *SILVER DIAMOND.* HOPEFULLY IT WILL SUCCESSFULLY COVER ALL THE CONFUSING CULTURAL AND LINGUAL ASPECTS OF THE SERIES AND HELP YOU ENJOY *SILVER DIAMOND* EVEN MORE!

JAPANESE USES HONORIFICS TO ADDRESS PEOPLE AND REFER TO THEM WITH RESPECT. SIMILAR TO "MR." AND "MRS." IN ENGLISH BUT THERE IS MORE VARIETY IN JAPANESE.

honorifics

THE MOST COMMON HONORIFICS SEEN IN *SILVER DIAMOND* ARE AS FOLLOWS:
- *SAN:* VERY COMMON IN JAPANESE AND IS A SIGN OF RESPECT.
- *KUN:* INFORMAL HONORIFIC USUALLY USED FOR MALES WHEN ADDRESSING SOMEONE YOUNGER THAN YOURSELF.
- *CHAN:* INFORMAL AND USUALLY USED FOR FEMALES OR CHILDREN.
- *SAMA:* MORE FORMAL THAN "-SAN." USED FOR PEOPLE HIGHER IN RANK, LIKE THE PRINCE.

p. 82 river beds

THE JAPANESE KANJI FOR RIVER IS 川 PRONOUNCED AS KAWA. WHEN THREE FUTONS ARE LAID OUT SIDE BY SIDE, IT IS SAID TO RESEMBLE THE CHARACTER FOR RIVER. THIS IS ALSO A SYMBOL FOR A HAPPY FAMILY WHERE EVERYONE SLEEPS TOGETHER IN THE SAME ROOM.

HERE'S THE KANJI FOR NARUSHIGE'S MOTHER, SHIGEKA SHIGEYUKI. YOU'LL ONCE AGAIN NOTE THE NAME TRADITION OF THE OTHER WORLD WHERE CHARACTERS SHARE THE SAME KANJI IN BOTH OF THEIR NAMES.

shigeyuki p. 41

重華重雪

AND HERE'S THE KANJI FOR HER DAUGHTER AND NARUSHIGE'S SISTER, SAE. THE FIRST KANJI IS THE SYMBOL FOR THE NUMBER THREE.(PRONOUNCED AS "SAN" WHEN BY ITSELF.)

三重

THE CHARACTERS WITH NUMBERS IN THEIR GIVEN NAMES SURE ARE TREATED POORLY IN THE OTHER WORLD!

Join us next time for more revealing tidbits in volume 4!

Silver Diamond
···Fanart···

Hope···Los Angeles

A beautiful picture of Rakan and Chigusa
surrounded by branches that seem to
be hugging them. Though why doesn't
Rakan seem to be enjoying it?!

Aira⋯Canada

Aira-chan has sent us a third piece of art and this one may be the best of the bunch. I just love the Prince/Kinrei relationship! Creepy but sexy!

Jessica⋯California

Chigusa seems to be getting a bit aggressive with Rakan in this picture by Jessica. Hey, I'm not complaining.

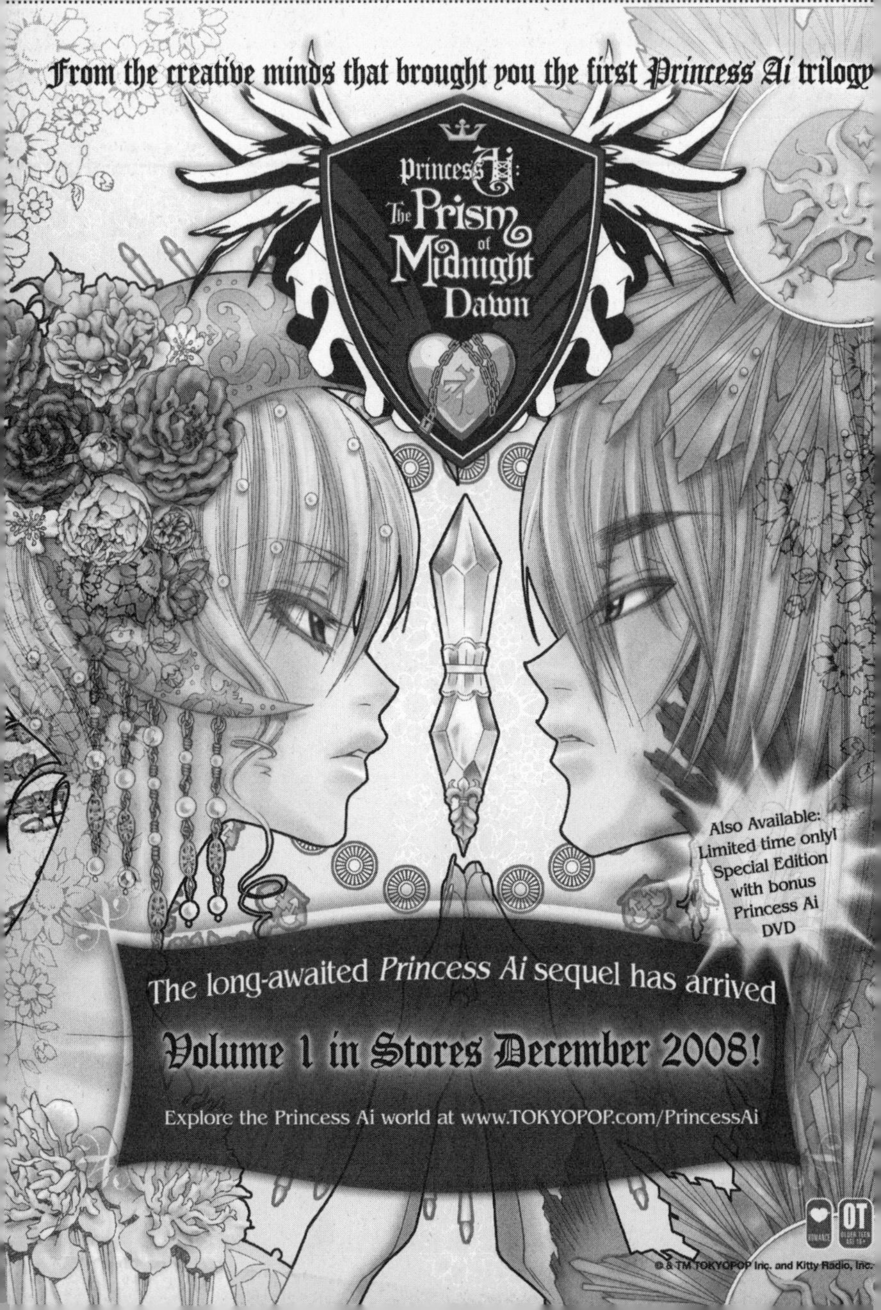
From the creative minds that brought you the first Princess Ai trilogy
Princess Ai: The Prism of Midnight Dawn
Also Available: Limited time only! Special Edition with bonus Princess Ai DVD
The long-awaited Princess Ai sequel has arrived
Volume 1 in Stores December 2008!
Explore the Princess Ai world at www.TOKYOPOP.com/PrincessAi
© & TM TOKYOPOP Inc. and Kitty Radio, Inc.

STOP!

This is the back of the book.
You wouldn't want to spoil a great ending!

This book is printed "manga-style," in the authentic Japanese right-to-left format. Since none of the artwork has been flipped or altered, readers get to experience the story just as the creator intended. You've been asking for it, so TOKYOPOP® delivered: authentic, hot-off-the-press, and far more fun!

DIRECTIONS

If this is your first time reading manga-style, here's a quick guide to help you understand how it works.

It's easy... just start in the top right panel and follow the numbers. Have fun, and look for more 100% authentic manga from TOKYOPOP®!